MARKETS, PRICES, AND INTERREGIONAL TRADE

MARKETS, PRICES, AND INTERREGIONAL TRADE

RAYMOND G. BRESSLER, Jr.

RICHARD A. KING

JOHN WILEY & SONS, INC.

NEW YORK · LONDON · SYDNEY · TORONTO

Library of Congress Catalogue Card Number: 70 112845

SBN 471 10305 5

Printed in the United States of America

10 9 8 7 6 5 4 3 2 1

FOR
RGB III, PAK, and friends

PREFACE

This book is devoted to the study of the central core of our economy — the marketing and pricing system. The operation of this unseen and largely automatic system directs the concurrent flows of resources to their myriad uses and of goods and services to their ultimate consumers. These flows include the production of services such as transportation, storage, and communication that bind the economy into an effective and integrated whole.

Although there are many social objectives to which marketing may contribute, the direct and fundamental goals for the marketing system are (1) to provide efficient and economical services and ownership transfers in the movement of commodities from producer to consumer, and (2) to provide an effective and efficient price-making mechanism. Only insofar as the prices that are established through the marketing system transmit the demands of consumers back to producers and transmit the supply conditions forward to consumers with a minimum of lags, imperfections, and distortions, can the economy achieve the efficient allocation and the economical use of resources in satisfying wants.

From this viewpoint, the first objective, relating to efficiency in the handling and the transferring of commodities, is simply a specific aspect of the second. The creation of marketing services does not differ from other productive processes in this respect, and the efficient operation of the pricing mechanism includes the economical allocation of resources to marketing uses. Thus, the real and direct contribution of the marketing system is to provide for and to participate in price formation, with the understanding that the pricing system will have as its prime functions the guiding of the allocation of resources into production (including marketing) and the rationing of goods and services in consumption.

Our objective has been to provide a textbook that emphasizes the interdependent nature of economic activities and the strategic role of marketing in the total economic system. Our approach is analytical and uses economic theory to interpret the essential nature of marketing processes, but with frequent illustrations and factual applications.

These illustrations are drawn largely from agriculture, and many center on the marketing of milk. For an illustration to be useful, it is important to understand the setting from which it is drawn. Most of us will be familiar with milk "factories," since cows are to be found in every state in the Union. Furthermore, although the marketing of milk may now involve some less familiar procedures than was true a few decades ago, the scope of milk problems extends through the space, time, and form dimensions of market price to encompass interesting problems of efficiency and public policy. Although some may believe that this is the milkman's approach to markets and trade, there is a large body of research data, readily available from studies during the past half century, from which we have drawn. Our goal, then, is not to train milk-marketing economists but to show the ready adaptability and power of the theoretical tools that are presented in the solution of a variety of problems that exist in the real world.

In Part I, we briefly discuss the growth and evolution of the American economy from the subsistence farming widespread in the Colonial period to the complex industrialized exchange economy of the 20th century. Our discussion serves the twofold purpose of providing illustrative material that can be drawn on later to clarify theoretical points and of encouraging the reader to view the economy of mid-20th century America as a snapshot of a complex and rapidly changing system.

In Part II, we examine the spatial dimension of market price. The theoretical framework treats an economy in which a specified set of commodities is available in given locations, although they may move from site to site in response to price incentives. The entire question of the location of economic activity revolves around the issue of how, if at all, the cost of doing business is affected by site — that is to say, the spatial characteristics of prices and costs. In this respect, this book differs from most economic treatises, which deal largely with a pinhead economy — that is, an economy that has no space, form, or time dimensions. In Part III, we introduce the form and time dimensions to produce an interdependent system of prices with three dimensions.

Part IV deals with regional specialization and trade. In this section, we consider an economy in which given bundles of resources may be used to produce a variety of sets of commodities in a given region. These commodities may then be moved from site to site in response to price differences. In Part V, we remove a final constraint and allow resources themselves to move from region to region. Here we examine an economy in which certain of the resources may be moved from one site to another to be used in the production of a variety of sets of commodities which, again, may be moved from site to site as the price conditions may dictate.

We close with a few remarks concerning the contributions of marketing to economic development and to the general welfare.

This text is directed toward advanced undergraduate students or, with appropriate supplementation, toward graduate students. We assume that these students have some knowledge both of economic theory and of facts descriptive of the economy in general and of marketing institutions in particular. However, we have attempted to provide factual and theoretical background material, that is adequate to offset any major deficiencies in these prerequisite areas.

It should be acknowledged that this book does not provide instruction on the merchandising activities of marketing agencies. Instead, it attempts to provide an understanding of the nature and of the operation of broad economic forces. As such, we offer it as the basis for a full-year course in the economics of marketing. Courses organized on the basis of a single semester or quarter will no doubt use only part of the material presented. Although the selection should depend primarily on the interests of the instructor and on the previous training of the students, we suggest that Parts I, II, III, and IV would be most appropriate for less advanced classes. Graduate students may well emphasize Parts IV and V, with only a brief consideration of the earlier chapters. Finally, some instructors prefer to emphasize the broad aspects of markets and pricing; for them, it would be appropriate to eliminate certain sections that treat in detail the problems of the marketing firm. Perhaps it is not too much to hope some of the excitement will be sensed that we have shared with our students as excess demand curves, transfer functions, price cones, market boundaries, and multiple-product price relationships have come to light in spatially separated markets such as Storrs, Connecticut; Berkeley, California; Raleigh, North Carolina; Naples, Italy; and Lima, Peru.

We are indebted to many individuals who have contributed directly or indirectly to this work. We thank particularly our present and former colleagues at the University of Connecticut, at North Carolina State University, and at the University of California.

CONTENTS

MARKETS, PRICES, AND INTERREGIONAL TRADE

PART I

PROLOGUE

chapter 1

THE AMERICAN ECONOMY: COLONIAL DAYS THROUGH THE CIVIL WAR

This Prologue consists of three chapters. The first chapter traces the changes in the American economy from the early settlement through the Civil War. The second chapter discusses the development of an advanced economy over the past century. The third chapter emphasizes the interdependence of economic activities and sketches briefly the interregional and international commodity flows that characterize mid-century America.

Economic theory is not only more palatable but also better understood when well mixed with examples that are relevant to the student. It is hoped that a review of development and regional specialization in the United States will provide a useful background for the theoretical models that constitute the main body of this book. However, Part I is not a prerequisite for an understanding of the material that follows. It may be omitted where time is a limitation, where students have a good grasp of the process of the growth of the American economy, or where examples drawn from another setting are more appropriate. This review is necessarily brief and incomplete but suggestions for additional reading have been provided for those students who wish to pursue in more depth some of the ideas that are presented.

1.1 THE COLONIAL POWERS IN NORTH AMERICA

From the beginning of the 16th century through the 18th century, the major European powers engaged in a struggle for colonial control of the North American continent. The drive for colonies had many motives, but central among them were economic considerations. Spain's great explorers of the late 15th century were searching for new routes to India and the Orient — routes that would circumvent Arabian control of the profitable trade in spices, silk, and gold. With the discovery of the Americas, objectives turned to the monopolization of trade and, under the mercantilist philosophy, the development of colonies that rounded out supplies of raw materials and guaranteed overseas markets within largely self-sufficient empires.

Spain's approach was primarily through military conquest, with plundering and exploitation to obtain gold and silver for the mother country. France moved largely by infiltration, developing friendly relations with many native tribes and capitalizing on the rich fur trade. England, on the other hand, began its colonization in North America through an extension of its fishing activities in the Grand Banks south of Newfoundland, coupled with a continuing search for a passageway through or around North America to northern China. Prominent, too, was the hope of developing important raw material sources and markets for manufactured goods. British long-range policies, therefore, contemplated several stages of development: (1) the establishment of outposts for exploration and experimentation; (2) the shipment of readily obtained native materials such as fish, furs, herbs, minerals, and naval stores; (3) the settlement of agricultural communities to produce sugar, wine, hides, and dyes; (4) the further development of industries based on forest and mineral resources; and (5) the eventual creation of a significant market for manufactures — especially woolen cloth — among the colonists and the Indians.

Spain led the race for American possessions by establishing a stronghold at Haiti at the beginning of the 16th century. From here the conquistadores spread out, and by 1536 they had established themselves in Puerto Rico, Jamaica, Cuba, Mexico, Peru, Bolivia, and Florida. In North America, however, they did not penetrate far inland, and their hold over these colonies by the end of the century depended mainly on sea power. This was broken by the English and Dutch in 1588 with the destruction of the Spanish Armada. But Spain continued to be an important colonial power in the New World, especially in South and Central America. In North America, its missions and settlements were pushed north of the Rio Grande and along the Pacific Coast to San Francisco until it was halted in 1821 by Mexico's declaration of independence.

With the seas cleared of the Spanish threat, France and England began a struggle for domination of North America. The French mounted a two-pronged attack — along the St. Lawrence River and the Great Lakes in the north and through the Mississippi River system from the south. Quebec was established in 1608 and Champlain had reached Georgian Bay on Lake Huron by 1615. The French policy of friendly relations with the Indians was largely successful, although Champlain's alliance with the Hurons against the powerful Iroquois proved to be a costly mistake in later conflicts between the French and the English. La Salle began his expeditions up the St. Lawrence and through the Great Lakes in 1669, by 1680 had reached the headwaters of the Mississippi, and within two years had moved down to the Gulf of Mexico. Outposts were established throughout all of this region by 1700, and the "west" was definitely French. Shortly thereafter, the Acadians were settling in Nova Scotia, Cape Breton Island, and the Gulf of St. Lawrence, and by 1755 the population of these settlements numbered approximately 9000. Meanwhile, the southern approach was not neglected: Fort Biloxi was established in 1699, New Orleans in 1718, and by 1731 the Louisiana country had a population of about 7000 Frenchmen. Mention should also be made of the migrations of the French Huguenots, especially after the Edict of Nantes in 1685. These Protestants were not welcome in the French colonies, however, and so for the most part served to swell the migration from England and the Low Countries to the British colonies.

After experiments during the 1580's in Newfoundland and North Carolina, England established its first permanent American colonies in Virginia in 1607 and Massachusetts in 1620. By the middle of the century, these settlements stretched in an almost continuous line along the Atlantic coast. With British stress on the colonies as sources of agricultural products and other raw materials and as markets for English manufactured goods, a policy of permanent settlement and of population growth was essential. This policy was implemented by aggressive promotional schemes emphasizing economic opportunity and political and religious freedom.

However, the Navigation Acts of 1651, 1660, and 1663 imposed three major restrictions on the American colonies. First, all trade between England and America had to be carried in English or colonial ships with English or colonial crews — this barred foreign ships from colonial ports. Second, all colonial imports, except wine and salt from southern Europe, had to come from England — this assured the colonial market for English traders and manufacturers. Third, certain colonial products that were enumerated or listed could be shipped only to England — this was designed to give England the products needed to round out her own economy, and also to give English traders the profits from reexporting surpluses to other European markets.

The number of settlers increased rapidly, and England soon had more settlers in North America than any other power. By 1750, the population of the English colonies exceeded 1,200,000, while France had managed to settle only 80,000. Growing rivalry and conflict with the French for the fisheries and fur trade were finally resolved by military power, with England the victor. By the Peace of Paris in 1763, France ceded Canada to the English and relinquished claims to territory west to the Mississippi River. By this same treaty, French claims beyond the Mississippi (including the Louisiana settlements and New Orleans) were turned over to Spain. As part of the implementation of the treaty, Britain deported approximately 6000 Acadians to the colonies to the south.

1.2 THE AMERICAN COLONIAL ECONOMY

Development of the English colonies, like the exploitation of the westward-moving frontier in the generations to follow, was in essence a gigantic speculation in natural resources. Here was a virgin and largely unexplored territory, with untold potential in terms of rich farming lands and mineral and forest resources. But to acquire value, these resources needed to be developed and connected with markets, and this required massive investments of capital and labor. To attract these investments, there had to be prospects of profits to pay returns on capital and to provide labor income for the purchase of European goods essential to existence as well as to a hoped-for increase in living standards in America. This meant that the colonial ventures needed exportable surpluses of goods keyed to the demands of European markets. Also, they had to contribute a maximum amount to their own subsistence and, especially in the early stages, to devote perhaps half of their energies to the creation of new capital through land improvement.

The dominant characteristic of colonial enterprise was its dependence on agriculture — perhaps 90 percent of the colonists made their living from farming, supplemented as well as possible by hunting and trapping, and this pattern persisted throughout the colonial period. Moreover, there was a high degree of economic self-sufficiency, with most households growing a large proportion of their food supplies and also weaving cloth, making clothes, curing meats, and carrying on crude manufacturing operations. Commercial agriculture soon developed, however, if defined in terms of the production of exportable surpluses. In this development, the production and trade patterns varied widely among the southern, middle, and northern colonies.

The tidewater regions of the southern colonies were well suited to large-scale farming, and soil and climate favored the production of crops such as tobacco, rice, and indigo. Commercial production quickly developed through the plantation system, with crops loaded directly on ships for the English market. England wanted these crops, so most of the products of the southern colonies were enumerated under the Navigation Acts. The South was thus restricted in its choice of markets, but it was able to build up a profitable "shuttle" trade with England by exchanging farm products and naval stores for British goods usually with a favorable balance of trade (Table 1.1). These colonies fit well into the British empire scheme, supplying needed products with surpluses for profitable reexport to other European markets. Tobacco was especially important and dominated exports in the colonial period. The southern colonial planters complained because the channeling of their crop through England returned them only a fraction of the world market price, but they also profited from the prohibition of tobacco production in southern England and from bounties paid on indigo and naval stores.

The middle and northern colonies needed the manufactured goods of England, but produced few products demanded by the mother country. Shipments to England included items such as furs and potashes from the middle colonies and masts and complete ships from New England. Fortunately, markets for the major products of these colonies were available in the "sugar islands" of the West Indies, where specialization on sugar

Table 1.1   Commerce of American Continental Colonies with England, 1701 to 1710 and 1761 to 1770[a]

Region	1701 to 1710			1761 to 1770		
	Exports	Imports	Balance	Exports	Imports	Balance
New England	37	86	− 49	113	358	− 245
Middle-Atlantic	22	37	− 15	97	644	− 547
Southern	219	150	+ 69	834	793	+ 41
Total	278	273	+ 5	1044	1795	− 751

[a]*Source.* Summarized from data reported by Robert C. Albion, "Colonial Commerce and Commercial Regulation," in Harold F. Williamson (Ed.), *Growth of the American Economy,* Prentice Hall, Inc., Englewood Cliffs, N.J., second edition, p. 48, 1951. Albion indicates that his data were compiled from D. Macpherson, *Annals of Commerce, passim,* and from J. S. Homans, *Historical and Statistical Account of the Foreign Commerce of the United States* (1857), pp. 6–7.

production had been carried to the point that imports of foods, horses, and lumber products were required. This gave rise to multilateral or triangular trade, the returns from which offset the unfavorable direct balances of the northern colonies with England. The middle colonies shipped flour and salted pork and beef to the Islands, while New England's contributions were fish and lumber. Cargoes of sugar were then moved to England, and manufactured goods returned to the colonies.

Rhode Island developed its own version of the sugar triangle — rum to Africa, slaves from Africa to the Islands, and molasses to Rhode Island to make more rum. At the peak of the rum and slave trade in 1763, about 150 vessels were bringing 14,000 hogsheads of molasses annually to 30 distilleries in Rhode Island — much of this from non-English sources to avoid payment of the duty. Other trade triangles linked the colonies with Spain and Portugal, permitted by the Navigation Acts for nonenumerated articles: fish, flour, and staves for wine casks were shipped to southern Europe with return trips through England or, perhaps, direct to the colonies with salt and wine. Finally, a coastal trade connected the tidewater regions of the colonies themselves, with movements of flour and livestock from the middle colonies, fish and lumber from New England.

Economic enterprise in the colonies was by no means limited to farming and foreign trade. Local communities were developing a considerable degree of specialization through craft shops, saw mills and grist mills, breweries and distilleries, and even iron furnaces. Near the end of the colonial period, real industries were developing. Mention has been made of shipbuilding; the colonies built 24,000 tons of sailing vessels in 1771 and by the Revolutionary War approximately one-third of all vessels in the British registry were of colonial build. Shoemaking and the textile industry developed under the "putting-out" system, with materials supplied to home workers. Blast furnaces, paper mills, tanneries, and glass works were not only established but were growing in size. These activities came increasingly in conflict with British policies, as did the competition of New England fishing fleets and the growing evasion of the Navigation Acts by colonial ships and traders. A series of new acts and proclamations attempted further to restrict colonial trade, to limit industrial development, and to prevent the expansion of the frontier beyond the Appalachian Mountains. They led to colonial agreements to boycott imports of British goods and, finally, to war.

1.3 TERRITORIAL EXPANSION OF THE NEW NATION

Open hostilities between England and the colonists started at Lexington and Concord in April of 1775, and on July 4th of the following year the members of the Continental Congress signed the Declaration of Independence. By 1778, the new United States had enlisted the aid of a number of European powers, particularly, through the treaty of alliance with France against England and the formation of the League of Armed Neutrality by Russia, Prussia, Denmark, Sweden, and Portugal to resist British sea power. The fighting ended with the defeat of the British at Yorktown in 1781, although the war was formally terminated with the signing of the Treaty of Paris in 1783. By this treaty, England granted the United States independence and title to all lands west to the Mississippi River and north to the Great Lakes. Spain still claimed Florida, the Gulf Coast, and the lands west of the Mississippi. Spanish control of the mouth of the Mississippi restricted the development of river traffic and trade with the region west of the Appalachian Mountains, but this was corrected by the Pinckney Treaty of 1795.

The United States thus controlled a far larger territory than it was immediately able to exploit. France had ceded the Louisiana territory to Spain after the French and Indian War, but Napoleon regained possession in 1800. This vast region was added to the United States through the Louisiana Purchase in 1803. English claims to the Red River basin in what is now Minnesota and North Dakota were relinquished about 1818. In the following year, Spain ceded Florida and a coastal strip in Louisiana. Russia, which had been developing the fur trade in Alaska and down the Pacific coast into California, agreed in 1824 to stay north of 54° 40′. The treaty of 1842 with England settled the northeastern boundary between the United States and Canada.

Meanwhile, Mexico had declared its independence from Spain in 1821, and Texas in turn gained its independence from Mexico in 1836. The Texas territory was annexed by the United States in 1845. In the northwest, the Oregon compromise of 1846 fixed the western boundary between the United States and Canada. Mexico ceded the southwestern territory including California in 1848, and the Gadsden Purchase (a small strip of land in southern Arizona) rounded out the borders of the nation in 1853.

The settlement of this vast territory was a much slower process, of course, involving exploration, the pushing back of the Indians, the growth and migration of population, the clearing and improvement of the land, and the development of transportation and marketing systems. At the end of the colonial period, the frontier of settlement followed the eastern slopes of the Appalachian Mountains with minor extensions through the Cumberland Gap to the Kentucky-Tennessee territory and through Pennsylvania to the Ohio River. The rough mountain country created an almost insurmountable barrier to transportation, and the bypassing of this barrier by "water-level" routes was blocked by the warlike Iroquois Indians in western New York and by the no less formidable Cherokees in the Georgia-Alabama district. But these restraints were overcome as the irresistable flood of population spilled over into the western territory.

By 1815 the frontier (defined as a settled population of two persons per square mile) had pushed well into eastern Ohio and down the Ohio River to the Wabash. Migration through the Cumberland Gap had settled Kentucky and much of Tennessee. To the south the Indians were still troublesome, but most of Georgia and the northern part of Alabama had been won. Also, the Louisiana Purchase had added an important southern beachhead that spread out from New Orleans (Figure 1.1). By 1840, the frontier was in southern Michigan and Wisconsin and, generally, extended across the first tier of states west of the Mississippi River. Progress through the Civil War period was relatively slow, but the frontier moved across Iowa and into eastern Nebraska, Kansas, and Texas. The gold rush created a rapidly growing population in California, and a new frontier was pushing eastward from the Pacific coast.

The twenty-five years from 1865 to 1890 carried agriculture into the semiarid prairie country and brought the settlement of Oregon and the Northwest. This was the period of rapid disposal of the Public Domain — through sale at low prices, through "free land" under the Homestead Act

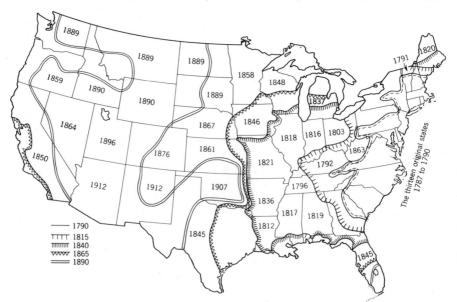

FIGURE 1.1 The moving frontier and the admission of states. (Based on Report of the Director of the Census, 1890.)

of 1862, and through land grants to the states for the support of education and to the railroads for their development. By the end of the 19th century, the government had no more good land to give away and the frontier period had come to an end. There remained large areas in the mountain states where population density was less than two persons per square mile. With limited economic opportunities, low population density has persisted in much of the intermountain area of the West until the present time.

With minor departures, such as the creation of West Virginia by the subdivision of Virginia in 1863, the formation of states closely followed the advancing frontier (Figure 1.1). The original thirteen states had ratified the Constitution by 1790, and by 1820 all states east of the Mississippi except Florida and Wisconsin had been admitted. Approximately 100,000 gold miners provided the basis for admitting California in 1850. Most of the mountain states were admitted about 1890, and the process was completed when Arizona and New Mexico became states in 1912.

The expansion of the frontier of settlement and the formation of states, however, by no means indicate the complete development of available resources. The westward movement was primarily agricultural, but only a small portion of the farmland was developed as the frontier advanced. This may be illustrated by comparing the improved land in farms in 1850 with the total cropland in 1950 (Figure 1.2). In the region between the original states and the Mississippi River, only 36 percent of the present cropland was improved in 1850, while in the first tier of states west of the river the ratio was less than 10 percent. Also, western competition resulted in decreases in cropland between 1850 and 1950 of more than 60 percent in New England and more than 20 percent in the New York to Virginia region.

1.4 TRANSPORTATION AND COMMUNICATION

At the close of the Revolutionary War, the United States found itself with a fairly well developed water transportation system along the coast and navigable rivers. Inland transportation was difficult and expensive, however, for the road network was little more than a collection of trails for pack horses and cattle. Where over-the-road transportation was available, service was slow and undependable.

With high freight costs, trade movements between inland points and seaports were limited to concentrated and valuable products such as furs, gunpowder, iron, salt, and whiskey. Animals provided their own transportation, and so could be moved economically for relatively long distances. Cattle and hogs were driven from west of the mountains in

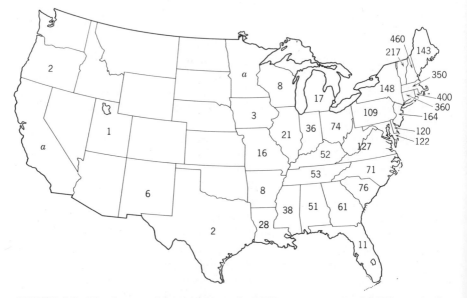

FIGURE 1.2 The improved land in farms in 1850 as a percent of 1950 cropland. [Calculated from data in Reports of the United States Bureau of the Census. (ªLess than one-half of one percent.)]

Ohio, Kentucky, and Tennessee to Baltimore, Philadelphia, and New York, and this practice continued well into the 19th century until the railroads served these areas and meat-packing developed along the Ohio River.

Several attempts were made to commit the federal government to a program of improved transportation—including the proposals of Secretary of the Treasury Gallatin and the "Bonus Act of 1816"—but they were rejected on constitutional grounds or because of diverse sectional interests. For the most part, road building was left to private initiative or to the states. Pennsylvania led the way by chartering private companies to construct toll roads. The success of the Philadelphia-Lancaster Turnpike —completed in 1794 and the first surfaced road in the Nation—led to the creation of literally thousands of such corporations. Private construction and operation under state charter and with supervision of tolls was typical in Pennsylvania and the states to the north, although in the southern states the fear of exploitation by private monopolies led to highway development by state and local governments. The federal government finally participated by constructing the National Pike or Cumberland Road from Cumberland Maryland to Wheeling in what is now West Virginia; this route was to connect with the Mississippi River at St. Louis and, actually, was extended as far as Vandalia, Illinois. These activities eventually linked together the eastern and northern states by a system of surfaced roads. By 1820 nearly 10,000 miles of surfaced roads had been completed, and this increased to 64,000 in 1840 and 88,000 in 1860.

A number of canals were constructed by private enterprise in the early years of the 19th century, but in 1817 the state of New York entered the field and began the construction of a comprehensive system connecting the Hudson River with Lake Champlain, with Lake Ontario, and with Lake Erie. The Erie Canal extended 363 miles from Albany to Buffalo, surmounting an altitude of 500 feet with 84 locks. When completed in 1825, the canal reduced the time required to move freight between Buffalo and New York City from 20 to eight days, and cut freight charges about 90 percent. It was an immediate financial success, and low-cost access to the hinterland did much to develop New York as the dominant city and seaport of the Atlantic Coast. By the same token, it was an immediate stimulus to commercial agriculture — and to land values — in the Great Lakes area, and the western competition profoundly influenced the agriculture of the Northeast.

Success of the Erie Canal coupled with the rivalry among New York, Philadelphia, and Baltimore as leading ports soon brought Pennsylvania and Maryland-Virginia into the canal-building ventures. The Pennsylvania Canal connected Philadelphia with the Ohio River at Pittsburgh in 1834 by a route that crossed the Allegheny Mountains at an elevation of 2300 feet.

The Chesapeake and Ohio Canal was the third major attempt to reach the West by canal. It was completed only to Cumberland over a route that covered 184 miles with 73 locks and had a maximum elevation of 609 feet. Meanwhile the Lake states and especially Ohio were completing a series of canals that joined the Ohio and Mississippi Rivers with the Great Lakes. By mid-century, the United States had nearly 4000 miles of canals in operation. But by that time the railroads were emerging as the major factor in inland transportation. Even the successful Erie Canal was surpassed by the railroads in volume of freight handled in New York by the end of the Civil War.

The first railroad in the United States was built in 1826 to haul stone for the Bunker Hill monument; the first common carrier was the Baltimore and Ohio Railroad, started in 1830. These and other early railroads were horse-drawn, but within several years steam was the universal traction power. Rail mileage increased to 2800 in 1840 and to 9000 in 1850. Early lines were built to complement water transportation, but the superiority of rail service was soon evident, and the building of a major network began. Track mileage increased to 31,000 by 1860 and to 53,000 by 1870. By the end of the Civil War, there existed a fairly comprehensive rail system in the northern states west to the Mississippi. The war had retarded construction in the South, but even there the major components of a network had been built. Finally, in 1869, a line was pushed across the continent to San Francisco.

The development of the system in this period and in the decades to follow was greatly stimulated by federal and state aid, particularly in the form of land grants. Between 1850 and 1871, when the practice was discontinued, the federal government granted nearly 160,000,000 acres of land to the railroad companies; approximately 130,000,000 acres were eventually patented by the railroads. In return for these grants, the companies agreed to construct roads in designated territories, primarily in the South and the West, and they also gave the government preferential rates on mail, troops, and government property.

The growing railroads by no means displaced coastal trade and inland water commerce on the Mississippi River and the Great Lakes. In 1807, Fulton's *Clermont* demonstrated the practicality of steam power for water transportation. The Pinckney Treaty with Spain in 1795 had opened up the Mississippi as a major trade route for the central regions of the United States, but this was almost entirely one-way, downstream traffic. However, the exploitation of steam power changed this and also greatly speeded the movement of traffic: the time from Louisville to New Orleans was reduced from 25 to less than five days. The first steamers were operating on the Mississippi shortly after 1810, and it has been estimated that 500 to 600 steamers were on the river by 1850. About 70 percent of outbound traffic from the Midwest flowed through the Mississippi system, while the balance went east by canal, railroad, and highway. Imported products were less bulky and more valuable, and riverboats handled considerably less than half of this trade. Meanwhile, coastal trade continued to expand and by the middle of the century still far exceeded the combined commerce of canals, railroads, and riverboats. The total gross tonnage of vessels in coastal and internal trade exceeded that in American foreign commerce in 1831 and remained well in the lead until World War I. In 1860, as a result of the growth of regional specialization and the rise of New York as the leading port, the value of commodities in the coastal trade was six times the value of American foreign trade.

Even a brief discussion of American transportation must mention the western trails, since they carried the bulk of the pioneers and early settlers. Routes through the Appalachian Mountains have already been described; there were several trails through western Pennsylvania and Maryland to the Ohio River and the "Wilderness Road" through Cumberland Gap to Kentucky and Tennessee. They were well developed by the end of the colonial period but were little used until the westward migrations after the Revolutionary War. As the frontier pushed across the Mississippi River, the great trails extended to the Far West. The Santa Fe Trail from St. Louis to New Mexico was developed during the 1820's as American traders began to supply the Spanish-Mexican outpost at Santa Fe (Figure 1.3). Later this was extended to southern California as the Spanish Trail. The first large migrations of settlers by the Oregon Trail came in the 1840's, and by the end of that decade the gold rush had created the California Trail as a southern branch. Salt Lake City was founded in 1847 and the Mormon Trail, roughly paralleling the Oregon Trail, brought settlers to the Utah area. Finally, the Butterfield Overland Mail swung south near the Mexican border: coaches carried mail and passengers to California in 25 days, until the trail was made obsolete by the completion of the transcontinental railroad in 1869.

Not all of the trails were for settlers, since many famous routes developed as cattle paths. Cattle droving was common practice in the colonies, and many special trails or roads were developed for this purpose. An example is the Ten Rod Road in Rhode Island—a tract 165 feet wide that extended from the western part of the colony to the Narragansett Bay. Cattle and hog drives across the Appalachian Mountains to the

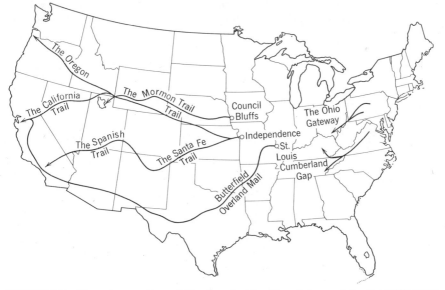

FIGURE 1.3   The gateways through the Appalachian Mountains, and the Great Western Trails. (Based primarily on Philip M. Overmeyer, "Westward Expansion before the Homestead Act," in Harold F. Williamson (Ed.), *Growth of the American Economy*, Prentice-Hall, Inc., Englewood Cliffs, N.J., second edition, 1951, p. 94.)

seaports were well established in the early 19th century. But it remained for Texas to develop the major trails of the 19th century, a good example of a frontier region reaching for adequate markets.

Cattle were first introduced north of the Rio Grande in the 1580's. The early Texas settlers from the United States crossed the "native" cattle with stock imported from northern Europe to develop the famous long-horned steer. It is estimated that there were more than 300,000 cattle in the area when Texas was admitted to the Union. They had increased to 1,400,000 in 1855 and to 3,800,000 in 1860. But the country was cattle-poor, since there were few markets except for hides and tallow. Sporadic drives were made between 1842 and 1861 in search for buyers in New Orleans, Shrevesport, and even in Ohio and New York. Several herds were driven to California during the gold rush; steers worth $10 in Texas brought $30 in California. Herds were also driven east to the Mississippi to provision the Confederate army until Grant captured Vicksburg in 1863.

The big drives started after the Civil War, and in the early years the movements were to railhead points in Kansas for shipment to markets and to the growing Union Stock Yards at Chicago. As the railroads were extended and as crop agriculture became established and forced the trail herds to the west, the major markets moved from Sedalia to Abilene, to Ellsworth, to Newton, to Wichita, and finally to Dodge City (Figure 1.4). Abilene was the northern terminus of the Chisholm Trail and between

FIGURE 1.4   The Texas cattle trails. (Based on Paul I. Wellman, *The Trampling Herd*, Garrick and Evans, Inc., New York, 1939.)

1867 and 1871, approximately 5,000,000 head of cattle passed through this outlet. Dodge City was the major center from 1875 to 1885 — as a railhead shipping point on the Santa Fe Railroad, as the headquarters for the buffalo hunters and, finally, as a major point on the Dodge City-Western Trail along which moved stocker cattle for the range in the Northwest territory. Probably 6,000,000 head of cattle and horses moved north through Dodge. Total shipments from Texas between 1867 and 1890 are estimated at 12,000,000 head with a total value of $250,000,000.

The economic incentive behind these trail drives was direct and simple. Cattle could be bought in Texas for $5 to $10 per head and sold at the market or railhead for $20 to $30. A drive from Texas to Montana would cover 3000 miles and take about six months — at a cost of about $1 per head. This left a profit sizable enough to fill the trails in spite of the risks of floods, blizzards, and the Comanche and Sioux Indians. Herds kept moving north until the frontier was closed and the land was covered with wheat ranches and fenced ranges.

The importance of communications was recognized in the Constitution, and Congress was given power to improve the postal service. A dependable mail service required dependable transportation, however, so improvement came slowly. Letter rates amounted to eight cents for 30 miles in 1820, but they were reduced to five cents for 300 miles by 1845 and to three cents for 3000 miles by 1851.

During this period, Samuel Morse invented the telegraph and in 1844 the first experimental line was completed between Washington and Baltimore. Telegraph lines connected New York with Chicago and Washington with New Orleans in 1850. In 1861, the first transcontinental line was completed and the first trans-Atlantic cable was laid. Immediately after the Civil War, the Western Union Company had 46,000 miles of pole lines and cables, 85,000 miles of wire, 2600 offices, and carried on an annual business in excess of $6,500,000.

The transportation and communication systems were far from complete, but substantial progress had been made in tying together the Nation. Dependable and low-cost mail service was a reality, and the telegraph provided almost instantaneous communications among all parts of the United States and with Europe. The transportation system of surfaced highways, canals and improved inland waterways, and railroads served all parts of the northeastern quarter of the country and was being extended rapidly in the southern and western sections. Transportation charges were a small fraction of the costs at the beginning of the 19th century (Table 1.2). From the standpoint of economic development, it was now possible to know of market opportunities, and it was economical to ship raw materials and finished products for long distances.

TABLE 1.2   Approximate Freight Rates in the United States during the 19th Century[a]

Type of Transportation	Period	Freight Rates or Costs Cents per Ton-Mile
Road	1800 to 1810	20 to 40
	1825 to 1840	10 to 15
Canal	1825 to 1840	1 to 3
Coastal	1800 to 1825	1 to 2
Railroad	1840	4 to 10
	1855	3
	1865	1.5 to 2
	1880	1.2
	1890	0.9

[a]Based on fragmentary reports from a variety of sources.

1.5   THE GROWTH OF ECONOMIC SPECIALIZATION

As settlement pushed westward, areas on the frontier evolved through a rather typical sequence. First came the hunters, explorers, fur traders, and the missionaries. Then came the "professional" pioneers — fighting Indians, clearing small plots for corn, and raising a few cattle. They were followed by the farmers, who frequently bought out the pioneers and settled down to occupy and to improve the land on a subsistence-farming basis. Villages developed as more settlers came to the area, and economic specialization had its start. Farming was by far the dominant occupation and a considerable degree of self-sufficiency persisted. But each community had men who specialized in the handcrafts (cabinetmaking, blacksmithing, harness and shoemaking) as well as millers, carpenters, printers, teachers, and merchants. In the days of high transport cost, each inland community was largely self-sufficient, and commercial contacts among these communities and with the seacoast was not extensive. Improving transportation made specialization possible on a larger scale and, by the mid-19th century, there was growing competition between "local" and "imported" products. Flour provides an excellent example: when local wheat production was important, flour making was in the hands of small grist mills. As transportation opened the western lands, wheat production moved more and more to the Great Lakes, large milling companies developed, and most eastern communities obtained their supplies from the west. By the Civil War, the monopoly of small industries in local markets had largely disappeared except in storekeeping and the service trades.

The growth of economic specialization during this period can best be summarized by considering the changes that were taking place in population and in employment. In 1790, only five percent of the population lived in urban communities with populations in excess of 2500 inhabitants; perhaps 90 percent of total gainful employment in the United States was in agriculture. By 1870, 26 percent of the population was urban and nearly half of the gainful employment was in nonagricultural lines. Data on the distribution of nonagricultural employment are not available for the earlier period, but in 1870 approximately 21 percent of the employed persons worked in manufacturing, the hand trades, and construction, 10 percent were involved in transportation and trade, and 13 percent in domestic and other service occupations. In terms of private income realized from production, the proportions originating in agriculture declined significantly from 40 percent in 1799 to 24 percent in 1869, while the proportions from manufacturing, trade, and service occupations increased. These changes are typical of growth in an advancing economy.

The effective British blockade during the War of 1812 did much to stimulate manufacturing in the United States. These new industries found it difficult to meet intense foreign competition following the War, however, and this led to the first protective tariff in 1816. Duties on imported goods averaged 20 percent, and rates were raised still further by 1833. The southern states were primarily interested in export markets for their major agricultural products rather than in manufacturing and, hence, generally opposed high tariffs. These differences in sectional interests resulted in rate reductions in 1833, increases in 1842, and reductions in 1846 and 1857. Duties averaged about 19 percent in 1861, but with southern opposition made ineffective by the Civil War, rates were raised to an average of 47 percent in 1864. With a growing and protected domestic market, manufacturing developed rapidly in the northern states and, especially, in the Northeast.

Iron smelting had developed in the early colonial period, but furnaces used wood and charcoal for fuel and were small in scale until the 1820's. The period from 1830 to 1870 saw a tenfold increase in the output of pig iron while coal production increased from virtually nothing to more than 33,000,000 tons per year. Textile mills were established in New England at the turn of the century, and soon they were producing cotton as well as woolen cloth. By 1860, more than 5,000,000 cotton spindles were operating, utilizing 845,000 bales or 22 percent of United States cotton production.

Agriculture was also keyed to the "industrial revolution" by becoming more specialized and commercialized. The urban and industrial population provided a growing market. In fact, the production of food supplies and agricultural raw materials were essential to industrial growth. The states in the Great Lakes region and the upper Mississippi Valley became the major grain producers (Figure 1.5). Livestock production moved to the rangelands, with "feeder" cattle often shipped from the range to the grain belt for fattening and finishing for market. Productive western lands and low freight rates forced northeastern farmers to turn to perishable and bulky products where closeness to urban markets gave them a real advantage—milk and dairy products, eggs, fruits and vegetables, and hay for the horses used in city transportation. The margin of cultivation in the Northeast retracted after 1850, and many acres that had been used as cropland reverted to forests.

Western competition was also a major influence on southeastern agriculture. Tobacco continued to be an important cash crop for foreign and domestic markets, but production increased little between 1800 and 1850. Indigo had been an important crop before the Revolution, but it disappeared quickly with the removal of the British subsidy. The big

FIGURE 1.5   The changes in the geographic centers for population, farm production, and manufacturing, 1850 to 1870. (*Source.* Population centers from *Statistical Abstract of the United States, 1956.*)

change came in cotton after Eli Whitney invented the gin in 1793. Production expanded rapidly to meet the demands of European and domestic markets — from less than 100,000 bales in 1800 to 1,350,000 in 1840 and more than 4,000,000 bales in 1870. Cotton rapidly depleted the soil, however, and soon the southeastern states were being displaced by new lands in Alabama, Mississippi, and Texas. With little opportunity to shift to market crops for the few urban centers in the area, agriculture declined while land eroded and was abandoned.

1.6 THE SITUATION AT THE CLOSE OF THE CIVIL WAR

In 250 years the American settlements had grown from a handful of isolated colonies clinging to the Atlantic Coast to a nation stretching from the Atlantic to the Pacific with a population of 35,000,000. Although still an agricultural economy, farm employment had declined to less than 60 percent of total employment. Manufacturing, construction, and trade were contributing increasingly large proportions to the national income. The transportation network had been developed through interconnected systems of highways, waterways, and railroads in the northeastern quarter of the country, and was rapidly expanding in other sections. Inland transportation costs (the big barrier to western growth and to interregional trade) had been reduced from 20 to 40 cents per ton-mile in the days of primitive roads to one to two cents per ton-mile on canals and railroads. Communication by mail and telegraph was helping to tie the country together and — through greatly improved information — was contributing to the growth of a market economy.

Agriculture had moved into the fertile lands of the Midwest, and regional specialization was developing to take advantage of favorable soil, climate, and location factors. Farm mechanization was underway, making more effective use of human and animal power. Household industries declined as farmers purchased more and more of their clothes, tools, furniture, and even food with money obtained from the sale of "cash" crops. Industrial cities were growing, particularly in the Northeast, and the migration of excess population from farms to cities and manufacturing occupations had started. International trade, though important, had declined somewhat in relative terms and was beginning to show the patterns characteristic of industrial instead of agricultural economies — increased imports of raw materials and exports of manufactured articles.

The stage had been set for this interrelated development of industry and commercial agriculture early in the 19th century. The United States had an abundance of unexploited natural resources, the necessary technology was being created by the industrial and agricultural revolutions, and the population and the labor supply were growing rapidly. This development would have been impossible, however, without the simultaneous advance of transportation, communication, and of the many occupations that make up the marketing system. By the close of the Civil War, these facilitating industries had been greatly improved and the evolution of a market-oriented enterprise economy was well under way.

SELECTED READINGS

The Early American Economy

Adams, James Truslow, *Provincial Society, 1690–1763*, The Macmillan Company, New York, (1927).

Bidwell, Percy W. and John I. Falconer, *History of Agriculture in the Northern United States, 1620–1860*. Carnegie Institute of Washington, 1925 (Peter Smith, New York, 1941).

Bragdon, Henry W. and Samuel P. McCutchen, *History of a Free People*, The Macmillan Company, New York (1954).

Craven, Wesley Frank, *The Southern Colonies in the Seventeenth Century*, Louisiana State University Press (1949).

Edwards, Everett E., "American Agriculture — The First 300 Years," in *Farmers in a Changing World, 1940 Yearbook of Agriculture*, USDA, Washington (1940). pp. 171–276.

Gray, Lewis C., *History of Agriculture in the Southern United States to 1860*, Vols. I and II. Carnegie Institute of Washington (1933). (Peter Smith, New York, 1941).

Jones, Howard Mumford, *America and French Culture, 1750–1848*, The University of North Carolina Press, Chapel Hill (1927).

Langdon, William Chauncy, *Everyday Things in American Life, 1776–1876*, Charles Scribner's & Sons, New York (1941).

Lewis, Oscar, *Sea Routes to the Gold Fields*, Alfred A. Knopf, New York (1949).

North, Douglass C., *The Economic Growth of the United States, 1790–1860*, Prentice-Hall Inc., Englewood Cliffs (1961).

Parker, William N. (ed.), *Trends in the American Economy in the Nineteenth Century*, NBER Studies in Income and Wealth. Vol. XXIV. Princeton University Press, Princeton (1960).

Wellman, Paul I., *The Trampling Herd*, Carrick and Evans, Inc., New York (1939).

chapter 2

DEVELOPMENT OF AN ADVANCED ECONOMY: 1870 TO THE 1960'S

During this period of nearly a century, the frontier has been closed and good farmlands brought under intensive cultivation. Agriculture has become more specialized and mechanized. The rail network has been completed and important new elements added to the transportation system through the automobile, the truck, and the airplane. Manufacturing has assumed a central role and the diversity of industrial output almost defies description. With these changes have come rapid increases in marketing and the emergence of the service occupations as a dominant feature of the economy. In this chapter we trace briefly how these changes, coupled with the growth of science and technology, have brought great increases in productivity and in the levels of income in the United States.

2.1 ECONOMIC SPECIALIZATION AND REGIONAL GROWTH

One hundred years ago the German economist Ernst Engel observed that, in working-class families, the proportion of income spent for food declined as total income increased. Years later the Australian economist

Colin Clark generalized Engel's law to describe conditions for economic progress among nations. Clark observed that, as countries advanced, *primary* or resource-based industries became relatively less important, that *secondary* industries such as manufacturing increased, and that well advanced countries devoted an increasing proportion of their resources to the *tertiary* industries — that is, to marketing, trade, and to professional, personal, and government services.

Although such a progression may not necessarily be inviolate in economic development, it certainly has characterized the growth of the American economy since the Civil War. Perloff, et al., have assembled a wide variety of data on the changes in the American economy during this period.[1] In the year 1870, resource industries employed more than 50 percent of the entire labor force of the United States. By 1910, this had dropped to 36 percent and by 1950 to 14 percent. Current estimates place the resource labor force at 5 to 6 percent (Table 2.1). Manufactures replaced agriculture as the largest single group in the mid-20th century with approximately one-fourth of the labor force engaged in these activities. This is a somewhat larger fraction than in the immediate post-Civil War period, and somewhat smaller than in the early 20th century. Service

[1]Harvey S. Perloff, Edgar S. Dunn, Jr., Eric E. Lampard, and Richard F. Muth, *Regions, Resources and Economic Growth*. Johns Hopkins Press: Baltimore, 1960.

TABLE 2.1   Distribution of Labor Force by Major Industry Group, United States, 1870 to 1967

Year	Resource Industries	Manufactures	Services
1870	54	21	25
1910	36	28	36
1950	14	24	62
1967	6	25	69

Sources. 1870, 1910, 1950 from Harvey S. Perloff, Edgar S. Dunn, Jr., Eric E. Lampard, and Richard F. Muth, *Regions, Resources, and Economic Growth*. Johns Hopkins Press, 1960. Table 30, p. 131 and Table 88, p. 234. 1967 estimated by projecting industry data for 1950 in Appendix Tables A-1 to A-7 to 1967 by using rates of change in employment reported in *Statistical Abstract of the United States, 1968,* Table 310, p. 215, Table 993, p. 652.

industries, however, have increased steadily and rapidly from 25 percent in 1870 to nearly 70 percent of the labor force in the late 1960's.

Clearly, this growth has not been uniform across the nation. The rapid shift in regional distribution of population is shown in Table 2.2. The

TABLE 2.2   Regional Distribution of Population, 1870, 1950, and 1967, and Total Personal Income, 1880, 1950, and 1967 (Percent of United States Total)

Region	Population			Total Personal Income		
	1870	1950	1967	1880	1950	1967
East						
New England	9	6	6	11	7	6
Mideast	24	22	21	33	26	24
Great Lakes	23	20	20	23	23	22
Southeast	29	23	22	14	15	17
Total	85	71	69	81	71	69
West						
Plains	10	9	8	11	9	8
Southwest	3	8	8	2	6	7
Rocky Mountains	a	2	2	1	2	2
Far West[b]	2	10	13	5	12	14
Total	15	29	31	19	29	31

Source.   Population 1870, 1950: Perloff, *op. cit.*, Table 1, p. 12.
Personal income 1880, 1950: Perloff, *op. cit.*, Table 8, p. 24.

Population 1967: *Statistical Abstract 1968*, Table 11, p. 12.
Personal income 1967: *Survey of Current Business*, April 1968, Volume 49, No. 4, Table 1, p. 20.

[a]Less than .05 percent.

[b]Excluding Alaska and Hawaii.

The current grouping of states used by Office of Business Economics, U.S. Department of Commerce, unless otherwise indicated.
New England: Me, N.H., Vt., Mass., R.I., Conn.
Mideast: N.Y., N.J., Penn., Del., Md., District of Columbia.
Great Lakes: Mich., Ohio, Ind., Ill., Wisc.
Plains: Minn., Iowa, Mo., N.D., S.D., Neb., Kan.
Southeast: Va., W. Va., Ky., Tenn., N.C., S.C., Ga., Fla., Ala., Miss., La., Ark.
Southwest: Okla., Texas., N.M., Ariz.
Rocky Mountain: Mont., Idaho, Wyo., Colo., Utah.
Far West: Wash., Ore., Nev., Calif., Alaska, Hawaii.

proportion of the total population living east of the Mississippi River declined from 85 percent in 1870 to less than 70 percent in the late 1960's. The shift in the center of population in the United States is graphically shown in Figure 2.1 for the period 1790 to 1960. The major area experiencing a relative increase in population, of course, has been the Far West, increasing from 2 percent in the post-Civil War period to more than 13 percent in the late 1960's.

In general, total personal income is distributed much as the population is distributed, but early differences arose with relatively high incomes in New England, the Mideast and in the Far West, while incomes were relatively low in the Southeast. At the close of this period the correlation between population and total personal income was much higher than earlier in the period, but differences still show through in lower fractions of total income being reported in the Southeast and somewhat higher fractions in the Mideast, the Great Lakes, and the Far West.

One reason for the regional differences in income can be found in the relative importance of agriculture in the economy of the several regions. In 1870, approximately 42 percent of the entire agricultural labor force was located in the Southeast, and 85 percent in the area east of the Mississippi. Agriculture rapidly moved west with the exception of the

FIGURE 2.1   The center of population for the United States, 1790 to 1980. Projections based on series 1B. Alaska and Hawaii included 1950 to 1980. (*Source.* United States Bureau of the Census, Current Population Reports, Series P-25, No. 388, "Summary of Demographic Projections".)

Southeast, which still employed a third of the agricultural labor force in the late 1960's. Manufactures, on the other hand, have been heavily concentrated in the East and, especially, in the Northeast. The Southeast accounted for only 10 percent of this industry group in 1870 and for less than 20 percent of all manufacturing in the late 1960's. Although the Mideast lost some of its dominance in manufactures, it still held a larger than proportional share of these jobs at the end of the period. Services, on the other hand, have consistently been highly correlated with population distribution, as will be noticed by comparing the distribution of the labor force shown in Table 2.3 with the distribution of population shown in the previous table.

TABLE 2.3   Regional Distribution of Labor Force by Major Industry Group, 1870, 1950, and 1967 (Percent of United States Total)

Region	Agriculture			Manufacture			Services		
	1870	1950	1967	1870	1950	1967	1870	1950	1967
East									
New England	5	2	2	22	10	8	11	6	6
Mideast	14	6	6	38	29	24	36	25	23
Great Lakes	24	15	17	20	29	26	20	19	19
Southeast	42	39	33	10	15	19	19	19	19
Total	85	62	58	90	83	77	86	69	67
West									
Plains	11	19	20	7	6	6	8	9	8
Southwest	3	10	10	1	3	5	2	8	8
Rocky Mountain	a	3	4	a	1	1	1	2	3
Far West[b]	1	6	8	2	7	11	3	12	14
Total	15	38	42	10	17	23	14	31	33

Source.   Agriculture 1870, 1950: Perloff, *op. cit.*, Table 34, p. 134 and Table 93, p. 238.
Manufacturing 1870, 1950: Perloff, *op. cit.*, Table 44, p. 152 and Table 102, p. 252.
Services 1870, 1950: Perloff, *op. cit.*, Table 50, p. 162 and Table 107, p. 257.
Agriculture 1967: *Agricultural Statistics, 1968*, Table 643, p. 445.
Manufacturing and services 1967: *Statistical Abstract 1968*, Table 319, p. 220.

[a]Less than .05 percent.
[b]Excluding Alaska and Hawaii.

2.2　INCREASING OUTPUT AND PRODUCTIVITY

This has been a period of tremendous increases in the physical output of the United States economy. When measured in terms of index numbers with 1899 as the base of 100, agricultural output increased from 42 in 1869 to 212 in 1949. Mining production advanced from 17 to 466, and the output of manufactured goods soared from 25 to 604 (Table 2.4). The combined index of all commodity production rose from 31 in 1869 to 443 in 1949. During this same period, population and employment in commodity production and distribution had increased about fourfold. As a result, productivity more than tripled: output per employee increased

TABLE 2.4　Changes in Population and Output in the United States, 1869 to 1949 (Index Numbers, 1899 = 100)

Item	Year				
	1869	1889	1909	1929	1949
Aggregate output					
Agriculture	42	79	115	145	212
Mining	17	57	184	389	466
Manufacturing	25	66	158	364	604
All commodities[a]	31	71	143	281	443
Population[b]	52	83	121	163	199
Employment[c]	44	82	122	153	178
Output per capita	60	86	118	172	223
Output per employee	70	87	117	184	249

Source. Harold Barger, Distribution's Place in the American Economy since 1869, National Bureau of Economic Research. Princeton University Press: Princeton, 1955, p. 22.

[a]Combined index based on agriculture, mining, and manufacturing indexes with 1899 value of products as weights.

[b]Estimates from U.S. Department of Commerce for total population residing in the United States, converted to index with 1899 as base.

[c]Employment in commodity production and distribution from Barger, op. cit., p. 4, converted to index numbers and moved from decennial years by interpolation.

from an index of 70 in 1869 to an index of 249 in 1949. Also, the real level of living was increasing by a comparable magnitude: per capita output of goods increased from indexes of 60 to 223.

Since the period covered by Barger's study, output and productivity have continued to increase rapidly.[2] From 1949 to 1968 farm output increased 29 percent, manufacturing output 137 percent, output of non-manufacturing industries 119 percent and population 30 percent. Output per employed person has advanced 176 percent, 76 percent and 51 percent in farm, manufacturing, and nonmanufacturing sections, respectively.

In fact, these comparisons understate the increase in levels of living in the United States. The average person spent many more years in school, began his work career at a later age, and had more leisure — the length of the average work week declined about 20 percent. Moreover, the content of living includes more than real goods, and the Nation was providing itself with more and more personal and professional services. Truly, the United States had moved far from the situation where the struggle for mere subsistence dominated the use of all resources.

For comparison purposes it is interesting to look at annual rates of change. Kuznets calculates population growth at 2.0 percent, product at 3.6 percent, and product per capita at 1.6 percent for the years 1840 to 1960 (Table 2.5). He finds United States population growth much higher, but product per capita very similar to rates of growth in the United Kingdom, France, and Germany during this period. However, product

[2]Compiled from *Statistics on Manpower*. U.S. Department of Labor. March, 1969. Table G-1, page 103.

TABLE 2.5 Rates of Growth of Population, Product, Labor Force, and Productivity in the United States, 1840 to 1960 (Percent per Year)

Item	Period			
	1840 to 1880	1880 to 1920	1920 to 1960	120-year period
Population	2.73	1.88	1.31	1.97
Gross national product	4.03	3.52	3.15	3.56
Product per capita	1.26	1.61	1.81	1.56
Labor force	2.96	2.23	1.28	2.15
Product per worker	1.04	1.26	1.84	1.38

Source. Simon Kuznets. "Notes on the Patterns of U.S. Economic Growth," in Edgar O. Edwards (ed.), *The Nation's Economic Objectives*. Chicago: University of Chicago Press, 1964. Table 1, p. 16.

per capita increased substantially more rapidly in Sweden, the USSR, and Japan (1.9 to 2.8 percent). In spite of this, increases in aggregate output in the United States have been exceptional and, given the initially high (relative) levels of income experienced in the early days of the American Republic, the absolute level of per capita income in this country continues to be among the highest in the world.

Strangely enough, the rapid increase in the output of consumer goods and services was possible because America could divert a significant proportion of its resources away from the immediate production of these items. This is the process of capital formation by which the productive capacity of the economy grows and provides the basis for still further increases in total output. In its most primitive stage, capital formation occurs when the level of living rises enough above subsistence to permit time and energy to be devoted to activities such as the fashioning of better tools and weapons, the clearing and improvement of land, and the domestication of animals. In a similar way, domestic capital formation—as distinct from investments of foreign capital—during the colonial and early national years was largely dominated by the creation of agricultural capital in the forms of land clearing and improvement, increasing livestock herds, and buildings and equipment. They continued to be important in the post-Civil War period.

Ever since the Civil War, the process of capital formation has proceeded rapidly in the United States. Although there have been variations in the rate in relation to general economic conditions, gross capital formation has averaged about 20 percent of the gross national product: in approximate terms, the economy has diverted one-fifth of its resources from the production of consumer goods to the production of producer goods.[3] This does not mean that the stock of capital goods has increased at this rate, however, for producer goods depreciate and wear out. With allowance for this, *net* capital formation has averaged about 10 percent of gross national product. The rate of net capital formation has been especially sensitive to economic conditions. During the depression years 1932 to 1934, for example, capital consumption actually exceeded gross capital formation and net capital formation was negative.

These estimates of capital formation neglect what is undoubtedly the most important factor of all—the improvement in the human resource. Although there are no simple indicators of the magnitude of this type of "capital" formation, it is clear that the population of the United States has been steadily improving in its abilities. In 1967 more than 84 percent of

[3]Simon Kuznets, *National Product Since 1869.* National Bureau of Economic Research, Inc., New York, 1946. Pages 50–54, 115–119.

the population 25 years old and over had completed at least eight years of schooling, 51 percent had completed at least four years of high school, and 20 percent had some college training. An increasing percentage of the labor force worked in skilled and semiskilled occupations, with corresponding decreases in the unskilled categories. This increase in American "know-how," coupled with net capital formation representing additional producer goods, has brought major technological advances and, hence, greatly expanded the productivity of both capital and labor.

2.3 THE MATURING TRANSPORTATION AND COMMUNICATIONS SYSTEMS

By the end of the Civil War, the United States had developed a reasonably good transportation system in the northeastern part of the country, based on networks of improved roads, railroads, and coastal and inland waterways. In the decades that followed, this expanded into a comprehensive system interconnecting all parts of the country. Railroad lines more than quadrupled. Waterways continued to be important, especially for heavy, nonperishable freight, and the Great Lakes soon became the dominant link in this system. At the turn of the century, the internal combustion engine was making its appearance and soon millions of automobiles, trucks, and buses were competing with older forms of transportation as surfaced highways replaced unpaved roads, providing effective service to areas not served by railroads or waterways. Pipelines were built for the long-distance transport of gas and petroleum products. Finally, the airplane ushered in the era of really fast transportation, and commercial airlines were developed to connect all major cities in the Nation as well as to tie the United States to other countries throughout the world. Today the United States has a highly complex and advanced transport system, and one that continues to evolve and to improve.

After the surge of turnpike building during the first half of the 19th century, highway construction and maintenance generally became the responsibility of local governments. Improvement came slowly — surfaced roads increased from 92,000 miles in 1870 to 128,000 miles in 1900. However, the new "horseless carriages" changed this by creating an insistent demand for more and better roads. The first decade of the 20th century brought most of the states into the fields of highway finance and construction, although the federal government became an active partner with the passage of the Federal-Aid Highway Act of 1916.

Federal participation in highway construction was further stimulated by the Federal-Aid Highway Act of 1944. This act created the National

System of Interstate Highways, an arterial system of strategic roads connecting all major cities in the country. In addition, the act provided for the Federal-Aid Secondary System—the "farm-to-market" highways—of important feeder routes. Of more than three million miles of roads, more than two million are now surfaced and nearly one million are federal-aid highways. About 85 percent of all farms, it can be pointed out, are now on or within two miles of all-weather roads.

Although the growth of the railroads was not as spectacular as the expansion of improved highways, it was nonetheless of great significance in the total transport situation. Operating roads increased from 53,000 miles in 1870 to a peak of 254,000 in 1916, and then declined slowly to 211,000 in 1965 as marginal lines were abandoned in the face of truck competition. The great agricultural and industrial mid-continent was completely blanketed by this expansion, and seven major lines were pushed to the Pacific Coast through gateways in Montana, Utah, and Arizona.

In the early period of railroad building, farmers were staunch supporters of public aid for new construction—believing that improved transportation and the consequent access to markets would be the cure-all for their economic problems. By the 1870's, it was clear that these hopes had been too optimistic, and at the same time the railroads themselves were generally charging high rates and were engaging in a variety of discriminatory practices. The farmers, spearheaded by the Grange, or Patrons of Husbandry, turned to political action to curb the railroads. Many states responded by passing legislation that regulated rates, outlawed certain practices, and established enforcement commissions. In 1886, however, the Supreme Court held that states did not have the right to regulate interstate commerce. This brought the federal government into the picture.

The Interstate Commerce Act of 1887 established the Interstate Commerce Commission, and when the commission's regulatory powers were weakened by court decisions, further legislation clarified its position in 1903, 1906, and 1910. The 1906 legislation also brought the petroleum and gas pipelines under commission jurisdiction. The railroads vigorously protested public regulation in the early stages, but by 1920 management recognized the possibilities of "stabilizing" competition through the commission's activities. Both management and labor from the railroads were active in urging state and federal regulation of the growing truck industry, and the highway common carriers were brought under commission regulation in 1935. Private carriers were not regulated, however and, hence, a competitive alternative to public highway and railroad carriers has remained through do-it-yourself ownership and operation of trucks.

Public regulation of the transport system was completed with the coverage of airlines in 1940, but in this case a new agency — the Civil Aeronautics Board — was established.

Although the development of railroad and highway transportation greatly reduced the strategic importance of coastal and inland waterways, nevertheless, these waterways still account for 15 to 20 percent of total domestic freight movements. Much of this bulk traffic is handled by special-purpose carriers such as tankers and ore boats. A similar development has been the building of pipelines for the transportation of petroleum products and, later, natural gas. The first lines were build from the Pennsylvania oilfields to the Atlantic coast in the 1870's as a direct answer to high rail freight rates. The feasibility of pipeline transmission of natural gas was demonstrated in 1891 with the completion of a line from northern Indiana to Chicago, but gas utilization remained essentially on a local basis until after World War I.

The airlines are newcomers to the transportation system, but they are fast growing and already have captured a dominant share of the first-class, long-distance passenger traffic. Starting after World War I, the scheduled routes within the United States increased to 105,000 miles in 1966. Domestic airlines carried 106,000,000 passengers in 1966 — a total of 69 billion passenger-miles as compared to 17 billion passenger-miles by the railroads.

To summarize, the railroads, although being pushed by more recent developments such as pipelines and highway trucks, remain the major factor in freight transportation. In 1966, for example, the rails carried 44 percent of total ton-miles of freight, trucks about 22 percent, inland waterways and pipelines 15 and 19 percent, respectively, while air freight increased to 13 percent from a negligible quantity 20 years earlier. In passenger traffic, however, the private automobile accounts for nearly 90 percent of total transportation. Among the common carriers, the railroads have dropped to third place behind the airlines and intercity buses.

When markets were largely confined to local communities, communication could be readily accomplished through direct contact. As improved transportation favored economic specialization, however, markets grew in geographic extent, becoming regional, national, or even international in character. This required a more formal and efficient system to develop and transmit information — to tie together and interrelate spatially separated producers, marketing agencies, and consumers. Communications were fairly well developed at the close of the Civil War with the improved mail service, the publication of numerous newspapers and magazines, and the newly developed telegraph system. These elements expanded rapidly with the subsequent growth of population and the settlement of the western regions, and to them were added the telephone, radio, and television.

The telephone was invented by Alexander Graham Bell in 1876 and, by 1900, there were more than 1,300,000 telephones in use in the United States. Early development was typically by local companies, but the compelling advantages of a unified system brought most of the major companies together under the American Telephone and Telegraph Company (the Bell System) during the first quarter of the 20th century. Today, the telephone system includes more than 100,000,000 telephones and nearly 500,000,000 miles of wire. This development of direct, two-way communication has been most strategic to the growth of the marketing system and, consequently, to the growth of the whole economy.

During the early part of the period under consideration, mass communication was limited to the newspapers and periodicals. By 1966, 1750 daily newspapers had a paid circulation aggregating more than 60,000,000 copies. Reliance on the written word was changed with the discovery of wireless telegraphy in 1901 and with the subsequent perfection of radio. The first commercial broadcasting station in the United States was built in Pittsburgh in 1920; today there are more than 6000 commercial stations on the air, and virtually every home has at least one receiving set. However, television, which had its start in the early 1940's, is the prime element in the communications system. Today, there are more than 600 broadcast stations, three major networks, and approximately nine households out of every ten in the United States receive horse operas and brand-name advertising in their living rooms.

In the farm sector of the economy, the United States Department of Agriculture has a most important role in communications. Crop and livestock reporting was established soon after the creation of the department in 1862, and now the department makes periodic reports on more than 150 crop and livestock enterprises. Work on market reporting (as distinct from production estimates) was initiated in 1915. Reports on market receipts and prices are compiled in the major markets throughout the country and are transmitted by teletype over an 11,000-mile leased-wire system for local distribution. Special reporting offices are established in major producing centers for seasonal crops. Timely crop and market reports are made available through the mails, newspapers, periodicals, radio, and television.

As an example of the combined effects of improvements in the transportation and communications network on prices and trade, we show in Table 2.6 the changes in regional differences in corn prices received by farmers in selected states in 1848 and 1966. In the pre-Civil War period,

TABLE 2.6   Regional Differences in Corn Prices Received by Farmers, Selected States, 1848 and 1966

Item	Price (Dollars per Bushel)		Index (Ohio = 100)	
	1848	1966	1848[a]	1966
New England				
Massachusetts	0.80 to 0.90	1.75	243	139
Vermont	0.50 to 1.00	1.75	214	139
Middle Atlantic				
Pennsylvania	0.33 to 1.00	1.50	189	119
New York	$0.37\frac{1}{2}$ to 0.75	1.43	163	113
Central				
Ohio	0.10 to 0.60	1.26	100	100
Illinois	$0.12\frac{1}{2}$ to 0.25	1.25	54	99
South Atlantic				
South Carolina	0.40 to 0.75	1.46	163	116
Georgia	0.20 to 0.40	1.46	86	116

Source. The 1848 Patent Office Report cited by Richard D. Easterlin, "Interregional Differences in Per Capita Income, Population and Total Income, 1840–1950." In *Trends in the American Economy in the Nineteenth Century*, NBER Studies in Income and Wealth, Volume 24. Princeton University Press, Princeton, 1960, Table B-2, p. 113, and *Agricultural Statistics, 1966*, U.S. Department of Agriculture. Washington, D.C., 1968, Table 37, p. 29.

[a]Computed for midpoint.

Massachusetts farmers received nearly $2\frac{1}{2}$ times as much for their corn as Ohio farmers who, in turn, obtained nearly twice that of Illinois farmers. Within-state differences were equally large. Today, roughly the same relative position is apparent, but absolute price differences have been drastically reduced as a single national market has developed.

2.4   THE AGRICULTURAL REVOLUTION

The most dramatic change in the American economy during the past century has been the decline in the relative importance of farming. As population grew from 40 million to 200 million between 1870 and the late 1960's, migration to the cities continued. By 1960, only 30 percent lived in rural areas and very small communities, as compared with more than 70 percent of the population in these communities 90 years earlier. Farm workers had declined from 53 to 5 percent of total gainful employment by 1967. In fact, after 1910, the decline occurred in absolute as well as relative terms, with workers in farm occupations dropping from 11.6 million to 3.8 million in 1967. Without going into detail as to how this modern agricultural sector developed, we shall find some of the highlights helpful to an understanding of the American economy of the mid-20th century.

At the close of the Civil War, the frontier of settlement had been pushed one tier of states west of the Mississippi River, with some additional advances into Texas, Kansas and Nebraska, and in California. Within this frontier, only a relatively small part of the potential cropland had been developed — perhaps 25 percent for the Mississippi Valley. The next 50 years brought not only the closing of the frontier but also the intensive development of agriculture. Total land in farms increased from 408,000,000 acres in 1870 to 956,000,000 in 1920. Acreage increased slowly to 1,206,000,000 in 1954 but has decreased slowly since then. Harvested cropland increased from 166,000,000 acres in 1879 to 360,000,000 in 1920, fluctuated around that level for several decades, but is now back to 300,000,000 acres.

The occupation of the western lands was accompanied by a decline in crop acreage in the Northeast, and the geographic centers of farm production moved steadily westward (Figure 2.2). The total number of farms increased roughly in proportion to the increase in farmlands, from 2,660,000 in 1870 to 6,448,000 in 1920. The average size of a farm was approximately constant at slightly less than 150 acres. Since World War I, however, there has been a marked consolidation: the number of farms fell to 4,782,000 in 1954 and 3,158,000 in 1964, while average size increased to 352 acres.

With the exception of the drought and depression years in the 1930's, agricultural output has increased rather steadily since 1870. Per capita farm output increased slowly until the reductions of the drought and depression years and then expanded rapidly during World War II and the postwar period. In 1950, the average farm worker supplied himself and 14 others, as compared with 4 others in 1870 and 3 others in 1820. By the late 1960's, he supplied more than 40 other persons.

Between 1950 and the late 1960's, cropland used for crops decreased 10 percent, crop production per acre increased 50 percent, the total number of man-hours used decreased 50 percent, and output per man-hour tripled. The increases in agricultural production and productivity resulted from increasing specialization and improved farm technology — from the substitution of inputs such as fertilizer, tractors, and gasoline purchased from the nonagricultural sectors of the economy for farmland

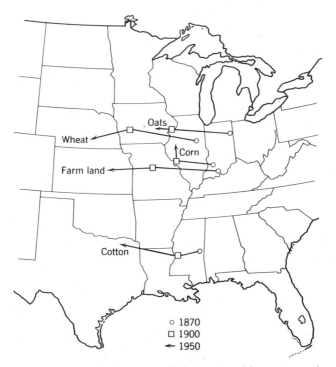

FIGURE 2.2 The westward movement of the geographic centers of agricultural production, 1870 to 1950. (Calculated from data by states, United States Bureau of the Census and United States Department of Agriculture.)

and farm labor, and the development of improved plant and animal strains.

The use of commercial fertilizers increased rapidly during the first half of the 20th century. The substitution of mechanical power for horse power reduced the acreage of cropland needed to produce workstock feed from 92,000,000 acres to less than 5,000,000 acres. This alone was the equivalent of a 30 percent increase in cropland available to produce food and fiber for human use. Hybrid corn began to be important on American farms in the late 1930's and is now planted throughout the country—a technological advance which has been a major factor in the increase of more than 40 percent in corn yields per acre.

Farm mechanization is by no means limited to the substitution of tractors for horses. Virtually all types of farm operations have been affected by the development of new and improved machines. This "industrial revolution" in agriculture had important beginnings in the mid-19th century with the invention of practical steel plows, threshing machines, mowing machines, and cultivators. During the last half of that century the development of gang plows, grain binders and the first combines, springtooth harrows, and cream separators occurred. With the 20th century, power came to the farm through electricity and the internal combustion motor. The result has been a sweeping change of farming methods brought on by the use of tractors, automobiles, trucks, grain combines, corn pickers, milking machines, mechanical cotton harvesters, and farmsteads fully equipped with running water, electricity, and telephone communication with neighboring communities — in short, a revolution both in farming methods and farming as a way of life.

2.5 THE EXPANSION AND RELOCATION OF MANUFACTURING

Manufacturing replaced agriculture as the largest single aggregate in the United States economy soon after the turn of the century. Whether measured in terms of employment or its contribution to national income, it still accounts for between one-fourth and one-third of total economic activity. It includes diverse enterprises such as sawmills and steel plants, textile mills and automobile plants, food processing, and the production of television sets, women's underwear, and hardware to carry men to the moon. As previously stated, the absolute increase in manufacturing output was tremendous: total output increased fourfold between 1869 and 1899; during the next 50 years manufacturing output increased sixfold, and during the period 1949 to 1968 manufacturing output again more than doubled.

The relative importance of the 20 major manufacturing industry groups in mid-century America is suggested by the data in Table 2.7. These industry groups may be divided roughly into durable manufactures and nondurable manufactures. In the first group, the nonelectrical and electrical machinery groups, together with transportation equipment, are of major importance in terms of both employment and value added. Among the nondurable manufactures, foods and beverages, apparel products, and textile-mill products dominate the total employment picture.

A notable feature of the modern American economy is the high concentration of individual industry activity within fairly small areas. One measure of this is the relative importance of the four leading states for each major manufacturing group shown in Table 2.7. The large state-to-state differences in the relative importance of manufacturing in terms of value added in 1963 is illustrated in Figure 2.3.

During the past quarter century, there has been a considerable shift in regional specialization in manufacturing. Both in terms of value added and total employment the heavy concentration formerly found in the north-

TABLE 2.7   Total Employment in 20 Manufacturing Industry Groups and Relative Importance of 4 Leading States, by Industry Group, 1929 and 1954

| Major Group | Total Employment | | | | Percent of Employment[b] in 4 Leading States | |
| | Thousands[a] | | Percent | | | |
	1929	1954	1929	1954	1929	1954
Durable Manufactures						
Primary metals	677	921	7.0	6.1	62.5	56.8
Fabricated metals	566	927	5.8	6.1	48.9	44.1
Machinery (non-electrical)	939	1946	9.7	12.9	45.9	45.2
Electrical machinery	421	959	4.4	6.4	59.9	49.0
Transportation equipment	642	1537	6.7	10.2	64.6	58.7
Instruments and related	100	272	1.0	1.8	69.0	59.9
Stone, clay and glass	378	492	3.9	3.3	44.7	41.1
Lumber and products	651	655	6.7	4.3	27.5	32.7
Furniture and fixtures	248	331	2.6	2.2	44.0	36.0
Miscellaneous manufactures	286	394	3.0	2.6	50.4	46.4
Total durables	4908	8434	50.8	55.9	–	–
Nondurable Manufactures						
Textile mill products	1163	1024	12.0	6.8	50.4	54.0
Apparel products	708	1203	7.3	8.0	62.8	56.4
Leather and products	351	356	3.6	2.4	59.5	54.8
Paper and products	268	530	2.8	3.5	44.4	32.6
Printing and publishing	561	804	5.8	5.3	51.2	47.6
Chemical products	382	863	4.0	5.7	38.5	33.8
Petroleum products	133	216	1.4	1.4	48.9	48.2
Rubber and plastics	172	246	1.8	1.6	68.0	51.6
Food and beverages	883	1347	9.2	8.9	38.5	33.8
Tobacco products	126	76	1.3	.5	56.4	68.4
Total nondurables	4747	6665	49.2	44.1	–	–
United States total	9655	15099	100.0	100.0	–	–

Source.   [a]Victor R. Fuchs. *Changes in the Location of Manufacturing in the United States Since 1929.* Yale University Press, New Haven, 1962. Table 8.2, p. 240.
[b]Fuchs, *op. cit.,* Table 9.3, p. 284.

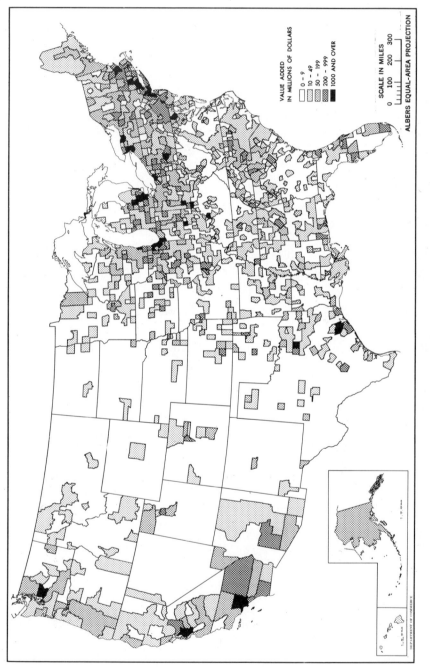

FIGURE 2.3   Industrial counties of the United States 1963. (*Source. 1963 Census of Manufactures.*)

eastern regions is diminishing while the upper and lower South and the western regions are increasing at a rapid rate (Table 2.8). Some of the reasons for the change in the relative importance of the several regions have been suggested by Fuchs.[4] The comparative losses experienced by New England are largely attributable to textiles which have been slow growing and have experienced a dramatic redistribution to the South. In the Mideast. as well. the redistribution of both textile and apparel industries has contributed to its relative decline as well as the more rapid growth elsewhere of the aircraft. electrical machinery. and chemicals industries. The decreasing relative importance of coal has also had an adverse effect as petroleum and natural gas. which are found mainly in other regions, have become important.

Relative growth of the upper and lower South is largely attributable to the rapid expansion of the textile industry. but also to the shift out of agriculture and to the relatively high expenditures by both civilian and military government operations. In the Southwest and Far West the chemical industries. aircraft and. more recently. the space program have been primarily responsible for the rapid growth that has occurred. although petroleum and related products have also been contributors.

2.6 EMERGENCE OF THE SERVICE INDUSTRIES

Since the end of World War II. the United States has become the world's first "service economy."[5] We have learned how the service industries as a group have increased from approximately one-fourth of the economic activity of the United States at the close of the Civil War to a position of prominence by the mid-20th century. Roughly 60 percent of the national income in the late 1960's originated there. as in 1930. although the fraction in 1950 was somewhat less (Table 2.9). Distribution activities accounted for roughly 70 percent of the service industry total in 1930 but has declined relative to other services during the past three decades. Professional and personal services remained constant. and the contribution of federal, state, and local government increased more than twofold. In 1967, government was approximately equal in importance to wholesale and retail trade, each representing about one-fourth of service industry activity.

[4]Victor R. Fuchs. *Changes in the Location of Manufacturing in the United States Since 1929*. Yale University Press. New Haven. 1962. For a discussion of earlier years see Frederic B. Garver. Francis M. Boddy. and A. J. Nixon. *The Location of Manufactures in the United States. 1899–1929*. University of Minnesota Press. Minneapolis. 1933.

[5]Victor R. Fuchs. *The Service Economy*. National Bureau of Economic Research. New York. 1968. p. 1.

TABLE 2.8 Regional Distribution of Manufacturing Output and Employment in 1954 and Comparative Growth Rates from 1920 to 1954

Region	Total Value Added (Millions of Dollars)	Total Manufacturing Employment (Thousands)	Proportion of United States Total (Percent)		Comparative Growth, 1929 to 1954 (Percent)	
			Value Added	Manufacturing Employment	Value Added	Total Employment
East						
New England	8,807	1,388	7.9	9.2	−21.3	−25.1
Middle Atlantic	31,258	4,247	27.9	28.1	−15.5	−9.9
Great Lakes	35,288	4,336	31.4	28.8	−0.2	−1.6
Upper South	5,224	730	4.7	4.8	+22.5	+13.3
Lower South	8,814	1,565	7.9	10.4	+21.1	+12.7
Total	89,391	12,266	79.8	81.3		
West						
Plains	6,566	874	5.9	5.8	+2.4	+9.2
Southwest	4,226	510	3.8	3.4	+46.7	+42.5
Rocky Mountains	1,069	136	1.0	0.9	+5.2	+3.0
Far West	10,653	1,300	9.5	8.6	+39.9	+38.7
Total	22,514	2,820	20.2	18.7		
United States total	111,905	15,086	100.0	100.0		

Source. Victor R. Fuchs, *Changes in the Location of Manufacturing in the United States since 1929.* Yale University Press, New Haven, 1962. Appendix B, Table B.2, p. 327.

TABLE 2.9 National Income Originating in the Service Industries in 1930, 1950, and 1967

Industry Group	National Income Originating in Group (Billion Dollars)			Proportion of All Service Industries (Percent)		
	1930	1950	1967	1930	1950	1967
Distribution						
Wholesale trade[a]	4.1	13.3	35.6	9.1	10.3	9.1
Retail trade[b]	8.3	27.6	61.2	18.4	21.4	15.6
Transportation	5.6	13.4	26.1	12.4	10.4	6.7
Communication	1.1	3.4	13.1	2.4	2.6	3.4
Electricity, gas, and sanitary services	1.6	3.9	12.9	3.5	3.0	3.3
Finance, insurance, real estate	10.7	22.0	70.9	23.8	17.1	18.2
Total	31.4	83.6	219.8	69.6	64.8	56.3
Professional and personal services						
Medical and health	1.5	4.4	19.6	3.3	3.4	5.0
Private households	1.5	2.6	4.3	3.3	2.0	1.1
Other	5.4	14.8	53.1	12.0	11.5	13.6
Total	8.4	21.8	77.0	18.6	16.9	19.7
Government						
Federal	1.5	12.7	41.7	3.3	9.8	10.7
State and Local	3.8	10.9	51.9	8.4	8.4	13.3
Total	5.3	23.6	93.6	11.7	18.3	24.0
All services	45.1	129.0	390.4	100.0	100.0	100.0
Total national income	75.4	241.1	652.9	—	—	—

Source. *The National Income and Product Accounts of the United States, 1929–65 Statistical Tables.* Washington, D.C., August 1966. Table 1.12, p. 18, and *Survey of Current Business*, July, 1968. Table 1.12, p. 23.

[a]Comparable data for 1869, .2 billion dollars; 1899, .8 billion dollars.
[b]Comparable data for 1869, .5 billion dollars; 1899, 1.3 billion dollars.

TABLE 2.10 Private Production Income and Labor Force in the Service Industries, United States, 1869 and 1910

Industry Group	Private Production Income[a]				Labor Force[b]			
	Total (Billion Dollars)		Percent of Total (Percent)		Number of Persons (Millions)		Percent of Total (Percent)	
	1869	1910	1869	1910	1869	1910	1869	1910
Services								
Distribution[c]	1.8	7.9	29	31	1.4	6.9	11	19
Professional services[d]	1.0	2.6	15	10	1.4	4.7	11	13
Government[e]	–	–	–	–	0.3	1.3	2	4
Other	0.4	1.8	7	7	0.2	0.8	1	2
All services	3.2	12.3	51	48	3.3	13.7	25	38
Resource[f]	1.6	6.5	26	25	6.7	12.6	52	34
Manufactures[g]	1.4	6.8	23	27	3.0	10.5	23	28
Total, all industries	6.3	25.6	100	100	12.9	36.9	100	100

[a]Private production income compiled from *Historical Statistics of the United States, 1789–1945*, U.S. Department of Commerce, 1949, p. 14. Items may not add to totals because of rounding.

[b]Based on data from Harold Barger, *Distribution's Place in the American Economy since 1869*, National Bureau of Economic Research, Princeton University Press, Princeton, 1955, p. 4.

[c]Includes wholesale and retail trade, transportation, communication, and finance in all years. Finance contribution to private production income was estimated for 1869 on basis of 1899 ratio of finance to "other" classification.

[d]Personal and professional services.

[e]Government not included in private production income.

[f]Includes agriculture, mining, and quarrying. Labor-force data include fishing as well.

[g]Includes manufacturing, construction, electricity, and gas.

Although the data for earlier years are somewhat sketchy, we can see that these trends began early in the period under consideration. Distribution occupied 11 percent of the labor force in 1869 and 19 percent in 1910 (Table 2.10). Government services increased from 2 to 4 percent of the labor force while the reduction in resource activities described earlier was moving very rapidly. With allowance for the fact that farm employees carried on a significant amount of nonagricultural activities in the earlier years, trends in the distribution of national income followed employment patterns rather closely.

In summary, then, we find the Colin Clark model describes rather well the experience in the United States during the past century. Resource-related activities have declined steadily and sharply. Production of manufactures rose early in the period and then declined slightly in relative importance. More recently, the service industries have increased dramatically as greater economic specialization has taken place and as rising levels of living have changed the distribution of goods and services demanded by United States consumers. In the chapters that follow we shall examine these changes in the level of economic activity and in its regional distribution in terms of market price relationships and the response of resource owners and users to changes in these prices.

SELECTED READINGS

Development of an Advanced Economy

Barger, Harold, *Distribution's Place in the American Economy Since 1869*, National Bureau of Economic Research. Princeton University Press, Princeton (1955).

Daggett, Stuart, *Principles of Inland Transportation*, Harper and Brothers, New York, fourth edition (1955).

Easterlin, Richard D., "Interregional Differences in Per Capita Income, Population and Total Income, 1840–1950," in *Trends in the American Economy in the Nineteenth Century*, NBER Studies in Income and Wealth, Vol. 24., Princeton University Press, Princeton (1960).

Fabricant, Solomon, *The Output of Manufacturing Industries, 1899–1937*, National Bureau of Economic Research, Inc., New York (1940).

Fuchs, Victor R., *Changes in the Location of Manufacturing in the United States Since 1929*. Yale University Press, New Haven (1962).

Fuchs, Victor R. (ed.), *Production and Productivity in the Service Industries*, National Bureau of Economic Research, Inc., New York, in press.

Fuchs, Victor R., *The Service Economy*, National Bureau of Economic Research, Inc., New York (1968).

Garver, Frederick B., Francis M. Boddy, and A. J. Nixon, *The Location of Manufactures in the United States, 1899–1929.* University of Minnesota Press, Minneapolis (1933).

Hathaway, Dale E., *People of Rural America*, United States Bureau of the Census, Washington (1968).

Kuznets, Simon, *National Product Since 1869*, National Bureau of Economic Research, Inc., New York (1946).

Kuznets, Simon, "Notes on the Patterns of U.S. Economic Growth" in Edgar O. Edwards (ed.), *The Nation's Economic Objectives.* University of Chicago Press (1964).

Maddox, James G. with E. E. Liebhafsky, Vivian W. Henderson, and Herbert M. Hamlin, *The Advancing South.* The Twentieth Century Fund, New York (1967).

North, Douglass C., *Growth and Welfare in the American Past*, Prentice-Hall Inc., Englewood Cliffs (1966).

President's National Advisory Commission on Rural Poverty, *The People Left Behind*, U.S. Government Printing Office, Washington (September 1967).

Perloff, Harvey S., Edgar S. Dunn, Eric E. Lampard, and Richard F. Muth, *Regions, Resources, and Economic Growth*, Part II, "Regional Economic Development 1870–1950," The Johns Hopkins Press, Baltimore (1960).

Williamson, Harold F. (ed.), *The Growth of the American Economy*, Prentice-Hall, Inc., Englewood Cliffs, second edition (1951).

chapter 3

ECONOMIC INTERDEPENDENCE
AND INTERREGIONAL TRADE

The previous chapters have described in some detail the evolution of the American economy from the largely subsistence agriculture of the early colonial period to the industrialized society of today. This evolution has been based on the growth of economic specialization—the division of labor. During the early days of this country each family did almost everything for itself (growing crops and livestock, storing grain and curing meat, grinding meal and flour, making butter and cheese, spinning yarn, weaving cloth, and making clothes) while selling or exchanging a few products in order to obtain the commodities that were difficult or impossible to produce at home.

Today very few families are self-sufficient in this way. Instead, they have become highly specialized cogs in a complex economic machine. The commercial farmer may produce a single crop or a relatively small number of products, and little, if any, of this production will be consumed directly by the farm household. The industrial worker may be even more specialized, perhaps performing a single operation in an assembly line or factory. Each obtains a flow of money income by means of these activities —income from the sale of products for the farmer and businessman and income from wages for the laborer. And each, in turn, uses his income to purchase goods and services made available through our exchange or market economy. In this chapter, we provide insights concerning these interrelated flows and their relevance to the development of a modern economic system.

3.1 INTERDEPENDENT ECONOMIC ACTIVITIES

Agriculture has been pictured as a broad aggregate within the economic system in which originates the flow of farm commodities within agriculture and, from agriculture, to other major industries or sectors. Also, there exists a reverse flow of goods and services (including labor) from these other sectors back to agriculture. Similar circular flows of inputs and outputs could be described for every sector and all of them interconnected to represent the flows of goods and services throughout the entire economic system. Needless to say, this representation would be very complex if it showed the interrelations among the major industrial sectors in the system and would be indescribably involved if it attempted to trace out the flows among millions of individuals as producers and consumers. An appreciation of these flows may be gained by thinking for a moment about the systems required to produce and to place thousands of commodities on the shelves of a modern supermarket.

Such detailed descriptions are far beyond the scope of this book, but the essential nature of the economic mechanism can be illustrated by simpler aggregations. Consider first a model of the total economy based on three large aggregates: (1) the production aggregate including farming, hunting and fishing, mining, construction, processing, and manufacturing activities; (2) the service aggregate including transportation, trade, communications, and all other business, personal, and professional service activities; and (3) the final demand aggregate including households, government, and foreign countries (this aggregate also represents the basic inputs of resources of land, labor, and capital owned by households, government services paid for by taxes, and the import of goods and services from foreign countries).

This highly aggregated model may be represented graphically by two circular flows: one showing the "sale" or input of goods and services from each aggregate to the succeeding aggregate and the other showing the "purchase" of goods and services by each aggregate from the preceding aggregate (Figure 3.1). To make our discussion more concrete, we use data from a study of the United States economy in the year 1947. The production aggregate sold $38 billion of commodities to the service aggregate and, in turn, purchased $41 billion of services. Also, production sold $120 billion to the final demand sector and bought $117 billion. Notice

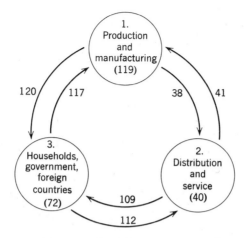

FIGURE 3.1   The flows of goods and services among three major sectors of the United States economy. All data are for the year 1947 and are given in billions of dollars. The figures in parentheses represent transfers within indicated sector. This diagram is based on Table 3.1.

that the sales and purchases between any two aggregates need not balance but that there is a balance between any single aggregate and the rest of the economy. Thus, the production aggregate had an *unfavorable* balance of purchases over sales with the service aggregate amounting to $3 billion and a compensating *favorable* balance of $3 billion with the final demand aggregate.

These interactions can be shown by an input–output table or matrix (Table 3.1). Here each aggregate appears as a "producing" or selling sector in the left-hand stub of the table and also as a "consuming" or purchasing sector at the top of the table. Each column shows the inputs from other industries to the particular purchasing industry; that is, (1) the production aggregate purchased $41 billion from (2) distribution and services and $117 billion from (3) the final demand or autonomous sector. Also, the production sector had internal transfers amounting to $119 billion and, hence, a total gross input of $277 billion. In a similar way, each row in such a table shows the distribution of the output of the indicated sector, or aggregate to all other sectors. The total gross output of the production aggregate — equal to the total gross input for the aggregate — was distributed as follows: (1) $119 billion transferred back into the production aggregate, (2) $38 billion sold to the service aggregate, and (3) $120 billion to the final demand aggregate.

Input–output tables permit the representation of far more detailed industry interactions than would be possible with graphic means. Tables

TABLE 3.1   Summary of the Flows of Goods and Services Among Three Major Sectors of the United States Economy, 1947

Producing Sectors and Total	Purchasing Sectors (Billion Dollars)			Total Gross Output[d]	Total Net Output[e]
	Production, Manufac-turing[a]	Distri-bution Service[b]	Final Demand[c]		
Production and manufacturing	119	38	120	277	158
Distribution and service	41	40	109	190	150
Autonomous sector payments	117	112	72	301	229
Total gross inputs	227	190	301	768	
Total net inputs	158	150	229		537

Source. Compiled from Wassily W. Leontief, "Input–Output Economics," *Scientific American*, Vol. 185, no. 4, October 1951, pp. 15–21, and from the aggregates based on Leontief by Ronald L. Mighell, *American Agriculture, Its Structure and Place in the Economy* (New York: John Wiley and Sons, 1955), p. 182.

[a]Agriculture, mining, fishing and hunting, construction, and all other manufacturing industries.

[b]Transportation, trade, communication, public utilities, finance, insurance, real estate, and all business, personal, and professional service industries.

[c]Households, government, foreign countries, inventory changes, and gross private capital formation.

[d]The sum of outputs (or inputs) for the three major sectors.

[e]The gross output (or input) less transfers within each major sector.

have been constructed dividing the United States economy into 500 sectors (an interindustry matrix with 500 rows and 500 columns). Although this huge table is still a tremendous simplification of the true economy, it nevertheless does give in considerable detail the interrelations and interdependencies in the economic system.

An "11-by-11" condensation of such a matrix is given in Table 3.2. Notice that Table 3.1 is simply a further condensation of this 11-industry table. The production aggregate in Table 3.1 represents the first three sectors of Table 3.2; the service aggregate combines sectors 4 through 7 in Table 3.2; and the final aggregate in Table 3.1 is the sum of sectors 8

TABLE 3.2 The Interchange of Goods and Services in the United States by Major Industry Groups, 1947 (Billion Dollars)

Producing Industry	Purchasing Industry[a]											Total Gross Output
	1	2	3	4	5	6	7	8	9	10	11	
1. Agriculture and fisheries	10.9	18.1	1.4	—[b]	—	—	1.1	1.0	1.3	0.6	9.9	44.3
2. Food, fiber, and related manufactures	2.6	20.6	4.2	0.4	0.8	0.5	12.8	2.2	3.4	1.4	37.8	86.7
3. All other manufactures[c]	1.9	5.1	54.4	4.2	0.7	4.9	12.3	30.7	7.0	7.9	16.6	145.6
4. Power, transportation, and communication	1.1	2.9	6.5	3.3	1.2	3.9	2.6	0.5	2.5	1.4	8.7	34.6
5. Trade	1.4	1.4	4.0	0.5	0.2	0.8	3.0	2.5	1.0	0.1	26.8	41.7
6. Finance, insurance, and real estate	2.6	0.7	1.3	0.8	3.0	2.7	2.1	0.8	0.1	0.2	27.3	41.6
7. Service industries	0.4	6.4	12.2	1.1	6.1	1.6	7.3	0.2	0.2	4.9	32.0	72.5
8. Inventory change[d]	2.7	0.8	0.5	—	—	—	0.4	—	—	—	—	4.4
9. Foreign countries[e]	0.7	3.4	1.9	0.7	—	0.1	0.1	—	—	1.3	1.3	9.5
10. Government	0.8	3.5	6.1	3.5	3.3	5.1	4.8	0.6	0.8	3.5	31.6	63.6
11. Households	19.2	23.8	53.2	20.1	26.4	22.0	25.9	—	0.9	30.1	2.1	223.7
Total gross input	44.3	86.7	145.6	34.6	41.7	41.6	72.5	38.5	17.2	51.4	194.1	768.2

Source. Ronald L. Mighell, *American Agriculture, Its Structure and Place in the Economy* (New York: John Wiley and Sons, 1955), p. 182

[a] Same definitions as producing industries.

[b] Dashes indicate no data available.

[c] Includes construction.

[d] Includes private capital formation; in "producing industries" this represents depletions, and in "purchasing industries" it signifies additions.

[e] Producing industry represents imports; purchasing industry represents exports.

through 11 in Table 3.2. It should be pointed out that total gross inputs and total gross outputs in Table 3.2 are equal for each of the first 7 sectors but are only equal in the aggregate for the last 4 sectors. Exports need not equal imports nor government expenditures equal tax receipts, for example, but in the aggregate these final sectors and the entire matrix must balance.

Before leaving these interindustry matrices, we must emphasize that they provide more than a convenient description of the national economy. These tables may be used to trace out the approximate impact of changes in certain sectors on the entire system. For example, suppose that the required output of agriculture and fisheries (row 1) increased by 10 percent. Barring changes in technology and in relative prices, this would mean a 10 percent increase in the inputs to agriculture and fisheries, that is, all entries in column 1 would be increased by approximately 10 percent. Corresponding to these changes, there would be upward adjustments in the total output of all other sectors which, in turn, would require input adjustments. In this way, the direct and indirect effects of the increase in agricultural and fisheries output can be traced through the whole economic system. For this reason, detailed input–output tables have been useful planning tools for diverse activities such as war strategy (to determine where strategic bombing will have the major disruptive effect on an economy) and the industrialization of underdeveloped countries (to check the internal consistency of proposed developments). Even the highly aggregated 11-industry model suggests the complex and interdependent nature of the economy: changes in any small sector spread out like ripples on a pond and have direct or indirect effects on all parts of the economic system.

3.2 INTERDEPENDENCIES WITHIN THE AGRICULTURAL SECTOR

Input–output analysis is also useful as a device for studying the relationships within as well as between sectors. Food, textile, and tobacco manufacturers are the primary receivers of farm products, but agriculture also sells directly to many other industries, to households, and to itself. Internal transfers in the form of feed, seed, and livestock amounted to more than $10 billion in 1947, or about 25 percent of the total gross output of the farming sector (Table 3.3). Three-quarters of this internal transfer was from the food and feed grain enterprises (row 4): $3,841 million went to the meat animal enterprise; $1,279 million to poultry and eggs; $1,755 million to dairy products; $817 million back to grain enterprises as seed and as feed for workstock; and the balance of $234

TABLE 3.3 Internal Purchases and Sales of the Farming Aggregate, 1947[a] (Millions of Dollars)

Producing Segment	Purchasing Segment[b]									Total Gross Sales
	1	2	3	4	5	6	7	8	9	
1. Meat animals and products	938									938
2. Poultry and eggs		308								308
3. Farm dairy products	130									130
4. Food grains and feed crops	3.841	1.279	1.755	817	33	20	33	85	63	7.926
5. Cotton	8		8		27					43
6. Tobacco										
7. Oil-bearing crops	3						93			96
8. Vegetables and fruits	80							121		201
9. All other agriculture	24	3	31	438	108		24	32	61	721
Total gross purchases	5.024	1.590	1.794	1.255	168	20	150	238	124	10.366

[a] *Source.* Davis and Goldberg, *A Concept of Agribusiness*, Division of Research, Harvard Business School, Boston, 1957, p. 33.

[b] Identical to the producing segment having same number.

million largely as workstock feed for other enterprises. On the other hand, the meat animal enterprise was the largest purchasing sector, accounting for about one-half of total gross purchases within agriculture (column 1).

Net of these internal transfers, about 45 percent of the value of farm products in 1947 was sold to the food processing industries and an additional 9 percent to the tobacco and textile industries. The chemical industry received about 4 percent, and a similar proportion was exported to foreign countries. Direct sales to households, including consumption on farms, accounted for 29 percent of net production. These households eventually receive virtually all farm products, but only after they have passed through various processing, manufacturing, and marketing channels (Table 3.4).

Farms not only sell to a variety of industrial outlets but also buy from or are serviced by many industries. The largest single purchase account is from households as payments for family-owned resources. This amounted to 57 percent of the net value of farm output in 1947, primarily representing farm family labor and hired labor. The food processing industry supplied the farm economy with products valued at 7 percent of the net value of farm products, and the petroleum, chemical, and power industries accounted for 4 percent. Transportation and trade services purchased by farmers in conjunction with purchased supplies amounted to 8 percent, and rental payments added another 7 percent.

These data provide a general picture of agriculture in relation to other major sectors of the economic system through the circular flow of the output of farms to other sectors and the inputs of goods and services from these other sectors into farm production. The data are for 1947, the immediate post-World War II period, and dollar values have substantially inflated during the ensuing years, to be sure, but the relative flows are reasonably stable, and therefore the overall picture is fairly typical of the mid-20th century.

3.3   SOME REASONS FOR REGIONAL SPECIALIZATION

As previously pointed out, the division of labor refers to the specialization of individuals (and firms) in certain lines of economic activity who depend on the market or exchange economy to sell their specialized products and services and, thus, to obtain income with which to purchase other goods and services. This takes place not because the individuals are necessarily interested in such specialization but rather because specialization permits a gain in efficiency or economy and, hence, leads to a greater total output

TABLE 3.4   Direct Sales and Purchases of Goods and Services by Agriculture with Other Major Industry Classifications, per $100 of Gross and Net Agricultural Output, 1947[a]

Industry	Sales per $100 Output		Purchases per $100 Output	
	Gross	Net[b]	Gross	Net[b]
1. Agriculture	$24.53	–	$24.53	–
2. Food and kindred	34.00	$45.04	5.37	$7.12
3. Tobacco, textiles, leather	6.58	8.71	0.14	0.19
4. Chemicals, petroleum, power	2.74	3.62	3.05	4.04
5. Machinery and equipment	0.01	0.01	0.59	0.79
6. Distribution[c]	0.04	0.05	6.02	7.98
7. Other services	0.26	0.35	0.85	1.13
8. Rental	–	–	5.41	7.16
9. Inventory changes	2.28	3.02	6.01	7.96
10. Miscellaneous	1.35	1.79	1.33	1.77
11. Foreign countries	2.88	3.82	1.56	2.07
12. Eating, drinking places	1.95	2.59	–	–
13. Government	1.29	1.70	1.84	2.43
14. Households (including farms)	22.11	29.29	43.30	57.37
Total	$100.00	$100.00	$100.00	$100.00

[a]Based on W. Duane Evans and Marvin Hoffenberg, "The Interindustry Relations Study for 1947," *The Review of Economics and Statistics*, Vol. XXXIV, No. 2 (May 1952), Tables 4 and 5 following p. 142.
[b]Net output is here defined as gross output less transfers within agriculture. Agriculture includes fisheries, but this industry's contribution was less than one percent of the agricultural total.
[c]Includes transportation, trade, communications, finance, and insurance.

from a given supply of basic resources. In very general terms, gains from specialization include the utilization of skills and resource qualities best adapted to the particular job, the development of additional skills and abilities through practice and experience, and a reduction in the waste of time and effort entailed in frequent changes in occupation. Geographic specialization occurs because regions, like individuals, are differently endowed with abilities—with basic resources such as soil, climate, mineral deposits, and (at least, during the short term) with human resources that differ in quantity and in quality.

Regional specialization occurs when a complex of economic forces (including the location of natural resources, market outlets, and transportation costs) makes it unusually profitable for a number of firms in the region to specialize in the same kind of activity. This is clearly evident in the primary production industries because of the direct relations to natural resources. Gold is where you find it. And so we have gold mines in South Dakota, California, Utah, Arizona, Colorado, and a few other states. The residents of North Carolina do not forgo mining for gold because they might dislike this occupation but simply because important deposits of this metal are not included in the natural endowments of that state. Texas is the leading state in the production of petroleum, natural gas, and sulfur because these minerals are in great demand in our industrial economy and because they have been deposited in great abundance in the Texas area. For equally obvious reasons, the major fishing industry exists along the Atlantic and Pacific Coasts and in the Gulf of Mexico, with minor freshwater fisheries contered on the Great Lakes and the Mississippi River system.

The basic localized resources for farm production are land and climate. These resources (coupled with available technology) determine the physical possibilities of production. Actual use of the resources, however, will depend on the markets for alternative farm commodities, on the location of urban centers of population, on the tastes and preferences of individual consumers, and on transfer costs from potential producing areas to markets. We have learned that the availability of abundant and excellent land and climatic resources in the Midwest was not sufficient in itself to bring about a highly developed agriculture, but that the combination of these resources plus growing urban markets along the Atlantic seaboard and improved transportation did result in a rapid westward movement of commercial agriculture and the actual abandonment of some areas already developed in the East. We also recognize that crops such as cotton and citrus fruits are produced in the southern part of the country because these plants cannot tolerate the rigorous winters and shorter growing seasons to the north.

Adjustments in farm production are readily understood when they involve the substitution of more favorable soils and climate for less favorable conditions. But what about the expansion of agriculture across the relatively unfavorable semiarid prairies of the west central states? North Dakota is the center of the spring wheat area, and Kansas is the dominant producer of winter wheat. Yet, yields in these states average 23 bushels per acre as compared to yields of approximately 35 bushels in the states from New York to Wisconsin. An understanding of this fact requires an economic analysis of comparative advantage based on location, alternative opportunities, market demands, and the prices of land and other resources. In brief, North Dakota produces wheat because it has few feasible alternatives, while the superior natural resources of the Great Lakes states are more profitably employed in other enterprises.

3.4 SOME EXAMPLES OF REGIONAL SPECIALIZATION

Farming. The working out of physical and economic forces has resulted in a fairly well-defined pattern of regional specialization in agriculture (Figure 3.2). The major wheat-producing areas are in the semi-arid plains that stretch south from North Dakota to Oklahoma and west through Montana to the Palouse area in eastern Washington. The Corn Belt (emphasizing feed grains and livestock) extends from Ohio west into Nebraska and South Dakota. The northeastern states and the Great Lakes states are predominantly dairy areas, with milk for urban markets the major factor in the northeast and manufactured dairy products the important outlet in Wisconsin and Minnesota. The Cotton Belt extends from North Carolina to Texas and, in irrigated valleys, on to California. Fruit and vegetable production tends to concentrate in areas such as New Jersey and Delaware, along the Great Lakes shores in New York, Ohio, and Michigan, in Florida and along the Gulf Coast, and in the irrigated areas of the Southwest and the Pacific Coast. Finally, the vast "intermountain" area of relatively low rainfall supports little intensive agriculture but is devoted primarily to range livestock production. It should be understood that these type-of-farming areas do not indicate areas of complete specialization; Iowa, for example, is in the heart of the Corn Belt, but it is one of the most important states in butter production. However, the type-of-farming map does give a good generalized picture of regional specialization in agriculture.

Mineral Industries. Primary production basic to the industrial economy is characterized by a high degree of regional specialization. Texas ranks first in total mineral production with a value of products of $3.7 billion in 1954. Petroleum, natural gas, and sulfur were the major components of this output. Petroleum, natural gas, and cement put California in second place with a value of $1.4 billion, although other important mineral-producing states include Louisiana, Pennsylvania, Oklahoma, West Virginia, and Illinois. The major petroleum fields in the United States are in Texas-Oklahoma-Kansas, California, along the Gulf in Louisiana and Texas, the Appalachian fields from Pennsylvania to

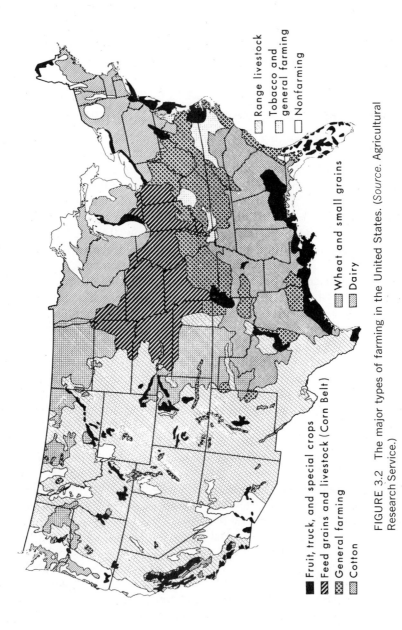

FIGURE 3.2 The major types of farming in the United States. (*Source.* Agricultural Research Service.)

Fruit, truck, and special crops

Feed grains and livestock (Corn Belt)

General farming

Cotton

Wheat and small grains

Dairy

Range livestock

Tobacco and general farming

Nonfarming

Tennessee, and scattered areas in Michigan, Ohio, Indiana, Illinois, and the Rocky Mountain states. Natural-gas supply areas correspond approximately with the geographic distribution of oil fields plus a large area in the Dakotas and eastern Montana. Coal deposits also follow this general pattern. The major supply of coal comes from the Appalachian field, including the anthracite beds in eastern Pennsylvania and the bituminous and semibituminous beds covering approximately 70,000 square miles. An important bituminous area lies in Illinois, Indiana, and western Kentucky, with extensions northeast into Michigan and southwest from Iowa to Texas. Deposits in the Rocky Mountain area are largely subbituminous coal and lignite and have been little developed except to serve local markets. Although not a mineral fuel, waterpower is an important source of mechanical and electrical energy in parts of the country. Important examples of major present and potential developments in hydroelectric power include the Niagara River, the Columbia River, and the Tennessee Valley.

Nonfuel and nonmetallic mineral industries include virtually ubiquitous activities such as stone quarries, sand and clay pits, and cement manufacturing. Although important variations in type and quality exist, usable deposits of these minerals are found in almost every part of the United States. However, other minerals in this category may be highly localized. Sulfur, in its natural form, is found in Louisiana and Texas. As metallic sulfides or pyrites, there are important deposits in Arizona and California, and some sulfur is obtained as a by-product of metal smelting and from natural and industrial gases. Phosphate rock, used chiefly in fertilizers, is found in large deposits in Florida, Tennessee, Utah, Wyoming, Idaho, and Montana. Salt, important as an industrial chemical as well as for food and feed, is produced from mines, deep wells, and the evaporation of seawater. Major salt-producing states in the United States are Michigan, New York, Louisiana, Ohio, and Texas.

Metallic minerals are widely scattered through the United States, although any particular mineral ore may be fairly well localized. Important iron ore fields are located in the Lake Superior region of Minnesota, Michigan, and Wisconsin, the Birmingham district in Alabama, the New York-New Jersey-Pennsylvania district, and scattered small deposits in many other states. Major copper deposits in the United States are in Montana, Utah, Arizona, Nevada, and New Mexico. Lead- and zinc-producing districts are found in Missouri, Kansas, Oklahoma, Idaho, Utah, New Jersey, Tennessee, and Virginia. Tin is an important metal in the United States, but domestic deposits of tin ore are insignificant. Aluminum is widely distributed in many types of rock and clay, but only bauxite ore is utilized commercially. Virtually the entire domestic supply of this ore comes from Arkansas. The most important United States deposits of precious metals are in South Dakota, California, and Colorado for gold, and in Idaho, Montana, Nevada, and Utah for silver. Uranium, the metal of the atomic age, occurs in all rocks but usually in too low a concentration to be significant. The chief commercial source in the United States is the carnotite deposits of the Colorado Plateau.

Agricultural Processing. Some agricultural processing industries are primarily oriented with reference to major farm production areas, although others tend to locate in relation to final markets. Thus, firms manufacturing ice cream and processing and distributing fluid milk with allowance for relatively low per capita consumption rates through the South are distributed approximately in line with the geographic distribution of population. On the other hand, plants manufacturing dairy products like butter and cheese are located mainly in the major milk-producing regions, especially in the western Great Lakes states. Wisconsin, Minnesota, and Iowa produce 56 percent of creamery butter and 60 percent of all nonfat dry milk in the United States. Wisconsin alone accounts for 43 percent of total cheese production.

Early grain milling centers in the United States were in the tidewater areas, but the westward movement of wheat production displaced the Atlantic Coast area with milling centers in Chicago and St. Louis. By 1900, Minneapolis had become the leading milling center in the world. A combination of cheap electrical power, water transportation, and strategic location with reference to Canadian wheat-producing areas and export markets favored Buffalo, however, and since 1930 this area has been the largest flour-producing center in the country. Minneapolis continues to be important in flour milling, and other major centers are located in Kansas and in the Pacific Northwest. Chicago emerged as the major meat-packing center after the improvement of rail transportation and the development of mechanical refrigeration. This still is the most important center, but decentralization (based in part on truck shipments) has been rapid in recent years. Other important meat-packing centers include cities such as Kansas City, St. Louis, Omaha, Fort Worth, Dallas, and South St. Paul. Vegetable oil mills are distributed throughout the country in close proximity to raw material supplies as are canneries and frozen food processing plants.

Aluminum Manufacturing. It is impractical to describe the locational pattern for every manufacturing industry, but two examples from the metals industries will illustrate the complex of factors involved and the differential importance of these factors. Bauxite ores, it has been pointed out, are basic to the manufacture of aluminum, and these ores are found in commercial significance principally in Arkansas within the United States.

These domestic deposits were supplemented by imports mainly from Guyana and Surinam in South America. The separation of aluminum from bauxite is a two-stage process: first, calcined aluminum oxide or alumina is recovered from the ore and, second, aluminum is produced from the alumina. The first stage requires about 2 tons of high-grade ore and flux material plus the heat from a ton of coal to produce 1 ton of alumina. Then, 10,000 kilowatt-hours of electrical energy — approximately equivalent to 4 tons of coal — plus 600 pounds of electrodes and 100 pounds of cryolite are required to convert the ton of alumina to $\frac{1}{2}$ ton of aluminum. The availability of cheap electrical power is a dominant consideration. Domestic or imported bauxite is converted to alumina at the source of supply or near the point of entry, primarily in the Gulf states. Alumina is then shipped to sources of hydroelectric power for the final step (to the Columbia River, the Tennessee Valley, and Niagara Falls). Finally, the aluminum metal is shipped to manufacturing plants located in several parts of the country but, especially, in Michigan, Illinois, and Pennsylvania. In this process, then, the location of the ore is the primary consideration in the location of alumina plants, although availability of low-priced electrical power is dominant in the final stages.

Iron and Steel Manufacturing.   The iron and steel industry is basic to much of our industrial economy, contributing essential semifinished materials to the automobile industry, construction and maintenance, the railroads, machinery tool production, and many other industries. Basic raw materials for this industry are iron ore, coal, limestone and, when available, iron and steel scrap. Approximate proportions in this "ingredient mix" to produce 1 ton of steel rolling-mill products are about 1.5 tons of ore, 1.5 tons of coal, 0.6 tons of limestone, and 0.3 tons of scrap, the proportions varying, of course, with variations in the quality of the ore and coal, the type of ore, and the amount of scrap available. Iron ore occurs in many localities of the United States, and high-grade ore is also imported from Canada and Venezuela; but the richest and most extensive deposits have been in the Mesabi Range in the Lake Superior region. Since 1900, about 85 percent of domestic iron ores have originated in this region, and 80 percent of steel capacity has been constructed in relation to these deposits and to the coking coal fields near Pittsburgh and in Indiana and Illinois. Other important but relatively minor centers are located in Alabama, Maryland-Pennsylvania-New Jersey, Utah-Colorado, and California.

In the early development of the iron industry, fuel supply was by far the dominant location factor. At the beginning of the 19th century, it required 7 to 8 tons of coal to produce 1 ton of pig iron. Technical improvements in furnace operation, however, led to important savings in fuel. In the United States, average coal consumption per ton of pig iron, which was about 2.1 tons in 1879, was only 1.27 tons in 1938. This has meant an increasing locational pull by ore sources and especially by final markets. (The market pull has been further reinforced by the fact that scrap iron is usually more available and cheaper at the major market centers.) These facts explain the early development of Pittsburgh as the major iron- and steel-producing region but also indicate why this district has been losing ground to centers such as Chicago-Gary, Cleveland, and Buffalo.

Pittsburgh has the most strategic location with reference to coal fields but has a serious disadvantage in terms of total transportation costs for raw material and finished products except in its own nearby market. The Pittsburgh district produced about 40 percent of the total United States output in 1900, when fuel requirements were substantially higher; but this had fallen to 25 percent by 1935. Bethlehem and Buffalo have transport advantages in serving eastern markets, while Detroit, Cleveland, and Chicago are best situated with respect to their important local markets. Birmingham has a site advantage for southern markets and can compete effectively in the Pacific Northwest, and Provo is well situated to serve the Mountain and western areas. Pacific Coast points are poorly located with reference to coal and ore; but the extensive use of scrap, estimated at 85 percent in 1944, enables steel plants in this region to compete effectively in producing a limited array of products for local markets. Locations on tidewater, such as Sparrows Point in Maryland, depend on the import of ores from Canada and Venezuela and will probably increase in importance as the high-grade ores of the Mesabi Range are exhausted.

The availability of low-cost transportation by water for raw materials and finished products is of major importance in determining the relative advantage of these alternative steel-producing centers. Lake Superior ores flow south and east through the Great Lakes, while coal flows from Pennsylvania and Ohio in the reverse direction. Pittsburgh's disadvantage lies primarily in that it must depend on rail shipments to reach eastern markets and on a combination of rail and water to reach the industrial centers at Detroit and Chicago. Freight rates on finished steel from Buffalo, Cleveland, and Detroit to New York City are about 50 percent lower by water through the New York State Barge Canal than by rail. Water shipment from Sparrows Point to New York costs less than one-third the rail rate.

3.5 INTERREGIONAL TRADE FLOWS

The foregoing pages have presented an abbreviated description of the geographic distribution of economic activities in the United States—the major locational patterns for selected agricultural and industrial activities. These producing areas are connected through trade flows with the major market centers. Market centers may represent the concentration points for secondary industry as in the flow of raw materials to manufacturing establishments; but, ultimately, the market for finished products corresponds closely with the geographic distribution of population. In other words, the primary determinant of the volume of goods and services consumed in any region is the number of consumers living in the region. Important modifying factors are interregional differences in levels of per capita income and purchasing power, population characteristics such as age, sex, and race and, interrelated with these factors, differences in aggregate consumer tastes and preferences.

Of course, geographic patterns of population, employment, and income are interrelated with industrial location. The availability of labor and the level of wages are important determinants of industrial location; and in turn, but with some lags, population moves in response to favorable employment opportunities. We have already discovered that the region stretching from Massachusetts to Illinois predominates in manufacturing activity. This 11-state region includes only 12 percent of the land area of the United States, but in it resides 45 percent of the total civilian population. Per capita income is relatively high in these states, so that residents of the region receive more than 50 percent of the total personal income in the United States. As a consequence, a substantial part of agricultural products, raw materials, and manufactured goods either originate in this region or flow to it through interregional trade.

Efforts have been made to break down the interindustry, input–output matrix for the United States into a set of interrelated regional matrices. Because of the complications involved in this procedure, presently available material is limited to an 11-industry matrix with three major regions: (I) the New England, Middle Atlantic, and South Atlantic states, (II) the North Central and South Central states, and (III) the Mountain and Pacific states. Even in this highly condensed form, the results are most interesting (Table 3.5). The eastern region, for example, produced only 47 percent of its requirements for the products of agriculture in 1947, received 32 percent from the Central states, 7 percent from the western region, and imported 14 percent from foreign countries. These *trade coefficients* show the proportions of the region's purchases (in value terms) that originated within the region and from interregional shipments

TABLE 3.5   Trade Coefficients for Major Regions in the United States, 1947

Industry	Producing Region	Consuming Region (Percent)		
		Region I	Region II	Region III
Products of agriculture	Region I	46.8	3.5	0.3
	Region II	32.4	84.8	10.1
	Region III	7.0	9.6	85.3
	Imports	13.8	2.2	4.3
Animals and products	Region I	36.9	8.4	1.8
	Region II	56.6	83.5	35.9
	Region III	2.9	8.1	60.1
	Imports	3.5	—[a]	2.2
Products of mines	Region I	79.4	19.5	0.2
	Region II	12.7	67.9	1.1
	Region III	0.3	2.4	98.6
	Imports	7.6	10.1	0.1
Products of forests	Region I	70.5	5.2	0.3
	Region II	10.4	68.6	1.6
	Region III	10.9	20.1	97.6
	Imports	8.2	6.1	0.5
Manufactures	Region I	73.5	20.3	8.6
	Region II	21.1	75.3	24.3
	Region III	1.5	3.3	64.9
	Imports	3.8	1.2	2.2
Petroleum and natural gas	Region I	16.7	1.1	–
	Region II	64.0	96.9	1.2
	Region III	3.7	1.8	56.4
	Imports	18.9	0.2	42.4
Electric light and power	Region I	100.0	–	–
	Region II	–	100.0	–
	Region III	–	–	100.0
	Imports	–	–	–
Transportation and communication	Region I	98.2	–	–
	Region II	–	99.5	–
	Region III	1.8	0.5	100.0
	Imports	–	–	–
Trade, finance, and banking	Region I	98.3	–	–
	Region II	1.7	100.0	2.3
	Region III	–	–	97.7
	Imports	–	–	–
Other services	Region I	100.0	3.5	–
	Region II	–	94.6	–
	Region III	–	1.9	100.0
	Imports	–	–	–

TABLE 3.5 *Continued*

Industry	Producing Region	Consuming Region (Percent)		
		Region I	Region II	Region III
Households	Region I	100.0	–	–
	Region II	–	100.0	–
	Region III	–	–	100.0
	Imports	–	–	–

Source. Leon N. Moses, "The Stability of Interregional Trading Patterns and Input–Output Analysis," *The American Economic Review*, Vol. XLV, No. 5, December 1955, pp. 803–832, (Table VI).

Regions include the following Census groups and correspond roughly to east, central and west.

Region I: New England, Middle Atlantic, and South Atlantic states.

Region II: East North Central, West North Central, East South Central, and West South Central states.

Region III: Mountain and Pacific states.

[a]Dashes indicate no data available.

and, hence, must add to 100 percent. Notice that Region I was deficit in the production of agricultural and livestock products and that this deficit was offset primarily by receipts from Region II and from foreign countries. Regions II and III each produced 85 percent of their own requirements of the products of agriculture, but because of regional specialization they did receive shipments from other regions and from foreign countries.

Shipments of coal and iron ore were responsible for much of the interdependence between Regions I and II in the products of mines. Region II clearly dominated in petroleum and gas, supplying not only its own requirements but 64 percent of the needs of Region I. Region III produced 56 percent of its oil and gas requirements and received 42 percent as imports from foreign countries. Notice that imports of petroleum also accounted for 19 percent of the supply for the eastern states. Finally, there is a group of important activities for which each region is self-sufficient or virtually so. They include the production of electric power, the service activities (transportation, communication, trade, finance, banking, and other professional and personal services) and of course, the household account.

Before leaving this set of trade coefficients, it should be emphasized that the degree of aggregation necessarily reduces the apparent importance of interdependencies. When the United States is combined into three major regions, many important trade movements are lost — coal from Pennsylvania to New England, cotton textiles from the South Atlantic states to New York, petroleum and gas from Texas to Chicago and Detroit, automobiles from Michigan to North Dakota, cattle from the range states to California, or citrus from Florida to the major metropolitan centers along the Atlantic Coast. A matrix based on 50 states would show substantially larger interstate shipments and correspondingly less important local production. Nevertheless, it is true that every area represents a combination of surplus, deficit, and self-sufficient situations. California is in the aggregate an important surplus-producing state for farm products, for example; but this aggregate combines large surpluses of many fruits and vegetables, deficits in meats and manufactured dairy products, and an approximate balance in fluid milk and cream production and consumption. In general, we can conclude that interregional and interstate trade is highly important in the United States but it is also clear that many significant activities, especially in the service field, are carried on with a close balance between *local* production and consumption.

3.6 THE MOBILITY OF PRODUCTION FACTORS

This chapter has reviewed the development of economic specialization — individual, industry, and region — and the concurrent development of commodity trade flows connecting specialized producers with each other and with consumers. Important effects of the geographic distribution of certain natural resources on production and, therefore, on trade have been stressed. It is true, of course, that natural resources such as coal and oil deposits, falling water for power, and land and climate are immobile and that production must adjust to the location of these natural factors of production. In these cases, the movements of products substitute for the movement of the resource. Changes in the effective location pattern of natural resources are possible through new discoveries and improved techniques of conservation and exploitation, but for the most part the location pattern at any time must be taken as given.

Capital and labor resources are not fixed in location, however, and thus move from place to place as required. We pointed out that these movements were essential to the early development of the American colonies — a massive movement of both capital and labor from Europe to America. In such movements the flows of capital are essentially flows of goods, since effective capital usually takes the form of producer goods such as machinery and equipment or of consumer goods needed for the sustenance of the labor force. Labor movements, on the other hand, are more familiar in the great migrations of population. There have been five main currents of intercontinental migration since the beginning of the 16th century: (1) from Europe to North America, (2) from southern Europe to Latin America, (3) from Great Britain to Africa and Australia, (4) the movement of slaves from Africa to the Americas, and (5) a variety of movements from China and India. Major internal or intracontinental flows have been (6) the westward movement in the United States, and (7) the eastward movement in Russia.

Since World War I, the internal migrations within the United States have been dominated by movements out of the Southeast, central and northern plains and Mountain states to the Pacific Coast and to the industrial area from southern New England to Illinois. A comparison of migration patterns with data on geographic differences in per capita personal incomes suggests that economic incentives are important basic causes of these internal migrations.

Differences in per capita incomes are shown in Table 3.6 for selected years from 1880 to 1968. Incomes in the Far West have exceeded those

TABLE 3.6   Regional Differences in Per Capita Personal Income, 1880 to 1968 (Dollars Per Capita)

Region	1880	1900	1920	1940	1960	1968
United States average	95	113	680	592	2215	3412

Index (United States average = 100)

	1880	1900	1920	1940	1960	1968
East						
New England	137	130	116	126	110	110
Mideast	122	123	123	133	116	113
Great Lakes	107	106	111	112	108	107
Southeast	58	56	53	57	73	77
West						
Plains	95	106	99	81	93	96
Southwest	67	78	88	70	87	87
Rocky Mountain	183	163	109	89	95	90
Far West	199	157	149	132	118	115

Source. 1880 to 1920: Hugh O. Nourse, *Regional Economics.* McGraw-Hill Book Company, New York, 1968. Table 6.5, p. 146.
1940 to 1968: *Survey of Current Business, April 1969*, Vol. 49, No. 4. Office of Business Economics, U.S. Department of Commerce, Washington, D.C.

in all other regions for the last century, but are now only 115 percent of the United States average instead of roughly double that figure in 1880. Incomes in the Southeast were between 50 and 60 percent of the United States average through 1940, but they have recently climbed to more than three-fourths the national average. As shown in Table 3.7, the Far West has shown a steady net in-migration while the Southeast has shown a steady out-migration throughout the period. For every other region, net migration rates have been consistent with the notion that people move in response to income differentials.

The causes of migration are by no means simple, and we have no desire to leave the impression that direct comparison of average levels of income provides a complete understanding. This is further emphasized by considering the three states of Florida, Arizona, and Nevada. These states and to some extent California and Colorado have unusually high increases in population through migration for reasons that are, at least in part, unrelated to employment opportunities—for example, the movements of retired people to these areas to take advantage of favorable climatic (and in some cases favorable tax) conditions.

The movement of population and labor force out of agriculture has been one of the important contributors to these internal movements. Farm population and the farm labor force have decreased relative to the United States totals, and in recent years there have been absolute as well as relative declines in farm population and farm employment. Data for the

TABLE 3.7   Net Regional Migration Per 1000 Average Population

Region	1880 to 1890	1900 to 1910	1920 to 1930	1940 to 1950
East				
New England	102	91	4	−1
Mideast	75	113	54	5
Great Lakes	37	33	55	13
Southeast	−26	−33	−64	−58
West				
Plains	170	−9	−56	−73
Southwest	98	176	27	−10
Rocky Mountain	548	289	−74	−13
Far West	396	481	307	284

Source. Perloff et al., *op. cit.* Table 199, p. 593. Attributed to Lee, Miller, Brainerd, and Easterlin, *Population Redistribution and Economic Growth, United States, 1870–1950* (Philadelphia: American Philosophical Society, 1957), Table P-1, pp. 107–231.

years since 1920 indicate that the movement from farms has usually far exceeded the movement to farms. However, two exceptions to this general observation are important. First, the decline in nonfarm employment opportunities during the depression years reduced the farm-to-nonfarm migration about 40 percent and, actually, resulted in a net migration to farms in 1932. Second, World War II drew unusually large numbers of men from farms into the armed forces or into war-plant production during 1941 to 1943, and the return of some of these men to the farms after the war resulted in a reversal of the usual farm-to-city migration pattern in 1945 and 1946. Since 1950 the trend has continued until only 7 percent of the population live on farms.

Whatever the basic causes, it is apparent that factors of production such as capital and labor do move between and within nations. The adjustments of these flows and of the flows of commodities through the development of production patterns related to basic natural resources are central problems in the operation of our economic system. They are considered in greater detail and more analytically in the chapters that follow.

SELECTED READINGS

Economic Interdependence

Barna, Tibor (ed.), *Structural Interdependence and Economic Development*, St. Martin's Press, New York (1963).

Chenery, Hollis B. and Paul G. Clark, *Interindustry Economics*, John Wiley and Sons, New York (1959).

Evans, W. Duane and Marvin Hoffenberg, "The Interindustry Relations Study for 1947," *The Review of Economics and Statistics*, Vol. XXXIV, No. 2 (May 1952). pp. 97–142.

Goldman, Morris R., Martin L. Marimont, and Beatrice N. Vaccara, "The Interindustry Structure of the United States, a Report on the 1958 Input/Output Study," *Survey of Current Business*, Vol. 44, No. 11 (November 1964) and Revisions, Vol. 45, No. 9 (September 1965).

Heady, Earl O. and Harold O. Carter, "Input–Output Models as Techniques of Analysis for Interregional Competition," *Journal of Farm Economics*, Vol. XLI, No. 5 (December 1959). pp. 978–991.

Isard, Walter, *Methods of Regional Analysis: An Introduction to Regional Science*, The M.I.T. Press, Cambridge (1960).

Leontief, Wassily W., "The Structure of the U.S. Economy," *Scientific American*, Vol. 212, No. 4 (April 1965). pp. 25–35.

Leontief, Wassily W., *Input–Output Economics*, Oxford University Press, New York (1966).

Leontief, Wassily W. and others, *Studies in the Structure of the American Economy*, Oxford University Press, New York (1953).

Miernyk, William H., *The Elements of Input–Output Analysis*, Random House, New York (1965).

Mighell, Ronald L., *American Agriculture, Its Structure and Place in the Economy*, John Wiley and Sons, New York (1955).

Moses, Leon N., "The Stability of Interregional Trading Patterns and Input–Output Analysis," *The American Economic Review*, Vol. XLV, No. 5 (December 1955). pp. 803–832.

Nourse, Hugh O., *Regional Economics*, Part II, "Measurement and Change in Regional Economic Activity," McGraw-Hill Book Company, New York (1968). pp. 129–207.

THE SPATIAL
DIMENSION OF
MARKET PRICE

chapter 4

MARKET PRICE IN AN EXCHANGE ECONOMY

4.1 INTRODUCTION

Primitive societies are characterized by a large degree of self-sufficiency: families and regions produce most of the goods and services that they require and depend only in small measure on the exchange of goods with other families and other regions. In an advanced economy, on the other hand, specialization is highly developed, giving rise to increases in productivity and, hence, to higher standards of living. This specialization would be impossible, however, without the development of a marketing system that binds the specialized activities into an effective and integrated whole. This system provides services such as transportation, storage, and the transfer of ownership.

Although the direct function of marketing is to provide the services and ownership transfers involved in the movement of commodities from producer to consumer, an even more essential role in a modern economy is price formulation or price discovery. In such an economy, prices direct the concurrent flows of resources into alternative uses and of goods and services to ultimate consumers. In this unseen and largely automatic system, prices guide producers in their choice of enterprises and in their purchase of factors of production, while they also ration the available supplies of goods and services among consumers. Only insofar as the prices established through the marketing system transmit demands back to producers and supply conditions forward to consumers with a minimum of lag, imperfection, and distortion can the economy achieve efficient allocation and economical use of its resources in satisfying wants.

The following chapters stress this interdependent nature of economic activity and the strategic role of marketing in the total economy. Our emphasis is on the system rather than on the individual firm and household. The first part of our discussion deals with markets in space, form, and time, and the later chapters elaborate this through the consideration of the theory of economic specialization and trade. Although the approach is from the viewpoint of marketing, the treatment necessarily involves important production economics problems such as the selection of enterprises and the allocation of basic resources among alternative uses. Our purpose is to provide the student with some of the analytical tools essential to an understanding of and research in marketing and in interregional competition.

4.2 CONCEPT OF THE MARKET

We have emphasized that marketing is primarily concerned with the creation of place, time, and ownership utilities (as a practical matter we may include aspects of form utility such as packaging and processing). The system involves the physical movement of goods (with the associated ownership transfers) from millions of producers, through thousands of middlemen or marketing agencies and, hence, eventually to many millions of final consumers.

We may classify these marketing activities as concentration, equalization, and dispersion. As the word implies, *concentration* refers to the collection or assembly of commodities from many producers and the channeling of these products into the wholesale markets. *Dispersion* is the reverse of concentration, taking goods from the wholesale markets and distributing them through retail outlets to final consumers. *Equalization* refers to the processes of adjusting the commodity flows in response to changing supply and demand conditions. The wholesale market may be thought of as a balancing reservoir, receiving fluctuating supplies from producers and releasing them as required to meet the changing needs and demands of consumers. In a capitalistic enterprise economy, like that of the United States, the process of equalization is accomplished more or less automatically through the marketing system.

A market may be loosely defined as an area or setting within which producers and consumers are in communication with one another, where supply and demand conditions operate, and the title to goods is transferred. The actual movement of goods in space or time is usually but not necessarily involved. In this communication process, prices are established, and these prices move up and down in response to changes in the underlying supply and demand forces. If an unusually large quantity of a commodity appears on the market, prices drop, and this encourages consumers to buy more and producers to offer less. This means a decrease in the relative profitability of producing the commodity in question, and eventually it leads to shifts in production patterns.

In this way prices, through a complex system of interrelated commodity and factor markets, become the primary directors of economic activity. On the production side, commodity prices interact on factor prices and thus serve to allocate scarce resources among alternative employments. On the consumption side, factor prices are prime determinants of income and its distribution, and income plus commodity prices serve to ration the available goods and services among consumers.

4.3 INDIVIDUAL AND AGGREGATE DEMAND

The quantity of a commodity that a consumer purchases depends on a complex of factors including the individual's tastes and preferences, the price of the commodity in question, the prices of other commodities, and his income. General observation suggests that, with income and other prices constant, an individual will usually buy less of a given commodity as its price increases and more when its price decreases. When expressed in quantitative terms, this inverse or negative relationship is called a demand schedule. From the above, it is clear that the individual consumer's demand schedule will shift or change with changes in his income, with changes in the prices of alternative products, and with changes (through time) in the consumer's tastes. Since different consumers characteristically have different tastes and incomes, it is also true that each individual has his own particular demand schedule for a given commodity. Some individuals will greatly adjust their purchases in response to price changes, but others will change their purchases very little. Some will buy relatively large quantities even at high prices, although others will purchase little or none even with the incentive of very low prices.

Such individual demand schedules are suggested graphically by the curves in the first section of Figure 4.1. These differ in shape, slope, and location. If consumers buy any of a commodity — and if the commodity has the ability to satisfy positive wants — then we shall expect the quantity

purchased to increase at least slightly as price decreases. The same holds
true for the sum or aggregate of consumers in a market. The aggregate or
market demand schedule represents the sum of the quantities that will
be purchased by all consumers at each level of prices. At very high
prices, only a few consumers will buy, and they will buy relatively small
amounts. As the price is lowered, these consumers will increase their
purchases, and new consumers will begin to buy. With many consumers
in the market, the aggregate can be expected to form a regular and
continuous schedule like the one suggested by the aggregate demand
curve in the second section of Figure 4.1.

Each commodity will have its characteristic demand schedule or
curve in a particular market, and these market demand curves will vary in

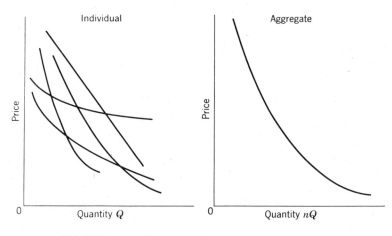

FIGURE 4.1   Individual and aggregate demand curves.

shape, slope, and location. Although we define the demand for any commodity as the price-quantity relation with incomes and other prices held
constant, we have observed that the particular demand schedule for any
commodity is dependent on the prices of other commodities. Consequently, to some degree, the demand schedules for all commodities in a
market are interdependent and interrelated.

4.4   INDIVIDUAL AND AGGREGATE SUPPLY

A brief resume of production and supply theory is provided at this point.
This theory parallels consumption and demand theory with a few important exceptions. The role of the consumer's indifference map is played by

the isoquant map showing the technology of factor substitution in the production of output. Unlike utility, output is readily measured in objective terms so isoquants have cardinal as well as ordinal values. Within the limits imposed by this technology, the production problem may be thought of as twofold: first, with given factor prices, to select the combinations of factors that will minimize costs for any level of output; second, with given product prices, to select the level of output that will maximize the positive difference between gross income (output × product price) and total cost (factor inputs × factor prices). Under competitive market conditions, the final adjustment for the firm is conveniently summarized in terms of the marginal cost curve with profit-maximizing output found where marginal cost equals product price.

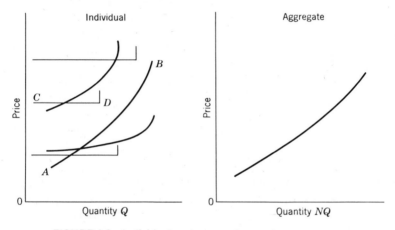

FIGURE 4.2   Individual and aggregate supply curves.

Marginal cost curves for a number of firms producing a given product for a given market are suggested by the first diagram in Figure 4.2. Here, we show a variety of curves differing with respect to both shape and position. In general, we expect that marginal costs will increase with increases in output because of intensification on fixed factors and the principle of diminishing marginal productivity. But this tendency for marginal costs to rise may be largely, if not entirely, offset through plant segmentation and by increasing the hours of plant operation. For this reason, the diagram illustrates some marginal cost curves that increase more or less regularly and others that are horizontal over a considerable range and then turn upward abruptly as output nears plant capacity.

In all cases, however, these marginal cost curves indicate the output response of individual firms to changes in product prices in the short run.

In the case of a firm with a marginal cost curve such as *AB*, output will be increased gradually as price increases. A plant with a curve similar to *CD*, however, will not enter the market if price is less than *OC*, although with prices of *OC* or greater, it will produce at capacity output *D*. If we start with a very low market price and increase gradually, it is possible to sum together the outputs of all firms and, hence, to obtain the aggregate market supply curve. This will be positively inclined — higher total output associated with higher price — for two reasons: (1) in the short run, higher prices will bring greater output from firms with positively inclined marginal cost curves and (2), in the long run, higher prices will bring new firms into the industry, attracting resources from other employments.

The aggregate supply curve shown in Figure 4.2 shows output increasing at a decreasing rate, but it should be recognized that this will not necessarily be true. Price increases may attract many new resources and firms to the industry and quite possibly may result in output that increases with price at an increasing rate. The only generalization that is possible is that the supply curve will be positively inclined. The exact shape will depend on factors such as the particular technology available, the nature of the resources involved, factor prices, prices of alternative products, and the net earnings in other industries.

4.5   PRICE EQUILIBRIUM

In a market for a particular commodity, equilibrium is achieved when a price is established at which the quantities offered for sale exactly equal the quantities demanded by purchasers. This is illustrated in Figure 4.3

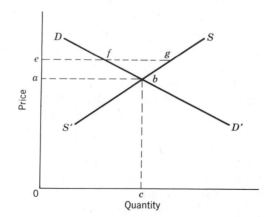

FIGURE 4.3   The equilibrium of demand and supply to determine market price.

where *DD'* represents a negatively inclined demand curve and *SS'* a positively inclined supply curve. They intersect at point *b* with price *oa* and with the quantity offered equal to the quantity demanded, *oc.* If the price in the market were higher than this level, say at *oe*, the quantity offered would exceed the quantity taken by some amount, such as *fg.* Competition among sellers would make this an unstable situation and force price down to the *oa* level. In a similar way, prices below the equilibrium level will be unstable and will be forced up by the bidding of prospective buyers.

This discussion has been based on the assumption that economic adjustments are made instantaneously, without time lags and frictions. But this is not true in real economic life. Consumers may take time to learn about and to adjust to changing quantity and price situations. Lags are even more important on the supply side. Here, we may identify three interrelated situations: (1) the *market* situation, with given supplies and no change in production possible, (2) the *short-run* situation, where producers may change output by moving along present marginal cost curves, and (3) the *long-run* situation, where producers (and resources) may enter or leave the industry and where existing producers can modify their productive facilities and so change their marginal cost curves.

Although these definitions are related to time lags, the actual calendar time involved is not the essential feature. Instead, they refer to the types of economic adjustments that are possible. In the first case, the product has been produced and is now available; the market supply curve, therefore, might be represented as a vertical line, perfectly inelastic, with the entire quantity placed on the market regardless of price. This is virtually true for perishable commodities, but with nonperishables the sellers have the option of placing their supplies on the market or of storing them in anticipation of better prices at a later date. Even with perishable products, producers may elect at very low prices to retain more of their crop for home consumption rather than to sell. In any event, it is clear that market supply curves will be relatively inelastic (Figure 4.4).

In the short run, present producers may increase or decrease the available quantities by moving up or down their marginal cost curves in response to price changes. These adjustments will result in short-run supply curves considerably more elastic than market-period curves.

Finally, the long run permits basic changes in resource allocation, with firms moving into the industry if prices and net returns are attractive or moving out if net returns are below normal. Since most industries use resources not particularly specialized to their production and account for only a small part of total resources, we can expect that long-run supply curves will be very elastic (Figure 4.4). This merely means that, given

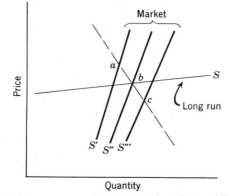

FIGURE 4.4 Market and long-run supply curves and market and "normal" equilibrium prices.

time for economic adjustments, most industries can expand output by increasing the number of firms and that, with new firms essentially similar to the old, this will require no large increase in price. If an industry depends on a highly specialized resource available in a limited supply (for instance, a small mineral deposit or a particular quality of soil) the long-run supply curve may be quite elastic up to the limit imposed by this resource but quite inelastic beyond that point. In these cases, the size of the industry relative to the resource in question may also have a pronounced effect on the resource price, and this bidding on the factor market can be expected to make the long-run supply for the commodity less elastic.

Differences between market and long-run supply situations explain much of the time-to-time fluctuation in commodity prices. To illustrate this, we compare a demand curve (assumed unchanging) with market and long-run supply curves in Figure 4.4. The several market supply curves — S', S'', and S''' — represent situations in different market periods, fluctuating or shifting in response to some factor, such as crop yields. As a consequence, market price may sometimes be high (a) and sometimes low (c). The relatively elastic curve S represents the long-run supply curve, and its intersection with the demand curve results in the "normal" equilibrium price (b). This is called the normal or long-run price because it represents a level of returns to resources employed in this industry that is in usual or normal relation to returns in other employments and, also, because it represents the equilibrium level around which market prices will fluctuate. Of course, the normal price will itself change in a dynamic economy as a result of fundamental shifts in demand or of technological changes in production.

4.6 JOINT DEMAND FOR GOODS AND SERVICES

In the paragraphs above, we have dealt with producers' supply and consumers' demand responses, indicating that market price results from the
equilibrium of supply and demand. It is apparent that this would be
correct only in very simple and primitive markets where original producers
and final consumers do, in fact, come face-to-face in the marketplace. In
most markets, however, producers and consumers are separated by many
intermediate marketing and processing agencies; and original production
and final sale may be separated both in space and in time. Consequently,
producers do not face directly the demands of consumers, nor do consumers come into direct contact with basic supply forces. Instead, these
forces are transmitted through the marketing system.

Suppose we lump together all marketing functions and consider the
simple case where producers and consumers are brought into contact
through a single marketing group. As in the previous example, there will
be a market demand function for the product in question, reflecting consumer responses to price changes. This is represented by the negatively
inclined demand curve D_r in Figure 4.5, and it refers to the exchange of
the commodity at the retail level as consumers make purchases from the
marketing agents. On the other hand, producers' reactions are represented by the "at the farm" supply curve S_f.

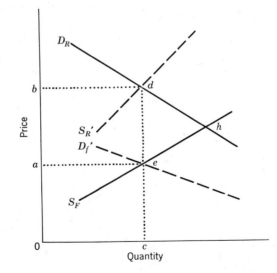

FIGURE 4.5   The original and derived demand and supply curves and price formation
at two stages in the marketing channel.

Now, it should be quite clear that the intersection of these two curves at point h has no real significance. At this point the retail price and the farm price would be equal, and marketing agents would be buying, selling, storing, packaging, transporting, and financing the distribution of the commodity at zero return. The performance of these functions requires inputs of resources and the bearing of risks; this will be true even if the services are performed by producers and consumers. In fact, if it were not more economical to have these functions performed by specialized marketing agencies, we would expect that the marketing process would bypass the marketers and connect producers directly with consumers.

The truth of the matter is that the consumer's demand function is not a demand for the product in question but a joint demand for the good plus the associated marketing services. There is no demand in Buffalo for wheat offered in Kansas City but instead a demand for wheat delivered to Buffalo when wanted and in the desired form. We can express this retail demand in terms of prices at the farm, however, by subtracting marketing price margins from the retail prices. Such a *derived* demand function is suggested by line D_f' in the diagram. In a similar way, the at-farm supply function can be projected to the retail level as line S_r'.

With these derived curves we can trace out the equilibrium of supply and demand and the determination of price. Apparently, this market is in equilibrium with the production and sale of quantity oc of the *product plus the associated marketing services*; this equilibrium involves a farm price of oa, a retail price to the consumer of ob, and a price margin to marketing agents equal to the difference, or ab. In any real market, of course, there may be several stages and alternative marketing channels with derived demand and supply curves and prices at every stage. Thus, we might define markets and observe prices at the point of communication between the farmer and the assembler, the assembler and the wholesaler, the wholesaler and the jobber, the jobber and the retailer, and finally between the retailer and the consumer.

We have referred to the derived demand and supply curves as differing from the basic demand and supply curves by the addition or the subtraction of marketing price margins. But we have also emphasized that the performance of marketing functions requires the committing of resources and the taking of risks, as does any economic production activity. Primary producers use resources to create a commodity; secondary or manufacturing industries use resources to modify the form of the commodity; marketing agencies use resources to produce services associated with commodities and necessary to their distribution—the creation of place, time, and ownership utilities. Now, if the returns from the sale of these services are very low, few agencies will offer to create them but, if the returns are high, many agencies will be willing to risk resources in such ventures. Consumers will also react; if marketing services are expensive, consumers will curtail their purchases and vice versa.

The essence of this is that there are demands for and supplies of marketing services just as there are for goods. Consumer demand, as has been indicated, is a joint demand for goods and services, and the supply curve *expressed at the retail level* is a joint supply of goods and services. The price spread between the retail and farm level, or any other stages in the marketing channel, is not a constant but varies as we would anticipate for demand and supply functions. This is indicated in Figure 4.6 where the differences between the original and derived functions from Figure 4.5 are shown as supply and demand functions for marketing services. With quantity *oc*, the derived demand for and supply of marketing services are in equilibrium at point *k* with price spread *oj*, which is equal to the amount *ab* in Figure 4.5.

Market equilibrium requires the simultaneous equating of the supply of and demand for goods *plus* services. In some cases this is evident from the fact that services are priced separately from the product itself and the consumer is given the option of taking or rejecting the service. In most situations, however, goods and services are completely intermingled, as in Figure 4.5, and the established prices refer to this goods-service composite.

4.7 MULTIPLE PRICE MARKETS

A market was defined earlier as an area or sphere of activity within which buyers and sellers are in intimate contact and where, with perfect knowledge, a single price will hold for a given commodity. We now are aware

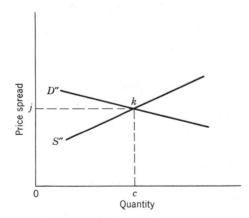

FIGURE 4.6   The derived demand for and supply of marketing services.

that a market may have multiple prices, all interdependent and simultaneously determined at various stages in the marketing channel from producer to consumer. We might consider the product at each stage or with each alternative combination of services as belonging to a separate market characterized by its unique price. However, the important concept to be grasped is that all of these stages and prices are interdependent and determined simultaneously in a single-market context — a single market with multiple prices.

The above illustration of multiple prices refers to the sequence of levels or stages in the marketing channel as a product moves from producer to consumer. In addition, there are multiple prices at any stage along dimensions corresponding to the traditional space, form, and time utilities. In a single market, all of these price structures are interrelated and simultaneously determined through transfer costs, processing costs, and storage costs. Thus, there is not a single price for a particular commodity at the farm level but a complex structure of prices reflecting geographic differences, form differences, and time differences.

Systematic relationships among these prices in isolated and in competing markets will be examined in detail in the following chapters. At this point it is important to recognize that every market has a space, form, and time dimension and that the operation of the market brings into equilibrium the whole complex of supply-demand relationships for goods and services. In a narrow sense, this concept refers directly to a particular commodity or to a family of commodities. When broadly conceived, however, it encompasses regional specialization, interregional trade and competition, the allocation of resources among alternative uses, the determination of product prices and factor prices and, therefore, approaches the concept of general interdependence and general equilibrium for the whole economy.

4.8   THE PERFECT MARKET CONCEPT

In most of the material that follows, we discuss "perfect" markets — markets characterized throughout by the conditions of perfect competition. The general nature of these market structures is familiar — perfect knowledge, no lags or frictions, large numbers of firms, standardized or homogeneous products, and no exercise of monopolistic power. Actually, the requirements for a perfect market are somewhat less restrictive. The essential conditions are: (1) perfect knowledge by all buyers and sellers, (2) each buyer and seller acts in an economically "rational" way, disregarding any influence of his actions on price, and (3) free entry in all directions.

Of course, all markets in real life operate with some degree of imperfect knowledge and with lags and frictions, and some have important elements of monopoly. In spite of this, the concept of the perfect market is an important tool for the economist. Its abstraction permits us to focus attention on and to understand the general nature of many market forces. It is a fair approximation to reality in some markets and, perhaps, especially for many agricultural markets. It has some "normative" values associated with the concept of economic efficiency and so may be useful in economic planning. Finally, it provides an essential background for the study of imperfect markets. Some modifications of this type will be discussed.

We conclude this chapter by pointing out that the basic ideas of specialization and trade grow out of the concept of the market in space, form, and time dimensions. The essential question is whether, given a number of points in space-form-time, they constitute a single, multiple-price market or a number of separate and competing markets.

As a preliminary definition that will be made more explicit later, we state that if such points are interconnected by trade, then they constitute a single market. The form and nature of these interconnections and the generalization of systematic relationships in the form of economic principles are the subject of later chapters.

SELECTED READINGS

Market Price Equilibrium

Braff, Allan J., *Microeconomic Analysis*, John Wiley and Sons Inc., New York (1969), Chapter 7, "The Purely Competitive Market," pp. 105–139.

Cochrane, Willard W., "The Market as a Unit of Inquiry in Agricultural Economics Research," *Journal of Farm Economics*, Vol. XXXIX, No. 1 (February 1957). pp. 21–39.

Grossman, Gregory, *Economic Systems*, "Anglia: The Perfect-Competition Model," Prentice-Hall Inc., Englewood Cliffs (1967). pp. 42–44.

Lloyd, Cliff, *Microeconomic Analysis*, Richard D. Irwin Inc. Homewood (1967), Chapter 5, "Competitive Markets," pp. 157–172.

Shepherd, Geoffrey S., *Marketing Farm Products* second edition, revised. Iowa State College Press, Ames (1947). Appendix A. "The Perfect Market in Time, Place, and Form." pp. 399–409.

PRICE EQUILIBRIUM IN SPATIALLY SEPARATED MARKETS

In the previous chapter we discussed the determination of price for a particular commodity as a result of the equilibrium of supply and demand in single and multiple price markets. In the present chapter we deal specifically with *prices* for a single commodity in several spatially separated markets and the *flows* of a single commodity in intermarket or interregional trade. Initially, we assume that transfer costs between markets are unimportant; then, that they are given. (Factors that determine transfer costs will be treated in detail in Chapter 6.)

The usage of the terms "market" and "region" may be puzzling. Region is used to refer to a readily identified geographic area. Whether such an area consists of one market, several markets, or is part of a larger, perhaps nationwide, market is an economic matter, not a geographical issue. Furthermore, although a region may be properly regarded as a market for one commodity, it may not be so regarded for others. When correctly described, the geographical features of a market will be clearly stated, so that there should be no cause for confusion.

5.1 THE TWO-REGION CASE

Consider first the simple case involving a single product produced and consumed in two regions. Supply and demand curves are given for each and, in the absence of trade between them, these curves determine the price for the commodity in each region. This is illustrated by the first two sections of Figure 5.1. In region X, the demand curve D_x and supply curve S_x intersect, resulting in a competitive price represented by oa. In region Y, on the other hand, the somewhat lower demand curve D_y and higher supply curve S_y result in the lower equilibrium price ob. In the absence of commercial contact between the two regions, these prices and the accompanying quantities produced and consumed would represent equilibrium conditions.

But suppose that traders from region Y make contact with region X. They discover that the price for this commodity is lower in Y than in X and that, ignoring transfer costs, they can buy in Y and sell in X at a profit. Traders will engage in such *arbitrage*, therefore, to their own profit. As part of the supply available in Y is transferred to X, however, the price in X will decline while that in Y increases. With the assumption of zero transfer cost, it follows that *arbitrage* will continue so long as the price in X exceeds that in Y. Eventually, the flow of the commodity from region Y to region X will be just large enough to result in the equalization of product prices and the establishment of a single market.

The opening of trade between regions has the effect of bringing the combined demand of the regions to bear on the combined supply conditions. This is illustrated by the third section of Figure 5.1, where the combined supply and demand curves for the two regions are shown. These curves have been added horizontally, combining the quantities that would

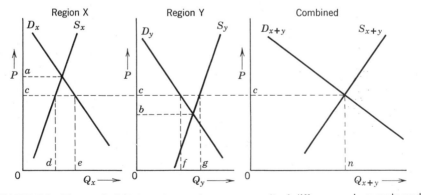

FIGURE 5.1   The trade between two regions as a result of differences in supply and demand functions.

be demanded (or supplied) in the two regions in response to selected levels of price. The intersection of the combined curves indicates a final equilibrium price of *oc* and total output *n*. Notice that this intersection will always occur between the prices that held in the regions in isolation and that it involves shipment of the commodity from the low-price region *Y* to the high-price region *X*. The amount shipped from *Y* is represented by *fg*, and the amount received in region *X* is shown by *de*. These two quantities must be equal, of course, at the equilibrium price *oc*.

An alternative and convenient presentation of the single-product, two-region case is the "back-to-back" diagram of Figure 5.2. Here, the supply and demand curves for region *Y* in Figure 5.1 are plotted on the right half of the diagram in conventional form, but the supply and demand curves for region *X* have been reversed on the left half of the figure: quantities are measured to the right of the origin *O* for region *Y* but to the left for region *X*. Now, suppose we plot an *excess supply* curve for each region, showing the amount by which the quantity offered for sale exceeds the quantity purchased or demanded at various levels of price. They are illustrated by the curves ES_x and ES_y, and their intersection at *j* represents the determination of the equilibrium price *oc* with trade. The distance *cj*, equal to *oh*, represents the quantity of the commodity exported from *Y* to *X*, and this is exactly equal to the *de* and *fg* quantities in this and in the previous diagram.

Observe that interregional trade will expand output in region *Y*, where supply conditions are more favorable, and contract output in region *X*. Also, the higher prices that will prevail in *Y* will reduce local or domestic consumption, while lower prices in *X* will expand consumption. It follows

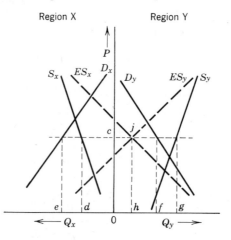

FIGURE 5.2   The equilibrium prices and trade illustrated by a "back-to-back" diagram.

that producers in region X will divert some of their productive resources into other uses and that those in region Y will allocate more resources to this commodity. On the other hand, consumers in region X will purchase more of this commodity and less of others, while consumers in region Y will make the opposite adjustment. Clearly, some resistance to such changes may arise in the real world as producer groups fight to protect their home market from producers in other regions. A full analysis of these effects must be delayed until two-commodity models are developed, but we can sense the general problem that new trading opportunities might create.

5.2 INTRODUCTION OF TRANSFER COSTS

We now indicate the modification that the insertion of transfer costs requires in the simple case of trade between two regions in a single product. We have discussed the aggregation of regional supply and demand curves to determine price and quantity traded under the assumption that the transfer costs were zero. We have observed that the two regions would have different prices in the absence of trade and that this difference would give rise to trade flows from region Y, where prices were low, to region X, where prices were high. This process would continue until prices in the two regions were equalized.

Obviously, this is an oversimplification—there are positive costs involved in the transfer of a commodity from one region to the other. It follows that trade will not completely equalize commodity prices; instead, the prices in the two regions will move toward each other until they differ exactly by the cost of transfer. It is a simple matter to indicate the modifications to the previous analysis that are required by the insertion of transfer costs.

In Figure 5.1, we used the horizontal summation of regional supply curves and demand curves to obtain aggregate functions for the combined regions. This procedure was appropriate in the absence of transfer costs because prices with trade would be identical in the several regions. With the addition of transfer costs, however, equilibrium prices will be lower in the exporting regions than in the importing regions (the difference equaling the transfer cost). In short, supply curves and demand curves can no longer be added directly but must be "positioned" or displaced to reflect this cost. This is indicated in Figure 5.3 where the supply and demand curves for region Y—the exporting region—have been moved upward by an amount t representing the unit cost of interregional transfer. Notice that, with this construction, any horizontal line across the diagrams no

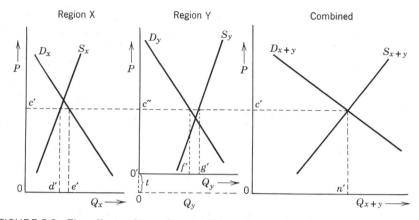

FIGURE 5.3   The effects of transfer cost (t) on prices and trade (compare with Figure 5.1).

longer represents equal prices in the two regions but, instead, prices that differ by transfer costs. Notice also that the combined curves in the final section of the diagram have been expressed in terms of prices in region X, but it is understood that the contributions of region Y are included at the lower level of prices which prevails in that region.

A similar modification can be made to Figure 5.2. Supply and demand curves for region Y, the region with lower prices, can be displaced upward by an amount t which represents the cost of interregional transfer (Figure 5.4). With this displacement, any horizontal line on the back-to-back diagram represents prices in the two regions that differ exactly by transfer cost. The analysis now proceeds as before: excess supply curves are constructed, and their intersection at j' defines the equilibrium prices with trade, equal to oc' in X and $o'c'$ in Y which differ by oo' or t. The distance $c'j'$ now represents the volume traded, and this is equal to the quantity $f'g'$ shipped by Y and $e'd'$ received by X. By simple extension of this argument, it should be clear that trade will take place between two regions only if the prices in isolation differ by more than transfer costs, and that prices in one region can differ from the ones in another by any amount within the range of plus or minus transfer costs without giving rise to commodity movement.

A comparison of Figures 5.2 and 5.4 indicates the general effects of transfer costs on trade. As stated above, commodity prices move toward equality, but equilibrium is reached when prices differ exactly by transfer costs (to go beyond this point would involve losses by the traders). The total volume of trade is reduced; the exact effect will depend on the shape of the two supply and demand curves, the price difference that exists in

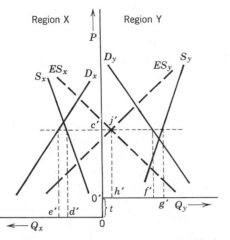

FIGURE 5.4   The effects of transfer cost (t) on prices and trade (compare with Figure 5.2)

the absence of trade, and the magnitude of the transfer cost. However, trade will be possible and profitable as long as the original difference in price is greater than the transfer costs.

A modification of Figure 5.2 will illustrate more clearly the relationship between transfer cost and trade movements. We reproduce in Figure 5.5 the excess supply curves ES_x and ES_y of Figure 5.2. Transfer cost

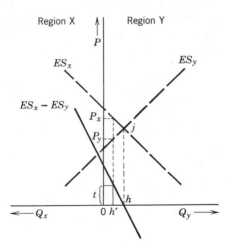

FIGURE 5.5   Equilibrium prices and trade illustrated by using differences between excess supply curves.

can be thought of as a block inserted from the left into the "V" formed by the two excess supply curves, the thickness of the block representing the level of transfer cost. Or, more simply, a new curve can be constructed that represents the vertical difference between the two, $ES_x - ES_y$. The transfer cost can now be measured along the vertical axis, and the quantity traded read off the horizontal axis. In particular, transfer cost of t per unit reduces the quantity shipped from region Y to region X from oh to oh'. A line drawn vertically through the point h' will indicate the equilibrium prices that will exist, namely, P_y and P_x.

As a corollary to this, it should be apparent that widely separated regions may not become connected by trade because the costs of transportation and handling the product exceed the price differences that exist in the absence of trade. Great distances and expensive transportation thus restrict trade, while technological developments that reduce transfer costs can be expected to increase trade. Before the development of modern highway and rail transportation, for example, trade was concentrated among regions situated along the seacoast or on navigable rivers. Notice also that improvements in transportation increase interregional competition and, in general, reduce the location advantage held by producers situated close to population centers.

The consideration of transportation costs greatly complicates the theoretical analysis of trade. In the absence of these costs, it is a simple matter to aggregate the supply curves and demand curves for many regions, to determine the equilibrium price that will hold in all regions, and to discover which regions will be exporters and which importers. All regions everywhere will be involved, and the actual trade flow patterns connecting exporters and importers will be unimportant, since transfer can be made without cost. With positive transfer costs, however, the multiple-region analysis is more complex. We observed previously that some regions will not be included in the trading system because price differences are less than transfer costs. Moreover, it will now be necessary to determine not only which regions export and which import but also the exact pattern of these flows. In order to combine regional supply curves and demand curves into composites for the single-market trading bloc, we must *know* the precise pattern of trade flows and the related transfer costs, yet, these patterns cannot be known until we complete our analysis! These difficulties will be resolved when we consider more complex location models.

5.3 MULTIREGION MODELS: PRODUCTION AND CONSUMPTION FIXED

A broad class of regional trade problems can be analyzed by using a relatively simple model in which it is assumed that given quantities of a homogeneous product are produced at m supply points and that given quantities of the same product are consumed at n demand points. Each pair of supply-demand points is connected by transportation facilities over which any amount of the product can be shipped at a given cost per unit which is specified for each pair of trading points.

A simple sketch of a two demand–three supply area problem is presented as a starting point. Let the quantities of cucumbers produced in California, North Carolina, and Maryland equal the unloads at Chicago and New York for a typical week – in this case, 200 carlots. Transfer costs are shown in dollars per bushel from each supply area to each market. As

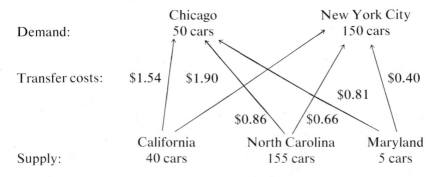

a tentative solution to the problem of selecting the optimum allocation of cucumbers, let California ship 40 cars to Chicago, Maryland ship 5 cars to New York City, and let North Carolina divide its supplies between the two, sending 10 to Chicago and 145 to New York City. Any such allocation implies a specific set of price relationships among producers and markets, as shown below, with New York City chosen as the base.

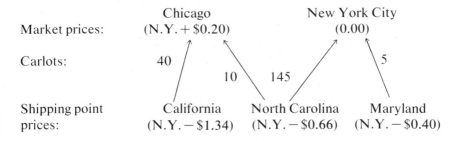

Markets and production areas are linked by transfer costs over active trading routes. If the trial allocation is, in fact, the optimum, no market will find it profitable to obtain supplies from any other producing area, and no producing area will be able to increase its price by shifting the markets to which it ships. In this example, Chicago is $0.20 above New York. Since Maryland would get $0.20 minus $0.81 or − $0.61 for cucumbers shipped to Chicago compared to − $0.40 in New York, there would be no incentive to shift. The same is true for California in considering shipment to New York, indicating that this allocation is in fact the optimum allocation.

Consider now the situation in which market price differences are given and notice the effect on alternative allocations of supplies. If Chicago is $0.25 above New York, all North Carolina supplies as well as all California supplies will move to Chicago while New York receives only 5 cars from Maryland. Obviously, this is not a "reasonable" allocation although it is "optimum" with the given market price differences. If Chicago fails to maintain a level $0.20 above New York, it will first lose all North Carolina supplies and eventually (N.Y. − $0.37) will lose California supplies as well.

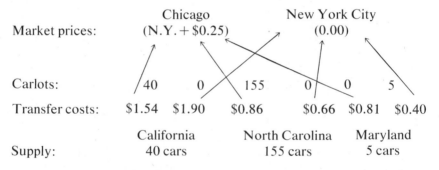

	Chicago	New York City
Market prices:	(N.Y. + $0.25)	(0.00)
Carlots:	40 0 155	0 0 5
Transfer costs:	$1.54 $1.90 $0.86	$0.66 $0.81 $0.40
	California	North Carolina Maryland
Supply:	40 cars	155 cars 5 cars

In short, product flows depend on transfer costs and relative market prices; market prices depend on demand and available supplies; product flows and market prices must be developed simultaneously. This process is described briefly in the following section.

5.4 MULTIREGION MODELS: PROGRAMMING SOLUTION

The "transportation problem," as it is often referred to, is a special case of linear programming which has certain features that allow a shortcut solution. Details of this procedure are not reproduced here in any detail, since excellent treatments are readily available.[1] Instead, emphasis is

[1]See reference to Dorfman, Samuelson, and Solow, for example.

placed on the types of information that may be obtained from the transportation problem formulation.

A larger version of the problem outlined in section 5.3 will illustrate the capabilities of this model. Table 5.1 summarizes transfer costs from 8 producing areas to each of 10 markets. In this example, transfer costs include transportation costs plus cartage charges for hauling cucumbers from rail sidings to wholesale market areas in each city. Total quantities available are shown in the last column (S_i) and quantities demanded are shown in the last row (D_j). Figures in parentheses are shipments which are consistent with the minimization of total transfer costs for all shipments. This optimum allocation is one of the useful pieces of information provided by this model.

Table 5.2 is the equilibrium cost matrix. In this table producer price differentials with sign changed, the $-u_i$'s, appear in the last column and market price differentials, the v_j's, appear in the last row.[2] The sum of these values for each route used in the equilibrium solution, identified in Table 5.2 by[a], must equal the unit cost, c_{ij}, for that route. We may select any supply area or market area as a base and may assign a zero price ($0.00) for that entry. The remaining values in the border row and border column are developed in a stepwise fashion by selecting values such that

$$c_{ij} = v_j + (-u_i)$$

In this example, New York was selected as the base and $0.00 entered in the v_j row. We know that the optimum shipping pattern calls for shipments from North Carolina to New York at a transfer cost of $0.66. Thus the entry for North Carolina is

$$\$0.66 = \$0.00 + (-u_i)$$

or $0.66 for $-u_{NC}$. The Philadelphia price can now be computed by using the North Carolina $-u_i$ as: $0.59 = v_j + \$0.66$ or $-0.07. This process is continued until all border cells are filled. Finally, the body of Table 5.2 is completed by adding the appropriate $-u_i$ and v_j values computed above.

Two types of information are provided by Table 5.2. The intermarket price comparisons can be made directly from the v_j row. For example, the Boston price is $0.14 above the one in New York. Also, comparisons of the returns in the several producing areas are readily made, although it is first necessary to change the sign of each element in the $-u_i$ column. For example, the California price is $1.44 *below* that in New York. A new

---

[2]By showing values for $-u_i$ instead of u_i, we are able to simplify the discussion somewhat. Since in the optimum solution it is necessary that $c_{ij} \geq v_j - v_i$, with u_i, $v_j \leq 0$, we may also write $c_{ij} \geq v_j + (-u_i)$. The equality holds true for all active routes and for any alternate routes that would not increase total transfer costs.

TABLE 5.1   Cost-Flow Matrix[a]

Exporting Region	Importing Region (Dollars per Bushel)										Surplus S_i (Carlots)
	Boston	New York	Phila- delphia	Pitts- burgh	Chicago	Atlanta	New Orleans	Denver	Los Angeles	San Francisco	
Salisbury, Maryland	0.57	0.40	0.31 (5)	0.49	0.81	0.77	1.06	1.32	1.75	1.86	5
Aurora, Illinois	0.95	0.86	0.81	0.61	0.21 (10)	0.76	0.90	0.93	1.52	1.54	10
Clinton, North Carolina	0.80 (75)	0.66 (150)	0.59 (55)	0.63 (5)	0.86	0.53	0.87	1.32	1.72	1.86	285
Columbia, South Carolina	0.89	0.76	0.70	0.69 (40)	0.82 (30)	0.40	0.77	1.26	1.69	1.83	70
Thomasville, Georgia	1.07	0.96	0.91	0.90	0.90	0.40 (10)	0.52	1.25	1.60	1.80	10
Sanford, Florida	1.11	1.01	0.96	0.96	1.02 (5)	0.59 (5)	0.75	1.38	1.71	1.85	10
San Antonio, Texas	1.48	1.37	1.33	1.19	1.06 (5)	0.96	0.66 (10)	0.90	1.13	1.33	15
Los Angeles, California	1.83	1.90	1.93	1.76	1.54 (5)	1.58	1.41	1.04 (10)	0.18 (50)	0.54 (15)	80
Deficit D_j (Carlots)	75	150	60	45	55	15	10	10	50	15	485

Source. Richard A. King, "Fixed Production–Fixed Consumption Models," *Interregional Competition Research Methods,* edited by Richard A. King, North Carolina Agricultural Policy Institute, Series 10 (Raleigh 1965), Chapter 2, p. 23.

[a]Optimum shipments expressed in carlots are shown in parentheses in the body of the table.

Exporting Region	Importing Region (Dollars per Bushel)										Producer Price Differentials, $-u_i$
	Boston	New York	Phila- delphia	Pitts- burgh	Chicago	Atlanta	New Orleans	Denver	Los Angeles	San Francisco	
Salisbury, Maryland	0.52	0.38	0.31[a]	0.35	0.48	0.05	0.08	−0.02	−0.88	−0.52	0.38
Aurora, Illinois	0.25	0.11	0.04	0.08	0.21[a]	−0.22	−0.19	−0.29	−1.15	−0.79	0.11
Clinton, North Carolina	0.80[a]	0.66[a]	0.59[a]	0.63[a]	0.76	0.33	0.36	0.26	−0.60	−0.24	0.66
Columbia, South Carolina	0.86	0.72	0.65	0.69[a]	0.82[a]	0.39	0.42	0.32	−0.54	−0.18	0.72
Thomasville, Georgia	0.87	0.73	0.66	0.70	0.83	0.40[a]	0.43	0.33	−0.53	−0.17	0.73
Sanford, Florida	1.06	0.92	0.85	0.89	1.02[a]	0.59[a]	0.62	0.52	−0.34	0.02	0.92
San Antonio, Texas	1.10	0.96	0.89	0.93	1.06[a]	0.63	0.66[a]	0.56	−0.30	0.06	0.96
Los Angeles, California	1.58	1.44	1.37	1.41	1.54[a]	1.11	1.14	1.04[a]	0.18[a]	0.54[a]	1.44
Market price differentials v_j	0.14	0.00	−0.07	−0.03	0.10	−0.33	−0.30	−0.40	−1.26	−0.90	

Source. Richard A. King, "Fixed Production–Fixed Consumption Models," *Interregional Competition Research Methods,* . . . Chapter 2. p. 25.

[a]Equilibrium cost matrix is derived from these values which correspond to transfer costs for active routes. New York is used as the base region.

base region is easily selected by adding to every element in the $-u_i$ column and the v_j row the quantity that will change to zero the border value for the new base region.

The cost of choosing a nonoptimum route is readily determined from Table 5.3. Elements in this table are obtained by subtracting from an element in Table 5.1 the corresponding element in Table 5.2. This provides a direct comparison of the amount that the "market" is willing to pay for products moving over a given route (Table 5.2) with the cost of providing this transfer (Table 5.1). Imputed prices for routes connecting trading pairs will exactly equal transfer cost and will result in zero entries in Table 5.3. In all other cases, transfer costs will be equal to or will exceed the equilibrium market price differentials. When zeros appear in Table 5.3 for routes that are not in use, this indicates that there are one or more alternate shipping plans which could be used without increasing total transfer costs.

The values in Table 5.3 represent costs that would have to be shared between buyer-seller pairs as a condition of making shipments along the indicated routes and so foregoing the trading opportunities indicated by the optimum solution. An alternative interpretation of these values is that they are "opportunity returns" to be shared between buyers and sellers if shipments that may currently prevail along the indicated routes are discontinued and trading diverted to routes for which opportunity costs are zero.

The usefulness of transportation models is increased when combined with side analyses. Location advantages or disadvantages of shippers in the various supply regions do not usually pass intact to raw material suppliers; differentials in processing or manufacturing costs may either offset or enhance the effects of location. Here is an opportunity to utilize information gained from studies of economies of scale, economies of concentration, and regional differentials in costs of factors used for processing or manufacturing. By summing production cost differentials and location advantages, with due regard to sign and by using the same base region throughout, differentials in net returns to raw material suppliers in the various regions may be obtained. The resulting information has implications for the growth or the decline of the industry in various locations.

Similarly, information from transportation models can be used in margins studies. Differences between prices paid by consumers and the ones received by farmers are partially explained by the location of consumers relative to location of their best sources of supplies. The transportation model effectively isolates contributions of transfer costs to farm-to-consumer margins for the various markets. Processing and

TABLE 5.3 Cost of Using Nonoptimum Routes[a]

Exporting Region	Importing Region (Dollars per Bushel)									
	Boston	New York	Phila-delphia	Pitts-burg	Chicago	Atlanta	New Orleans	Denver	Los Angeles	San Francisco
Salisbury, Maryland	0.05	0.02	0.00	0.14	0.33	0.72	0.98	1.34	2.63	2.38
Aurora, Illinois	0.70	0.75	0.77	0.53	0.00	0.98	1.09	1.22	2.67	2.33
Clinton, North Carolina	0.00	0.00	0.00	0.00	0.10	0.20	0.51	1.06	2.32	2.10
Columbia, South Carolina	0.03	0.04	0.05	0.00	0.00	0.01	0.35	0.94	2.23	2.01
Thomasville, Georgia	0.20	0.23	0.25	0.20	0.07	0.00	0.09	0.92	2.13	1.97
Sanford, Florida	0.05	0.09	0.11	0.07	0.00	0.00	0.13	0.86	2.05	1.83
San Antonio, Texas	0.38	0.41	0.44	0.26	0.00	0.33	0.00	0.34	1.43	1.27
Los Angeles, California	0.25	0.46	0.56	0.35	0.00	0.47	0.27	0.00	0.00	0.00

Source. Richard A. King, "Fixed Production—Fixed Consumption Models," *Interregional Competition Research Methods*, ... Chapter 2, p. 26.

[a]Transfer cost (Table 5.1) less corresponding element in equilibrium cost matrix (Table 5.2).

distribution costs can be added in side analyses to determine minimum margins consistent with competitive equilibria. When compared with margins observed in the actual commodity market, those studies could provide indications of inefficiencies and/or the absence of effective competition in certain sectors of the commodity market.

5.5 PRODUCTION AND CONSUMPTION VARIABLE[3]

Reactive programming makes it possible to obtain solutions to spatial equilibrium problems by maximizing net returns at each shipping point for specified forms of competition. Each supply point is considered as a shipper and, by evaluating the demand function in each of the outlets, a set of gross prices is established. From these gross prices the appropriate transfer costs are deducted to obtain a set of net prices, and supplies are allocated to the outlets that offer the highest net prices. This process is repeated for each shipper in turn, with each making the most profitable allocation possible. When it is not profitable for any shipper to reallocate his supplies among the outlets, the equilibrium solution has been obtained. If supplies at a particular supply point are so large that the equilibrium net price is zero, the surplus quantity remains unallocated. Given the conditions of perfect competition, the equilibrium solution is such that the net revenue to each shipper at the several supply points has been maximized.

Demand Functions with Uniform Slopes — Predetermined Supplies. We first assume uniform slopes for all demand functions to illustrate the reactive programming procedure. A demand function of the form $P = a + bQ$ is needed for each of the consumer centers. Consider the receipts and the corresponding prices shown in Table 5.4B as points on market demand functions. Suppose the results of a demand analysis established that the coefficient b, measuring the effect of quantity on price, was -2.0 in each market. With this information, unique demand functions can be established for each of the centers, since the only unknown is the value of a, which can be readily estimated. For consumer center W, $P = \$150$, $Q = 35$, and $b = -2$. Substituting into the demand equation, $P = a + bQ$, we have: $150 = a + (-2)\ (35)$ or $a = 150 + (2)\ (35) = 220$. The demand equation is thus $P_w = 220 - 2Q_w$. Demand equations for other outlets are established in the same manner and are shown in the last line of Table 5.4B.

[3]Based on A. D. Seale, Jr., and Thomas E. Tramel, "Reactive Programming Models," *Interregional Competition Research Methods* . . . Chapter 4, pp. 47–58.

By using the transportation cost data specified in Table 5.4A and the allocation in Table 5.4B as a starting basis, the equilibrium shipments, receipts, prices, and revenues can be determined. The results are shown in Tables 5.4C and D.

The inspection of the net prices shown in Table 5.4D will reveal that the net returns to each of the individual shippers are at equilibrium levels. For each shipping point, the available supplies were allocated to the outlets offering the highest net price; for multiple outlets, the net prices were equated. There is no incentive for any individual shipper to reallocate supplies because any change in the solution would reduce the net returns to the individual shipper making the change. Thus, it is an equilibrium solution.

TABLE 5.4   Reactive Programming: Demand Functions with Uniform Slopes and Predetermined Supplies

A. Transportation Cost[a]

Shipping Point	Consumer Center (Dollars per Carlot)			
	W	X	Y	Z
A	105	230	180	100
B	90	140	100	175
C	200	140	120	110

B. Initial Situation

Shipping Point	Consumer Center (Shipments in Carlots)				Supplies[a]
	W	X	Y	Z	
A	5				5
B	30	10	20		60
C			15	25	40
Receipts	35	10	35	25	105
Prices	150	180	160	150	–
Demand[a]	$P = 220 - 2Q$	$P = 200 - 2Q$	$P = 230 - 2Q$	$P = 200 - 2Q$	–

TABLE 5.4 Continued

C. Equilibrium Solution

Shipping Point	Consumer Center (Shipments in Carlots)				Supplies
	W	X	Y	Z	
A				5	5
B	35		25		60
C		10	10	20	40
Receipts	35	10	35	25	105
Prices	150	180	160	150	–
Demand	$P = 220 - 2Q$	$P = 200 - 2Q$	$P = 230 - 2Q$	$P = 200 - 2Q$	–

D. Equilibrium Prices and Net Revenue

Shipping Point	Consumer Center (Net Prices, Dollars per Carlot)				Net Revenue
	W	X	Y	Z	
A	45.00	−50.00	−20.00	50.00[b]	250.00
B	60.00[b]	40.00	60.00[b]	−25.00	3,600.00
C	−50.00	40.00[b]	40.00[b]	40.00[b]	1,600.00
Prices	150.00	180.00	160.00	150.00	–

Source. A. D. Seale, Jr., and Thomas E. Tramel, "Reactive Programming Models," *Interregional Competition Research Methods* . . . Chapter 4, Table 2, p. 51.

[a]Denotes required input data.
[b]Net prices for shipping routes actually used.

Demand Functions with Different Slopes – Predetermined Supplies. In the previous example, it was assumed that we had access to only one estimate of the effect of quantity on price and that this slope coefficient was appropriate for each of the outlets. Now it is assumed that the effect of quantity on price at each market is different. All input data used earlier are also used here except for the effect of quantity on price. The equilibrium solution for this problem, shown in Table 5.5, is quite different from the previous problem. From an inspection of the net prices, it is clear that an equilibrium solution has been obtained because any reallocation would reduce the net returns to any individual shipper making such a change.

TABLE 5.5   Reactive Programming: Demand Functions with Different Slopes and Predetermined Supplies

A. Transportation Cost[a]

Shipping Point	Consumer Center (Cost per Carlot)			
	W	X	Y	Z
A	105	230	180	100
B	90	140	100	175
C	200	140	120	110

B. Initial Situation

Shipping Point	Consumer Center (Shipments in Carlots)				Supplies [a]
	W	X	Y	Z	
A	5				5
B	30	10	20		60
C			15	25	40
Receipts	35	10	35	25	105
Prices	185	180	125	100	—
Demand[a]	$P=220-1Q$	$P=200-2Q$	$P=230-3Q$	$P=200-4Q$	

C. Equilibrium Solution

Shipping Point	Consumer Center (Shipments in Carlots)				Supplies
	W	X	Y	Z	
A	2.2			2.8	5.0
B	60.0				60.0
C		8.6	22.4	9.0	40.0
Receipts	62.2	8.6	22.4	11.8	105.0
Prices	157.80	182.80	162.80	152.80	—
Demand	$P=220-1Q$	$P=220-2Q$	$P=230-3Q$	$P=200-4Q$	—

TABLE 5.5 Continued

D. Equilibrium Prices and Net Revenue

Shipping Point	Consumer Center (Net Prices, Dollars per Carlot)				Net Revenue
	W	X	Y	Z	
A	52.80[b]	−47.20	−17.20	52.80[b]	264.00
B	67.80[b]	42.80	62.80	−22.20	4,068,00
C	−42.20	42.80[b]	42.80[b]	42.80[b]	1,712.00
Prices	157.80	182.80	162.80	152.80	−

Source. A. D. Seale, Jr., and Thomas E. Tramel, "Reactive Programming Models," *Interregional Competition Research Methods* . . . Chapter 4, Table 3, p. 52.

[a]Denotes required input data.

[b]Net prices for shipping routes actually used.

Demand and Supply Functions with Different Slopes. Up to this point, we have assumed a fixed supply at each of the supply points. In reality, available supplies are a function of the net prices received by producers, and equilibrium levels of these supplies must also be determined. This determination requires the use of supply functions.

In a competitive situation, the equilibrium level of supplies is the level at which net profits or economic rent is zero. Although there are no undistributed supplies in problems of this type, the cost matrix must include all costs incurred between the supply points and the level of demand at the consumer centers in order to compute the equilibrium levels of supplies.

It is assumed that the results of a demand study in each consumer center and cost studies for each of the supply points are available. The demand functions and the production cost functions (provided by these studies) are shown in Tables 5.6*A* and 5.6*B*. The equilibrium levels of supplies, shipments, and receipts, as well as the prices and revenues, can be simultaneously determined by the procedure outlined earlier. They are shown in Tables 5.6*C* and 5.6*D*. A comparison of the net prices and production costs shows that the equilibrium levels of supplies have been determined.

TABLE 5.6 Reactive Programming: Demand and Supply Functions with Different Slopes

A. Transportation Cost[a]

Shipping Point	Consumer Center (Dollars per Carlot)				Production Cost Functions[a]
	W	X	Y	Z	
A	105	230	180	100	$C = 35 + 3S$
B	90	140	100	175	$C = 5 + 1S$
C	200	140	120	110	$C = 0 + 2S$

B. Initial Situation

Shipping Point	Consumer Center (Shipments in Carlots)				Supplies
	W	X	Y	Z	
A	5				5
B	30	10	20		60
C			15	25	40
Receipts	35	10	35	25	105
Prices	185	180	125	100	—
Demand[a]	$P=220-1Q$	$P=200-2Q$	$P=230-3Q$	$P=200-4Q$	—

C. Equilibrium Solution

Shipping Point	Consumer Center (Shipments in Carlots)				Supplies
	W	X	Y	Z	
A				8.05	8.05
B	60.84		3.31		64.15
C		5.43	16.98	2.17	24.58
Receipts	60.84	5.43	20.29	10.22	96.78
Prices	159.15	189.14	169.15	159.14	—
Demand	$P=220-1Q$	$P=200-2Q$	$P=230-3Q$	$P=200-4Q$	—

TABLE 5.6 Continued

D. Equilibrium Prices and Net Revenue

Shipping Point	Consumer Center (Net Prices, Dollars per Carlot)				Production Cost	Economic Rent
	W	X	Y	Z		
A	−4.98	−100.00	−69.99	0[b]	59.14	0
B	0[b]	−20.00	0[a]	−85.00	69.15	0
C	−89.99	0[b]	0[b]	0[b]	49.14	0
Prices	159.15	189.14	169.15	159.14	−	−

Source. A. D. Seale, Jr., and Thomas E. Tramel, "Reactive Programming Models," *Interregional Competition Research Methods*... Chapter 4, Table 4, p. 54.

[a]Denotes required input data.
[b]Net prices for shipping routes actually used.

5.6 LIMITATIONS OF SINGLE-PRODUCT ANALYSIS

We have now demonstrated how it is possible to extend the analysis of spatially separated regions with perfectly inelastic demand and supply curves (outlined in sections 5.3 and 5.4) to deal with cases where either or both quantity demanded and supplied are treated as a function of price. These mathematical procedures also accomplish what we were unable to do graphically in section 5.2 because of the difficulty of knowing which pairs of regions would be engaged in trade and, therefore, by what amount *t* the price axes for each exporting region should be shifted upward.

However, the student may have become disturbed by the oversimplified analysis of trade in terms of the supply and demand for a single commodity. Clearly, traders will profit from arbitrage as long as prices in any two regions differ by more than transfer costs. It is also apparent that, as a result, producers in an exporting region Y will receive higher prices, while consumers in an importing region X will benefit from lower prices. But what of producers in X and consumers in Y? Does trade result in a general benefit or work only to the advantage of a few in each region? And what of the payment for the goods imported by X? Apparently, the flow of goods from Y to X means a compensating flow of money from X to Y. Yet, money itself is merely a claim on goods, and where are the goods that the producers in region Y will buy with this added income? An understanding of the operation of exchange, either within a region or among regions, requires a more elaborate analytical device than that afforded by supply and demand curves for a single commodity. We shall be concerned with this elaboration in later chapters.

SELECTED READINGS

Spatially Separated Markets

Dantzig, G. B., "Application of the Simplex Method to a Transportation Problem," in *Activity Analysis of Production and Allocation*. T. C. Koopmans (ed.), John Wiley and Sons, Inc., New York (1951).

Dorfman, Robert, Paul A. Samuelson, and Robert M. Solow, *Linear Programming and Economic Analysis*, McGraw-Hill Book Co., Inc., New York (1958), Chapter 5, "The Transportation Problem," pp. 106–128.

Hitchcock, F. L., "The Distribution of a Product from Several Sources to Numerous Localities," *Journal of Mathematics and Physics*, Vol. 20 (1941). pp. 224–230.

Samuelson, Paul A., "Spatial Price Equilibrium and Linear Programming," *American Economic Review*, Vol. 42 (June 1952). pp. 283–303.

Snodgrass, Milton M. and Charles E. French, "Simplified Presentation of Transportation Problem Procedure in Linear Programming," *Journal of Farm Economics*, Vol. XXXIX, No. 1. (February 1957). pp. 40–51.

Tramel, Thomas E. and A. D. Seale, Jr., "Reactive Programming of Supply and Demand Relations—Applications to Fresh Vegetables," *Journal of Farm Economics*, Vol. XLI, No. 5 (December 1959). pp. 1012–1022.

chapter 6

SPACE AND TRANSFER COST

Our analysis of marketing and prices in Chapter 4 proceeded on the assumption that producers and consumers are located at a single point. Within such a point market, of course, there are no costs of moving products through space! We first assumed in Chapter 5 that transfer costs were zero and, hence, concluded that product prices would equalize completely and perfectly in the several regions connected through trade. We then developed a more realistic model which included the costs associated with the spatial distribution and segregation of production and consumption. Now we turn to a more detailed consideration of transfer costs and the impact of these costs on economic specialization and trade.

6.1 COMPONENTS OF TRANSFER COST

With production and consumption carried on at spatially separated locations, the transfer of products — raw materials and semifinished and finished goods — provides a necessary and essential connection. These transfer services may include activities such as the assembly or collection from small producing sites, loading and other terminal activities, the transportation to major market centers, and the distribution to wholesalers, retailers, and final consumers. Some of these activities are not directly related to space or length of haul, but the costs of performing other services are clearly a function of the distance involved. The complex of all of these costs of movement we call *transfer cost*. The costs that are directly related to length of haul are usually called *transportation costs*, but the fixed or constant costs we shall call *terminal costs*.

6.2   DISTANCE-COST RELATIONSHIPS

The relationship between length of haul and cost of transfer services is called a *transfer cost function*. Several commonly observed types of distance-transfer cost relationships are illustrated in Figure 6.1. Type A is a horizontal line suggesting that transfer charges are a constant T_a regardless of distance. An example is the structure of first-class postal rates in the United States where the entire country is blanketed by a single zone within which charges are constant regardless of the distance involved. Type B is a more conventional zone-rate system where charges increase with distance but through a series of discontinuous steps. The familiar zone charges for parcel post illustrate this type. Many rail freight tariff schedules are also based on this scheme. Notice that we have drawn this function with a relatively high initial charge T_b; this "intercept" value covers terminal and other costs not associated with distance. Type C is a continuous function with an initial charge T_c to cover nondistance factors plus a straight-line relationship to cover transportation costs which are a linear function of distance. Such a linear function is frequently encountered when all factors other than distance (including size and type of equipment) are held constant.

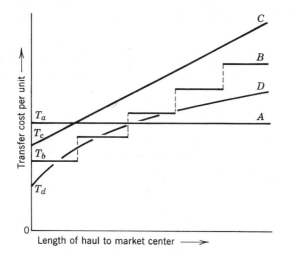

FIGURE 6.1   Alternative transfer cost-distance relationships.

Type D is also a continuous function but one which describes a situation where costs or charges increase at a decreasing rate with distance. Such a less-than-proportional schedule commonly describes commercial transportation rates. It may also be expected when transfer conditions or the type of carrier used changes with distance. For example, the transportation of milk to a large metropolitan center may be performed (1) with direct delivery from farms to market by small trucks from nearby zones, (2) with initial assembly from farms by small trucks for concentration at country receiving stations and transportation to the city in large trucks from intermediate zones, and (3) with the operation of country stations and rail transport from distant zones. In each location, the most economical transfer arrangement tends to dominate, with the result that the complex of transfer costs will usually be found to increase with distance at a decreasing rate.

Moreover, transfer costs and charges are influenced by many factors. Certainly conditions such as terrain and topography are important, as are the type of carrier and the total amount of traffic. In fact, transport facilities are themselves subject to change over time and, in the long run, reflect changes in both the demand for and the techniques for providing transport services. The characteristics of the product are important (bulkiness, value, perishability, type of container, and size of lot).

The institutional setting will have an important effect on charges (if not on costs) through the type of competition that is permitted among carriers and the decisions of public rate-establishing agencies. The type A flat charge for first-class mail is a good example of this institutional influence. Early mail rates were steeply graduated with distance, but with improvements in transportation this influence was reduced. Finally, and certainly on an arbitrary basis in relation to real costs, the federal government established a single rate for all except local mail, and eventually this single rate was expanded to cover all domestic first-class mail service. No doubt, terminal costs are more important than transportation costs in the modern mail service, and possibly a system of zoned rates would even increase these terminal costs; but the flat-rate system generally involves some subsidization of distant shippers by nearby shippers. The same is true of any zone system. Shippers near the inner boundary of a given zone subsidize shippers near the outer boundary, but this may be slight relative to the gain in simplicity in applying a zoned rather than a point-to-point rate schedule.

6.3 TRANSFER COST SURFACE

Suppose that transfer cost for a given product can be expressed as a linear or curvilinear function of airline distance. Consider one localized market with product supplies situated at points scattered over a completely uniform and flat geographic area. Let us assume further that, as far as transport distances and costs are concerned, this plain is appropriately surfaced (with concrete or asphalt connections) so as to make travel in any direction equally feasible. The resulting spatial pattern of transfer costs from every point on this plain to the market is called a *transfer cost surface*.

A transfer cost surface can be described in either cross-section or plan view. Given a linear transfer function like type C in Figure 6.1, the cost of moving a product to market will increase at a constant rate as distance to market increases. This case, illustrated for the cross section along the line RS in Figure 6.2, has a very simple interpretation. A shipment originating at D_1 will incur a transfer cost of T_1 per unit of product, at D_2 a cost of T_2 per unit of product, etc. Alternatively, we may represent the transfer cost surface in plan view by connecting those sites where a given outlay is required to transport a unit of product to market. In our simplified model these equal-transfer-cost contours consist of a series of concentric circles. An *isocost contour* represents the locus of points on a plain where equal transfer costs will be incurred when shipping a given product to a given market center.

If the transfer cost function takes the shape of type D in Figure 6.1, the resulting isocost contours are concentric circles but with radii that increase at an increasing rate rather than at a constant rate, as is the case with a type C function. To illustrate, the isocost contours in Figure 6.2 are drawn to represent equal increments to transfer cost from one contour to the next; that is, $T_1 - T_0 = T_2 - T_1$, etc., for each pair of contour lines. With a linear transfer cost function, these contours are equally spaced on the plain and distances D_1, D_2, etc., represent equal increments in terms of miles to market. However, with a type D cost function the distance between D_1 and D_2, D_2 and D_3, etc., becomes greater and greater because the cost surface rises at a decreasing rate.

In much of the material that follows, we utilize a transfer cost function of type D. Furthermore, we usually express transfer costs as a simple and regular function of airline distance. These assumptions simplify the presentation and permit emphasis on the major influences of location on price. They are admittedly unrealistic assumptions, however, as will be shown. Bear in mind that any application to a real-world situation will involve the use of actual rates and rate structures appropriate to that

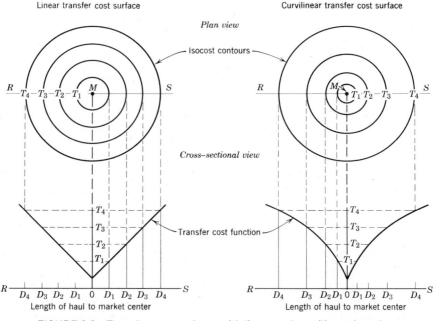

FIGURE 6.2 Transfer cost surfaces with linear and curvilinear functions.

situation. Such actual rate structures typically result in final solutions that are less smooth and symmetrical than the ones suggested here, but the underlying principles and generalizations will not be affected.

6.4 EFFECT OF TRANSPORT NETWORK ON COST

Any real geographic area will be characterized by a complex of non-uniform topography — hills and valleys, mountain ranges, rivers, and streams. These topographic influences, interacting with nonuniform spatial distributions of resources, will give rise to particular spatial distributions of human populations — a complex of major cities and sub-urban areas, secondary cities, towns, villages, and rural districts. Inter-connecting these population distributions, and developing simultaneously with them, will be particular networks of transportation routes — the grid of major and secondary highways, rural roads, trunk-line and feeder railroad routes, water transport by major rivers, canals, lakes, and coastal ocean routes, plus the complex of scheduled and chartered airline routes.

The obvious impact of the real-world rail and road networks is to distort the relationship between transfer costs and airline distances.

Under many circumstances, this distortion may be slight. In Connecticut, for example, comparison of airline and highway mileages for selected points indicates that highway mileage H may be represented as a function of airline mileage A with a correlation of 0.99: $H = 2.4 + 1.02A$. In other circumstances where natural barriers are more formidable, the location of mountain passes and bridges over major rivers will represent "gateways" that may seriously affect point-to-point transport distances and costs. This suggests that equal-cost contours will be irregular instead of forming concentric circles.

Even when the relation between airline and highway distance is not greatly affected, topographic features may significantly change cost relations. Thus, we expect that the near-level topography of Iowa or of the Central Valley of California will result in lower trucking costs per ton-mile than the rugged terrain through the Rocky Mountains west of Denver or the mountain passes between Nevada and California.

These distance and cost distortions can be expected to destroy the smoothness and symmetry of locational solutions suggested by our theoretical discussions, but not the basic concepts. Given any irregular pattern of transport costs, it will still be possible to define appropriate transport cost contours for materials and products. Population and production densities will also affect transfer costs, since they determine the aggregate volume of products shipped and the availability of "back-haul" loads and, hence, influence the utilization of the available capacity of existing transport systems.

The square or rectangular network of transport routes is common enough to justify specific comment here; these regular networks are approximated by the section and township roads in many parts of the United States as well as by the street patterns in many cities. Such a grid is suggested in Figure 6.3; equal-distance contours will now be a

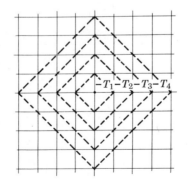

FIGURE 6.3   The effects of a square highway grid on the pattern of isotims.

system of squares centered on the point in question, with these squares rotated 45 degrees in relation to the underlying transport grid. Price surfaces will also reflect this pattern of concentric squares.

6.5 ALTERNATIVE MODES OF TRANSPORTATION

Not only are transport cost contours distorted from circular form by topography and transport grids but also by alternative transport systems or technologies. We have mentioned the complex of roads, railroads, waterways, and air routes as examples of four major forms of transportation. Each will be characterized by its own particular grid of routes and, also, by appropriately different cost functions. Without attempting a detailed treatment, we point out that more "sophisticated" transport systems frequently involve relatively large investments and high fixed or terminal costs per ton but much lower operating costs per ton-mile for actual transportation. This very general situation is illustrated in Figure 6.4 where line ab represents the costs for the relatively simple system T_1 and line cd represents the costs for the more complex or sophisticated system T_2. Such a comparison should be appropriate for various pairs of systems—wagon versus truck, small truck versus large truck, large truck versus rail, and so on.

One consequence of these alternative transport technologies is that there may be zones within which each will have the advantage of lowest cost. In Figure 6.4 it is clear that the simple system will be most advantageous for transportation within the zone oe—for short hauls near the market—while the more complex system will show lower costs for long hauls. In general, we may expect a progression from small trucks to large

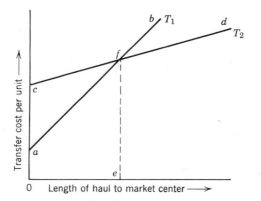

FIGURE 6.4   Transfer costs with two alternative transportation systems.

trucks to rail, as transport distance increases. Correspondingly, the appropriate aggregate transfer cost function will show a general tendency to increase with distance but at a decreasing rate; the discontinuous function *afd* illustrates this for the two-technology case.

Let us consider the alternatives represented by trucks of varying size and capacity. As truck size increases, both fixed and variable truck costs will increase. At least within limits, however, these cost increases will not be in direct proportion to the increases in capacity; that is, fixed truck costs per ton and variable truck costs per ton-mile will decrease. With larger trucks, however, the costs per customer associated with direct loading and unloading services will usually increase. Considering all elements, we can expect to find that average route costs per unit of product will show higher "intercepts" and lower "slopes" as truck size increases. This is indicated graphically in Figure 6.5. It is immediately apparent that there will be zones around the market within which a particular technology or size of truck will be optimum. Notice that this does not mean that every possible technology will be utilized; we have illustrated one case where the combination of high intercept and high slope results in costs that are never as low as the costs possible with other organizations.

We have observed that increasing truck size will often be associated with decreasing unit truck costs—fixed costs per ton and variable costs per ton-mile—but that these advantages tend to be offset by increasing costs of direct customer service. In plain words, this means that very large equipment, for example, the truck-and-trailer combination, is quite economical for over-the-highway transportation involving long distances but is very costly for the stop-and-go operations characteristic of collection or delivery routes. In fact, it may be physically impossible for this

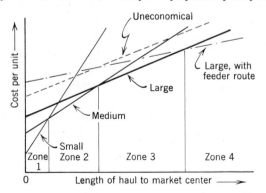

FIGURE 6.5   The cost-distance relationships for various transport technologies and the determination of zones within which a particular technology is optimum.

large equipment to perform collection or delivery services. At-farm collection will often involve driving through narrow roads or lanes, off the main highway to farmsteads, and delivery operations also may involve narrow streets that would be difficult or impossible to negotiate with large-scale equipment. Moreover, the time required to make individual collection or delivery stops places an outside limit on the total volume that can be handled on any route — a volume often far short of physical truck capacity.

6.6 COMBINED MODES OF TRANSPORTATION

The availability of a railway (waterway or major highway) along a particular route through a region will affect transport costs by elongating the isocost contours along the axis of the low-cost route. Moreover, this will usually permit the economical combination of two transport systems. A farm located off a main highway may be most economically served by a small truck on a "stub" or "feeder" route. With such a system of feeder or stub routes, at-farm collection will be made by small trucks that deliver their volume, not to the market but to main highways where it is loaded on large trucks for transport to market. This has the effect of lowering the fixed cost for large-truck operation and, thus, permitting lower combined costs that would be possible with any system based on single trucks. This is suggested in Figure 6.5 by the relationship labeled feeder technology.

The general influence of a low-cost transport route, such as a waterway, was first pointed out by von Thünen in 1826, but the feeder route-main route case was given formal mathematical treatment by Launhardt in 1882.[1] The Launhardt analysis is illustrated in Figure 6.6 where the localized material is at point A, the market at point B, and where the main-line, low-cost transport route is represented by the line CB. The shortest distance from point A to the market at point B is a straight line representing the use of feeder route transportation only. However, with main line transportation costs r_2 lower than feeder route costs r_1, it is clear that this would not represent the minimum cost method for all material sources. Instead, the minimum cost arrangement will involve transportation from A by feeder route to some point D with final transport to market from D to B along the main route.

[1]This section draws heavily on R. O. Been, "A Reconstruction of the Classical Theory of Location" (unpublished Ph.D. dissertation, Department of Agricultural Economics, University of California, Berkeley, 1965).

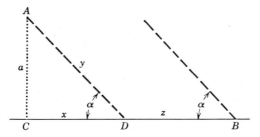
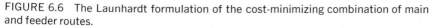

FIGURE 6.6   The Launhardt formulation of the cost-minimizing combination of main and feeder routes.

Assume that two modes of transport are available, truck and rail, at rates of r_1 and r_2 dollars per ton-mile. In Figure 6.6 we let the line CB represent the rail line, a the distance from point A to the line CB, and b the distance between the intersection of the perpendicular bisector from A to CB and the point B. The distance traveled by truck is represented by y and the distance traveled by rail is represented by z. In the event that the two modes are used, special costs of transferring cargo from one mode to the other, amounting to C dollars per ton, are incurred.

We may write out these conditions as follows.

$$\text{Direct (Mode 1)} \; TC_t = r_1\sqrt{a^2 + b^2}. \tag{6.1}$$

$$\text{Combined (Modes 1 and 2)} \; TC_c = r_1 y + r_2 z + C. \tag{6.2}$$

The minimum cost route from A to B by combined modes involves travel by truck along the line AD, transhipment to rail at point D, and rail shipment from D to B. It will be shown that the lines AD and CB form the angle α such that $\cos \alpha = r_2/r_1$. We let $z = b - x$ and rewrite Equation 6.2 as

$$TC_c = r_1\sqrt{a^2 + z^2} + r_2(b - x) + C. \tag{6.3}$$

Since all the terms in Equation 6.3 except x are fixed, we can find that value for x that will minimize total cost by taking the derivative of Equation 6.3 with respect to x and setting this equal to zero:

$$\frac{dTC_c}{dx} = r_1 \frac{x}{\sqrt{a^2 + x^2}} - r_2 = 0$$

or

$$= r_1 \cos \alpha - r_2 = 0$$

$$\cos \alpha = \frac{r_2}{r_1} \tag{6.4}$$

The cost-minimizing location for changing transport modes is that point D where the cosine of angle α is equal to the ratio of the transport rates.

It is possible to generalize concerning the choice of direct or combined modes by using the relationships developed above. By using relation (6.4), we may write

$$\frac{x}{y} = \frac{r_2}{r_1} \quad \text{or} \quad x = \frac{r_2}{r_1} y. \tag{6.5}$$

Since

$$\sin \alpha = \frac{a}{y} \quad \text{or} \quad y = \frac{a}{\sin \alpha} \tag{6.6}$$

we rewrite Equation 6.2, by using relations (6.5) and (6.6), as

$$\min TC_c = r_1 \frac{a}{\sin \alpha} + r_2 b - \frac{r_2^2}{r_1} \frac{a}{\sin \alpha} + C \tag{6.7}$$

We may now write the equation for the curve representing locations where the costs of truck and combined modes are identical by using relations (6.1) and (6.7) as

$$TC_t = \min TC_c$$

$$r_1 \sqrt{a^2 + b^2} = r_1 \frac{a}{\sin \alpha} + r_2 b - \frac{r_2^2}{r_1} \frac{a}{\sin \alpha} + C \tag{6.8}$$

To find the point on the line CB where truck and combined modes are equally costly, we let $a = 0$ and rewrite Equation 6.8 as

$$r_1 b = r_2 b + C$$

$$b = \frac{C}{r_1 - r_2}$$

That is, the distance from point B in miles is equal to the special cost C divided by the difference in the two rates. If $C = 0$, the equal cost boundary is the straight line through B, forming angle α with CB. If $C \neq 0$, the boundary described by Equation 6.8 will not be a straight line. Notice that isocost contours for truck transport will be arcs of circles as shown in Equation 6.1. Isocost contours for combined modes are readily constructed from relation (6.7). The reader can verify for himself that these isocost contours are straight lines having the same slope as line AD but opposite sign.

6.7 COLLECTION AND DELIVERY ROUTES

When the outputs of individual firms (or the purchases of individual households) are small relative to the available capacities of transportation units and when transportation costs per unit of product decrease with increases in capacity, local transportation will be most advantageously organized in collection (or delivery) routes. Rather than point-to-point transportation, then, we will have routes that serve a number of producers and that haul the combined loads to market. The general principle that governs route organization resembles that for the allocation of market areas. The collection section of each route should be a concentrated and exclusive territory, for this will eliminate route duplication and thus permit minimum transfer costs.

That these nonduplicating collection or delivery areas will minimize transportation costs can be demonstrated by a simple example. Consider a number of producers evenly spaced along a single road extending from market. Assume that these farms are located every mile along the road in the pattern suggested below:

$$M(\text{o o o o o}) \ (\text{o o o o o}) \ (\text{o o o} \ldots$$
$$\text{Route 1} \quad \text{Route 2} \quad \text{Route.} \ldots$$

Here, M represents the location of the market and o the location of the farms, spaced one mile apart along the road from market. Suppose that transportation to market is performed by truck and that collection trucks have a capacity equal to the output of five farms. Following the principle of exclusive collection areas, we organize routes as indicated: Route 1 collects from the first five farms; Route 2 collects from the second five farms; and so on. Consider any two routes, for example, Routes 1 and 2. Route 1 involves a total round-trip travel of 10 miles; Route 2 travels a total of 20 miles; thus, the combined travel is 30 miles.

We now inquire as to the effects on total mileage (and, hence, on total transfer costs) of compensating shifts of farms between these two routes since, if it is possible to reduce distance by these changes, then the exclusive areas will not represent the cost-minimizing solution. Suppose we exchange Farms 5 and 6. This will leave travel for Route 2 unchanged at 20 miles, increase Route 1 to 12 miles, and so increase the total from 30 to 32 miles. We can only reduce the travel for Route 2 by substituting nearby farms for the most distant farms on the route. If we exchange Farm 5 for Farm 10, travel by Route 2 will be reduced to 18 miles; but now Route 1 must collect from Farm 10, and so its travel is increased to 20 miles; the total mileage is thus increased to 38. In this way, we discover that no alternate route assignment of farms that maintains each route at capacity load will permit total mileage or total transportation cost lower than the one that is involved with the exclusive collection areas.

Although the structure of competition and of joint costs poses problems in this situation, it is informative to explore the geographic structure of hauling charges that might evolve with this system of route organization. The costs of operating a truck route with fixed volume and number of customers can be represented quite realistically by a linear function where the "fixed" component represents overhead costs plus the fixed costs associated with direct customer services (such as the actual loading and unloading operations at each farmstead) and the "slope" component represents the variable operating costs per mile traveled. We ignore the fact that cost per mile will increase somewhat as the load on the truck increases from zero to capacity. Insofar as this is important, the minimum-cost organization of the route will require that the truck start its collection at the most distant producer and that it accumulate the full load on the return trip to market. With this understanding, the simplification of using a single, average cost per mile is not serious. For any route, then, the average cost per unit of product hauled will be represented by

$$C = a + 2bD$$

where a = the nonvariable costs divided by route volume
b = the variable cost per mile divided by route volume
$2D$ = the round-trip mileage between the market and the most distant customer.

We assume that competition among routes or potential competition from operators willing to enter this market will be such as to keep rates charged for transport service in line with costs: for every route, the sum of the charges levied for the service will exactly equal total operating costs including necessary profits. Although many irregular patterns of charges within a given route might satisfy this requirement, we consider only linear rate structures. The rate for any location i within the collection area of a given route, then, may be represented by

$$R_i = a + 2bD + e\left(D_i - \frac{D_n + D_m}{2}\right)$$

where D_i = the distance from market to the customer in question
D_n and D_m = the distances to the nearest and most distant customers served by the route
e = the slope or inclination of the rate structure in cents per mile; if $e = 0$, all customers served by the route will be charged a flat rate equal to the average route costs.

If this rate equation is applied to the two routes in our earlier example, the specific rate structures would be as follows.

$$Route\ 1.\ R_i = a + 10b + (D_i - 3)e$$
$$Route\ 2.\ R_j = a + 20b + (D_j - 8)e$$

By construction, these rate systems will equate total route revenue to total route cost for either route. There remains the question, however, of the possibility of increased profits by an exchange of customers. The operator of Route 2 might drop the customer located 10 miles from market and add the customer from Route 1, located 5 miles from market. Changes in net revenue for Route 2, then, would be

$$\Delta Y_2 = + R_5 - R_{10} + 10b$$

where the last term represents the *reduction* in route travel costs associated with the dropping of the most distant customer. Substituting the above specific rate equations gives the change in net revenue as

$$\Delta Y_2 = a + 10b + 2e - a - 20b - 2e + 10b = 0.$$

For this possible exchange, therefore, there would be no gain for Route 2. If Route 2 dropped customer 6 and added customer 5, however, the change in net revenue would be

$$\Delta Y_2 = a + 10b + 2e - a - 20b + 2e = 4e - 10b.$$

This exchange would be profitable for the operator of Route 2, apparently, if e is positive and greater than $2.5b$.

By making other calculations of this type, we can arrive at the following general conclusions.

1. If e is negative, the rate structures will provide profitable opportunities for interroute customer exchanges. The resulting competitive scramble will make these rate structures unstable and force it to a flat-rate structure where $e = 0$.

2. If e is positive and falls within the range from 0 to 2.5, operators will not be able to improve net revenue by shifting customers, and the rate structures will be stable.

3. If e is positive and greater than 2.5, possibilities for increased net revenue through customer shifts will exist, the rate structures and route organization will be unstable, and competition will force the structures back to positions where e is not greater than 2.5.

These limits are illustrated in Figure 6.7. Apparently, the efficient organization of collection routes will be stable as long as the transportation rates or charges fall within the limits indicated above. Observe that

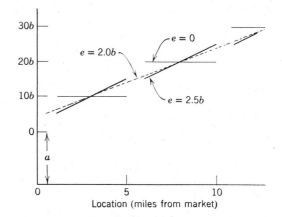

FIGURE 6.7 The competitive limits to the structures of rates charged by collection routes.

a smooth and continuous system of rates, extending across all routes and increasing in line with the increases in average costs ($e = 2.0$), falls within these limits. This may seem to be the most reasonable and equitable system and, if instituted, it should be stable; but there is no reason to expect that this particular system will result automatically from free competition. Notice also that, although our discussion has assumed linear and continuous rate structures within routes, individual charges may vary erratically as long as they fall within limits where between-route shifts are unprofitable.

A logical extension of the feeder-route system involves the use of shipping stations or plants where volume is concentrated from a number of local collection routes and held for large-volume shipment to market. In addition to the advantages inherent in feeder routes, this type of organization may permit the consolidation of volumes from a number of shippers and, thus, gain advantages from bulk instead of individual shipment. The addition of plant operations adds a new element of cost — an element that tends to increase the "intercept" or fixed component in the cost-distance relationship. If such a system is economical, however, the added cost is more than offset by lower direct collection costs and by lower cost per ton-mile for transport from plant to market.

It is not our intention to suggest here that any particular form or type of transport is economical for a particular situation; that is, after all, a matter of empirical fact. Instead, the above theoretical treatment suggests how the problem of the selection of least-cost transport technology should be approached under various circumstances. The theory can be used, as indicated, to outline the approach to such problems, but the final solution must rest on the real facts of cost relationships for alternative systems of collection and transportation.

SELECTED READINGS

Transfer Costs

Bressler, R. G. Jr., *City Milk Distribution*, Harvard University Press, Cambridge (1952), Chapter 9, "Delivery Truck Costs," pp. 110–139. Chapter 10, "Route Labor Requirements and Costs," pp. 140–176.

Caves, Richard, *Air Transport and Its Regulation*, Harvard University Press, Cambridge (1962).

Fogel, Robert W., "A Quantitative Approach to the Study of Railroads in American Economic Growth," *The Journal of Economic History*, Vol. XXII, No. 2 (June 1962). pp. 163–197.

Hassler, James B., *Transportation Rates and Other Pricing Factors Affecting the California Swine Industry*, California Agricultural Experiment Station Bulletin 754. Berkeley (June 1956).

Isard, Walter, *Location and Space-Economy*, The M.I.T. Press, Cambridge (1956) Chapter 4. "Transport Inputs and Related Spatial Concepts." pp. 77–90.

Meyer, J. R., M. S. Peck, J. Stenason, and C. Zwick, *The Economics of Competition in the Transportation Industries*, Harvard University Press, Cambridge (1959).

Weber, Alfred, *Theory of the Location of Industries*, Translated with an Introduction and notes by Carl J. Friedrich, University of Chicago Press, Chicago (1929). Chapter 3, "Transport Orientation." pp. 41–94.

chapter 7

MARKETS WITH SPATIALLY DISPERSED PRODUCTION

7.1 SPATIAL DISPERSION

In Chapter 5, we discussed price and trade relationships involving localized product sources and localized markets. This treatment of point-trading models can be extended readily to situations in which resources are for the most part ubiquitous, where production is widely dispersed through space, and where consumers also are scattered over a broad geographic expanse rather than concentrated at a single point.

In agricultural production the basic resource is land, so that farming by its very nature is carried on at a multitude of points in space – at millions of farmsteads. Thus, any particular market for a given commodity may be served by thousands of farms distributed through hundreds of square miles of farming country. In manufacturing, as in agriculture, the customers for a particular plant may include wholesale and retail distributors scattered across a very large geographic area, while final consumers are even farther dispersed and segregated through space. Economic models that treat explicitly the spatial dimension of market price are, therefore, of widespread interest.

7.2   SITE-PRICE SURFACE

For convenience, we use the term *site price* to refer to the price of a product at a particular location or site. A product site price is derived from a particular base market price; that is, it is the market price less transfer cost from the particular site in question. We can think of a *site-price surface* as a representation of the spatial pattern of site prices oriented to a given market or set of markets.

Consider first the case of an isolated market surrounded by an agricultural area in which only one product is grown. The site-price surface for such an area is illustrated in plan view and in cross-section view in Figure 7.1. Let us suppose that a single uniform price P_m is established for this crop at the market center, indicated as 25 cents per pound (point *a*) in the cross-section view. Farm-to-market transfer costs also are taken as given. The price P_f at any farm location is therefore equal to the market price less the appropriate transfer cost t which, in turn, is a function of distance from market $f(D)$. The resulting *site-price function* may be written as

$$P_f = P_m - T = P_m - f(D). \tag{7.1}$$

This site-price function is illustrated for the cross-section at RS in the upper diagram of Figure 7.1, where farm prices are shown to be decreasing with distance from market.

The cone-shaped, site-price surface can also be represented in plan view, as in the lower diagram. Here, the concentric circles represent contours of equal farm prices. An *isotim* (Palander) is the locus of points corresponding to the sites for which a specified transfer cost is required to move a unit of product to a particular market center and is, therefore, a special type of isoprice contour. Since the isotims in Figure 7.1 reflect a given market price less transfer costs that increase with distance at a decreasing rate, the farm price structure falls off with distance from market, but at a decreasing rate. For this reason, the more distant isotims are drawn with radii that increase at an increasing rate to reflect the longer distances covered with a given increment in transfer cost. Notice also that the farm price immediately adjacent to the market is *not* equal to the market price but differs from it at least by terminal charges *ab*.

At present, we defer any discussion of the case of a concentrated production point surrounded by scattered consumers, but the reader will recognize the similarity between the production area and the market area cases. In the latter, prices *delivered* to consumers will represent the central price *plus* transfer costs, and the site-price surface will resemble an inverted cone or funnel.

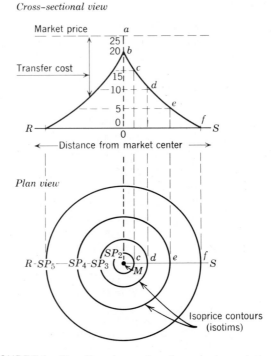

FIGURE 7.1   The site-price surface for a single market.

7.3 THE LAW OF MARKET AREAS

Up to this point we have treated the case of an isolated market in an agricultural region. Consider now the case involving several markets which compete for available supplies. What principles govern the allocation of the producing territory among these markets?

Suppose that you were a farmer in a region producing a crop that could be sold in any one of several markets. For each alternative market outlet the price at your farm would be represented by the market price less the appropriate transfer cost. Should one of these site prices be higher than any other, you, operating on a free-choice basis and in your own best interest, would select it as the market to which you would ship your crop. Notice that this decision involves only market prices and transfer costs, since your production costs are unaffected by the market selection.

By chance, a farmer may find that a particular set of market prices and transfer costs for two alternative markets result in exactly identical net prices at his farm location. Under these conditions, the choice between these two markets would be a matter of indifference to him. A neighboring farmer located a little closer to market A would find a slight advantage in shipping to A, although a neighbor on the other side would find an advantage in market B. Apparently, this farmer is located on the competitive margin or boundary between the two markets. This free-choice principle gives rise to what Fetter has called the "law of market areas." This law asserts that the boundary between two competing markets is the locus of points so situated that the site prices (market price net of transfer cost) for shipments made to the competing markets are equal. In algebraic terms, this law can be expressed as follows:

$$P_a - t_a = P_b - t_b \tag{7.2}$$

or, in terms of market price difference, as

$$P_a - P_b = t_a - t_b \tag{7.3}$$

where

P = market price

t = farm-to-market transfer cost.

and

subscripts = alternative markets, A and B

Notice that in equation (7.3) the law is restated in such a way that the boundary between any two markets is the locus of points for which the difference in transfer cost to each market is a constant and is equal to the given difference in market prices.

7.4 BOUNDARIES BETWEEN COMPETING MARKETS

Intermarket competition for a single product is illustrated in Figure 7.2. The diagram is comparable to Figure 7.1, but here we show the site-price surface of farm prices around two competing markets, A and B. We assume that the price in market A is fixed, and we illustrate the effects of three different levels of price at market B: (1) the price at B equal to the price at A with a maximum site price of c, (2) the price at B somewhat lower than at A with a maximum site price of d, and (3) the price at B considerably lower with a maximum site price of e. Notice that again in this diagram the market price lies above the peak on the site-price surface because of terminal costs (equal to Bc, etc). At points f and g transfer costs are equal to market price, and site prices are zero.

We first examine case 1. From Equation 7.3 we may conclude that with equal prices in the two markets the competitive boundary will

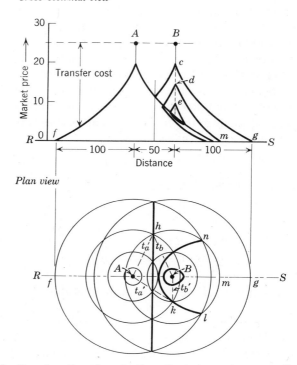

Cross–sectional view

Plan view

FIGURE 7.2 The allocation of production sites between two competing markets.

consist of all points where the difference in transfer costs is equal to zero — that is, where the transfer cost to A is exactly equal to the transfer cost to B. Therefore, so long as the transfer cost-distance function holds true for shipments made in any direction and regardless of the particular form of this function, the boundary must be the locus of points where the *distances* to the two markets are equal. This is indicated in the plan view of the diagram by points such as *h*. Here, the alternative distances are equal; the alternative transfer costs are equal; and, hence, the alternative site prices must be equal. Furthermore, it follows that this market boundary is the perpendicular bisector of the straight line connecting markets A and B.

If the price in market B falls below that in market A, as in case 2, the market boundary is pushed toward B. Some producers to the "east" of the perpendicular bisector now find it profitable to ship to A rather than to B. The new boundary is again the locus of points for which the difference in alternative transfer costs is constant and equal to the difference in market prices, but these points are no longer equidistant from the two markets. If transfer costs are a linear function of distance, the boundary can be restated in terms of a constant difference in distances to the two markets, and the market boundary would be a hyperbola. But with a curvilinear transfer cost function, the controlling factor is a constant difference in transfer cost and not a constant difference in distance. The resulting curve is not a hyperbola although, under the circumstances, it might well be called an *economic hyperbola*. This is illustrated by point k on the line *lkn* with transfer costs t'_a and t'_b. Notice that this boundary extends to the zero price edge of the area for market A at points l and n (actually, only to the no-rent margin, as we shall show later when we consider production costs) and that the "eastern" boundary for market B is a segment *lmn* of the circle centered on B that represents sites having zero at-farm prices.

In those situations in which transfer costs are properly expressed as a curvilinear function of distance throughout their entire range and in which production areas extend over long distances, these economic hyperbolas will eventually completely enclose the market with the lower price; that is, the high-price market will extend beyond the outer margin of the supply area for the low-price market. This is illustrated by case 3 where the price at B is quite low relative to A. With a maximum price of e, the site-price surface around B now resembles a secondary cone on the flank of a large volcano, as the cross-section view along the line *RS* shows. The plan view illustrates how the small supply area for B is completely surrounded by the supply area for A.

Observe that the encirclement of a lower priced market stems from the different slope or gradient of the two price surfaces. If the transfer function were linear, the margin between the two markets would be a hyperbola, as discussed above, and the larger market would never encircle the smaller; the limit would be where the price cone for the lower price market just touches the cone for the higher price market, and the supply area for the smaller market becomes a straight line starting at B and extending infinitely away from A. This straight line would represent the path of tangency between the two price cones, possible only with linear transfer functions. On the other hand, if transfer costs are linear but with a steeper slope for the low-price market than for the high-price market, the boundary will be a perfect circle centered somewhat to the "east" of B. With curvilinear functions the boundaries will completely close, as indicated above, and the particular shapes will depend on the curvilinearity of the price surfaces in the relevant ranges. The only generalization than can be made is that market boundaries will *always* be economic hyperbolas with all points representing constant differences in transfer costs to the two competing markets.

7.5 AN EXAMPLE OF INTERRELATED MARKETS

The prewar geographic patterns of milk consumption and production in New England are indicated in Figure 7.3. These maps are based on production and consumption estimates by towns and show the surplus or deficit of production relative to consumption. As such, the data are comparable to the "excess supply functions" discussed in Chapter 5 but with the assumption that demands and supplies are perfectly inelastic — a not too unrealistic assumption in the short run. The boundaries to theoretical milksheds consistent with competitive market prices and minimum transfer costs are shown in Figure 7.4. Although this analysis is oversimplified by using airline distances, by combining milk and cream and by assuming that only whole milk will be delivered to market, and by representing an average situation instead of showing seasonal variations, the empirical results are nonetheless of considerable interest.

The major markets, Boston and Providence, were surrounded in the theoretical analysis by a semicircle of secondary markets in Connecticut, central Massachusetts, and nearby New Hampshire and Maine. Although some supplies were obtained locally for the major markets, competition forced them to reach beyond to surround the secondary markets and to compete directly with New York City in western Vermont. Actual milk-

FIGURE 7.3 The milk production–consumption balance in New England, 1939. Each dot equals 500,000 lb of milk per year. [*Source.* Kasten Gailius, "The Price and Supply Interrelationships for New England Milk Markets" (unpublished master's thesis, Department of Agricultural Economics, University of Connecticut, 1941).]

FIGURE 7.4   The theoretical milksheds for New England markets, 1939. *1*, Boston; *2*, Providence; *3*, New Haven; *4*, Springfield; *5*, Lowell-Lawrence; *6*, Hartford; *7*, Bridge-port; *8*, Worcester; *9*, Portland; *10*, Manchester; *11*, Fitchburg; *12*, Pittsfield; *13*, Lewiston; *14*, Nashua; *15*, Burlington; *16*, Bangor; *17*, Berlin; and *18*, New York City. [*Source.* Kasten Gailius, "The Price and Supply Interrelationships for New England Milk Markets" (unpublished master's thesis, Department of Agricultural Economics, University of Connecticut, 1941).]

sheds were found to overlap to a considerable extent, but the general pattern in New England in 1939 was remarkably similar to this theoretical and simplified allocation of milk supplies. A comparison of actual and theoretical market prices, however, revealed persistent and quite signi-ficant deviations: a situation that was not surprising in light of the general dependence of the fluid milk industry at that time on noncompetitive pricing mechanisms.

For a completely general treatment with a number of competing markets, the final equilibrium will involve the demand functions in every market, the transfer functions, the location of producing areas, production cost conditions, and the resulting patterns of production density. Supply functions for each market will represent the aggregation of producers' marginal cost curves, but the allocation of producers and producing terri-tory will involve prices in all markets and not simply the price in a given market. The result will be an interdependent set of supply relationships so that an increase in the price in any market will influence the quantities received in all markets and, thus, will influence all market prices. The equilibrium set of market prices will involve an interrelated set of free-choice supply areas consistent with the economic law of market areas.

7.6 MINIMIZING TRANSFER COSTS

The law of market areas has focused our attention on prices in competing markets, on the geographic structure of prices around these markets, and on the allocation of producing or consuming territories through the free-choice response of firms and individuals to these prices. A valuable characteristic of these competitive market or supply areas, however, is that they involve the lowest possible pooled transfer costs for all markets under consideration.

Consider a farm located at any point Y in the area serving two markets, A and B. From our earlier discussion, we know that this point will lie on the boundary between the two markets if the difference in transfer costs to the alternative markets is exactly offset by differences in market prices and that it will fall in one or the other market supply area if transfer cost differences are more than or less than price differences. In equation form these conditions are given by

$$\text{point } Y \text{ on boundary: } t_{yb} - t_{ya} = P_b - P_a \qquad (7.4)$$
$$\text{point } Y \text{ in A's area: } \quad t_{yb} - t_{ya} > P_b - P_a \qquad (7.5)$$
$$\text{point } Y \text{ in B's area: } \quad t_{ya} - t_{yb} > P_a - P_b \qquad (7.6)$$

where $\quad P = $ price at market center
$\quad\quad t = $ transfer cost from farm to market
a and $b = $ the markets
$\quad\quad y = $ the farm.

Through these free choices, the entire area will be allocated among competing markets. Demand and supply will be in equilibrium in each market, and the competitive equilibrium will involve a particular set of market prices and the associated system of boundaries among supply areas.

To demonstrate that this allocation minimizes aggregate transfer costs, subject, of course, to the constraint that the supply-demand equilibria in the two markets are maintained, it is necessary to show that no exchanges of producers among markets will reduce transfer costs. Suppose that point Y is located in the supply area for market A and that another point Z is located somewhere in B's area. Within the areas, these locations are quite general—they refer to any locations. Now let us reassign a unit of production at Y from market A to market B and, to compensate and so maintain market equilibria, reassign an equal unit of production at Z from B to A. Changes in transfer costs (Δt) then will be

$$\text{for point } Y: \ \Delta t_y = t_{yb} - t_{ya} > P_b - P_a \qquad (7.7)$$
$$\text{for point } Z: \ \Delta t_z = t_{za} - t_{zb} > P_a - P_b \qquad (7.8)$$
$$\text{combined: } \ \Delta t_y + \Delta t_z = t_{yb} - t_{ya} + t_{za} - t_{zb} > 0. \qquad (7.9)$$

In words, we state that the change in transfer cost resulting from the shift of point Y must be greater than the amount by which the price at B exceeds the price at A; if this were not true, Y would not have been in A's area. Similarly, the shift of point Z involves a change in costs greater than the price at A less the price at B. The combined change in transfer cost, therefore, must always be greater than zero. Consequently, the free-choice boundary does involve minimum transfer costs. By testing more elaborate but similar systems of transfers among several markets, we discover that any system of transfers that maintains the competitive balance in all markets will result in transfer costs higher than the ones possible with the competitive areas.

Actually, we can proceed directly to transfer cost minimization without reference to market prices. Take the simple case of four regions where two have net surpluses of a particular commodity available for export, and the other two have net deficits that must be met through imports. To be specific, assume that regions A and B have deficits of 300 and 400 units, respectively, while regions C and D have surpluses of 200 and 500 units. It costs $10 per unit to transfer the product from C to A, $25 from C to B, $15 from D to A, and $20 from D to B. What pattern of shipments will minimize total transfer costs and also meet the restraints imposed by the above regional surpluses and deficits?

Clearly region C cannot fully supply either importing region and the surplus at region D is larger than the requirements at either A or B. Several shipment patterns are possible: (1) C could ship its entire surplus to A, while D supplied the balance required at A and completely supplied B; (2) C could ship its entire surplus to B, while D supplied the balance needed at B and completely supplied A; or (3) both surplus regions could ship to both deficit regions — there being, of course, an infinite variety of such combinations. From our familiarity with location theory and an inspection of the above market requirements and transfer costs, it appears probable that the first alternative is the cost-minimizing solution. This involves shipping 200 units from C to A at a cost of $10 per unit, 100 units from D to A at $15, and 400 from D to B at $20 for a combined transfer cost of $11,500. Similar calculations for alternative (2) indicate a higher total cost of $13,500.

Alternative (3) provides a limitless opportunity for such calculations. Let us consider the case where C ships 100 units to each of the two deficit regions with the balances coming from D; this would entail a combined transfer cost of $12,500. The fact that shipping a product from C to A results in lower total transfer costs than when all of C's surplus goes to B strengthens our belief that alternative (1) is the optimum. To be certain, however, let us consider changing this alternative by shifting a single pair of production units. If one unit from C is shipped to B rather than to A, transfer costs will increase from $10 to $25; also, a compensating shift of one unit from D will involve a transfer cost of $15 rather than $20. The net effect, therefore, is an *increase* in total transfer cost of $10, thus, finally confirming that alternative (1) involves the lowest possible transfer costs.

Alternative (1) is diagrammed in Figure 7.5 where the four regions are positioned at distances proportional to the assumed transfer costs. Although the indicated solution is based entirely on transfer costs and market surpluses or deficits, there is a "dual" solution in terms of competitive prices. If we consider the price at D as the base, the prices at A and B will exceed this base price by the unit costs of transfer or $15 and $20, respectively. Moreover, the price at C is linked to A through transfer costs and must be $5 above the base price. Thus the transfer cost-minimizing solution also involves the determination of the competitive price structure. Here, we have indicated only the prices relative to the base; but if production costs (or supply functions) were given for the surplus regions, this would determine absolute prices. Suppose that production cost at C is equal to that at D, say, $10 per unit. Then the competitive prices will be $10 at D, $15 at C, $25 at A, and $30 at B. And notice that the amount by which the price at C exceeds production cost represents economic rent per unit of product.

Mention of production costs emphasizes that competitive allocations not only minimize transfer costs but also the combination of production and transfer costs. If production costs differ from location to location, this must be considered in determining market prices and the allocation of territories. By including production costs or costs for other appropriate functions such as processing, warehousing, and marketing, the aggregate of these costs will be minimized. Moreover, these market equilibria and allocations will represent the *maximum* aggregate returns to producers

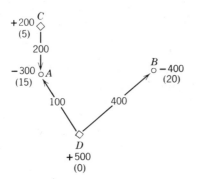

FIGURE 7.5 The flow of a commodity among points in space illustrating transfer cost minimization (figures in parentheses represent competitive price differences).

that are possible with the restraints of perfect competition and also the *minimum* aggregate expenditures by consumers.

Although it was a simple matter to discover the cost-minimizing solution in the previous example, this would not be true if many alternative sources and markets were involved. To determine the cost-minimizing shipments of dressed broilers from 14 major producing centers to 43 important markets in the United States, for example, would be most time-consuming and complex if approached by such direct comparisons. Fortunately, the transportation model (Chapter 5) for dealing with point-trading problems makes it possible to consider such involved situations and to select the program that is optimum and consistent with our market and transfer cost theory. The results of a 1955 programming study of the broiler industry are illustrated by the shipment patterns in Figure 7.6.

We now find that our discussion of spatially dispersed production and consumption leads us back to our earlier treatment of point-trading models. This is as it should be, since there exist an infinite number of combinations of production points and consumption points. In some situations, the spatial dispersion approach used in the present chapter will be most efficient in dealing with real-world problems. In others, the use of point-trading models will be preferable. The point to be made here is that

FIGURE 7.6 The transportation-cost-minimizing shipments of broilers among 14 producing centers and 43 deficit areas in the United States, 1955. [*Source.* W. R. Henry and C. E. Bishop, *North Carolina Broilers in Interregional Competition*].

the economic framework underlying the two is identical, and the choice will be based purely on the grounds of computational convenience.

We have pointed out that the theory of competitive intermarket prices has a dual solution in terms of the allocation of areas and the minimization of transfer costs. We have also pointed out that minimizing transfer costs can be approached directly, in which case the dual solution is the structure of competitive market prices. However, it must be emphasized that they are only "shadow" prices and that they are not essential to the transfer cost-minimizing solution. Even if actual prices depart materially from the shadow prices (and so from competitive market prices), costs will be minimized through the system of area allocations consistent with competitive prices. In this event, however, it will no longer be true that aggregate producer returns are maximized or aggregate consumer expenditures minimized.

7.7   PRODUCTION COSTS AND IRREGULAR TRANSFER COSTS

When production costs are included in the analysis, we have suggested that it is possible to determine absolute prices rather than prices relative to one market taken as base and, also, that the allocations among markets will then minimize combined production and transportation costs. The inclusion of production costs, however, will *not* change the location of the competitive boundaries among markets. Let us assume that each section in our earlier problem is characterized by a particular production cost (as in the case of production itself, we assume that the production cost is uniform within sections and varies between sections). At some point Y, the production costs are given and may be represented by c_y. The condition for point Y to fall on the competitive boundary between markets A and B, then, is given by

$$P_a - t_{ya} - c_y = P_b - t_{yb} - c_y. \qquad (7.10)$$

With the constant c_y appearing on both sides of this equation, it is apparent that boundary conditions are the same as in the case that involves only transfer costs: the boundary is the locus of points where the difference in transportation costs to the two markets is a constant and equal to the difference in market prices.

Notice that this same conclusion holds true for erratic differences in transfer costs *if* the differences affect equally the transfer costs to alternative markets. A good example is afforded by the influence of production density costs. Transportation from farm to city often involves truck routes that collect the product from a number of points. With such collection routes rather than point-to-point transportation, transfer costs will have two components: (1) the direct hauling component, involving the travel of the truck from a distant producing area to and from the market; and (2) the collection component, related to the farm-to-farm movement in the producing area as load is assembled. The first component is comparable to the point-to-point transportation that we have been using, and transfer costs can thus be regular functions of distance from market. The second component, however, is not related to distance from market, since it involves movements only in the distant producing district, but is definitely influenced by the density of production.

Suppose that a truck has capacity for 100 units of product. In a district where density is high (say, 20 units per mile of road) collection mileage will be relatively low and, therefore, the second transportation cost component will be low. With low density, however, collection mileage and costs will be high. But these high or low collection costs will hold true regardless of the market destination and, hence, will not influence the competitive allocation of producing territories among markets.

In algebraic terms, the difference in transfer costs to two markets is $t_{yb} - t_{ya}$ and will become $(t_{yb} + k_y) - (t_{ya} + k_y)$; but since the collection cost term k_y is the same regardless of market destination, this reduces to the original form.

Irregularities in the transfer cost and distance relationship can result from factors other than collection densities, of course, and some of these factors will affect different markets in different ways. This is equivalent to saying that the isotims around each market will not be regular circles centered on the market. These irregularities will certainly modify the shape and the location of competitive boundaries between markets. But these changes are in results and not in method or principle; the boundaries will still represent the locus of points where differences in transfer costs are equal to differences in market prices. The graphic determination of these boundaries will be more complicated, since it will be necessary to draw irregular systems of contours representing transfer costs around each market rather than to use concentric circles; but, with this modification, the determination of boundaries proceeds as above.

7.8 APPLICABILITY TO REAL MARKETS

We have developed in some detail the pure theory of markets in space and have discovered that, under perfectly competitive conditions, the equilibrium of a system of these markets involves, on the one hand, a set of interdependent and interrelated market prices and price surfaces surrounding markets and, on the other, a complex of market area or supply area boundaries within which transfer costs (and as appropriate, other costs) are minimized, returns to sellers in the aggregate are maximized (within the structure of perfect competition), and aggregate expenditures by consumers minimized. Whether this theory has relevance to real markets depends in large measure on the similarity of conditions in real markets to the ones essential to perfect competition. They include items such as the absence of monopoly elements, the homogeneity of the products under consideration, and the general availability of perfect knowledge about supply, demand, and price conditions in all alternative markets. Even without the more careful analysis of real markets that will be developed in later chapters, we can state with assurance that the conditions of perfect markets are never completely satisfied by conditions in real markets.

In spite of this fact, our theoretical models do provide important insights into the operation of the real market and pricing systems. Many individuals make careers of *arbitrage* — buying in one market in the expectation of selling at a profit at another market location. A wholesaler on the strawberry auctions in Connecticut buys berries for resale in upstate New York. A butter merchant in Iowa watches price quotations at New York, Chicago, and San Francisco and makes shipments when he believes that the prices at those markets will more than cover the Iowa price plus transfer costs. A Sunkist cooperative rolls a car of oranges eastward toward Chicago, but changes in market conditions en route may dictate a final destination in New Orleans, St. Louis, or Boston.

Arbitrage is thus viewed as part of the free-choice mechanism that determines prices and production-consumption allocations. Even under the best of real conditions, however, it is clear that knowledge is imperfect, that intermarket transfers cannot be made instantaneously, and that marketing decisions involve a considerable amount of risk and uncertainty. The strawberry buyer may arrive in Syracuse to find a brisk market and may sell his load at an unexpectedly high profit; or he may find that many other truckers have arrived in Syracuse with strawberries, and the perishability of his product leaves him little alternative but to sell for what he can get, even though this represents a substantial loss. The car of citrus may hit a favorable market or, even with several reroutings, it may reach "the end of the line" only to find a local glut. Sales in eastern markets at prices too low to cover freight charges are not novel experiences for California growers.

Under these conditions, intermarket prices cannot be kept in perfect alignment through marketing decisions. Although arbitrage is an effective adjustor, prices must move out of line by some amount to bring this mechanism to life. Consequently, prices tend to oscillate around normal relationships following a type of "cobweb" like that we discussed in an earlier chapter. Perhaps, this matter can be explained best by a physical parallel: arbitrage is similar to the thermostat that regulates temperatures in your home. Variations in temperature operate through the thermostat to turn your furnace on and off, but some actual drop in temperature is required to activate the system. Moreover, after the furnace starts there is a time lag before room temperatures respond. The result is that temperatures, like market prices, fluctuate around or "hunt" for the equilibrium level without actually achieving it except for brief and sporadic periods.

An examination of many actual markets reveals marked regularity in the space economy — regularity reflecting the operation of the forces considered in the foregoing theory. Of course, in some cases, there are major departures between the actual and the theoretical structures of perfect competition, but, as we shall learn, these differences may in themselves be of great interest.

SELECTED READINGS

Spatially Dispersed Production

Cootner, Paul F., "The Role of the Railroads in United States Economic Growth," *The Journal of Economic History*, Vol. XXIII, No. 4., pp. 477–524.

Fetter, Frank A., "The Economic Law of Market Areas," *Quarterly Journal of Economics*, Vol. XXXVI, No. 3 (May 1924). pp. 520–529.

Hoover, Edgar M. Jr., *Location Theory and the Shoe and Leather Industries*. Harvard University Press, Cambridge (1937). pp. 6–23.

Isard, Walter, *Location and Space-Economy*. The M.I.T. Press, Cambridge (1956), Chapter 7, "Market and Supply Area Analysis." pp. 143–171.

Johnson, Stewart and Arthur D. Little, *Intermarket Milk Price Relationships. I. Factors Determining the Boundaries of the Connecticut Milkshed*. Bulletin 266, University of Connecticut, Storrs Agricultural Experiment Station (January 1951).

Pred, Allan, *Behavior and Location: Foundations for a Geographic and Dynamic Location Theory, Part I*. Royal University of Lund Studies in Geography, Series B, No. 27, Lund (1967).

Schneider, Erich, *Pricing and Equilibrium*, (English version by Esra Bennathan) The Macmillan Co. New York (1962). pp. 62–70.

chapter 8

EFFICIENT ORGANIZATION WITHIN MARKET AREAS[1]

8.1 EFFICIENT PRODUCT ASSEMBLY

Economical assembly of a product from scattered producing units may well involve a combination of plant and transportation operations. In fact, commodity marketing will frequently involve plant operations, either as an adjunct to the collection operation or for involved processing. The marketing of farm products affords many examples of such plant facilities — packing houses, canneries, cotton gins, country grain elevators, creameries, and cheese factories to mention but a few. We now examine the problem of the economical and efficient organization of plants plus transportation when there are many scattered sources for the raw product or destinations for the finished goods.

Although earlier chapters have dealt with the allocation of producing territories among competing markets, the same general principles apply to

[1]In this chapter the mathematical formulation of plant location model is based on John F. Stollsteimer, "A Working Model for Plant Numbers and Locations," *Journal of Farm Economics*, Vol. 45, No. 3 (August, 1963), pp. 631–645. Empirical data on the sweet potato industry are drawn from Gene A. Mathia and Richard A. King, *Planning Data for the Sweet Potato Industry: 3. Selection of the Optimum Number, Size and Location of Processing Plants in Eastern North Carolina*, North Carolina State College, A. E. Information Series No. 97 (Raleigh, 1962), 75 pp.

the allocation of producing territories among local marketing facilities. Two important adjustments to the analysis are required: (1) the market demand function is replaced by a plant cost curve or, in the long run, by a curve representing economies of scale and (2) the number, size, and location of plants are variables rather than fixed as in the given geographic distribution of cities.

The economical organization of a system that is concerned with processing plants involves the simultaneous consideration of three main components of total cost: (1) the costs of collection from scattered origins to the point of plant location, (2) the costs of plant operation, and (3) the costs of plant-to-market transportation. All of these components can be expected to vary with variations in the total volume handled by the plant, and the most economical organization will involve the selection of that plant volume which will result in minimum *combined* costs for the three component operations. In the following discussion, however, we stress the combination of collection and plant operations. This does not mean that plant-to-market transportation is unimportant; instead, it is omitted for simplicity and because the insertion of this element in the analysis is not difficult.[2]

8.2 ISOLATED PLANT SITES

Consider a plant located in the middle of a large producing territory. This plant is in essence a very small market, and to attract larger and larger volumes it will be necessary to offer higher and higher prices for the product delivered to the plant door. As long as the plant is isolated from other plants, its supply or producing territory will take the form of a circle centered on the plant. If the density of production is held constant, it is clear that the volume delivered to the plant will be a direct function of the circular area and, hence, of the square of the radius of this area (r^2). Collection costs will tend to increase with distance at a constant rate, but because of the quadratic relation between distance and volume the marginal costs of collection will increase with volume at a decreasing rate. Total collection costs, it follows will be related to the cube of the radius (r^3).

The specific relationship between total volume and collection costs will depend on the particular geographic pattern of production, since this pattern will determine the extent of the plant area for any selected volume but, in general, it can be expected to resemble the curves given in Figure 8.1. They illustrate three different situations: (1) relatively high density,

[2]Miller and King (1964) discuss a variety of models which are appropriate for more complicated situations.

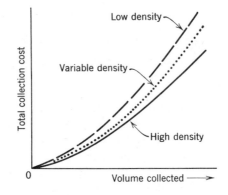

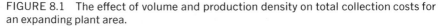

FIGURE 8.1   The effect of volume and production density on total collection costs for an expanding plant area.

constant throughout the producing territory, (2) constant density but at a lower level (actually, we have illustrated the case where density is one-half that in the first case), and (3) variable density, graduated from high density near the plant location to low density in distant sections. In all cases, the relationship indicates that total collection costs increase with total volume at an increasing rate: the rate increase is more rapid as density is lowered, reflecting the proportionately greater distances involved in obtaining a fixed increment to plant volume.

If there were no economies of scale in plant operation — if plant costs per unit of product were constant and unaffected by plant size — then, clearly, optimum organization would involve a plant at every production location. But plants are subject to economies — and perhaps diseconomies — of scale; at least within limits, larger plants with a volume well adjusted to the available capacity will operate with lower average costs than smaller plants. Optimum organization, therefore, involves a balancing of the decreasing average plant costs against the increasing collection costs. This is suggested by the diagram in Figure 8.2 where we show the total long-run cost and volume relationship for plant operation in conventional sigmoid form. This relationship suggests that unit costs for plant operation will decrease over a considerable range in scale and output and eventually increase. When combined with the relationship for collection costs, we can indicate the point b that represents the lowest possible costs per unit for the collection plus plant operations.

This combination of plant and collection costs is also shown in terms of average costs in Figure 8.3. Notice that plant costs alone are at lowest levels at point a and that combined costs are minimized at a lower volume as represented by point b. A consideration of the several diagrams should

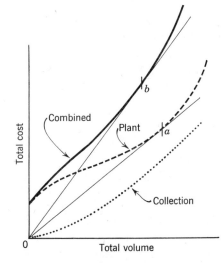

FIGURE 8.2   The combination of collection costs and long-run plant costs to determine optimum organization.

indicate that minimum combined costs will involve lower volumes as density is decreased, although the reduction in volume with lower densities will usually involve expansions in the geographic area served by the plant. In this isolated situation, in any event, optimum organization will involve balancing off plant and collection costs; and the final adjustment will entail a plant located in the center of a circular supply area.[3]

[3]An interesting empirical example is provided by Henry, Chappell and Seagraves (1960).

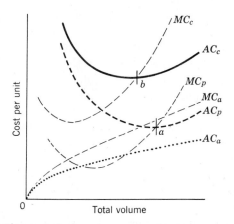

FIGURE 8.3   Collection and plant costs expressed in terms of average costs per unit of product handled.

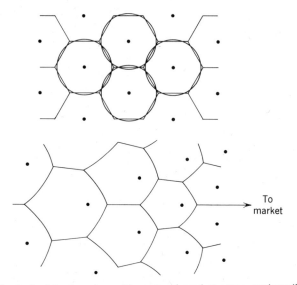

FIGURE 8.4   A regular Lösch system of hexagonal market areas, and modifications to represent supply areas around country marketing plants.

8.3 COMPETING PLANTS

With the development of competing plants to service an entire producing region, free-choice areas would allocate the region among plants much as in the case of competing markets; but now the final equilibrium would determine the location, size, and number of plants as well as the allocation of territory among them. Since a system of circular areas cannot completely cover a region without overlapping and since such overlapping would be eliminated by producers in making their free choice of most favorable outlets, the idealized solution to the problem of plant size and location would appear to involve a regular system of hexagonal plant areas as shown in the upper half of Figure 8.4. But plants located at varying distances from the central market will necessarily have differing at-plant prices. This would distort the interplant boundaries somewhat as suggested in Figures 8.5 and 8.6. Further deviations from the regular hexagonal pattern would result from variations in production densities and from the peculiarities of local road networks. With these complications and with the infinite set of alternative volume-number-location possibilities, a rigorous theoretical solution to this problem may well be impossible. Practical and at least near-optimum solutions can be obtained, however, by determining the cost-minimizing volumes appropriate for

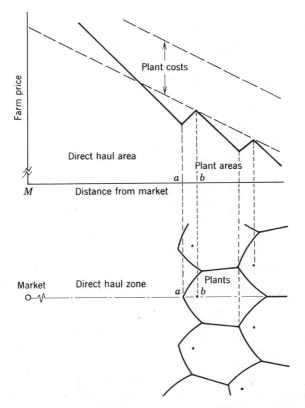

FIGURE 8.5   A cross-section of price surface in a market area with direct haul and plant-plus-transportation zones.

FIGURE 8.6   The allocation of direct haul and plant areas within a market area.

isolated plants in various parts of the market territory and then by using these results as guides in establishing a somewhat arbitrary pattern of plant locations and the associated systems of plant areas and volumes for the entire region.

8.4   PROCESSING PLANT NUMBERS AND COSTS

An analysis of the sweet potato processing industry in Eastern North Carolina will be used to illustrate how the number, size, and location of processing plants can be selected that will minimize combined assembly and processing costs. The production density pattern is regarded as predetermined. The assembly costs would be expected to decline as the number of plants increases because the size of the supply area for particular plants and total distance required for assembly are reduced. This effect is illustrated in Figure 8.7 where *TAC* represents the minimum total assembly costs associated with assembling a fixed volume of raw product with varying numbers of plants.

The effect of the number of processing plants on total season processing costs, *TSPC* is illustrated in Figure 8.8. The *TSPC* curve should not be confused with the usual total cost function where cost is expressed as a function of *plant* volume. A positive sloping *TSPC* function reflects higher costs that are associated with processing a given volume of raw material in two or more plants as compared with the processing of the same volume in any one plant. Two plants would each process one-half the volume handled by a one plant organization of the region. The slope of *TSPC*, thus, reflects the added annual costs of building and operating the processing sector as the number of plants is increased from j to $j+1$. This assumes that plants can be designed for any output and that they will be operated at a specified proportion (100 percent?) of capacity.

The summation of these two relationships results in a combined assembly and processing function that is useful in evaluating the efficiency of the marketing system. The procedure for summing the assembly and processing relationships is described in a mathematical note at the end of this chapter. The combined cost function *TC* and a hypothetical two-plant optimum solution are shown in Figure 8.8. The optimum number and location of plants are determined when the reduction in assembly costs is just offset by the increase in processing costs as the number of plants increases.

The total assembly costs are minimized for a given set of plants by

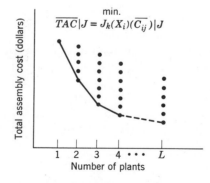

$$\overline{TAC}|J = \overset{min.}{J_k(X_i)(\overline{C_{ij}})}|J$$

Total assembly cost (dollars)

1 2 3 4 ••• L
Number of plants

FIGURE 8.7 The minimized total assembly costs for fixed volume of raw product. (See Section 8.7 for details and definitions of terms.)

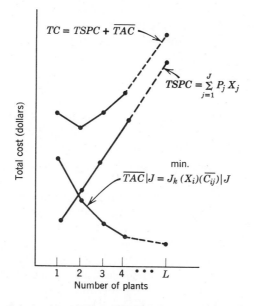

FIGURE 8.8   The minimized total assembly and the processing plant cost for a fixed volume of raw product. (See Section 8.7 for details and definitions of terms.)

assigning the fixed supplies of raw potatoes at each production origin to that plant which minimizes assembly costs from that origin. This is possible because of the assumption of equal FOB plant prices (see Mathia and King, 1962). The assembly cost-distance relationship in terms of road miles for a two-ton truck is estimated as follows:

$$C = \$5.14 + \$.176D_R \qquad (8.1)$$

where C is total assembly costs in dollars per load and D_R is distance in road miles, round trip.

The important variables affecting total season processing cost are rate of plant operation, length of operating season, percent trim and peel loss, percent of rated capacity, and length of planning horizon. On the assumption of full capacity operations and a 10-year planning horizon, the processing cost equation fitted by least-squares regression to the data for the four model plants described by Hammond (1961) is as follows:

$$TSPC = 30{,}560.00 + 26.73H + 173.50R + \qquad (8.2)$$
$$226.50T + 2.324HR + .02662HRT$$

where $TSPC$ = total season processing costs
      H = hours of operation per season
      R = rate of operation in cases per hour
      T = percent trim and peel loss.

The procedure used for determining the optimum rates of output and lengths of season for varying volumes processed is shown in the mathematical note. The linear total cost equation fitted by least-squares regression to estimated $TSPC$ for varying rates of output and lengths of season with trim and peel loss of 40 percent is

$$TSPC^* = \$82,781 + \$3.4906V \qquad (8.3)$$

where $TSPC^*$ is minimum total season processing costs and V is volume of output in cases per season. The intercept value of $82,781$ represents an estimate of the minimum annual cost of establishing and maintaining a processing plant. This minimum value is used in determining the number of plants required to minimize combined assembly and processing costs.

To estimate the minimum costs of assembling sweet potatoes with varying numbers of plants is a sizable computational task. If 22 possible plant sites are considered and one site is to be selected, the minimum assembly cost is selected by assigning the total volume to each of the 22 plants in succession and by selecting the plant site representing the minimum costs. When considering two or more plants, all possible combinations of the given number of plants must be compared by assigning the production at each supply origin among plants so as to obtain minimum total assembly costs.

The assumption of constant and equal marginal costs of processing in all plants simplifies the problem of deriving a processing cost relationship with respect to plant numbers. This assumption concerning marginal costs makes it possible to state the relationship between the total season processing costs and the number of plants as follows:

$$TSPC = bV + aN \qquad (8.4)$$

where $TSPC$ = total season processing costs
      b = marginal cost per case of processing sweet potatoes
      V = total volume to be processed in cases per season
      a = minimum season cost of establishing and maintaining a processing plant
      N = number of plants in operation.

Appropriate values of V and N were substituted in Equation 8.4 to derive each $TSPC$ by using the parameters of Equation 8.3.

The final step in determining the optimum number, size, and location of plants involves estimating total assembly and processing costs for varying numbers of plants. The relationship between the combined cost and the numbers of sweet potato processing plants in eastern North Carolina is presented in Table 8.1. Notice that one plant constitutes the optimum.

TABLE 8.1   The Relationship Between Number of Plants, Total Assembly Cost, Total Season Processing Cost, Total Combined Cost, and Average Combined Cost

Number of Plants	Total Assembly Cost	Total Season Processing Cost	Total Combined Cost	Average Combined Cost
	1,000 Dollars per Season			Dollars per Case
1	109.0	1,987.5	2,096.5	3.842
2	77.3	2,070.3	2,147.6	3.936
3	58.4	2,153.1	2,211.5	4.053
4	53.2	2,235.8	2,289.0	4.195

Since all possible plant sites were considered to have equal processing-input prices, including the price of green sweet potatoes, assembly costs and the production density pattern are the only factors that determine the optimum locations of plants. The location of plants is automatically specified in the process of determining the optimum number of plants.

The optimum location for one plant was Faison, which was the location with the lowest combined costs of $3.84 per case. Optimum location of plants in the 2-, 3-, and 4-plant industries increased the average cost by 9 cents, 27 cents, and 35 cents, respectively. The raw product supply areas and isotims that indicate the net farm prices associated with the four situations are shown in Figure 8.9a to d.

8.5   EFFICIENT DISTRIBUTION SYSTEMS

Similar methods can be used to evaluate the efficiency of distribution systems. A 1942 study undertaken to evaluate potential savings of tires, gasoline, and labor required by 55 dealers distributing milk in the metropolitan area of New Haven, Connecticut, indicated that alternate-day

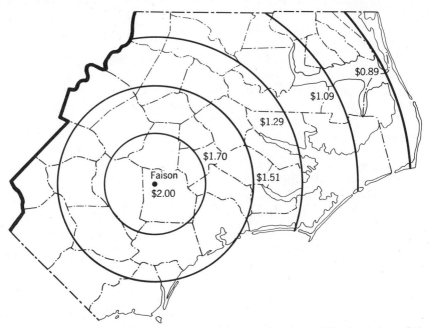

FIGURE 8.9*a* The net farm prices received by producers and the boundary of the supply area for the one best plant located at Faison, North Carolina, 1960.

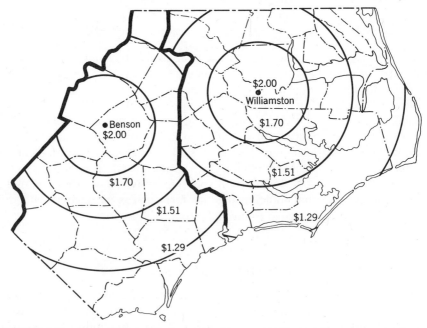

FIGURE 8.9*b* The net farm prices received by producers and the supply area boundaries for the best two plants located at Benson and Williamston, North Carolina, 1960.

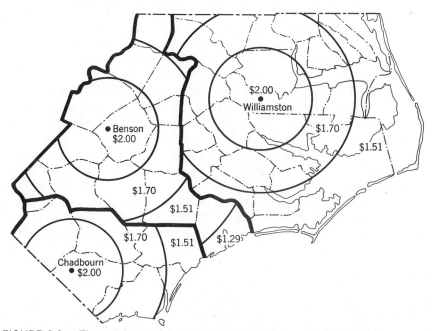

FIGURE 8.9c The net farm prices received by producers and the supply area boundaries for the best three plants located at Benson, Chadbourn, and Williamston, North Carolina, 1960.

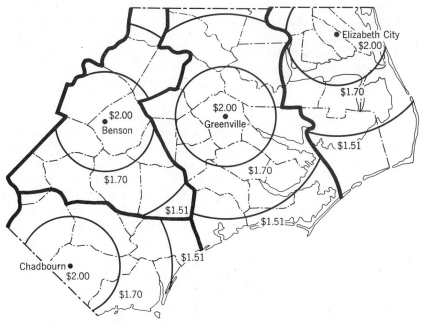

FIGURE 8.9d The net farm prices received by producers and the supply area boundaries for the best four plants located at Benson, Chadbourn, Greenville, and Elizabeth City, North Carolina, 1960.

delivery involved 72,936 quarts of milk, 217 routes, and a total route distance of 5284 miles per day. Customers were charged a uniform price regardless of location, and routes duplicated and overlapped to a considerable extent — the 5284 miles of truck travel involved only 700 miles of city streets. If existing dealer plant locations and volumes were maintained but deliveries were allocated through a system of efficient and exclusive territories, the resulting reorganization of routes would have accomplished the total delivery function with 123 routes and 829 miles of daily route travel. Estimated delivery costs could have been reduced from approximately 4.4 to 2.5 cents per quart, a savings of 42 percent representing in the aggregate more than $500,000 per year. This situation in New Haven, it should be emphasized, is by no means abnormal in the field of city milk distribution.

Savings in delivery costs will be maximized if all dealers in a market are involved, yet significant savings are available to smaller subgroups. In New Haven, three small dealers located in different sections of the area were studied. The delivery operations of these three firms were duplicated only in part because their small size and location had resulted in a degree of natural segregation. An exchange that involved 30 percent of all customers would have eliminated this duplication, and with route reorganization truck travel could have been reduced from 242 to 134 miles per day. Delivery costs could have been reduced from an average of 4.5 cents to 3.5 cents per quart — a savings of 22 percent. This would amount to nearly $12,000 per year, an impressive sum for three small firms handling an aggregate of only 3183 quarts of milk daily. Maps that show the actual and theoretical delivery territories are given in Figure 8.10.

Such duplication in distribution routes reflects imperfections in the competitive market structure and, especially, the segmentation of decisions where many firms are involved. Within a particular firm, however, principles of efficient organization may be followed much more precisely. Although routes of all dealers in a milk market overlap and duplicate, the routes operated by a single dealer are normally planned quite rationally and with minimum duplication. In a similar way, routes assemblying or collecting products from farms will usually involve important inefficiencies in duplication and less than optimum size, yet the routes operated by a particular firm will show compact and nonoverlapping areas within the confines imposed by the geographic scatter of the farms selling to this firm. In many cases, then, individual firms may be well adjusted to approximate cost-minimizing allocations, and yet the aggregate situation for the entire market may be quite inefficient. Stated in another way, the principles of location theory and competitive market or supply areas

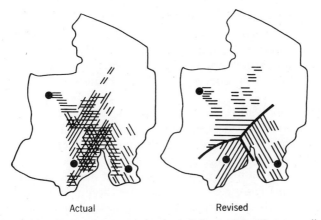

Actual   Revised

FIGURE 8.10   The actual and reorganized market areas for three small milk distributors in New Haven, Connecticut, 1942. [*Source*. R. G. Bressler, Jr., *City Milk Distribution* ("Harvard Economic Studies," Vol. XCI; Cambridge: Harvard University Press,
1952), p. 278.]

frequently will fail to describe conditions in actual markets, but they would
be good descriptions if the entire market operation were placed under a
single agency.

8.6 SPATIAL MONOPOLY

Our theoretical models have been based on competitive assumptions, yet
we have concluded that efficient organizations of market areas, collection
and delivery routes, and local plants all require the allocation of exclusive
territories. With such exclusive territories, the number of buyers (or
sellers) will be strictly limited, and the local market structure certainly
will depart seriously from the competitive assumptions. In short, there is
an inherent and unavoidable conflict between competition and efficiency
that stems from the element of spatial monopoly. To have even a very
limited number of buyers available at every location must mean duplication with unnecessarily high costs for all operators. However, the
assigning of exclusive territories to obtain efficiency leaves customers
confronted by a single operator and, hence, subject, to some degree, to
monopolistic exploitation.

That this is not unrealistic is suggested by the frequent use of devices
to absorb freight and hauling charges whereby operators discriminate
against nearby producers and subsidize the ones located at a distance
from plant. If farm-to-plant transportation is under the control of the plant

manager, this may take the form of a flat charge for transportation to all producers regardless of location. Or the competition for producers along the boundaries between plants may actually result in an inverted price structure: distant producers receive high prices in order to gain their trade, while nearby producers with limited alternative outlets receive lower prices.

Spatial monopoly also may be a major element leading to the development of inefficient instead of efficient organizations. Let us suppose that we have an industry organized in a regular and efficient system of hexagonal plant areas where the number and size of areas is consistent with the requirement of minimizing combined plant and transport costs. Such a grid is given in Figure 8.11. Consider the three plants located at *A*, *B*, and *C*; prices for the product *delivered* to these plants will be equal and, consequently, at-farm prices will be lowest at intermediate points such as *D*. Now, if a new operator were to consider entering this field, he might reasonably choose this low-price point for his location. Such actions by a number of newcomers would result in reallocating the area into triangular plant areas with twice the original number of plants. Moreover, low prices at points such as *E* would encourage the continuation of entry, resulting in small hexagonal areas that involved plants with one-third the original volume.

Apparently this process could continue until finally the costs would be so high that a single operator (perhaps a producer cooperative) would find it advantageous to buy out all plants in a section and reestablish the original, cost-minimizing organization. The important issue here is not the

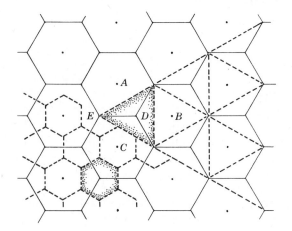

FIGURE 8.11   The degeneration of efficient plant organization as a consequence of the nature of spatial competition.

particular developments that might be involved in this decomposition, but rather that the nature of competition is such that the entry of an excessive number of firms is possible. These firms force inefficiency and high costs on the original plants and, hence, restrict their abilities to compete. When new plants enter, they reduce volumes and increase unit costs for existing plants. Similarly, the overlapping and duplication of collection routes results in excess capacity for all operators in lowered effective collection density and, thus, in higher than optimum costs. This tendency for efficient arrangements to decompose has sometimes been called the "law of mediocracy": because of spatial aspects, competition results in a uniform but unnecessarily high level of costs for all firms instead of the uniform level of low costs that could be achieved through efficient organization. Under these circumstances, location theory can be used to devise efficient organizations, but apparently the implementation and maintenance of them must require direct control by government (public ownership or public utility) or complete monopoly of the entire local marketing function by a single firm.

8.7   MATHEMATICAL NOTE ON EFFICIENT SPATIAL ALLOCATION

The analytical procedure for determining the number, size, and location of processing plants that minimize the combined assembly and processing costs requires statements of the relationships of these two functions to volume of output. The following model adapts the economic logic of location theory to the empirical analysis required in determining the optimum number, size, and location of processing plants.

Given I raw material origins each of which produces a specified quantity X_i of the raw material to be assembled and processed at one of L possible processing plant locations in the supply area, what are the number, size, and location of plants that will minimize the costs of assembling and processing the total quantity of raw material produced in the supply area?

Let

TC = total processing and assembly costs
TAC = total assembly cost
$TSPC$ = total season processing costs
L_j = location of plant j
P_j = unit processing cost of plant j
    $(j = 1, \ldots, J \leqslant L)$ located at L_j
X_j = quantity of raw material processed at plant j

X_i = quantity of raw material produced at origin i per production period

X = total quantity of raw material produced in supply area

X_{ij} = quantity of raw material transported from origin i to plant j located at L_j

C_{ij} = unit cost of transporting the raw product from origin i to plant j located at L_j and

J_k = one combination of locations for J plants among the $\binom{L}{J}$ possible combinations of locations for J plants, given L potential plant locations.

The assembly cost relationship is stated algebraically as

$$\underset{(J,J_k)}{TAC} = \sum_{i=1}^{I} \sum_{j=1}^{J} X_{ij} C_{ij} | J_k. \tag{8.5}$$

The total season processing-cost relationship is expressed as

$$\underset{(J,J_k)}{TSPC} = \sum_{j=1}^{J} P_j X_j | J_k \tag{8.6}$$

These two relationships are stated algebraically as a sum. The procedure is to minimize the combined function

$$\underset{(J,J_k)}{TC} = \sum_{j=1}^{J} P_j X_j \bigg| J_k + \sum_{i=1}^{I} \sum_{j=1}^{J} X_{ij} C_{ij} \bigg| J_k \tag{8.7}$$

with respect to plant numbers J $(J \leqslant L)$ and locations J_k $[k = 1, \ldots, \binom{L}{J}]$ subject to

$$\sum_{j=1}^{J} X_{ij} = X_i \tag{8.8}$$

$$\sum_{i=1}^{I} X_{ij} = X_j \tag{8.9}$$

$$\sum_{i=1}^{I} X_i = \sum_{j=1}^{J} X_j = X \tag{8.10}$$

$$X_{ij} \geqslant 0 \tag{8.11}$$

$$X_j \geqslant 0. \tag{8.12}$$

The procedure followed in minimizing Equation 8.7 with respect to plant numbers and locations is affected by the presence or absence of economies of scale in processing and the effects of plant location on processing costs. Four possible cases of processing relationships and their effects on the optimum number, size, and location of processing plants are discussed by Stollsteimer (1961). For the purpose of this example, it is assumed that (1) economies of scale in processing exist and (2) processing costs are independent of plant location.

The total plant cost function is assumed to be linear and positively sloping with a positive intercept, and plants at each possible location use the same production techniques. These limiting assumptions simplify the analytical procedure. French et al. (1956), showed that these assumptions are consistent with the cost-output relationship found in many processing operations. It is assumed that this type of relationship is satisfactory for long-run planning purposes.

Under these circumstances, the problem of minimizing Equation 8.7 with respect to plant numbers (J) and locations (J_k) is a three-step process. The first step is to compute a transfer cost function that is minimized with respect to plant locations for varying values of J. For a specified number of plants J there are $\binom{L}{J}$ possible combinations of locations.

The transportation cost table or matrix C_{ij} can be partitioned into a submatrix $(C_{ij}^*)|J_k$ for each combination of locations J_k. This submatrix $(C_{ij}^*)|J_k$ will be (IxJ), with the elements of the J columns representing the assembly costs from each origin to one of the plant locations being considered. A $(I \times 1)$ column vector $(C_{ij}|J_k)$ is obtained by selecting the minimum C_{ij} from each row of the submatrix $(C_{ij}|J_k)$. Minimum total transfer cost with J plants at a specified combination of locations J_k is the product of the row vector (X_i) whose elements X_i represent the quantities of raw material available at each of the I origins and the column vector $C_{ij}|J_k$. For each value of J there are $\binom{L}{J}$ values of $(X_i)C_{ij}|J_k$. The minimum of these values over J_k is the minimum point on an assembly cost function minimized with respect to plant location. This takes on the functional form of

$$\overline{TAC}|J = \overset{\text{min.}}{J_k}(X_i)\overline{C_{ij}}|J \qquad (8.13)$$

where $\overline{TAC}$ = total assembly cost minimized with respect to plant locations for each value of J ($J = 1, \ldots, L$)
(X_i) = a $(1 \times I)$ vector whose entries X_i represent the raw material produced at each of the I origins

and $(C_{ij})|J_k =$ a vector whose entries c_{ij} represent minimum transfer cost between each origin and a specified combination of locations J_k for J plants.

The second step in determining the optimum number, size, and location of processing plants is to derive the relationship between the cost of processing a fixed quantity of raw material and varying numbers of plants. With constant and equal marginal processing costs for all plants and a positive intercept in the plant cost function, the total cost of processing a fixed quantity of raw material X will increase by an amount equal to the intercept value of the plant cost function with each additional plant.

The intercept value of the plant cost function does not necessarily represent only the cost of durable goods associated with short-run fixed costs. A better description of this intercept value is that it represents the minimum costs associated with establishing and maintaining a processing plant.

The final step in this three-step process is to derive a total combined cost function by adding the total assembly cost function $\overline{TAC}$ and the total processing cost function $TSPC$ for varying numbers of plants. The number of plants which minimizes this total cost function (TC) depends on the rates of change in $\overline{TAC}$ and $TSPC$. Since the $\overline{TAC}$ function would be expected to decline and $TSPC$ to increase as the number of plants increases, TC would fall only if the decrease in $\overline{TAC}$ was greater than the increase in $TSPC$. Figures 8.7 and 8.8 present an example of the expected shapes of the three functions and illustrate a two-plant optimum solution.

The amount processed in each plant is equal to $\sum_{i=1}^{I} X_{ij} = X_j$ for each value of J.

The procedure for estimating the optimum rates of output and lengths of season for varying levels of output (V) to minimize processing costs is a constrained-minimization problem. Total processing costs are minimized subject to the constraint that rate of output (R) times length of season (H) equals V.

The procedure to determine the optimum rates of output and lengths of season can be demonstrated for the total season processing cost function, $TSPC = a + b_1 R + b_2 H + b_3 HR$, where a, b_1, b_2, and b_3 are parameters.

First, form the function

$$Z = a + b_1 R + b_2 H + b_3 HR + \lambda \ (V - RH) \qquad (8.14)$$

where λ is an undetermined Lagrange multiplier.

Second, set the partial derivatives of Z with respect to H, R, and λ equal to zero and solve for the three unknowns simultaneously.

$$\frac{\partial Z}{\partial R} = b_1 + b_3 H - \lambda H = 0 \tag{8.15}$$

$$\frac{\partial Z}{\partial H} = b_2 + b_3 R - \lambda R = 0 \tag{8.16}$$

$$\frac{\partial Z}{\partial \lambda} = V - RH = 0. \tag{8.17}$$

Solve Equations 8.15 and 8.16 for λ

$$\lambda = b_3 + \frac{b_1}{H} = b_3 + \frac{b_2}{R}. \tag{8.18}$$

Solve Equation 8.18 for H

$$H = \frac{b_1 R}{b_2}. \tag{8.19}$$

Solve Equation 8.17 for R

$$R = \frac{V}{H}. \tag{8.20}$$

Substitute Equation 8.20 for R in Equation 8.19 and solve for H

$$H = \sqrt{\frac{b_1 V}{b_2}}. \tag{8.21}$$

Substitute Equation 8.21 for H in Equation 8.20 and solve for R

$$R = \sqrt{\frac{b_2 V}{b_1}}. \tag{8.22}$$

For any predetermined level of output V, total season processing costs are minimized when length of season H and rate of output R are given by Equations 8.21 and 8.22.

SELECTED READINGS

Efficient Area Organization

French, Ben C., "Some Considerations in Estimating Assembly Cost Functions for Agricultural Processing Operations," *Journal of Farm Economics*, Vol. 42, No. 4. (November 1960). pp. 767–778.

Henry, William R., J. S. Chappell, and J. A. Seagraves, *Broiler Production Density, Plant Size, Alternative Operating Plans and Total Unit Cost.* North Carolina Agricultural Experiment Station Technical Bulletin 144. Raleigh (June 1960).

Lösch, August, *The Economics of Location* (Translated by William H. Woglom with the assistance of Wolfgang F. Stolper). Yale University Press, New Haven (1954) Chapter 10, "The Network of Markets." pp. 109–123.

MacLeod, Alan and Miller, C. J., *Efficiency of Milk Marketing in Connecticut: 7. Milk Delivery in Rural Connecticut.* University of Connecticut, Storrs Agricultural Experiment Station, Bulletin 249 (July 1943).

Miller, B. R. and R. A. King, *Models for Measuring the Impact of Technological Change on Location of Marketing Facilities*, North Carolina State University, Agricultural Economics Information Series No. 115, Raleigh (September 1964).

Olson, Fred L., "Location Theory as Applied to Milk Processing Plants," *Journal of Farm Economics*, Vol. XLI, No. 5 (December 1959). pp. 1546–1556.

Seaver, S. K. and R. G. Bressler, Jr., *Efficiency of Milk Marketing in Connecticut: 8. Possible Milk Delivery Economies in Secondary Markets.* University of Connecticut, Storrs Agricultural Experiment Station Bulletin 252 (May 1944).

Stollsteimer, John F., "A Working Model for Plant Numbers and Locations," *Journal of Farm Economics* 45, No. 36 (August 1963). pp. 631–645.

Williamson, J. C., "Equilibrium Size of Marketing Plants," *Journal of Farm Economics* Vol. 44, No. 4 (November 1962), pp. 953–967.

PART III

FORM, TIME, AND SPACE DIMENSIONS OF MARKET PRICE

chapter 9

PRICE EQUILIBRIUM WITH ALTERNATIVE PRODUCT FORMS

In Part II we discovered that a single market may extend over a large geographic area with a market-wide structure of prices interrelated through transfer costs. In a similar way, a market may be viewed as extending through alternative and successive forms of a product with a consistent structure of prices interrelated through processing costs—the costs of changing product form. The changes in product form to which we refer result from operations performed on a given basic product or raw material. They may be relatively minor, as in the packaging of a product, or they may be quite substantial, as in the processing of wheat into flour and the baking of flour into bread or a variety of other finished products. In a perfect market these man-made differences in form would be reflected in price differences, with prices for the raw product, semifinished, and finished goods all interrelated through processing costs.

9.1 PRODUCT FORM CHOICES

Consider alternative uses for a raw product at a particular geographic location with any particular use yielding n units of finished product per unit of raw material at a cost c per unit of finished product. If it is

163

economical to produce this product, competition in a perfect market will keep the price of the finished product (p) and of the raw material (P) in line so that the net value of the finished product less processing costs will equal the price of the raw material

$$P = n(p-c). \tag{9.1}$$

Again, notice that this equality will hold true in a perfect market if it is economical to process the product. If p is lower than specified in the Equation 9.1, processors would incur losses, and the product would not be made; if higher, the abnormal profits would attract firms to this enterprise until the equilibrium relationship is restored.

With a number of alternative finished products (m) from the given raw material (r), each would be characterized by such a net value equation:

$$\begin{aligned} P_r &= n_1(p_1 - c_1) \\ P_r &= n_2(p_2 - c_2) \\ &\cdots \cdots \\ P_r &= n_m(p_m - c_m). \end{aligned} \tag{9.2}$$

Since all net values will equal the price of the raw material P_r, in equilibrium, the net values in all uses must be equal, or

$$n_1(p_1 - c_1) = n_2(p_2 - c_2) = \cdots = n_m(p_m - c_m). \tag{9.3}$$

9.2 PRODUCT PRICE BOUNDARIES

The student will recognize the similarity between this formulation and the price equations for markets in space. By parallel argument, if the net value for the raw product in finished product 1 is higher than in any other form, then the material falls in the market for product 1; if lower, then the raw material is not in the market for product 1 but for some other finished product i; and if exactly equal, then the material falls on the "boundary of indifference" between two finished product markets.

To use a specific example, a supply of milk from a number of farms is available at a particular plant. This milk supply can be used in a variety of ways. It can be shipped as whole milk, separated into cream, or manufactured into various products such as butter or cheese. If we neglect by-products for the moment, we might convert 100 pounds of milk testing 4.0 percent butterfat into any of these alternatives (the indicated yields are only approximate): 100 pounds of whole milk, 20 pounds of 20 percent butterfat cream, 10 pounds of 40 percent cream, 5 pounds of butter, 10 pounds of cheese, or 47 pounds of canned evaporated milk.

Assume that the raw product is identical in quality for all uses with a price delivered to the plant of \$3.00 per hundredweight. And suppose that the following not unrealistic processing costs *per pound of final product* are involved: whole milk, 0.3 cents; 20 percent cream, 2.0 cents; 40 percent cream, 4.0 cents; butter, 8.0 cents; cheese, 10.0 cents; and evaporated milk, 4.5 cents. Under perfect market conditions, the prices for finished products at this plant will reflect exactly the raw product costs and processing charges. This is illustrated in Table 9.1. The first column gives the product yields (n_i) per hundredweight of the raw product. The second column shows the raw product cost per pound of the various finished products; the third column summarizes the processing costs per pound of finished product (c_i); and the final column shows the summation of raw product and processing costs to indicate the competitive prices (p_i) per pound of finished product. Thus, 100 pounds of milk can be converted into 10 pounds of cheese with a raw product cost of 30 cents per pound of cheese. Adding processing costs of 10 cents results in a final product price of 40 cents per pound of cheese.

Actually, the alternative uses in this case and in many others do not always result in single products. Instead, there are alternative plant operations with yields of products and of by-products. A plant that converts milk into cream or butter will have substantial by-products in the form of skim milk, and this in turn may be processed into products such as skim milk powder or condensed skim. The cheese operation will have a by-product in the form of whey or whey solids and with standardized

TABLE 9.1 Calculation of Hypothetical Competitive Prices for Dairy Products at a Single Location

Final Product	Yield per Hundredweight of Raw Milk (Pounds)	Cost Per Pound of Final Product (Cents per Pound)		Competitive Price of Final Product[b] (Cents per Pound)
		Raw Product[a]	Processing Costs	
Whole milk	100	3.0	0.3	3.3
20 percent cream	20	15.0	2.0	17.0
40 percent cream	10	30.0	4.0	34.0
Butter	5	60.0	8.0	68.0
Cheese	10	30.0	10.0	40.0
Evaporated milk	47	6.4	4.5	10.9

[a]Assuming that raw milk price, delivered to plant, is \$3.00 per hundredweight.
[b]Set of fluid product prices such that the six products are equally profitable at the selected location.

operations will normally yield a small butterfat by-product. Evaporated milk will have minor by-products in the form of cream, skim, or products manufactured from these items. The costs and values of these by-products, of course, will influence the competitive levels of all product prices.

9.3   ROLE OF PROCESSING COSTS

If all dairy processing plants had exactly the same processing costs (and if location and transfer costs are neglected), the manufacturing dairy industry would be in equilibrium when the above prices were realized. This equilibrium would occur through the interactions of quantities manufactured and the several market demand functions. As long as equilibrium prices have not been attained, processors would find it to their advantage to shift utilization of the raw product from those uses with relatively low net values for the raw product to those with relatively high values, and this shifting would continue until the net values for the raw product are exactly equal in all uses. In equilibrium, and with the conditions assumed, each plant would find itself indifferent to the use made of the raw product. It would be a rather precarious equilibrium, to be sure. In equilibrium, every plant would be without a basis for selection among uses, but out-of-equilibrium conditions would provide incentives for all plants to move in identical directions.

This extrasensitive equilibrating system could be "dampened" in its more or less random oscillations by lags in adjustment by some firms, so that only a few would be involved in the correction processes. Even under perfect market conditions, however, the market will result in precise and stable adjustments if we drop the assumption that all plants have equal and identical processing costs. If plant costs vary, and if some are especially efficient along one line while others have low costs in other alternatives, the interdependent supply and demand equilibria will not only determine the pattern of products processed and the equilibrium prices but also the particular allocations of plant processing facilities among the various alternative products.

Consider plants with differing costs of processing. By arraying these plants according to their relative processing costs (butter to cheese, etc.), we can develop the equivalent of an opportunity cost curve for the industry. In addition to differences in production or processing costs, plants will also differ with respect to location, and the resulting differences in transfer costs will be important determinants in the final industry equilibrium. The subject of markets in form and space, however, will be developed in some detail in following chapters.

9.4 SHORT-RUN PLANT COSTS

Price equilibrium with alternative product forms depends directly on processing costs for each. The theoretical foundation for analyzing processing costs will be sketched briefly here.

We define a plant as consisting of a collection of stages or operations that are carried on under a single roof or at one location under the direction of a plant manager. The short run is that period of time during which the plant — equipment, layout, and buildings — is taken as essentially fixed and during which choices are limited to the selection of proper levels of application of the variable factors of production. For simplicity, we first assume that this plant produces only a single product or multiple products in fixed proportions, thereby avoiding choices among products in addition to input levels.

Under any given set of technological conditions, production can be characterized by a functional relationship between output and the several input factors, a relationship that tells us what *flow* of physical output will result from the combination of any specified *flows* of physical inputs. The cost of producing this output flow then will be defined simply as the sum of the expenditures for the factors or the physical input flows multiplied by the appropriate factor prices. But notice that this will not define a *unique* set of input or cost flows for any specified rate of output. Rather, there will ordinarily be a large number of factor combinations that would yield this output (defined by the substitution possibilities inherent in the production function), and they in turn would be reflected in even larger numbers of cost possibilities depending on the factor prices.

For any given production function, the efficient organization will be represented by that factor combination that will minimize costs for any given output. This will be achieved when the marginal increments of product per dollar of factor expenditure are equal for all factors involved or when the ratios of marginal productivities are equated to the ratios at factor prices. These conditions define a unique set of outputs and associated inputs such that for any output the total cost will be minimized or, conversely, for any level of total cost the output will be maximized.

It is convenient to illustrate these procedures graphically. Figure 9.1 represents a physical production function where X_1 and X_2 are two variable input factors, and the curves ($Y_1, Y_2, \ldots$) show the ways in which the factors may be combined in producing the product. We assume that they are the only two factors involved. The same principles will apply for more factors, but mathematical instead of graphic treatment would be required. Each curve shows all possible factor combinations that will yield a particular output, there being one such isoproduct curve for every

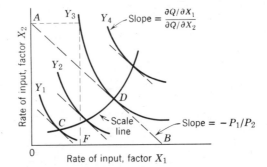

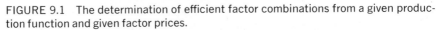

FIGURE 9.1 The determination of efficient factor combinations from a given production function and given factor prices.

possible level of output. The slope at any point on an isoproduct curve (dX_2/dX_1) represents the negative (inverse) ratio of marginal productivities $(\partial Q/\partial X_1 / \partial Q/\partial X_2)$, since it shows the increase in one factor that is required to offset the production effects of a decrease in the other. The specific shape of these curves will be defined by the production relationship—in the diagram we illustrate the principle of diminishing returns.

Any combination of X_1 and X_2 in this diagram represents a production possibility. With the given technology, the input of these factors will result in the indicated product. With any given factor prices, therefore, each level of output will be associated with a wide range of possible costs. This is suggested by the scatter of cost-output points in Figure 9.2. In addition, inefficient management may fail to exploit the technological possibilities. This would mean higher costs and a wider scatter of points in Figure 9.2. The problem of the efficient combination of factors is solved

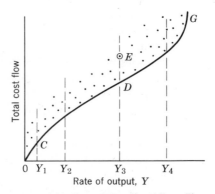

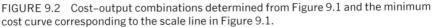

FIGURE 9.2 Cost–output combinations determined from Figure 9.1 and the minimum cost curve corresponding to the scale line in Figure 9.1.

by the selection of those combinations that will minimize costs for any output.

Returning to Figure 9.1, we find that any given total cost or outlay for specified factor prices may be represented by a straight line such as AB. The quantity OA represents the possible purchase of factor X_2 if the given expenditure were used entirely for this factor or the total expenditure divided by the price of factor 2. In a similar way OB represents the maximum quantity of factor X_1 if only that factor were purchased, while intermediate points between A and B represent the various purchase combinations that are possible with the given total expenditure and the given factor prices. Notice that the slope of AB represents the (inverse) ratio of factor prices. Clearly, the most efficient combination of factors along line AB will be at point D since here output is a maximum, that is, this point lies on the highest possible isoproduct curve. By similar construction, it is possible to determine the most efficient combination of factors for every output. The locus of these combinations is the "scale" line CD. As pointed out, each of these combinations will represent a point of tangency between isoproduct curves and isooutlay lines. This means that the (inverse) ratio of marginal productivities has been equated to the (inverse) ratio of factor prices—the condition for efficiency described in earlier paragraphs.

Cost and output combinations from the contact line CD in Figure 9.1 when transferred to Figure 9.2 trace out the total cost curve OCDG. In line with our definition of efficiency, this set of points represents the minimum costs for any output, given technology and factor prices and, hence, takes the form of an envelope defining the lower limit of the individual cost-output possibilities. It is true, of course, that changes in factor prices will modify all cost points and will define a new set of efficient factor combinations and so a new minimum cost curve. But for each of these possible conditions, the efficient organization will be determined as indicated.

9.5 MEASUREMENT OF PLANT COSTS

The foregoing should serve as a general framework, but it requires modification to be useful as a guide to problems of quantification and measurement. For these purposes we must consider how actual plants are organized and operated. For any given plant, certain elements of technology and factor inputs have been selected from the many possibilities suggested in the foregoing section. Investments have been made, buildings constructed, equipment purchased and installed, and they define the technology within which the plant will operate. With this particular set of technology and fixed inputs, there will be a number of alternative production possibilities, although the ranges in inputs and outputs have been greatly limited. These are the short-run problems that face the decision maker.

We may represent the plant production function in much the same way as before. Assume that there are several variable factors; then the production possibilities will be reflected in a set of isoproduct curves. They are illustrated in Figure 9.3 and resemble the functions in Figure 9.1, except that they exist only within a limited range of input flows and for a limited range in the rate of output. With highly mechanized and integrated organization, these ranges may be very narrow, reducing in some cases to a unique expansion line or path or even to a single point. Within the limits imposed by this production function, efficient organizations will be defined as before in terms of marginal productivities and factor prices. It is clear that adjustments to changes in factor prices are now quite circumscribed and that the most efficient organization *possible* for the given plant may necessarily fail to equate the ratio of marginal productivities and factor prices. In Figure 9.3, for example, the efficient adjustments follow the contract line from A to B but then are restricted by the physical limits inherent in the plant itself. To expand production beyond Y_3, the most efficient adjustments possible with given prices will follow the limit BC. In this zone the ratios of marginal productivities are not equated to factor price ratios, but this adjustment is approached as closely as permitted by the production limitations.

These efficient combinations may be converted to a total *variable* cost curve as shown in Figure 9.4. Notice that there will be a discontinuity or "kink" at point B and that the impossibility of complete adjustment in

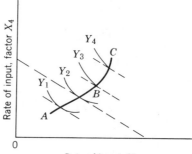

FIGURE 9.3 The instantaneous production function and scale line for a particular plant, illustrating the limited substitution and expansion possibilities.

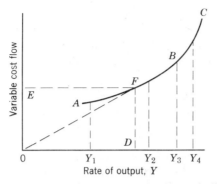

FIGURE 9.4   The instantaneous variable cost curve for an individual plant, derived from the production function and factor prices given in Figure 9.3.

factor combinations will result in more rapidly increasing costs beyond that point. Also, notice that the output range will usually be restricted at both low and high rates, as compared to the general production and cost functions discussed in the previous section.

It should be emphasized that Figure 9.4 shows only the sum of *variable* costs and does not include the costs for the "fixed" factors of production. These fixed factors are durable or semidurable capital goods, such as buildings and equipment, and to incorporate their costs into the analysis will require a consideration of the nature of capital and of the flows of inputs and outputs in production. It will be recalled that our discussion has been in terms of flows of resources — instantaneous rates in the case of continuous processes such as characterize most "factory" type production or rates per "production period" for discontinuous operations. When we speak of applying 50 bushels of seed and three tons of fertilizer to an acre of ground, we imply that this is in one season or production period. Similarly, we speak of combining factors in terms of rates of inputs in a plant, and the changes in output that result are, in turn, instantaneous rates (not the result of running the plant for longer hours or more days). The inputs of capital goods must be considered as rates or flows, there-fore, where the real input is the use or service of the capital good. Thus, our inputs are in terms of so many laborers, so much fertilizer, and the use of so much land and equipment during a season.

This creates real difficulty in defining the "prices" for the services of capital goods, since they are not completely consumed during the produc-tion process or the production period. It seems clear that over the useful life of the capital good these prices (multiplied by the inputs or use) must in the aggregate repay the original investment, must pay interest on the capital, including a return for risk, and must keep the equipment in a useful state of repair. In addition, government services are financed in part by property taxes levied on the basis of a valuation of these investments, and they are costs that also must be covered. To summarize, the capital goods will give rise to certain "fixed" costs, including depreciation, interest, insurance (part of risk payment), repairs, and taxes. To further complicate matters, depreciation consists of several components: (1) obsolescence because of technological changes, (2) depreciation as a function of time, such as would result from exposure to the elements, and (3) actual wear and tear associated with use—Keynes' "user costs." Moreover, there is an interaction between repair costs and the magnitude of the last two categories of depreciation costs.

9.6 HARMONY AMONG STAGES

Our discussion in Chapter 9 has thus far assumed that plant cost curves change smoothly with changes in output. However, we pointed out in Chapter 6 that some inputs are not perfectly divisible with the result that some stage cost curves increase in a stair-step fashion. The aggregation of two or more stages to derive a plant cost curve may also reflect such discontinuities. These discontinuities very likely will not occur at identical output levels at each stage. In a study by Rogers and Bardwell, we find that the 45 holding batteries used in the 2400-bird poultry processing plant are adequate for plants varying from 2400 to 10,000 broilers per hour, the two fork trucks from 2400 to 5000 broilers per hour, the three mechanical pickers for either 1800 or 2400 bird plants, although a second gizzard skinner is not needed until 5000 or more birds are processed hourly.

The effect of these differences in stage capacities is to introduce lack of harmony among the stages (Figure 9.5). At levels Y_1 and Y_2, stages 2 and 3 are in harmony in the sense that each is operating at capacity of the durable inputs, although output must reach Y_2 before all three stages reach harmony. This is one way of stating that at output Y_2 all stages are operating at full capacity, but at any other rate of output one or more stages will have unused capacity. In designing plants for least-cost operation, it will clearly be advantageous to minimize the excess capacity or lack of harmony in the several stages. Also, certain types of equipment may be more suitable for later expansion should this prove to be profitable.

A second reason for discontinuities in plant cost curves is the frequent use of two or more "lines" of equipment, each line representing essentially a duplicate set of equipment. Grading lines at a fruit cannery, bottling machines in a fluid milk plant, multiple "stands" in a cotton gin, and grad-

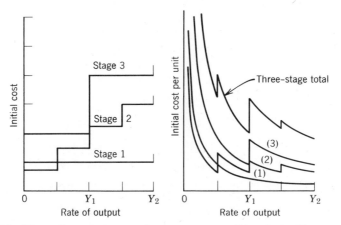

FIGURE 9.5   Discontinuous stage cost curves may result in a lack of harmony among stages.

ing and candling lines in egg packing plants are common examples. When multiple lines use some common items of equipment, such as retorts, homogenizers, suction unloaders, or forklift trucks, we again meet the problem of lack of harmony, making it desirable to schedule plant operations so as to take full advantage of the low points on the total average cost curve.

9.7   TIME VERSUS RATE DIMENSIONS OF PLANT OUTPUT

For any given plant, we have the type of instantaneous production function illustrated earlier in Figure 9.3. By following the procedures already discussed, we can determine the most efficient combinations of variable factors and derive the variable cost function as shown in Figure 9.4. Moreover, we can now select the most efficient rate of output where average variable costs are a minimum. This would be the rate of output OD in Figure 9.4.

Now let us consider the fact that this plant is operating through time. At any point in time the optimum rate of output is OD with corresponding rate of variable costs OE. Volume per unit of *time* (not the *production* period) may then be varied simply by varying the number of hours or days of operation at the efficient rate defined in Figure 9.4. Notice that external factors may sometimes prevent a plant from achieving this rate, in which event they would try to operate elsewhere on the efficient cost curve. For example, a sudden increase in the receipts of a highly perishable product at the plant may require a more intensive rate of operation than at point F. The results will be a variable cost curve like the one

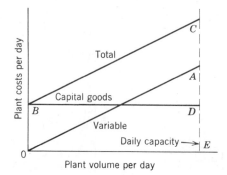

FIGURE 9.6   The variable and total cost relations for an individual plant where output is increased by operating for longer time periods.

illustrated by OA in Figure 9.6. The slope of OA is the same as the slope of OF in Figure 9.4, the minimum average variable cost per unit of output. Observe that, in expanding output by expanding the period of operation, we will not expect to find increasing marginal costs. In other words, if we operate a plant today exactly as we did yesterday, the average (and marginal) variable costs will be equal. The doubling of the total volume of output has not meant a real intensification on the fixed factors.

In terms of this concept of plant costs, it is not difficult to introduce the costs for capital goods, since both axes measure the aggregates (of cost or output) during a specified time period. Costs associated with the capital goods may then be expressed as a constant for the time period regardless of actual usage and will appear as a uniform addition to the variable cost relationship. Elements of "user costs" associated with capital goods, of course, will be included with variable costs. In Figure 9.6, BD represents the constant capital goods costs. Notice that this function is linear, that marginal costs are constant throughout the volume range up to "daily" capacity (OE), and that average total costs per unit decrease throughout this range as a consequence of the spreading of the constant capital goods costs. The use of the term daily in this and following discussions merely stresses the time dimension and does not imply that the day will always be the appropriate time span to use.

We stress that these findings do not disprove the principle of diminishing returns but merely refer to a situation where the flow rates of factors have been combined in efficient proportions and where volume is expanded by producing at this rate for longer periods of time. If the period of operation were fixed, say, at eight hours per day, then variations in output would involve changes in proportions with results comparable to Figure 9.4. Most empirical studies of plant costs have reported linear (or

nearly linear) total cost functions largely as a result of the above conditions. This will be especially true for highly mechanized plants with
assembly-line type of integration where the combination of factors and
the rate of operation are both fixed within narrow limits. Even when
variations in rates are possible, the alternatives may largely rule out
diminishing returns. In certain types of packinghouses, for example,
there are a number of packing "tubs" or "stations." The rate of pack may
be changed by increasing or decreasing the number of packers employed,
but this should not affect packing labor efficiency, since each station is an
isolated area independent of all others. This is comparable to saying that
we have available an acre of land and will vary output by using more or
less of it, always maintaining the *rate* of seeding per acre.

A three-dimensional illustration of the rate-time-cost relationship is
presented in Figure 9.7. Diminishing marginal returns to the fixed factors
are reflected in the sharply rising total cost curve in the rate dimension at
levels above Y_2. On the other hand, costs rise linearly in the time dimension. Costs of the fixed factors are reflected in the height of the "base" on
which the curvilinear surface rests. It is clear that marginal costs (changes
in the slope of the surface) and average variable costs are independent of
the size (height) of fixed costs.

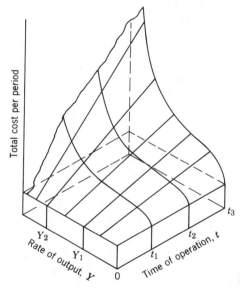

FIGURE 9.7   The total cost as a function of rate of output and time of operation.
[*Source.* B. C. French, L. L. Sammet, and R. G. Bressler, "Economic Efficiency in Plant
Operations with Special Reference to the Marketing of California Pears," *Hilgardia*,
Vol. XXIV, No. 19 (July, 1956), p. 573.]

9.8 MULTIPLE SERVICE PLANTS

The above discussion refers to situations where output is a single homogeneous good or service. In many, if not most, productive activities, however, several outputs are involved. The effects of multiple products on the organization of production can be clarified by considering five general cases: (1) joint services in fixed proportion, (2) outputs with varying composition, (3) independent services from a single plant, (4) single services that may be applied to several physical commodities, and (5) joint services with variable proportions.

1. Joint products in fixed proportions require no important change in the foregoing analysis. If production always results in a constant ratio of the outputs of service Y_1 to service Y_2, we can and should combine them into a composite output with units defined to include a units of Y_1 and b units of Y_2, a/b representing the fixed proportion. Having done this, our analysis of efficient factor combinations and minimum costs will proceed exactly as before. We point out, however that, although this procedure will permit the determination of average costs for the composite unit, any attempt to obtain average costs for each of the separate components must be based on entirely arbitrary allocations.

2. The second category of multiple products represents the case where there is one direct output but where the component parts of this output have separate importance and vary in proportion as the total output increases. This is frequently true of growth through time of plants and animals. Thus, the total "pounds" of a tree increase through time; and the proportions of saw timber, cordwood, and waste change as the total weight increases. Or we feed a hog through time and witness a typical growth reaction in terms of total weight, but the proportions of bone and waste, fat, and lean meat change along with the increase in the total. However, the peculiar aspect of this situation, is that there will be (for any particular "technology") a unique combination of component outputs for each point on the total output curve. Our efficiency problem may now be resolved as follows: (1) the combination of factors will be determined by the production function for the "total" output — this will define a total cost curve; (2) the revenue function will be obtained by adding together the revenues for each component part; and (3) efficient production will be determined by equating the addition to total combined revenue that would accompany the production and sale of one more unit of total product to the marginal cost of producing that unit.

3. The classification of several essentially independent services produced in a single plant may be visualized as the combination of two or more separate plants into a single producing unit. An extreme case would

be where a building was used to pack or process one commodity during part of the year (the harvest season for this commodity) and then was completely reequipped for a different packing operation during another part of the year. Less extreme examples would include plants receiving a single agricultural product, such as milk or fresh fruit, performing certain operations on the commodity, and eventually sorting or separating it into two or more components where the following processes are independent for each component. The essential character of these operations is that, although sharing certain common costs, beyond a certain point where the raw material is split into components the operations and costs for each component product are independent of other operations.

Figure 9.8 illustrates the situation for the extreme case of two

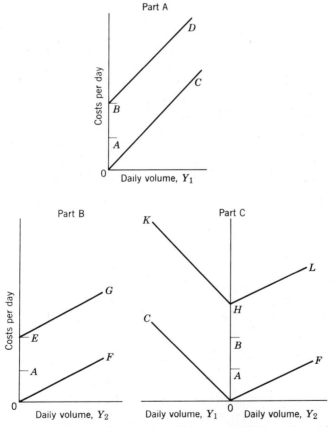

FIGURE 9.8   Independent services produced in separate plants and combined in one plant.

processes sharing the same building but with all other inputs and costs specialized for each process. Parts A and B show efficient variable and total cost functions for two specialized plants, and Part C shows the results of combining the two into a single producing unit. This back-to-back diagram emphasizes that the variable costs (slopes of the cost curves) are unaffected by this combination. Notice, however, that the combined fixed costs OH are less than the sum of fixed costs OB and OE for two specialized plants. If this were not the case, there would be no reason for combination. We have drawn these curves on the assumption that the buildings used for either specialized operation would be essentially similar to the building for the combined plant. The fixed building costs may be represented in all three cases then by an amount such as OA. Other fixed costs are related to equipment: AB in the first case, AE in the second, and AH (equal to AB plus AE) in the combined plant. In short, the operations are independent, and efficient combinations of variable factors will be determined for each "line" independently, but there will be some economics of combination that result from indivisibilities and the consequent unutilized capacity for some factors in the specialized plants. However, the "meshing" of the two operations will permit more complete utilization of these factors and hence, will lower combined costs.

Although it would be possible to illustrate graphically the case where certain plant operations are performed on the common raw material before it is divided into separate and independent operations, the ideas involved are similar to the ones already expressed. The nature of the problem is more readily revealed by a mathematical formula:

$$C = a + (a_1 + b_1 X_1) + (a_2 + b_2 X_2) + (a_3 + b_3 X_3) \ldots$$

where

$$C = \text{the daily total costs}$$
$$X_1 = \text{the volume of raw material}$$
$$X_2 = \text{the volume of one component product}$$
$$X_3 = \text{the volume of the other component}$$
$$a = \text{the common fixed costs}$$
$$a_1, \ldots, a_3 = \text{the fixed costs specialized to each operation}$$

and $b_1, \ldots, b_3 = \text{the variable costs for each operation or process.}$

The independent nature of the processes is revealed by the fact that this is an additive function and that, except for the common cost a, each line is independent and unaffected by changes in the other operations.

4. The fourth category of multiple product organizations turns out to be a case of single product production when the real output of the organiz-

ation is recognized. Many marketing activities create services where the service may in turn be *applied to* a large number of alternative commodities. This application, however, does not make the productive process a multiple service one — any more than the application makes a paint factory a producer of houses, barns, and battleships. A trucking firm is engaged in the production of transportation services, and its operations should be so analyzed regardless as to the variety of commodities transported. This is not to say that certain spatial costs may not be attached to particular commodities (containers, refrigeration, etc.), but they may be assessed directly to the commodities in question. And finally, the costs of certain loading, checking, and inventorying operations will undoubtedly be influenced by the number and diversity of commodities transported (or sold in a retail shop); but these operations can be analyzed as illustrated in the previous cases. In terms of average costs, this means that we can compute average costs for the services, but that any allocation to commodities will be arbitrary.

5. We come at last to the case of joint services with variable proportions. This is usually presented as the "realistic" case, although theoretical treatments have been most inadequate. One procedure is to assume that the cost function is given and available with the several outputs as independent variables determining total costs. Such a function will define a set of equal total cost or "isocost" curves as in Figure 9.9, here reflecting increasing marginal costs with increases in either output variable. From this point, the analysis is concerned with determining the optimum combination of products — optimum defined in terms of equating the ratio of marginal costs to the ratio of product prices (with competitive product markets). In the diagram, contact line DE will trace the locus of economical output combinations, and for each of them the appropriate costs are

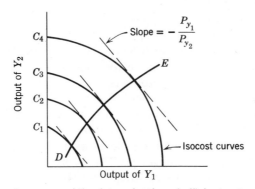

FIGURE 9.9   Isocost curves and the determination of efficient output combinations.

indicated. But this approach completely avoids the basic problem: *How are factors combined in order to determine the unique "given" cost function?*

A more sophisticated approach is to conceive the production function as $Q_1 = f(a, b, \ldots, n, Q_2, \ldots)$, where Q_1 and Q_2 are the joint services and $a, b, \ldots, n$ the factor inputs. This formulation at least has the merit of specifying the nature of the problem of joint products with variable proportions. It says in effect that there is, with any given technology, a functional relationship among several outputs and several inputs. By transferring all outputs save one to the right (independent) side of the equation and fixing them at some specified level (Q_2), we can vary inputs and trace out a consistent production pattern for Q_1. Other levels of Q_2 will result in different but consistent production patterns for Q_1, and for any of them it will be possible to define efficient combinations of factors by the conventional methods. By computing costs under these efficient organizations for all levels of Q_2, we can completely specify the cost function assumed in the previous case. At first glance this appears to be a reasonable and productive approach to the problem.

An apparently insurmountable obstacle arises, however, on further consideration. How are we to hold one output constant while permitting inputs and the other output to vary? What kind of a real production relationship would permit this? Or, if we conceive that it is possible to fix one set of outputs, then we must admit the possibility of *not* fixing it, in which case our production function explodes! What kind of a productive process (reflected in a production function) could take a given and unique technology, combine it with a given and unique set of factor inputs, and then result in a nonunique set of outputs? True enough, it is supposed that the several outputs would follow some specified substitution function, but we would never know just what particular combination of the possibilities would result.

Imagine, if you can, a cow that today might give 5 gallons of skim milk, or 2 quarts of whipping cream, or any combination of the two! We find it impossible to visualize such a cow, or such a function, or to admit that one could exist. Yet, the above formulation correctly specifies the nature of the problem of joint products with variable proportions. Consequently, we are forced to the conclusion that the problem itself cannot exist—that this is a "straw man" with no counterpart in real life. If this is correct, then it must follow that situations which appear to illustrate this joint products problem will, on closer examination, be found to fall under one of the foregoing categories. This is obviously true of the time-honored textbook illustrations of wheat and straw or wool and mutton. Proportions are not varied through a continuous function but by discrete changes in technology, changes in cultural practices, in breeds and varieties of crops and livestock, in crop rotation, and so on. We have been unable to find a single case where, with a given set of technology and inputs, anything but a unique set of outputs would result.

SELECTED READINGS

Alternative Product Forms

Alchian, Armen A. and William R. Allen, *University Economics*, Wadsworth Pub. Co. Belmont (second edition 1967) Chapter 14, "Costs and Output Programs," pp. 221–243.

Braff, Allan, *op. cit.* pp. 46–78, 140–154.

French, B. C., L. L. Sammet, and R. G. Bressler Jr., *Economic Efficiency in Plant Operations with Special Reference to the Marketing of California Pears, Hilgardia*, Vol. XXIV, No. 19., Berkeley (July 1956).

Lloyd, Cliff, *op. cit.* pp. 101–151.

Schneider, Erich, *op. cit.* pp. 70–109.

chapter 10

MULTIPLE PRODUCT FORMS AND SPATIALLY SEPARATED MARKETS

It became apparent in Chapter 9 that under competitive conditions the prices of all finished products derived from a common raw material must come into a particular equilibrium reflecting product yields and processing costs. If the price of one product form (or a set of products and by-products) falls below this equilibrium level, it will be unprofitable for firms to sell the raw material in that form and, hence, the product will not be produced. On the other hand, if a product price is above the equilibrium level, the raw material will be diverted from all other uses into this use. Such diversions of a raw product continue until prices are forced into perfect alignment through processing costs and equal net values for the raw material. Just as with spatially separated markets, the equilibrium mechanism is *arbitrage*; but here the arbitrage takes place in relation to alternative product forms.

It also became clear from our dairy products example that a given commodity will often yield products that differ widely in concentration, bulkiness, and value per pound. Thus, alternative uses of a hundredweight of raw milk included 5 pounds of butter worth 68 cents per pound, 10 pounds of cheese worth 40 cents per pound, 20 pounds of cream worth 17 cents per pound, or 47 pounds of evaporated milk with a market price of less than 11 cents per pound. It follows that transportation costs have a differing impact on each of the alternatives and that the simultaneous consideration of alternative product forms and the space dimension of price will establish an optimum pattern of production organization around a given market.

10.1 NET VALUES OF THE RAW PRODUCT

We begin our discussion of a market in form and space by first considering a very simple model where we neglect processing costs and by-product values. Suppose that we consider whole milk, light cream (20 percent butterfat), and butter as the only alternative uses. The first step is to find a meaningful way to compare the different market prices. For this purpose, we calculate an equivalent raw product price R_i for each by multiplying the market price P_i times the yield of the ith product per unit of raw product (in this case one hundredweight) k_i. In our example these equivalent raw product prices are $100P_m$, $20P_c$, and $5P_b$ for milk, cream, and butter, respectively.

Now we can compare the profitability of these alternatives at any location by expressing each in terms of the net value per unit of the raw product. Under our simplifying assumptions, this involves only the market price of each form, the product yields, and the transfer-cost function.

The net value of the raw product in each form can be written as follows:

$$N_m = 100P_m - 100(tD)$$
$$N_c = 20P_c - 20(tD)$$
$$N_b = 5P_b - 5(tD)$$

$$(10.1)$$

where m, c and $b =$ the milk, cream, and butter alternatives,

$N =$ the net value per hundredweight of raw product at a given location
$P =$ the product price per pound at the market
$D =$ the distance from the given location to market
$T =$ the transport cost per pound-mile of raw product.

The constants 100, 20, and 5 represent the several product yields in pounds per hundredweight of raw milk. We assume that transfer cost increases with distance but is identical per pound-mile for all products. Here we use a linear relationship with distance tD, but it is understood that transfer cost will normally increase with distance at a decreasing rate and that the transfer functions may differ for the several products.

In more general terms, we might write these net values as

$$N_i = k_i P_i - k_i t_i D \qquad (10.2)$$

where k_i = yield of the ith product per unit of raw product
$\quad P_i$ = the market price
$\quad t_i$ = transport cost per pound-mile for the ith product.

The reader will recognize these functions as similar to the single-product examples developed in Chapter 7. In each case, we visualize a geographic structure of net values or "at-farm" prices for the raw product, centered on the market and declining in all directions by an amount equal to transfer costs. Moreover, this geographic structure of net values will fall off rapidly in the case of a bulky product because of the relatively large quantities to be transported but very slowly for concentrated products where the total weight to be transported per unit of raw product is small.

These net value or equivalent price cones are illustrated by the cross-section diagram at the top of Figure 10.1. Here we show the fluid milk

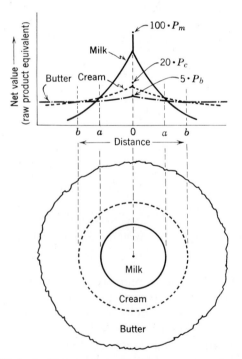

FIGURE 10.1 Efficient milk, cream, and butter zones around an isolated market.

price as high at the market center but declining rapidly with distance. Cream prices per hundredweight of raw product equivalent are lower but decline with distance at a more gradual rate. The market price for butter (again in terms of the equivalent raw product) is lowest of all, and for this concentrated product the geographic price structure is nearly flat.

10.2 IDENTIFICATION OF PRODUCT BOUNDARIES

Given market prices and transport costs, it is apparent that shippers near the market will choose to ship whole milk since the net value obtained from this use is higher than other alternatives. Farther from market, the cream alternative will be most profitable, although butter will be the optimum utilization at distant points. In this way, competition will bring about a system of product zones around the market as shown at the bottom of Figure 10.1. The boundary between any two products, such as the set of points a or b, is found where the net values of the two alternatives are equal. The boundary between the milk and the cream zones, for example, will be represented by the set of points a where the following equality holds true:

$$N_m = N_c. \tag{10.3}$$

By using the data from our earlier example, Equation 10.1, this can be written as

$$100P_m - 100(tD) = 20P_c - 20(tD) \tag{10.4}$$

or as

$$100P_m - 20P_c = 100(tD) - 20(tD). \tag{10.4'}$$

In short, the boundary is found at that distance where the difference in the market values (per hundredweight of raw product equivalent) is exactly offset by the difference in transfer costs. This principle will hold true for the boundary between every pair of products.

By solving Equation 10.4 for D, we find that the milk-cream boundary, in terms of miles from market, can be expressed as a ratio:

$$D_{m-c} = \frac{100P_m - 20P_c}{100t - 20t} \tag{10.5}$$

or, more generally, as

$$D_{i-j} = \frac{k_i P_i - k_j P_j}{k_i t - k_j t}. \tag{10.6}$$

It is now a simple matter to allow for differences in processing costs in this formulation since we merely subtract the appropriate costs from the net value equations. If processing costs are expressed in terms of *raw* product equivalents, Equation 10.5 becomes

$$D_{m-c} = \frac{(100P_m - C_m) - (20P_c - C_c)}{100t - 20t}. \tag{10.7}$$

However, frequently it is more convenient to express processing costs in terms of cost per unit of *final* product, as was done earlier in Table 9.1. In this case, the milk-cream boundary would be written

$$D_{mc} = \frac{100(P_m - c_m) - 20(P_c - c_c)}{100t - 20t} \tag{10.8}$$

or, more generally,

$$D_{i-j} = \frac{k_i(P_i - c_i) - k_j(P_j - c_j)}{k_i t - k_j t}. \tag{10.9}$$

A summary of the definitions used is provided in Table 10.1 to assist the reader in shifting between final product units and equivalent raw product units.

We observe here a general tendency of markets in form and space: bulky products will have relatively high prices at the market (in terms of equivalent raw product) and will be produced adjacent to the market, but concentrated products will have relatively low at-market raw product values and will be produced at a greater distance from the market. If this were not true, then there would be no location within the producing area where it would be profitable to produce the bulky product; the milk price cone in Figure 10.1 would always be below the cream price cone, and therefore the market would be unable to obtain a supply of this bulky product.

10.3 ROLE OF MARKET DEMANDS AND SUPPLIES

We have assumed that prices at the market were fixed and given and have proceeded to determine the optimum allocation of the producing area among the alternative products consistent with these given prices. It should be clear, however, that market prices and the allocation of product zones are, themselves, part of a multiple-price, *single-market* equilibrium. There exist various demands for products at the market center, each with its characteristic elasticity. The geographic production pattern for the basic raw material also will change with changes in effective at-farm

TABLE 10.1 Identification of Variables Used in Multiple-Form Analysis

Product Form	Market Price (in Final Product Units)	Final Product Yield per Unit of Raw Product	Equivalent Raw Product Price (R_i)	Volume of Output of Product i		Total Variable Cost for Product i	
				Equivalent Raw Product Units	Final Product Units (Q_i)	Equivalent Raw Product Units	Final Product Units
Milk	P_m	k_m	$k_m P_m$	V_m	$k_m V_m$	$C_m V_m$	$c_m k_m V_m$
Cream	P_c	k_c	$k_c P_c$	V_c	$k_c V_c$	$C_c V_c$	$c_c k_c V_c$
Butter	P_b	k_b	$k_b P_b$	V_b	$k_b V_b$	$C_b V_b$	$c_b k_b V_b$
Generalized	P_i	k_i	$k_i P_i$	V_i	$k_i V_i$	$C_i V_i$	$c_i k_i V_i$

Equalities:

Plant volume, $V = \Sigma V_i$.

Output of final product i, $Q_i = k_i V_i$.

Variable cost per unit equivalent raw product, $C_i = c_i k_i$.

Total variable cost for product i, $C_i V_i = c_i k_i V_i = c_i Q_i$.

Equivalent raw product price, $R_i = k_i P_i$.

Contribution of ith product to net income:

In raw product units: $NR_i = R_i V_i - C_i V_i = (R_i - C_i)V_i$

In final product units: $NR_i = k_i P_i V_i - k_i c_i V_i = (P - c_i)k_i V_i = P_i Q_i - cQ_i = (P_i - c_i)Q_i.$

prices. Market equilibrium will then balance off supplies and demands for each product, and the supply functions (and perhaps the demand functions) will be interrelated.

In final equilibrium, the supply function for each product will involve not only the prices and transfer costs for that product but the prices, transfer costs, and processing costs for all products. The quantity of cream delivered to market, for example, will increase if we raise the cream price relative to other prices. On the other hand, it will decrease if we raise either the milk or butter price. One can visualize the effects of such price changes as raising or lowering a price cone and observe the effects on the boundaries with other price cones in the system. Similarly, changes in transfer costs or processing costs will influence not only the product directly involved but also the supplies of all products. In this important way, then, the whole structure of product prices and zones is interrelated and interdependent.

It is easy to demonstrate that in a perfect market these equilibrium product zones will result in the lowest aggregate transfer cost for all products consistent with meeting market requirements of the several products. Suppose that we consider shifting one unit of raw product located at some point X in the milk zone from milk to cream use and that we compensate for this by shifting a unit of raw product from cream to milk use at any point Y in the cream zone. Notice that milk is the bulky product and subject to higher transfer cost per unit of distance in terms of raw product equivalent—it costs more to ship 100 pounds of milk than 20 pounds of cream. Point Y, therefore, must be farther from market than point X. Now, the indicated shifts represent a net increase in the distance that the unit of milk is shipped and an exactly equal decrease in the distance that the unit of cream is shipped. But, since it costs more to ship the raw product equivalent as milk than as cream, the net effect must be an increase in transfer cost. This will be true for any pair of points that we choose and for any pair of products and, hence, the competitive product zones must *minimize* transfer costs for the aggregate market.

Not only do these product boundaries define the most efficient allocation from the standpoint of transfer costs but they also represent the *maximum* aggregate returns to producers consistent with perfect competition. In our example above, point X is in the milk zone and this is closer to market than point Y in the cream zone. We know that the net value is higher for milk than for cream at point X, although the reverse is true at point Y. Shifting point X to cream would thus reduce net value, while shifting point Y to milk would also reduce net value. On both scores, then, such shifts would reduce the net value of the raw product. Since net values represent producer payments (at-the-plant), clearly, the competitive or free-choice zones permit consumers at the market center to obtain the demanded quantities of the several products at the *lowest* aggregate expenditure.

10.4 POINT TRADING, SPACE-FORM MODELS

To introduce the idea of two or more competing markets with several alternative product forms required in each, we use a modification of the transportation model that was discussed earlier (Chapter 5). As described there, the transportation model was a single-dimension model because shipping and receiving points were separated from each other in the single dimension of space. Now we make use of a multiple-dimension model in which shipping and receiving points are separated not only in space but also with respect to the form in which the product is delivered.

Transfer costs in this multiple-dimension model contain other charges in addition to transportation cost. The cost matrix now includes not only the cost of transfer between shipping point and destination but also the cost of transformation or processing. In this way we can simultaneously determine optimum locations for processing and interregional commodity movements.

To illustrate a two-dimension transportation model, a fluid milk example that uses six regions and two product forms is presented in Table 10.2. Surplus quantities may be moved to market from exporting regions in either conventional or concentrated form. Producers are indifferent as to the form in which the milk is sold, since the competitive market equalizes net returns from each after deduction of processing costs. Consumers, on the other hand, regard the two forms as different products. Requirements for each of the two forms are known for each of the importing regions. It is possible to allow for differences among surplus regions in the costs of converting milk into the concentrated form as well as in the proportion by which costs of transfer are reduced as a result of such processing. Transfer costs, then, for the concentrated form consist of the sum of the cost of processing and the cost of transportation, although the transfer costs for the conventional product include only the usual transportation costs.

An examination of the flow matrix in section 2*a* shows that the equilibrium solution to this problem contains a new item of information. By summing the quantities in the columns labeled "concentrated," we obtain an estimate of the processing capacity needed in each surplus region with the market in equilibrium. In section 2*b* the u_i values again indicate relative prices in the three exporting regions (before sign change), and v_j

TABLE 10.2 Six-Region, Two-Dimension Model (Space-Form)

Exporting Region	New England		South Atlantic		California		Surplus (S_i)
	Conventional	Concentrated	Conventional	Concentrated	Conventional	Concentrated	

Dollars per Hundredweight — Physical Units

2a. Cost-flow Matrix

Exporting Region	New England Conventional	New England Concentrated	South Atlantic Conventional	South Atlantic Concentrated	California Conventional	California Concentrated	Surplus (S_i)
Minnesota	2.70	0.50	3.20	0.54	4.00	0.60	
					$(7.5)^a$	(1.1)	8.6
Wisconsin	2.25	0.46	2.70	0.52	4.50	0.63	
		(1.6)	(4.0)	(4.0)		(6.4)	16.0
New York	0.55	0.30	2.60	0.45	8.00	0.75	
	(2.5)	(0.9)					3.4
Deficit, D_j (physical units)	2.5	2.5	4.0	4.0	7.5	7.5	28.0

2b. Equilibrium Cost Matrix

	New England Conventional	New England Concentrated	South Atlantic Conventional	South Atlantic Concentrated	California Conventional	California Concentrated	$-u_i^b$
Minnesota	0.68	0.43	2.67	0.49	4.00	0.60	0.00
Wisconsin	0.71	0.46	2.70	0.52	4.03	0.63	0.03
New York	0.55	0.30	2.54	0.36	3.87	0.47	−0.13
v_j^c	0.68	0.43	2.67	0.49	4.00	0.60	

2c. Cost of Using Nonoptimum Routes

	New England Conventional	New England Concentrated	South Atlantic Conventional	South Atlantic Concentrated	California Conventional	California Concentrated
Minnesota	2.02	0.07	0.53	0.05	0.00	0.00
Wisconsin	1.54	0.00	0.00	0.00	0.47	0.00
New York	0.00	0.00	0.06	0.09	4.13	0.28

Source. Richard A. King and William R. Henry, "Transportation Models in Studies of Interregional Competition," *Journal of Farm Economics*, Vol. XLI, No. 5 (December, 1959), p. 1004.
[a] Numbers in parentheses are optimum supply allocations in physical units.
[b] Producer price differentials before sign change.
[c] Consumer price differentials.

entries in the same section show price differentials between each market and the base region, not only for the conventional form but also for the concentrated form. Notice that Minnesota has been selected as the base region in this example. As in the earlier example, section 2c shows the cost of using nonoptimum routes which, in this case, provide information on the added cost of locating processing facilities in certain areas as well as the cost of selecting routes that do not enter the minimum transportation cost solution.

This space-form version of the transportation model has been used in a variety of empirical studies. For example, Snodgrass and French used this model to determine optimum locations of processing facilities in a study of the national dairy products market. The trade patterns shown in Figure 10.2 are not actual trade patterns for milk in fluid form or as evaporated milk, cheese, or butter. Instead, the calculated movements among 24 regions in the United States are the ones that would minimize processing and transportation costs. Movements within regions are not included. Notice that this map clearly indicates the dominant position of

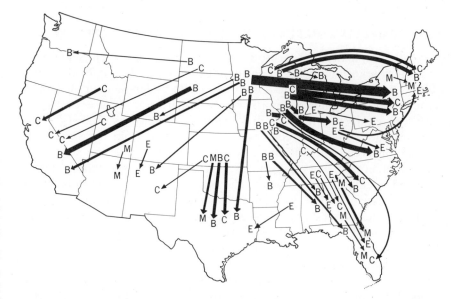

FIGURE 10.2   The optimum interregional movements of dairy products to minimize processing and transportation costs, 1953. M, fluid milk; E, evaporated milk; C, cheese; and B, butter. All movements in terms of milk equivalent. [*Source.* Milton M. Snodgrass, "Linear Programming Approach to Optimum Resource Use in Dairying" (unpublished Ph.D. dissertation, Department of Agricultural Economics, Purdue University, 1956), Table 23, p. 99.]

Iowa, Wisconsin, and Minnesota in the market for dairy products with product flows radiating out from this focal center. Butter is the predominant product in Minnesota and Iowa with cheese shipments intermingling with butter at the periphery of the central core. Virtually all regions other than the ones in the North Central States are deficit with respect to dairy products. Massive shipments are made to the population centers along the Atlantic seaboard, and smaller but important movements fan out to the southern and western states. Evaporated milk shipments are minor relative to butter and cheese and, for the most part, originate from the zones beyond the major butter-cheese producing areas. Interregional shipments of whole milk for fluid purposes would not be large as a consequence of bulkiness and high transfer costs, but some shipments are indicated to meet needs in New England, Florida, Texas, and the Southwest. Although the complete details of actual movements are not available to compare with these calculated and efficient patterns, the general organization of the industry is remarkably consistent with the model results.

10.5 COMPETING MARKETS WITH PRODUCTION DISPERSED

The full complexity of interproduct boundaries discussed in section 10.2 and intermarket boundaries considered in Chapter 9 is difficult to visualize. Therefore, to provide a more complete understanding of the price structure of multiple-form markets, we illustrate in Figure 10.3 a case with four competing markets or "dealers" identified as A, B, C, and D. Each of these markets receives milk and cream from the surrounding production area, with the most distant area serving as the supply area for manufactured dairy products. A variety of transportation methods are used, including direct haul to the plant, the shipment of milk by tank truck and cream by rail. In Figure 10.3, we find a reproduction of the type of price cones illustrated in Figure 10.1 except that now we have multiple cones surrounding each of the four markets.

The upper section of Figure 10.3 represents the net farm price surface for alternative products. Net farm prices are shown as cones centered on each market. The lower section of the diagram delineates the product supply areas for each of these markets. Sufficient milk is provided to each market to meet their fluid milk and cream requirements, with any remaining supplies sold in manufactured form. It is assumed that this is a deficit area with regard to manufactured dairy products so that it is not necessary to consider equilibrium prices for milk other than that needed for milk and cream purposes. Plants that ship fluid milk or cream

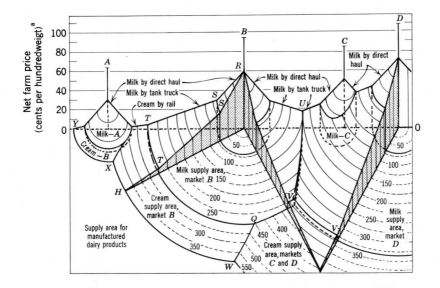

FIGURE 10.3   The net farm prices and supply areas for fluid milk, cream, and manufactured milk products, four-market model. [a]Relative to base price for milk sold in manufacturing outlets. [*Source.* William Bredo and Anthony S. Rojko, *Prices and Milksheds of Northeastern Markets*].

are located nearer to the markets of this region and pay a higher price to induce farmers to shift from selling milk to local manufacturing plants.

Markets B and D are the major markets in the region. Both compete for the same milk supply areas. Since the demand for milk in market D is large and D is the most distant from the surplus-milk producing area (being located on the edge of the region), prices in this market are higher than in market B. The farm price surface is higher around D than around B to permit both the milk and cream supply areas of D to encroach on the supply area of B. In this example, the milk supply area for market D extends approximately 330 miles with the line *UV* forming the market boundary with the milk supply area of market B. The cream supply area of market D is in contact with both the milk and cream supply areas of market B along the boundary *VQW*. The cream supply area of D extends 550 miles, whereas that of B extends 350 miles.

The milk supply area of market C, a small secondary market, is completely surrounded by the milk supply area for D. The price of milk in C is lower than but is directly related to the milk price in D. On the intermarket boundary, the milk producer chooses between shipping direct to the city plant at C or selling to a country receiving plant which in turn ships milk to D. The cream requirements of market C are obtained from the same general area as the cream supply area of D.

These intermarket boundaries could now be defined in algebraic form as was done earlier for product boundaries. Clearly, it would be necessary to add a subscript referring to market as well as a subscript identifying product form. This, however, will be left to the interested reader to do for himself. The theory is clear—so long as the net price for a particular product form in one market exceeds that of all other forms in that market as well as that for every form in all other markets, producers will choose the first alternative. Whenever it becomes profitable to change form or to shift to another market, the producer will do so under competitive conditions. The set of points at which net prices of products shipped to any two markets are equal will form the intermarket boundaries shown in Figure 10.3. In some cases, for instance, in the case of market boundary *UV*, the market boundary will divide a given product zone, such as the area engaged in the shipment of fluid milk by tank truck. In other cases, however, such as the eastern edge of the milk market around A, the boundary will separate fluid milk shipped to one market, A, from cream shipped to another market, B.

An empirical example of the usefulness of this model is provided in Figure 10.4. Because of substantial differences in milk supplies in fall and

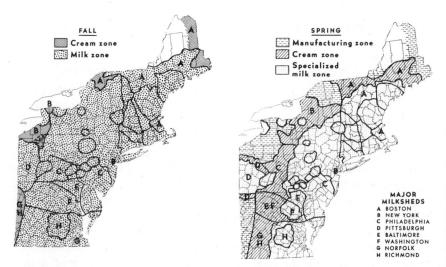

FIGURE 10.4 The location of milk utilization zones in the northeast milksheds. Major milksheds: *A*, Boston; *B*, New York; *C*, Philadelphia; *D*, Pittsburgh; *E*, Baltimore; *F*, Washington; *G*, Norfolk; and *H*, Richmond. [*Source.* William Bredo and Anthony S. Rojko, *Prices and Milksheds of Northeastern Markets*].

spring months, it was necessary to calculate the shape of the several milksheds for these two periods separately. At the time that the study was made, very nearly the entire supply of milk produced during the fall months was shipped as fluid milk. However, with heavier production in the spring, some areas shifted to cream and, in a few cases, to the production of manufactured milk products. Associated with these product zones are a set of imputed intermarket price differences that reflect demands in each market and the availability of supplies to meet these demands.

We now repeat certain generalizations concerning interrelated market prices. A change in the price of any product form in any market will influence not only the supply areas for other forms of that product in the given market but will also have effects on the boundaries between that market and every other market in the interconnected system.

10.6 SEASONAL VARIATION IN PRODUCT BOUNDARIES

Recognizing that demands and supplies vary seasonally for many products, we now inquire in more detail into the effects of such changes on plant operations. As suggested in Figure 10.4, seasonal supply and demand changes give rise to seasonal changes in product prices; and they, in turn, affect the boundaries between product zones. With a boundary between two product zones that varies from month to month, the result must be one zone that is specialized throughout the year in the shipment of a product such as milk, a more distant specialized cream zone, and a third intermediate, diversified zone that sometimes ships milk and sometimes cream. The general outlines of these zones are suggested in Figure 10.5. Our earlier illustration drawn from a study of northeastern milk markets shows that these diversified zones are not simply a theoretical possibility. Figure 10.6 identifies the geographic areas where the most efficient use of raw milk changes from season to season.

We now investigate the particular problems posed for plants located in these diversified regions. Let us consider the situation confronting the manager of a plant located in the milk-cream diversified zone, noticing that the general findings for this location are appropriate for other two-product diversified zones. We assume that the market is characterized by perfect competition. We also assume that managers act intelligently in their own self-interest and are not misled by some common accounting folklore with respect to fixed costs (although this is more a warning to our readers than a separate assumption, since it is implicit in the assumption of a perfect market).

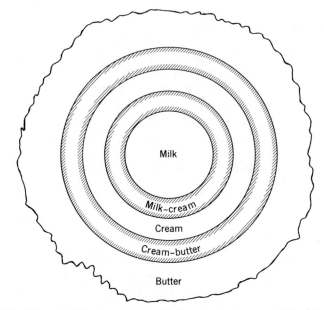

FIGURE 10.5   The specialized and diversified product zones resulting from seasonal supply and demand fluctuations.

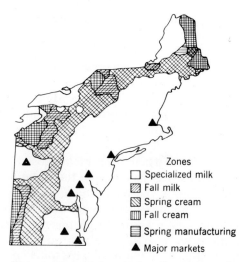

FIGURE 10.6   The efficient seasonal changes in milk, cream, and manufacturing zones for major northeastern milk markets, 1947 to 1948. [*Source.* William Bredo and Anthony S. Rojko, *Prices and Milksheds of Northeastern Markets*].

We assume that the plant in question serves a given number of producers located near the plant and that this number is constant throughout the year. Production per farm varies seasonally, however, so that even under ideal conditions the plant will handle volumes less than capacity during the fall and winter months. We assume that the plant is equipped with appropriate facilities so that it can divert its entire volume to milk or to cream shipment. Market prices for milk and cream vary seasonally, and to meet demands in the low-production period, milk prices change more than cream prices. With given plant location and transportation costs to market, this means that the manager is faced with seasonally changing milk and cream prices f.o.b. his plant. Our problem is to indicate the effects of these changes on plant output.

10.7 SELECTION OF PRODUCT FORM

Consider first the cost function for a plant. We assume that variable costs are constant per unit of output and that output of either product can be expanded at the specified variable cost per unit up to the limits imposed by plant equipment (capacity) and available raw product. This constant variable cost assumption simplifies the presentation and is, in fact, a good approximation to the situation in many plants.

In addition to variable costs, the plant operation involves certain fixed or overhead costs. They are independent of the volume of the several products but reflect the particular pattern of plant facilities and investments. As far as these fixed costs are concerned, the several outputs must be recognized as joint products. Although there are a number of ways in which these fixed costs might be allocated among the joint products, all are arbitrary.

Fortunately, such allocations of fixed costs are not necessary to the determination of firm policy concerning the selection of optimum production patterns. In fact, fixed-cost allocations would only serve to confuse the issue. We take fixed costs as given in total for the year, although even this is arbitrary, for the outputs of any two years are also joint products. The pertinent idea is that the firm should recover its investment over appropriate life periods. If it does not, it will not continue to operate over the long run; if it more than recovers investments plus associated costs, then the abnormal level of profits will induce the entry of new firms and return profits to the normal level. Many of the usual fixed costs are institutionally connected with the fiscal year, however, and for this reason the treatment of total fixed costs on a yearly basis seems appropriate.

Examples include annual interest charges, annual taxes, and annual salaries for management and key personnel.

In terms of total costs per year, we visualize a surface corresponding to a function of the type

$$TC = A + C_1 V_1 + C_2 V_2 \qquad (10.9)$$

where
A = annual fixed costs
V_1 and V_2 = annual output of each product
C_1 = variable cost per unit for product 1
C_2 = variable cost per unit for product 2,

all expressed in terms of the raw product equivalent. If we wish to express total costs in terms of the final products, we would write Equation 10.9 as

$$TC = A + c_1 k_1 V_1 + c_2 k_2 V_2 \qquad (10.9')$$

where c_1 and c_2 are variable costs per unit of final product, and k_1 and k_2 are final product yields per unit of raw product.

Total revenue to the plant is represented by product outputs multiplied by f.o.b. plant prices, or

$$TR = k_1(P_1 - t_1 D)V_1 + k_2(P_2 - t_2 D)V_2 \qquad (10.10)$$

where P and t represent market prices and unit transport costs — again multiplied by k_1 and k_2 to convert to raw product equivalent terms. Net returns, or the net value of the raw product, is represented by total revenue minus total costs, or

$$NR = TR - TC$$
$$NR = k_1(P_1 - t_1 D)V_1 + k_2(P_2 - t_2 D)V_2 - A - C_1 V_1 - C_2 V_2. \qquad (10.11)$$

If the manager wishes to maximize his net return (and under perfect competition he has no alternative if he is to remain in business), then he can calculate his optimum adjustments by using familiar methods. To determine the net-revenue maximizing adjustments, we take partial derivatives of the net-revenue function, Equation 10.11, with respect to each product, set each equal to zero, and solve:

$$\frac{\partial NR}{\partial V_1} = k_1(P_1 - t_1 D) - C_1 = 0$$

$$\frac{\partial NR}{\partial V_2} = k_2(P_2 - t_2 D) - C_2 = 0. \qquad (10.12)$$

We may substitute for C_1 and C_2 in Equation 10.12 the values c_1k_1 and c_2k_2. We also substitute the f.o.b. plant prices P'_1 and P'_2 for the corresponding market prices less transfer cost. The partial derivatives may now be written

$$\frac{\partial NR}{\partial V_1} = k_1 P'_1 - k_1 c_1 = 0$$

$$\frac{\partial NR}{\partial V_2} = k_2 P'_2 - k_2 c_2 = 0. \tag{10.13}$$

This merely confirms what we already know—that to maximize net returns, the manager should expand each line of production so long as f.o.b. prices exceed marginal processing costs. Notice that this optimum decision is in no way dependent on fixed costs or on any arbitrary allocation of these fixed costs.

But, under the assumed conditions, marginal costs are constant; and, at any time, f.o.b. plant prices are also constant. Apparently, the above equations do not define equilibrium adjustments involving the combined output of the two products. Instead, they tell the manager not to produce a product if price is less than marginal cost and to produce to the limit of plant capacity and available raw product if price exceeds marginal cost. For any set of prices, one or the other product will be more profitable, and the entire output of the plant will be in the more profitable alternative. In algebraic terms, we state the following rules for the manager.

$$\begin{aligned} &\text{If } (P'_1 - c_1)k_1 > (P'_2 - c_2)k_2, \quad \text{ship only product 1.} \\ &\text{If } (P'_1 - c_1)k_1 < (P'_2 - c_2)k_2, \quad \text{ship only product 2.} \qquad (10.14) \\ &\text{If } (P'_1 - c_1)k_1 = (P'_2 - c_2)k_2, \quad \text{ship either 1 or 2.} \end{aligned}$$

Since we have assumed that this plant is located in the milk-cream diversified zone, it follows that prices will make milk shipment the more attractive alternative during part of the year, and cream will be more profitable in other seasons.

We have assumed that product prices will vary seasonally and have observed that milk prices will vary more than cream prices. We have also assumed that the marginal or variable unit costs c_1 and c_2 are given and constant. We may restate the above profit-maximizing conditions as rules for the manager.[1]

---

[1]This is done by equating the partial derivatives in Equation 10.13, dividing through by $k_2 P'_2$, substituting to eliminate the two terms on the right-hand side, and finally multiplying the remaining terms by k_2/k_1.

$$\text{When} \frac{P'_1}{P'_2} > \frac{c_1}{c_2}, \quad \text{ship product 1.}$$

$$\text{When} \frac{P'_1}{P'_2} < \frac{c_1}{c_2}, \quad \text{ship product 2.} \qquad (10.15)$$

$$\text{When} \frac{P'_1}{P'_2} = \frac{c_1}{c_2}, \quad \text{ship either product.}$$

The manager will watch the ratio of f.o.b. plant prices and compare them with his marginal cost ratio. If the price ratio always exceeds the cost ratio, the plant should always ship whole milk and, thus, be in the specialized milk zone. If the price ratio always is lower than the marginal cost ratio, optimum operation calls for specialized cream shipments at all times. But if this plant is, in fact, located in the diversified milk-cream zone, then during some of the fall and winter months the price ratio will exceed the marginal cost ratio and the plant will ship milk. But during the spring and summer months, milk prices will decline relative to cream prices, the price ratio will fall below the marginal cost ratio, and cream shipment will be more profitable. Day by day and week by week the manager will make these decisions, and the result will be a particular seasonal pattern of milk and cream shipments. If the plant is located near the inner boundary of the milk-cream diversified zone, then it will ship milk during most of the year and cream for only a few days or weeks during the peak production period. Conversely, a location near the outer boundary of this zone will dictate cream shipments during most of the year with milk the more profitable alternative for a short period when production for the market is very low.

10.8 LONG-RUN ADJUSTMENT TO SEASONAL VARIATIONS

It may be protested that the foregoing analysis is incorrect because a plant that uses its separating equipment for only a few days must have very high cream costs. This is a common misunderstanding; it arises from the practice of allocating fixed costs to particular products. Nevertheless, a grain of truth is involved, and it can be correctly interpreted by considering the alternatives of specialized milk plant or milk-cream diversification near the milk and milk-cream boundary.

We have learned that the net value of raw product for the diversified plant can be represented by

$$NR_d = k_1 P'_1 V_1 + k_2 P'_2 V_2 - A_d - C_1 V_1 - C_2 V_2. \qquad (10.16)$$

In a similar way, we represent net values for the specialized milk plant as

$$NR_s = k_1 P_1' V_1 - A_s - C_1 V_1 \tag{10.17}$$

in which A_s represents the fixed costs for a specialized milk plant and C_1 the variable costs. We assume that the variable costs of shipping milk are the same in the two types of plant, although this may not be true and is not essential to our argument.

In our equations, prices are given in terms of the milk equivalent of the whole milk or cream and are expressed at country plant location. By remembering that the at-plant price is market price less transportation cost to market and that transportation costs are functions of distance, we can use these costs to define the economic boundary between the specialized milk plant zone and the transition milk-cream zone. For simplicity, we represent the transportation costs by $t_1 D$ and $t_2 D$ and give the expression for the distance to the boundary of indifference below:

$$D_{d-s} = \frac{(k_1 P_1 - C_1) - (k_2 P_2 - C_2) + (A_d - A_s)/V_2}{t_1 - t_2}. \tag{10.18}$$

Notice that this boundary is long run in nature; it defines the distance within which it will not be economical to provide separating facilities but beyond which plants will be built with these facilities.[2] The short-run situation would be represented by the margin between specialized milk shipment and diversified milk-cream shipments *where all plants are already equipped to handle both products*. From the material given earlier, it is clear that the equation for the short-run boundary will be exactly the same as the long-run equation, *except* that the fixed costs term $(A_d - A_s)/V_2$ will be eliminated. From this it follows that the long-run boundary will be farther from market than the short-run boundary. If a market has reached stable equilibrium, separating facilities will not be provided until a substantial volume of milk can be separated.

The actual determination of these boundaries will depend on the specific magnitudes of the several fixed and variable cost coefficients, the patterns of seasonal production, the relative transfer costs, and the patterns of seasonal price changes. Ideally, all of them interact to give a total equilibrium for the market. We may illustrate the solution, however, by assuming values for the various parameters and seasonal patterns. This has been done, with the results shown in Figure 10.7. Here we have

---

[2] We assume that equipment will have adequate capacity to handle total plant volume. The possibility remains that a plant would provide some equipment for a particular product but less than enough to permit complete diversion. As equipment investments and operating costs normally increase less rapidly than capacity, it usually will pay to provide equipment to permit complete diversion of plant volume if it pays to diversify at all.

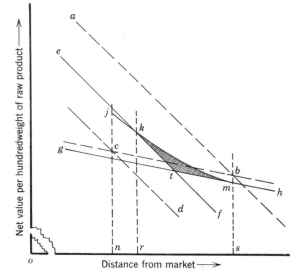

FIGURE 10.7 Seasonal price fluctuations and the boundaries of the diversified milk–cream zone.

assumed that fluid milk prices change seasonally; the prices minus unit variable costs at country points are represented by line *ab* for the high-price season and line *cd* for the low-price season. We have assumed that cream prices are constant. Although this is not strictly correct, it will permit us to indicate the final solution in somewhat less complicated form than otherwise would be necessary. The geographic structure of cream prices less direct variable costs is represented by line *cb*. Apparently, the short-run boundary between the specialized milk zone and the milk-cream zone would be at distance *on*, since at point *c* net raw product values would be equal in either alternative. Similarly, the outer short-run margin between the milk-cream zone and the specialized cream zone would be at distance *os*.

Consider the long-run situation where decisions as to plant and equipment are involved. For convenience, express all net values in terms of the averages for the entire year. The net value of raw product from specialized milk plants is represented by line *ef*. This line is a weighted average of lines such as *ab* and *cd*, each weighted by the quantity of milk handled at that particular price. The line represents the seasonal weighted-average price minus direct variable cost *and minus* annual average fixed costs A_s/V per unit of raw product. In other words, this net value line is long run in that it shows the effects of fixed costs as well as variable costs and seasonal price and production changes. Similarly, line *gh* represents long-run net value of raw product in specialized cream plants differing from cb by the subtraction of average fixed costs A_d/V. Apparently, the economic boundary between specialized milk and specialized cream plants would be at point t *if we prohibited diversified operations.* But we know that plants equipped with separators would find it economical to diversify seasonally in zone ns.

The increase in net value realized by cream plants through seasonal milk shipments is represented by the curved line *jkm* in the diagram. As we start at point m on the outer boundary of the diversified zone and move to plants located closer to market, an increasing proportion of the raw product during any given year will be shipped to market as whole milk. These milk shipments occur during the low-production season, as milk prices are then at their highest levels. Observe that these plants are covering total costs, including the costs for fixed separating equipment, even though a smaller and smaller volume of milk is separated. That is, the dominant consideration in this situation is the opportunity for higher net values through milk shipments — and not higher costs based on an arbitrary allocation of certain fixed costs to a diminishing volume of cream. Notice also that, under competitive conditions, plants must make this shift to milk shipment. Otherwise, they could not compete for raw product and, hence, would be forced out of business.

Although plants equipped with separating equipment would find it economical to ship small volumes of cream in the low-price period, even from the zone nr, the gains would not be adequate to cover the long-run costs of supplying separating equipment. This means that specialized milk plants (without separating equipment and so with lower fixed costs) are more economical in this zone. This is indicated by the fact that line *jkm* falls below the net value line *ef* for specialized milk plants in the *jk* segment. The boundary specified by our long-run equation is found at distance *or*, where net long-run values are equal to *rk* for both specialized milk plants and for diversified plants. Plants at this boundary would find it economical to ship cream for a month or two each year if they shipped cream at all. This abrupt change from specialized milk plants to plants shipping a fairly substantial volume of cream is a reflection of the added fixed costs, and this represents the previously mentioned grain of truth in the usual statements about the high plant costs involved in shipping low volumes of cream or similar products.

SELECTED READINGS

Multiple Product Forms and Spatially Separated Markets

Bredo, William and Anthony S. Rojko, *Prices and Milksheds of Northeastern Markets*, University of Massachusetts Agricultural Experiment Station Bulletin No. 470, Amherst (1952).

Cassels, John M., *A Study of Fluid Milk Prices*. Harvard University Press, Cambridge (1937). pp. 9–40.

Hammerberg, D. O., L. W. Parker, and R. G. Bressler, Jr., *Efficiency of Milk Marketing in Connecticut: 1. Supply and Price Interrelationships for Fluid Milk Markets*. University of Connecticut, Storrs Agricultural Experiment Station Bulletin 237 (February 1942).

Hassler, J. B. "Pricing Efficiency in the Manufactured Dairy Product Industry," *Hilgardia*, Vol. 22, No. 8, California Agricultural Experiment Station. Berkeley (August 1953). pp. 235–334.

King, Richard A. and William R. Henry, "Transportation Models in Studies of Interregional Competition," *Journal of Farm Economics*, Vol. XLI, No. 5 (December 1959). pp. 997–1011.

Leuthold, Raymond M. and D. Lee Bawden, *An Annotated Bibliography of Spatial Studies*, University of Wisconsin, Agricultural Experiment Station Research Report No. 25, Madison (August 1965).

West, D. A. and G. E. Brandow, "Space-Product Equilibrium in the Dairy Industry of the Northeastern and North Central Regions," *Journal of Farm Economics*, Vol. 46, No. 4 (November 1964). pp. 719–731.

chapter 11

TEMPORAL MARKET PRICE RELATIONSHIPS

In the preceeding chapters of Parts II and III, we discussed markets in space and form, observing that prices in these markets would be interconnected through transfer and processing costs. We now consider markets in time and to the parallel concept of market prices interrelated through storage costs.

11.1 THE TIME DIMENSION AND STORAGE COSTS

Just as production and consumption are most commonly carried on at points widely separated in space, so production and consumption are usually separated in time, and perhaps by relatively long periods of time. In some instances, for example, in many personal services, production and consumption are and must be simultaneous. The dentist produces his services and at the same time these services are "consumed"—a good example despite the fact that some teeth need not accompany the owner. Similarly, electrical power is generated and consumed almost simultaneously except in those cases that involve batteries for "storage." But in most cases there is a time lag between production and consumption, and the creation of *time utility* in bridging this gap is a productive activity (storage) that can be accomplished only at a cost in terms of resources.

We need not be especially concerned here about the particular nature of storage costs other than to point out that the operation usually involves providing certain physical facilities (warehouses, grain elevators, or storage vats and tanks) and that operating costs will normally be a function of the length of time period. Fixed costs will include the usual types of overhead expenses associated with the physical facilities plus certain handling costs, such as placing and removing the products, that will be necessary without regard to the length of storage period. Variable costs will include continuing items such as protection expenses, handling expenses related to storage time (for example, turning the product), fuel and power expenses in connection with heat or refrigeration, and interest on the inventory. The similarity between transport costs and storage costs should be clear, but it should also be recognized that storage refers to the time dimension and that some costs, normally considered as fixed in the usual production sense, will properly be considered as variable in this time dimension.

In addition to the direct *costs* of storage, changes in product characteristics during storage must be considered as a cost in terms of depreciated product *values*. Thus, commodities such as butter and eggs deteriorate in storage even under the best of conditions, and therefore the stored products will have somewhat lower market values than the equivalent fresh products. In addition to quality deterioration, there may be loss of weight or volume through evaporation, loss of weight and quality through insect damage, and so on.

Similar losses through time are the corrosion of metals and the degeneration of rubber and other materials. In some instances, of course, storage may enhance market value — as in aged cheeses and wines — but even here the product will degenerate if kept in storage for too long a period. All of these product changes (deterioration or improvement) can be expressed in terms of changes in market values and counted as part of storage costs. This is suggested in very simple terms by the diagrams in Figure 11.1.

11.2   TWO-PERIOD DEMAND CASE

The back-to-back diagram used to illustrate the two-region spatial equilibrium model in section 5.1 is equally helpful in understanding a two-period storage case. Suppose that a product is produced in period 1, say the harvest period, and may be consumed either in period 1 or in period 2 when no production takes place. We assume in Figure 11.2 that supply is perfectly inelastic, although this is not necessary to our argument. In the absence of storage of this product from the harvest period to period 2, the

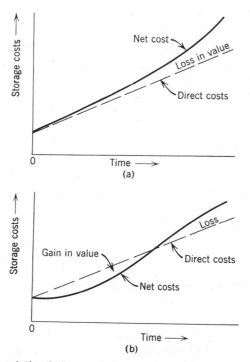

FIGURE 11.1 The relation between storage costs and the length of storage period including (a) Product deterioration; (b) Product improvement.

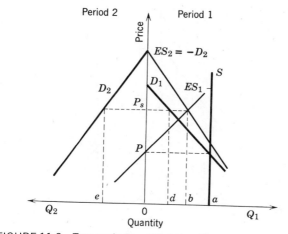

FIGURE 11.2 Two-period equilibrium with zero storage costs.

quantity a is consumed at harvest time at the equilibrium price P. We now construct an excess supply curve for period 1 just as was done in chapter 5. This excess supply curve passes through point P, is positively sloped, and represents the amount by which supply exceeds (or falls short of) the quantity demanded at every price.

The construction of an excess supply curve for period 2 follows our earlier instructions; namely, this excess supply curve represents the amount by which the available supply, in this case zero, exceeds the quantity demanded at each price. The obvious result of this subtraction is to produce an excess supply curve for period 2, each point on which is the negative of the corresponding point on the demand curve and, therefore, lies to the right of the price axis. (The reader is reminded that the quantity axis for period 1 is measured to the right of the origin and for period 2 to the left of the origin.) In Figure 11.2 the excess supply curve for period 2 is, thus, the negative of the demand curve for period 2; that is, ES_2 is the mirror image of D_2.

With storage, but in the absence of storage costs, the equilibrium price is found where these two excess supply curves intersect, or price P_s in Figure 11.2. Of the total supply a, the amount d will be consumed in period 1 and the amount b will be stored in period 1 for consumption in period 2. The obvious effect of storage has been to raise the price in period 1 and to limit consumption during that period while making possible consumption of the product in period 2.

We now modify Figure 11.2 to facilitate the introduction of storage costs. In Figure 11.3, we reproduce the earlier demand curves and the

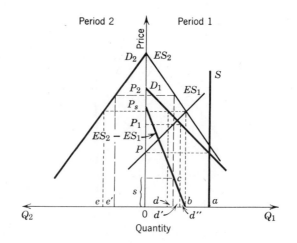

FIGURE 11.3   Two-period equilibrium with storage costs introduced.

supply curve and add a new curve representing the difference between the two excess supply curves labeled $ES_2 - ES_1$. As in our earlier spatial analysis, each point on this curve represents the vertical difference between the two excess supply curves. Now suppose that the storage cost per unit is represented by the amount s. We measure horizontally from point s on the price axis to our excess supply difference curve and find that this intersection occurs at quantity c. Reading vertically, we find that this quantity intersects ES_1 at price P_1 and ES_2 at price P_2 for period 1 and period 2, respectively. Again, reading horizontally from these prices, we find that the total supply is allocated between the two time periods in such a way that quantity od'' is consumed in the first period and od', which is equal to oe' by construction, is consumed in the second period. Equilibrium prices in the two periods are thus separated by the cost of storage, a result that is exactly comparable to our earlier analyses in which we found that the prices in two regions that engage in trade will differ exactly by transfer cost and that the prices of two forms of a given raw product will differ exactly by differences in the cost of processing.

It is also possible to analyze the temporal dimension of market price by using a slight modification of the transportation model. In Table 11.1, we show a six-region, space-time model in which the three exporting regions, Minnesota, Wisconsin, and New York, sell a given product (milk?) in three importing regions, New England, South Atlantic, and California, in each of the two periods. In this formulation the transfer cost from a given exporting region to a given importing region differs from period 1 to period 2 by the cost of storage. Any special costs required to prepare the product for storage would also be included. Here we have a perfectly inelastic demand curve in each region in each time period and a given quantity of output in each exporting region which is to be allocated among regions and between the two time periods.

The transportation-model solution provides information comparable to that described earlier. Section 1b summarizes the equilibrium cost matrix. The row identified as v_j represents intermarket price differences with the additional information concerning intertemporal price differences. For example, in New England, the equilibrium price, relative to the base region, in period 1 is \$1.85 and in period 2 is \$1.95, or a 10-cent differential between the two time periods. As in the earlier example, the $-u_i$ column represents export region price differences before the sign has been changed. Finally, Section 1c illustrates the cost of using nonoptimum routes, some of which here represent nonoptimum periods for storage. By summing the quantities in each period-two column in a given row, it is possible to determine the amount of storage needed in an exporting region. This example is vastly oversimplified, but it can be extended to larger,

TABLE 11.1   Hypothetical Six-Region, Two-Dimension Model (Space-Time)

	Importing Region and Time of Consumption						
	New England		South Atlantic		California		Surplus
Exporting Region	Period 1	Period 2	Period 1	Period 2	Period 1	Period 2	(S_i)
	Dollars per Hundredweight						Physical Units
1a. Cost-Flow Matrix							
Minnesota	2.70	2.80	3.20	3.25	4.00	4.20	
					(7.5)[a]	(1.1)	8.6
Wisconsin	2.25	2.30	2.70	2.80	4.50	4.55	
		(1.6)	(4.0)	(4.0)		(6.4)	16.0
New York	0.55	0.65	2.60	2.65	8.00	8.30	
	(2.5)	(0.9)					3.4
Deficit D_j (physical units)	2.5	2.5	4.0	4.0	7.5	7.5	28.0
1b. Equilibrium Cost Matrix							$-u_i$[b]
Minnesota	1.85	1.95	2.35	2.45	4.00[c]	4.20[c]	0.00
Wisconsin	2.20	2.30[c]	2.70[c]	2.80[c]	4.35	4.55[c]	0.35
New York	0.55[c]	0.65[c]	1.05	1.15	2.70	2.90	−1.30
v_j[d]	1.85	1.95	2.35	2.45	4.00	4.20	
1c. Cost of Using Nonoptimum Routes							
Minnesota	0.85	0.85	0.85	0.80	0.00	0.00	
Wisconsin	0.05	0.00	0.00	0.00	0.15	0.00	
New York	0.00	0.00	1.55	1.50	5.30	5.40	

Source. Richard A. King and William R. Henry, "Transportation Models in Studies of Interregional Competition," *Journal of Farm Economics*, Vol. XLI, No. 5 (December, 1959), p. 1005.

[a]Numbers in parentheses are optimum allocations of supplies in physical units.
[b]Producer price differentials before sign change.
[c]Transfer cost for active route used in developing equilibrium cost matrix.
[d]Consumer price differentials relative to Minnesota base.

more interesting problems including simultaneous treatment of form, time, and space.

11.3 MULTI-PERIOD DEMAND CASE

Arbitrage is the name given to the activities of individuals who buy in one market in the expectation of selling in another market at a profit, and we have illustrated how this is the effective mechanism that brings consistency to market prices through space. *Speculation* is the term used to describe arbitrage between markets in time. Thus, through the speculative actions of individuals, prices through time are interrelated by storage costs.

If we assume perfect knowledge as to the future (an admittedly unrealistic assumption to be discussed later), then traders will be informed about present and future supply and demand conditions. If the outlook is for significantly higher prices, products will be put into storage. This will reduce supplies currently on the market and, thus, force present prices up; it also increases potential supplies in the future and so will force future prices down. Speculation and storage operations will continue as long as the difference between future and present prices exceeds storage costs, since this excess will represent potential profits.

In equilibrium, then, future and present prices will differ by exactly the costs of storage, including normal profits. But notice that this is a one-way process always moving from the present to the future. If future prospects are for higher prices, storage operations can bring future and present prices into alignment. But if for any reason the prospect is for lower future prices, the discrepancies must remain because of the impossibility of inverse storage. The only moderation of the differential between present and future prices, then, would come from shifts in consumer demands through decisions to defer consumption until the later lower-priced period.

The relation between storage costs and prices is perhaps most apparent in connection with the seasonal production of nonperishable products. Most agricultural products are harvested during a relatively short period during the summer or fall months while consumption tends to be spread throughout the year. After the harvest there is no opportunity to change the available supply, but there are alternatives in terms of the distribution of the given supply through storage and sales operations. Consider the case with a given crop harvested in September with no carry-over from year to year, and with identical demand curves month-by-month through the year. Assume that storage costs involve a fixed "warehouse" charge plus a variable cost per month. For ease in presentation, we make the not unrealistic assumption that variable cost per month is constant. Under these conditions and with perfect knowledge, what patterns of storage movements, prices, and consumption will result?

The essentials of this problem are indicated in Figure 11.4 where DD' represents the demand curve for the product in any month. Month-by-month prices are represented by $P_1, P_2, \ldots, P_{12}$. Here P_1 represents the price in the market in month 1 (the harvest month, September) on the assumption that the product goes into consumption without storage. The price P_2 represents month 2, and is higher than P_1 by an amount equaling the fixed warehouse charge plus variable storage costs for one month. Prices $P_3, P_4, \ldots, P_{12}$ increase each month by the variable storage costs per month. Each of these monthly prices interact with the demand to determine the quantity to be sold $Q_1, Q_2, \ldots Q_{12}$ within the stated restraint that the total of the monthly sales must exactly equal the fixed quantity available from the harvest.

Consideration of this problem will indicate that the opening price P_1 is not *given*, as suggested in this diagram, but instead that this price — and, hence, the whole seasonal price structure — is determined by the available harvest, by the demands, and by the requirement that the amount available, and exactly this amount, will be distributed and sold throughout the season. This can be made clear by reexpressing our storage problem in equation form.[1]

We have given the following.

$$\text{Quantity harvested} = Q$$
$$\text{Monthly demand} = D_t = a - bP_t$$
$$\text{Storage costs} = C = d + eT$$

where Q = constant for the season in question
T = number of months in storage
t = the months from month 1 through month 12.

We assume a perfect market, and so we know that the following price relationship must hold true:

$$P_t = P_1 + d + eT.$$

In short, the price in any month must be the price at harvest plus storage costs. Finally, we know that the sum of the monthly quantities sold must equal the supply available from the harvest, or

$$Q = D_1 + D_2 + \cdots + D_{12}.$$

---

[1]For ease in presentation and comprehension, specific linear equation forms are employed. The analysis is general in nature, however, and not dependent on these particular forms.

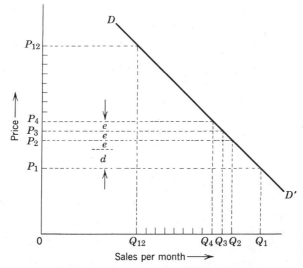

FIGURE 11.4 The seasonal prices and quantities sold, illustrating the storage problem with uniform demand across months.

Now, each of the monthly quantities in the last equation can be redefined in terms of the appropriate monthly prices as indicated by the demand equation, and each monthly price can be defined in terms of the opening price P_1 and the appropriate storage costs. With these substitutions, we obtain:

$$Q = [a - bP_1] + [a - b(P_1 + d + e)] + [a - b(P_1 + d + 2e)]$$
$$+ \cdots + [a - b(P_1 + d + 11e)]$$
$$Q = 12a - 12bP_1 - 11bd - 66be.$$

Notice that in this formulation we have simplified matters by assuming that storage and storage charges would be by one-month periods — in essence, that all quantities taken out of storage would be removed at a single time each month. With this, we have obtained an equation that contains the given total harvest Q, the given cost parameters a, b, d, and e, and the single unknown price P_1. For any assigned values for the constant terms, it would be a simple matter to solve for the opening price P_1 and to determine from this the prices and the quantities removed from storage and sold every month.

The general nature of the results of this process can be illustrated readily. The top diagram in Figure 11.5 shows the seasonal price and sales patterns and is drawn with price and quantity scales one-half those in Figure 11.4. Notice that prices increase abruptly between the harvest month and the first month of storage, as a result of the fixed warehouse

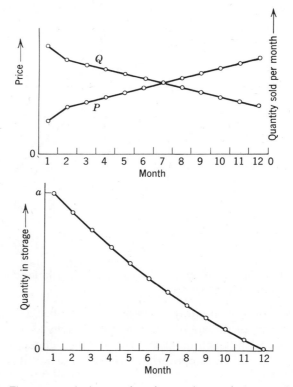

FIGURE 11.5 The seasonal changes in prices, sales, and storage stocks. (*Source.* Derived from Figure 11.4.)

charge, and then more gradually and regularly through the remainder of the season. Quantities consumed are highest during the harvest season of low prices and then fall off in conformity with the increasing price and the demand function. The lower diagram in this figure shows the total quantity in storage, with a quantity scale one-tenth that of the upper diagram. Obviously, the largest quantity in storage will occur immediately following the harvest, here represented by the quantity *oa*, and then the amount in storage falls off at a decreasing rate as smaller and smaller monthly withdrawals are made. Finally, the last remaining quantity in storage is withdrawn in the twelfth month and the cycle has been completed.

Figure 11.6 shows seasonal price cycles for a number of years on the assumption that all conditions including the quantity harvested remain constant from year to year. It should be understood that these examples have magnified storage costs relative to product price levels to emphasize the price and cost relationships involved. In many real situations, storage

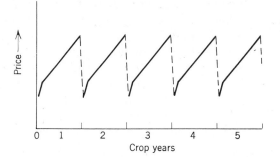

FIGURE 11.6   The seasonal price cycles over a number of years with uniform harvests and constant demand.

costs would be relatively small and seasonal price patterns corresponding-ly would be reduced in amplitude.

In some cases, storable products result from a continuous or year-round production pattern, but with seasonal changes in the quantities produced, in demand, or both. A familiar example is found in butter

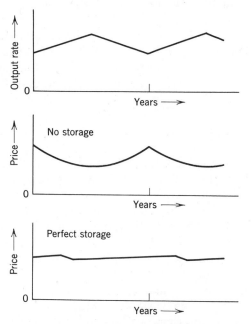

FIGURE 11.7   The price variations for a product having a seasonal pattern of production. (*Note.* The "no storage" price cycles reflect curvilinear demand functions.) [*Source.* J. B. Hassler, "Pricing Efficiency in the Manufactured Dairy Products Industry," *Hilgardia*, Vol. 22, No. 8 (August, 1953), Figure 3, p. 250.]

production where the flow of the raw material from dairy farms continues throughout the year but with wide variations between the spring and fall months. Without storage operations, these seasonal production patterns would give rise to substantial price fluctuations. But butter can be and is stored, and into-storage movements from April through July and out-of-storage movements from September through March level out the seasonal price pattern. This is suggested by the diagrams in Figure 11.7. The particular patterns for any commodity, of course, will depend on the production patterns, on the demands, and on storage costs.

11.4 CARRY-OVER BETWEEN PRODUCTION PERIODS

Clearly a carry-over of a commodity from one year to the following year will not occur if production and demand are constant, since identical price patterns year after year will not permit storage at a profit. But, if a large crop is followed by a small crop, the whole seasonal price pattern will be increased in the second year, and this difference in price may be sufficient for profitable storage with a carry-over from the first to the second year.

This situation is similar to trade possibilities between regions; trade depends on differences in prices, and these differences must be great enough to pay for interregional transfer costs. In the case of markets in time, however, "trade" must always go in one direction—from present to future time periods. This means that interyear trade under conditions of perfect knowledge can bring prices into perfect alignment when high-price seasons follow low-price seasons but cannot be effective when low-price seasons follow high-price seasons.

We have already explored the case of interseason storage; only minor modifications are required to cover the between-year situation. The basic idea is suggested by the construction in Figure 11.8. We assume two successive years and start by considering the case in which these years are isolated—in which no trade or storage occurs between the two. Suppose that the first production period has been characterized by abundant yields for the crop in question and that the second has been less favorable. The seasonal price pattern for the first year is indicated by the solid line to the left in the diagram. This has been developed as explained in the previous section; the shape or slope of this line is entirely dependent on the nature of storage costs, and its level reflects the total quantity available and the demand conditions. Seasonal price patterns for the second year are also depicted by solid lines in this diagram: Case A represents a situation in which yields are only moderately lower than in the first year

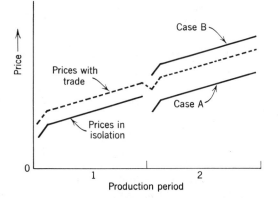

FIGURE 11.8   Interyear price differences with and without interyear trade.

and prices only moderately higher, and Case B represents a situation in which the available supply is substantially reduced with prices thus substantially higher.

When we remember that the slope of these seasonal price lines represents storage costs, it is easy to understand that interperiod trade will not be economical in Case A but that it will be in Case B. Prices are higher in Case A than in the preceding year, *but the difference is not as large as storage costs*. In Case B, however, the increase in price is greater than the costs of storage and, hence, trade between the two periods (that is to say, storage with a carry-over from the first to the second period) will be profitable. When trade is established between these two markets in time, the aggregate supplies available are brought to bear on the aggregate demands with price results as indicated by the broken line.

It may be revealing to trace out the general interactions by an extension of the equations used in the previous section. With the particular demand and storage cost functions specified earlier, the condition that the aggregate quantities consumed during a single year must equal the size of the crop available resulted in the following equation:

$$Q = 12a - 12bP_1 - 11bd - 66be.$$

All quantities in this equation except the opening price P_1 are given, so it is relatively easy to solve for P_1 and from this determine the entire seasonal price pattern and, hence, the seasonal storage and consumption patterns.

When two years are joined through storage into a single market in time, the appropriate equation becomes

$$Q + Q' = 2(12a - 12bP_1 - 11bd - 66be) - 12(12be).$$

The last term in this equation simply modifies (or displaces) the prices during the second season by the appropriate storage costs. With this expression, it is again a straightforward matter to solve for the opening price P_1, and from this generate the entire price structure over the two seasons. In turn, these prices will interact with the demand functions to determine month-by-month consumption, and they can be accumulated to show the patterns of stocks in storage and the carry-over between seasons.

The interperiod trade patterns are suggested in Figure 11.9 for a hypothetical case involving eight successive years. Crop yields in years 1, 4, and 8 are at "normal" levels. Years 2 and 5 have high production and, if trade between seasons were not possible, this would mean low prices in year 2 and especially low prices in year 5. Year 6 has production slightly lower and prices slightly higher than normal. Years 3 and 7 represent years of low production and relatively high prices. Let us trace out the changing situation through this span of years.

Prices drop between year 1 and year 2 and storage operations cannot influence this drop because of the impossibility of storing from a present to a past period. Prices rise between year 2 and year 3, however, and this

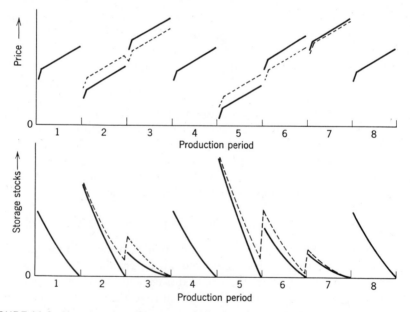

FIGURE 11.9   Year-to-year price changes and the effects of interperiod trade on prices and storage stocks. (*Note.* Solid lines show years in "isolation," broken lines interyear trade.)

rise is more than enough to cover interseasonal storage costs. The broken line spanning the two years represents the prices that will hold with storage and carry-over — this is the case illustrated in the previous Figure 11.8. The decline in prices from year 3 to year 5 again prohibits profitable storage operations, but prices move upward during years 5, 6, and 7. These three years provide an interesting example: prices in year 6 are well above those in year 5 and, hence, encourage storage operations. Prices in year 7, however, are little higher than in year 6, and this would seem to preclude any carry-over of stocks between these two years. Notice that prices in year 7 are high enough relative to year 5 to justify storage over the three-year period. More to the point, prices in year 7 exceed the price levels for years 5 and 6 *combined* by more than the added storage costs. Consequently, these three seasons will be united through storage into a single market in time, with prices throughout the period as shown by the broken line. Finally, production and prices return to normal levels in year 8.

The lower part of Figure 11.9 summarizes changes in storage stocks for these eight years. As in the upper diagram, solid lines represent the storage patterns for each year in isolation. The broken lines show the modifications that would result from interperiod trade in the cases where this would be economical. Notice that these with-trade patterns show stocks building up to higher levels than in the isolated cases. When interperiod trade is established, part of the supplies available in the low-price season (or seasons) is transferred and used to satisfy demands in the high-price years.

Prices are increased in the early years, consumption curtailed, and stocks correspondingly increased. The stocks remaining at the end of the first year are carried over to become part of the supply available during the following year. Observe the carry-overs at the end of years 2, 5, and 6.

11.5 FAT YEARS AND LEAN

A somewhat different type of interperiod storage is represented by the Biblical story of the seven lean years. It will be remembered that Pharaoh dreamed that seven well-favored and fat-fleshed kine came up out of the river and that they were followed and devoured by seven ill-favored and lean-fleshed kine. Joseph correctly interpreted this dream as foretelling seven years of plenty to be followed by seven years of famine. Pharaoh thereupon set Joseph over all the land of Egypt and Joseph took up and stored a fifth part of all the grain produced during the seven fat years and in all the land of Egypt there was bread during the seven lean years.

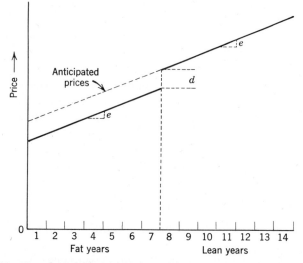

FIGURE 11.10 The perfect market price changes during seven "fat" and seven "lean" years.

In terms of our analysis of the perfect market in time, this story represents a period of high production and low prices followed by a period of low production and high prices. With perfect knowledge of future production, and with a given storage cost relationship, these fat and lean years could be interrelated as indicated in Figure 11.10. Figure 11.11

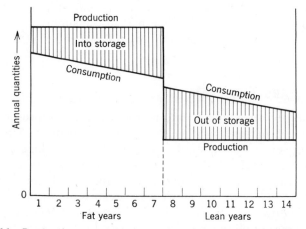

FIGURE 11.11 Production, consumption, and storage movements during seven "fat" and seven "lean" years.

shows the corresponding patterns of production, of storage operations, and of consumption. In this diagram the shaded area to the left represents the economical movement into storage during the fat years, and the equivalent area to the right represents the withdrawal from storage during the lean years. Consumption declines steadily throughout the period, even though the effects of the famine years are greatly moderated by the storage program. The pattern of consumption throughout the period would be more uniform, of course, if storage costs were lower or demands were more inelastic.

11.6   A SPATIAL AND SEASONAL ILLUSTRATION[2]

This example is drawn from a study of temporal and spatial corn prices in three North Carolina market areas—the northeastern Coastal Plain, the central Coastal Plain, and the Piedmont. The perfect market concept was used as a bench mark for developing hypotheses that describe the expected behavior of prices in the selected North Carolina markets. Theoretical price limits were developed for each pricing point by adding transfer costs to prices in markets from which purchases were made and by subtracting transfer costs from prices in markets to which corn was shipped. Out-of-state shipping destinations selected for surplus Coastal Plain corn were Norfolk, Baltimore, and Harrisonburg. Cincinnati was used as a pricing point to represent corn coming into the state from the Midwest.

Theoretical price models were developed for each of the three areas selected for study. To compare reported corn prices with expected prices based on these models, it was necessary to develop a framework for looking at several markets simultaneously in different seasons of the crop year.

At a specified time, prices in two markets trading with each other may be expected to be equal except for transfer costs between the markets. Harvest period prices in a particular market will be equal to postharvest prices except for the addition of storage costs. Differences in form or grade are reflected in premiums and discounts from a standard grade. Thus, by using storage costs and transfer costs between a local market and a central market, price limits for the local market can be obtained for a specific grade of corn.

Although prices in a local area may be correlated with the ones in

[2]This section draws on a study by Travis D. Phillips and Richard A. King, "A Spatial and Seasonal Analysis of Corn Prices in North Carolina," North Carolina State College, Agricultural Economics Information Series No. 95 (Raleigh, 1962).

central markets, the equilibrium price in a local market depends on the local supply and demand and the costs of bringing corn in or shipping it out. The procedure for deriving theoretical price limits over a season for a simplified two-market situation is illustrated in Figure 11.12. Price in a deficit area *aa'* will approach the major supplying area's price plus transfer costs. The price paid for corn from a smaller nearby surplus area may be *less* than the delivered price from the major surplus producing area but *not more* because purchasers can obtain all their needs from the major supplying area at the going price represented by points on *aa'*.

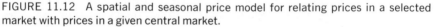

FIGURE 11.12 A spatial and seasonal price model for relating prices in a selected market with prices in a given central market.

Prices in a surplus area may go as low as the receiving area's price minus transfer costs *cc'*. Shippers in surplus areas, such as eastern North Carolina, may be able to obtain a higher price than this lower limit by shipping to a nearby deficit area. However, theoretical prices in the surplus area will not fall below this floor because all that is shipped could be sold at the going price represented by points on *cc'*.

The above model is highly oversimplified because an area may well be buying from or selling to several markets at a time. The slopes of *aa'* and *cc'* which represent storage charges should contain, in general, some curvature because of the high initial handling charges and possible economies from longer periods of storage. Also, although there has been little research that compares costs in different parts of the country, storage costs in buying and selling markets may not be the same. Therefore, the two lines would not be parallel. Adjustment for spatial differences allows a direct comparison of the observed prices with the appropriate theoretical selling or buying limit.

The perfect-market idea of a uniform price after adjustments have been made for form, time, and space offers a convenient framework for the development of theoretical price limits to be used as bench marks for understanding observed price relationships. This does not imply that the existing marketing structure operates as a perfect market, or that it should

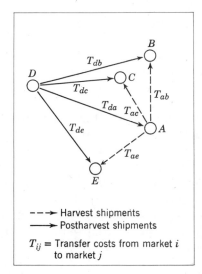

FIGURE 11.13   A simplified model of the seasonal shipment pattern of North Carolina corn markets.

so operate. To be consistent with the perfect market, observed prices may vary by amounts less than the extremes set by the theoretical price limits; price fluctuations that exceed the limits reflect changes in expectations or imply imperfection in the marketing system.

By integrating the theory of the behavior of prices in a single market with our knowledge of corn movements and marketing practices in North Carolina, we developed the hypothetical price relationships among markets. The relationships are shown graphically in Figure 11.13. The arrows indicate the major flows in each of two seasons. Market A represents a Coastal Plain market shipping to the Piedmont (market E) and to Virginia and the Baltimore areas (markets B and C). Market D represents the Cincinnati area, which supplies the deficit requirements during the postharvest period. Transfer costs T_{ij} represent the adjustment factors required to make prices among markets comparable.

The Coastal Plain furnishes roughly three-fourths of western North Carolina supplies during the harvest period and also ships large quantities to neighboring deficit areas to the north. In recent years, these shipments have gone to Norfolk and Harrisonburg in Virginia and to Baltimore and its vicinity. The remaining requirements for the Piedmont are met by imports from the Ohio-Indiana area. Although the quantity received during the harvest period is small, shipments from Cincinnati establish the upper limit to prices offered in the Piedmont for corn from the Coastal Plain. When large quantities of Coastal Plain corn are available, harvest-period prices in the Piedmont for corn from the Coastal Plain may be several cents per bushel lower than that from Cincinnati. During the postharvest period more than one-half of the corn fed in the Piedmont comes from the Midwest; therefore, prices in the Piedmont would theoretically be expected to follow closely the price of corn delivered from Cincinnati.

Much of the early corn produced in the northeastern Coastal Plain area is shipped out during the harvest period, so that later in the season small quantities are required from the Midwest. Under these conditions, postharvest prices in this part of the Coastal Plain should approach the ones for corn delivered from Cincinnati. The central Coastal Plain continues shipping small quantities of corn to the Piedmont throughout the year. These shipments to the Piedmont are too small to influence prices there; consequently, corn delivered from the Coastal Plain sells for roughly the same price as that delivered from Cincinnati. As surplus corn in the central area disappears, even though no in-shipments from Cincinnati occur, prices in the area approach the price of corn delivered from Cincinnati.

Although the perfect-market model implies a specific price at a particular time for a given market, a "price region" was used, indicated by the shaded areas of the models shown. Since prices in a market area would not be expected to change abruptly from the lower selling limit to the upper buying limit, the shaded area allows for gradual price adjustment as the type of marketing transaction changes.

Northeastern Coastal Plain. The northeastern Coastal Plain area is a surplus-producing, deficit-storage area with some corn brought back into the area during the postharvest period. The model for the northeastern area, shown in Figure 11.14a reflects the practice of pushing up the harvest date to take advantage of high prices still being paid in the Delmarva area for old-crop corn. The vertical distance *ag* reflects storage charges for corn produced the previous year and the prices paid in the

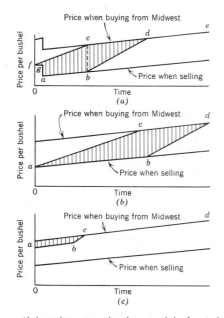

FIGURE 11.14   The spatial and seasonal price models for selected North Carolina corn marketing areas. (*a*) Northeastern Coastal Plain. (*b*) Central Coastal Plain. (*c*) Piedmont.

Delmarva area. The distance *ag* represents the gains from early harvest. Of course, prices received for corn in the Delmarva area would not be expected to change abruptly from *fg* to *ab* but would follow a relatively smooth path. The horizontal distance between the line *ag* and the price axis represents the length of time by which harvest in the northeastern area precedes harvest in major surplus areas that supply the Delmarva area.

The area *abcfg* represents the possible price range during the harvest period when corn is being shipped from the area. The transitional period between harvest and the period when corn becomes deficit and the importing activities increase is illustrated by the triangular area *bcd*. Toward the end of the crop year when some corn is shipped in, price is represented by the line *de*. These limits differ for each production, utilization, and storage situation and also depend on factors such as the disappearance rates and the mobility of corn stored within the area. The possible range for point *d* might be anywhere from point *c* to point *e*.

Central Coastal Plain. Storage relations for the Central Coastal Plain area were difficult to quantify. Since no corn was found coming back into the area during the postharvest period, it was concluded that sufficient farm and commercial storage capacity exists to satisfy local requirements. The fact that some corn continues to move out of the area in the post-harvest period indicates that storage capacity is, in fact, somewhat above this minimum level.

Theoretical limits for this area are presented in Figure 11.14*b*. Prices would be expected to lie along the lower limit *ab* for much of the crop year. However, as shipments to the Piedmont decline, prices in the area would be expected to rise toward the ones that would prevail if corn were brought in from the Midwest. These prices are represented by *cd*. To the extent that this rise is anticipated, a gradual price increase represented by line *ac* may be evident.

Piedmont. There appeared to be no need to investigate the case of deficit storage for local production in the Piedmont because practically all of the corn produced in the area is currently farm-stored and fed. Only about 1 percent of this corn, according to the survey, finds its way into marketing channels. The Piedmont is an area possessing more than adequate storage capacity for local production, but having far less production than that needed to meet feeding requirements.

As long as storage capacity does not exceed requirements, expected prices will lie along the upper price limit, since the only transactions with other areas will be purchases. Corn in the form of manufactured feed is shipped out of the area. However, the lower or selling limit has little meaning in this case, since corn alone is not shipped.

The price of corn in the Piedmont area theoretically would be expected to follow rather closely the upper import price line of Figure 11.14*c*. The price for corn shipped from the central Coastal Plain area to the Piedmont has an upper limit established by the midwestern shipped-in price. However, if the price for corn from the surplus Coastal Plain area is depressed during the harvest period because of a shortage of storage capacity, Piedmont paying price might drop to a somewhat lower level indicated by line *ab*. After this harvest glut, during which time surplus Coastal Plain corn is moved into storage or northward to export buyers or to broiler production areas, prices readjust to the upper limit along line *bc*.

These hypotheses of how market price relationships are expected to behave provide a basis for evaluating observed price relationships. Although reported prices generally conformed to the theoretical price limits, weekly prices often fluctuated widely. Movement of large quantities of corn from the Coastal Plain to the Piedmont during a relatively short period of time during harvest depressed Piedmont prices as compared to delivered prices from Cincinnati. The downward pressure on prices was positively correlated with the size of the Coastal Plain crop.

Several problems confronting individuals engaged in corn production and trade come to light as a result of these price analyses. First, wide weekly price fluctuations between prices paid producers and prices received by dealers arise during harvest in the Coastal Plain, apparently because dealers are buying on the basis of central market prices in areas to which they ship are influenced by local conditions. Changes over the harvest period in returns to dealers also may be associated with a shortage of drying facilities to condition high-moisture corn.

Second, although no data are available to determine the adequacy of present storage facilities, storage from harvest until the following summer in the Coastal Plain would have paid quite well in three of the five years studied. The price analyses indicate that forces outside the area cause seasonal prices to be quite unpredictable. Farmers and dealers may prefer a low harvest price to taking the risk of an unfavorable seasonal price pattern. The strong influence of central market prices in determining North Carolina seasonal price patterns independent of local conditions points up the need for a seasonal price predictor at the central market level.

Third, the question arises as to why Coastal Plain dealers and farmers do not spread their shipments to deficit markets over a few more weeks in order to prevent depressing harvest prices so far below the ones for corn from the Midwest. The analyses indicate that unless there is a shortage of storage facilities, this action would be worth several cents per bushel in years of large crops. However, Coastal Plain "losses" may be offset by Piedmont "gains" in terms of cheaper feed.

11.7 CONCLUDING OBSERVATIONS

Let us summarize in terms of several generalizations about markets in time. We have pointed out that the increase in prices through time will reflect the costs of storage, although the level of prices results from the interaction of available supplies with the aggregated demand functions. From this we can conclude that perfect markets will be interrelated through relatively short time periods if storage costs are relatively high, but through relatively long time periods if storage costs are low. In the limit, as storage costs approach zero, prices approach a single constant level, and the time span covered by a single market approaches infinity. This is equivalent, in markets in space, to the conclusion that product prices completely equalize and all regions become part of a single market if transport costs are zero. Second, the time span of markets will depend on the elasticity of demand—the time span increasing as demands become more inelastic. This merely means that decreases in available supplies will generate relatively large increases in prices and, hence, will cover storage costs for longer time periods. In the limit, with elasticity approaching zero, consumption will approach a completely uniform pattern through time even though prices vary in accordance with storage costs. Finally, trade between time periods may result either from changes in available production or shifts in demand, since either will give rise to price differences and, thus, will provide the economic incentive for storage operations. The parallels with interregional trade should be clear.

SELECTED READINGS

Temporal Market Price Relationships

Bell, Duran Jr. *Models of Commodity Transfer*, Giannini Foundation Monograph No. 20., California Agricultural Experiment Station, Berkeley (October 1967).

Brownlee, O. H. and John A. Buttrick, *Producer, Consumer, and Social Choice*, McGraw-Hill Book Co., New York (1968), Chapter 11, "Decisions That Unavoidably Involve Time," pp. 165–186.

Hadley, George and T. M. Whitin, *Analysis of Inventory Systems*, Prentice-Hall Inc., Englewood Cliffs (1963).

Hassler, James B., "Interregional Competition in Agriculture: Principal Forces, Normative Models and Reality," *Journal of Farm Economics*, Vol. XLI, No. 5 (December 1959). pp. 959–968.

Leath, Mack N, and James E. Martin, "Formulation of a Transhipment Problem Involving Time," *Agricultural Economics Research*, Vol. XIX, No. 1 (January 1967). Pp. 7–14.

Samuelson, Paul A. "Intertemporal Price Equilibrium: A Prologue to the Theory of Speculation" Reprinted in *The Collected Scientific Papers of Paul Samuelson*, The M.I.T. Press, Cambridge (1966). pp. 946–984.

Schneider, Erich, *op. cit.* pp. 239–271.

Waugh, Frederick V., "Cobweb Models," *Journal of Farm Economics*, Vol. 46, No. 4 (November 1964). pp. 732.

chapter 12

PRICE DISCRIMINATION
AMONG MARKETS

In the preceding chapters, we assume that prices achieve an equilibrium so that prices at spatially separated points differ at most by cost of transfer; that prices of different products made from a common raw product source differ at most by cost of transformation; and that prices at one time period differ from prices in an earlier time period at most by costs of storage from the earlier time period to the later time period. This perfect-market model is a useful approximation of the real world, but we need not be satisfied with it as a final analytical device. In this chapter, we investigate market price relationships when price discrimination among markets is possible.

12.1 TYPES OF PRICE DISCRIMINATION

Price discrimination may take a variety of forms. First, it is possible that spatially separated markets, in fact, may be cut into two or more independent units, and supplies may be allocated in such a way that prices will differ by more than costs of transfer. Clearly, such a division would be effective only if leakage could be prevented; that is, firms in the market in which a lower price was established must be restrained from reselling the product in the higher priced market. A second possibility is that the market for a raw product sold in two or more forms may be separated in such a way that the price of the product in one form exceeds the prices of other product forms by more than the cost of transformation. A third possibility is that temporal separation of markets is feasible, making it possible to raise the price in one time period by more than the cost of storage from earlier time periods. Other possibilities include the separation of markets according to user group, that is, of charging one group of customers a higher price for a given product at a given point in time at a given geographic location than is charged other groups. Or there may be an opportunity for price discrimination according to the use to which a particular product is put, such as the division of the market for a particular product between industrial and home users.

None of these possibilities is admissible under pure competition (the market situation in which no firm is sufficiently large to influence the price of the product by its output decisions or sufficiently important to have its actions be of any concern to other producers of a similar product). We now examine alternative modes of behavior of the firm in order to identify situations in which price discrimination opportunities might be considered.

12.2 MODES OF BEHAVIOR OF THE FIRM

In this section we concentrate on the modes of behavior of selling firms, although a comparable analysis of buying firms could easily be provided. Schneider has identified five modes of behavior which are useful in this analysis. We now briefly discuss each of these types of firms.

The Quantity Adjuster. The quantity adjuster is faced with a decision concerning the quantity of goods to be sold at the ruling price. Such a seller is too small to influence price and, therefore, the only variable in the plan of the firm which he is able to manipulate is the quantity he wishes to sell. This is the type of firm that populates the world of pure competition.

The Price Fixer. The price fixer has as his action parameter the price at which he wishes to sell his product. This decision is based on the expected price-sales relation which he perceives for his product. He takes as his expectation parameter the quantity which can be sold at alternative prices and chooses his price in such a way as to maximize revenue or to achieve some other goal which has been selected.

Several classes of price fixers can be identified. If the sales of a particular firm depend only on the price established by the firm in question, his behavior can be described as that of a monopolist. However, it is possible that his sales also depend on the prices established by other firms. If it is assumed that other firms will not modify their prices in response to changes in his price, his behavior will be polypolistic. Of course, it is possible that his sales depend on prices fixed by others and, furthermore, that other firms will react to changes that he makes in his price. In this situation, he will behave as an oligopolist.

The Quantity Fixer. As suggested by the title of this class of firm, their action parameter consists of the quantity of output they wish to offer for sale. This quantity is selected on the basis of an expected price-sales relation as in the price-fixer mode with the price at which a given quantity can be sold resting with the buyer. Again, we can identify three subclasses of quantity fixers — those for which the outcome is influenced solely by the quantity they choose, those firms whose price-sales relation also is affected by the actions of others and, finally, that class of firm for which the actions of other firms influence their price-sales relation and which need to be concerned about possible reactions by other firms to choices they make concerning the quantity to be sold.

The Fixer of Options. Firms in this class have, as their action parameter, the setting of both price and quantity. Obviously, this is not to be thought of as dictating what the consumer will choose. Instead, such a firm establishes an option that the buyer of his product is free to accept or reject. Clearly, the willingness of buyers to accept or reject a particular option depends on the price and quantity characteristics of the offer. The types of options that are proposed, therefore, will reflect the expected response by these buyers to alternative price-quantity combinations.

The Economic Warrior. It is necessary to include this fifth class in order to allow for the possibility that the behavior of firms will no longer consist of the type of peaceful adaptation provided for in the first four classes. Here, we find ourselves in the world of strategy and maneuver on the part of individual firms — the relevant variables including not only the behavior of rivals, given the fact that peaceful coexistence is to be maintained, but also the recognition that the choices open to a particular firm may include some that in the long run will defeat competitors and will leave a larger share of the market to the firm engaging in this behavior.

We now observe that it is only the first class of sellers, the quantity adjusters, whose behavior will automatically bring about a set of market prices such as those described by the perfect market model that we have used thus far. Furthermore, introductory economics texts to the contrary, the agricultural sector of the United States is ill-defined in terms of quantity adjusters alone. In fact, the existence of cooperative and other groups of firms that band together to influence prices and sales and the role of state and federal governments in price-setting and quantity-regulating decisions in agriculture are sufficiently important to require our careful attention.

Price discrimination is perhaps the most common tool used to regulate markets in order to provide for an orderly flow of products to consumers and to benefit selected groups of producers over a short- or longer run period. Before examining specific types of price discrimination, we review briefly some analytical tools that will help to clarify the basis for price discrimination.

12.3 PRICE ELASTICITY REVIEWED

Elasticity is a pure measure that relates proportional changes in dependent and independent variables for any function. In approximate terms, elasticity may be defined as the percent change in a variable Y that results from a 1 percent change in variable X. Suppose that we have given two points (X_1, Y_1) and (X_2, Y_2) on a particular function (Figure 12.1). The change in Y is apparently $(Y_2 - Y_1)$, and the corresponding change in X is $(X_2 - X_1)$. These changes must be expressed in relative terms, and this creates a problem: Shall we use the X_1 and Y_1 values or the X_2 and Y_2 values? Inspection of the diagram indicates that the straight line connecting point 1 and point 2 does not represent the slope or the rate of change in the curve at either point. The slope of this straight line, however, is about the same as the slope of the curve at a point midway between the two points. For this reason, we select an arbitrary and approximate rule — the changes in Y and X shall be expressed relative to the average values for these variables.

Following this rule, expressions for elasticity are given below:

$$E = \frac{\text{percent change in } Y}{\text{percent change in } X}$$

$$E = \frac{(Y_1 - Y_2)/(Y_1 + Y_2)/2}{(X_1 - X_2)/(X_1 + X_2)/2}$$

$$E = \frac{(Y_1 - Y_2)/(Y_1 + Y_2)}{(X_1 - X_2)/(X_1 + X_2)}.$$

It should be clear from the diagram that this is only an approximate procedure, measuring roughly the average elasticity between two points on the function. Such a measure is called *arc elasticity*. A precise measure defining elasticity at a selected point on the function is called *point elasticity*.

Suppose that we reexpress the above formulas by using ΔY and ΔX to represent the changes in Y and X and that we simply use Y and X to

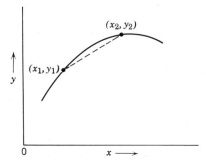

FIGURE 12.1   Points selected on a curve to measure arc elasticity.

denote the average values for these variables. We then have

$$E = \frac{\Delta Y/Y}{\Delta X/X}$$

$$E = \frac{\Delta Y}{\Delta X} \cdot \frac{X}{Y}.$$

This is a convenient form for it expresses elasticity as the slope of the straight line connecting the two points multiplied by the ratio of X to Y. And notice that as ΔX and ΔY become smaller and smaller, the slope of the line segment approaches closer and closer to the true slope of the function. The limit to this is the slope of the tangent at a single point on the function, and the correct expression for elasticity is

$$E = \frac{dy}{dx} \cdot \frac{X}{Y}$$

where dy/dx represents the slope of the tangent.[1]

[1]While dy/dx represents the slope of the tangent to the function at any point, it is no longer a ratio as was $\Delta Y/\Delta X$ but a compound symbol representing the first derivative of the function. For functions that are or can be expressed in algebraic terms, the simplest and only precise procedure for determining elasticity is to use the above equation and to quantify it from the algebraic function. Consider the function

$$Y = a + bX - cX^2$$

a function, in general, similar to that shown in Figure 12.1. The derivative is

$$dy/dx = b - 2cX$$

and elasticity is, therefore,

$$E = \frac{dy}{dx} \cdot \frac{X}{Y} = \frac{(b - 2cX)X}{a + bX - cX^2}.$$

With this expression, it is a simple matter to select any value for X and to evaluate E exactly by substitution.

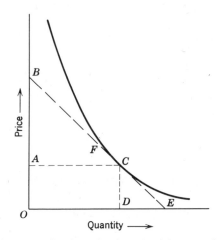

FIGURE 12.2   A graphic determination of price elasticity at point C on a demand curve.

As these expressions for elasticity hold true for any function, it should be relatively simply to apply them to demand and supply relationships. Suppose that we are given a demand curve as in Figure 12.2 and want to evaluate elasticity at some point C. Tangent BE has the same slope as the demand curve at point C and should permit us to define elasticity without difficulty. Notice, however, that elasticity expresses the proportionate change in the dependent variable Y to the proportionate change in the independent variable X, and that, by convention, price is taken as independent and quantity as dependent in demand and supply functions, even though American custom plots price on the Y axis as shown. With this in mind, the expression for the elasticity of demand with respect to price is

$$n_p = \frac{dQ}{dP} \cdot \frac{P}{Q}.$$

In terms of our diagram, the slope $dQ/dP = DE/CD$, $P = OA = CD$, and $Q = OD$. The expression for elasticity, thus, is equivalent to

$$n_p = \frac{DE}{CD} \cdot \frac{CD}{OD} = \frac{DE}{OD}$$

and, by similar triangles,

$$n_p = \frac{DE}{OD} = \frac{CE}{BC} = \frac{OA}{AB}$$

Thus, the geometric or graphic determination of price elasticity of demand involves construction of a tangent such as *BE* to the demand curve at given point *C* and the determination of the proportions *CE* to *BC* into which the tangent is divided by point *C*. Alternatively, the corresponding proportions for line segments *OE* and *OB* may be used. In the present example, the elasticity at point *C* is approximately −0.5 with the negative sign reflecting the negative slope of the demand curve.

Let us consider the case of a linear or straight-line demand curve (line *BE* in the previous diagram). From the above, we know that the price elasticity at any point on this line will be represented by the proportions into which the point divides the line. Thus, at point *C* the elasticity is represented by *CE/BC*, at point *F* by *EF/BF*, and so on. From this, it is clear that elasticity at the midpoint *F* on such a linear demand curve must have a value of −1.0 *unit elasticity*. Points between *F* and *E* will have elasticities between −1.0 and 0; such points are called *inelastic*. And as the selected point approaches *E*, the value for elasticity approaches 0. A vertical line on this diagram will have zero elasticity throughout and so be *perfectly inelastic*. At the other extreme, points between *F* and *B* will have elasticities ranging from −1.0 and approaching −∞ as the point selected approaches *B*. These points are called *elastic*, but a horizontal line with elasticity of −∞ is termed *perfectly elastic*. The study of this diagram will indicate why all linear demand curves through *B* will have identical elasticity values for any selected price, just as all linear demand curves through point *E* will have identical elasticities for any selected quantity. These curves are called isoelastic with respect to price or to quantity.

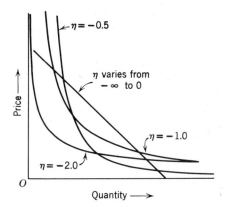

FIGURE 12.3   Curves showing constant price elasticities of −0.5, −1.0, and −2.0, and a straight-line demand curve with elasticity ranging from −∞ to 0.

The straight-line demand curve may also serve to eliminate confusion between elasticity and the slope of a curve. Often a curve that appears steep is thought to be inelastic, just as one that is relatively flat is judged to be elastic. Yet here we find that on a single line with constant slope throughout, elasticity actually ranges from 0 to $-\infty$. This point is also stressed by the curves given in Figure 12.3. Here, we have plotted a straight-line demand curve together with curves having constant elasticities of -0.5, -1.0, and -2.0. In spite of the fact that these last curves have constant elasticities, each has very steep and very flat segments.[2]

12.4   REVENUE FUNCTIONS REVIEWED

Although demand functions summarize the reactions of buyers to price changes, to sellers they represent schedules of potential revenue. The prices paid by consumers are received by producers and, hence, represent their *average revenue* per unit of sale. Total revenue, then, is the product PQ, or the average revenue multiplied by the quantity sold. In a conventional demand diagram, price or average revenue is measured along the vertical axis — for example, the dimensions OD, OE, or OF in Figure 12.4. Corresponding to these prices are quantities purchased (and sold) — OG,

---

[2]These three curves are based on the equations $Q = kP^{-0.5}$, $Q = kP^{-1.0}$, and $Q = kP^{-2.0}$. The student may wish to take derivatives of these functions and demonstrate to himself that constant elasticities are involved.

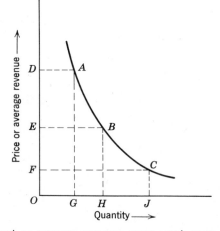

FIGURE 12.4   Demand or average revenue curve, and areas that represent total revenue.

OH, and *OJ*. Apparently, the total revenue obtained from the sale of any quantity may then be represented by the area of these rectangles as *ODAG*, *OEBH*, and *OFCJ*.

Elasticity of demand coefficients are especially interesting in their relation to revenue. It will be recalled that these coefficients are the relative change in quantity divided by the relative change in price. We observe that the demand curve shown in Figure 12.4 is somewhat inelastic in the *B–C* range; coefficients have numerical values ranging from less than −0.5 to about −0.75. They indicate that a one percent change in price will result in a 0.5 to 0.75 percent change in quantity or, conversely, that one percent quantity changes will accompany price changes ranging from about 2.0 to 1.3 percent. From them, it is clear that increases in the quantity sold will bring more than proportionate decreases in price and that quantity increases will be associated with actual decreases in the total revenue to sellers. This can be confirmed by comparing the total revenue area *OEBH* with the area *OFCJ*. In a similar way, we may conclude that, with elastic demand curves, total revenue will increase with increases in the quantity sold. Finally, if demand has unit elasticity, changes in quantity will be exactly compensated by changes in price or average revenue, and total revenue will be constant regardless of the volume of sales.

Total revenue curves based on the demand or average revenue curves from Figure 12.3 are shown in Figure 12.5. They confirm the generalizations just made with respect to the relation between demand elasticity and total revenue. The demand curve with unit elasticity results in a

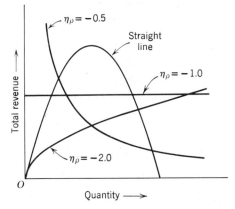

FIGURE 12.5   The total revenue curves that correspond to the demand or average revenue curves in Figure 12.3. (*Note.* The labels identify the average revenue curves in Figure 12.3 and do not indicate the elasticities of the total revenue functions.)

horizontal total revenue function; total revenue is constant for all values of sales. The inelastic demand results in a negatively sloping total revenue function, just as the elastic demand corresponds to a positively inclined total revenue curve. Finally, the straight-line demand curve yields a total revenue curve that starts at zero, increases as quantity increases in the elastic portion of the demand curve, reaches a peak when elasticity is −1.0 at the midpoint, and then declines to zero through the range of inelastic demand.[3]

Marginal revenue is the rate of change or slope of the total revenue function. From the above discussion, plus an examination of the graphs of total revenue functions, it is clear that marginal revenue is positive when demand is elastic with respect to price, negative for inelastic demand functions, and zero when demand has unit elasticity. Marginal revenue curves derived from the total revenue curves in Figure 12.5 are given in Figure 12.6. These values may be determined graphically by constructing tangents to points on total revenue curves, but a somewhat more convenient approach based on average revenue curves (demand curves) is illustrated in Figure 12.7. Suppose that we are given the linear average revenue curve BE and wish to determine the marginal revenue corresponding to a point C (output OD). Find point G bisecting line OE (or any horizontal line such as AC) and construct a straight line through points

---

[3]Perhaps these relationships may be better understood in algebraic rather than geometric terms. Consider the linear demand function,

$$Q = a - bP.$$

This may readily be converted to the form,

$$P = c - dQ,$$

where $c = a/b$ and $d = 1/b$. The total revenue function then will be

$$PQ = cQ - dQ^2.$$

This is the general form of the revenue function shown in Figure 12.5.

The general form for the constant elasticity demand equation is

$$Q = kP^\eta.$$

This may be transformed to show quantity as the independent variable,

$$P = Q^{(1/\eta)}/K^{(1/\eta)}.$$

Total revenue then will be represented as

$$PQ = Q^{(1+1/\eta)}/K^{(1/\eta)}.$$

From this, it is clear that with values of η greater than −1.0, the total revenue function will be positive; with values less than −1.0, the revenue function will be negative (reciprocal); but with unit elasticity, the revenue function reduces to a constant.

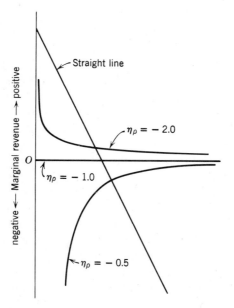

FIGURE 12.6 The marginal revenue curves that correspond to the average and total revenue curves in Figures 12.3 and 12.5.

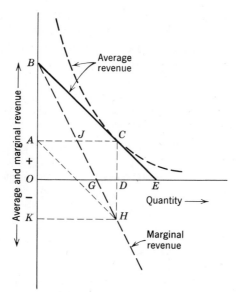

FIGURE 12.7 The graphic determination of marginal revenue.

B and *G*. Drop perpendicular *CD* to the *Q* axis and extend as required to intersect line *BG* at point *H*. This point indicates the required marginal revenue; here, -*DH* or -*OK*. An inspection of the diagram will indicate that all points of marginal revenue corresponding to the linear average revenue line *BE* will fall along this line *BGH* with positive values where the average curve is elastic, zero value at unit elasticity, and negative values for the inelastic portion of the average revenue curve. An alternative graphic determination involves dropping perpendiculars from *C* to both average revenue and quantity axes and constructing line *AH* through *A* and parallel to *BE*. Point *H* at the intersection of *AH* and *CH* again is the required marginal revenue.

Graphic determination of marginal curves corresponding to curvilinear average revenue functions proceeds by drawing the tangent to a selected point on the curve, determining the marginal revenue for that point, and repeating the process for other points until enough marginal revenue points have been obtained to smooth in the entire marginal revenue curve. This is suggested in Figure 12.7 by point *C* on the straight line *BE* and, also, on the curvilinear average revenue function tangent at this point.[4]

12.5   PRICE DIFFERENTIATION AMONG MARKETS – SPACE

In our discussion of price discrimination, it will be convenient to refer to specific empirical studies. Hopefully, this approach will assist the reader to realize that the topic is of more than theoretical interest, not only in the United States but throughout the world.

---

[4]Since the marginal revenue represents the slope of the total revenue curve, it is readily expressed in algebraic terms as the first derivative of the total revenue function. With total revenue defined as the product of price P and quantity Q, marginal revenue will be

$$MR = \frac{dPQ}{dQ} = P + Q\frac{dP}{dQ} = P + P\left(\frac{Q}{P}\frac{dP}{dQ}\right).$$

The price elasticity of demand is the relative slope of the average revenue curve, or

$$\eta_p = \frac{dQ}{dP}\frac{P}{Q}.$$

By substituting in the above equation for marginal revenue, we have

$$MR = P + \frac{P}{\eta_p} = P\left(1 + \frac{1}{\eta_p}\right).$$

Remembering that the price elasticity of demand will be negative, the above equation makes it clear that marginal revenue will be positive when η_p falls between -1.0 and $-\infty$, negative when η_p falls between -1.0 and zero, and equal to zero when η_p is exactly equal to -1.0.

Our first example consists of an examination of the domestic and export markets for cotton produced in the United States—a case of spatially separated markets. A recent study has provided an estimate of the demand for United States cotton in these two markets for the year 1975. Figure 12.8 is a three-part diagram that provides the following information: the demand curves for the domestic and export markets (part *a*), the relationship between price and total revenue (part *b*), and the relationship between quantity sold in each market and total revenue (part *c*). This presentation makes it possible to compare total revenue relationships with price choices by using parts *a* and *b* and to view the relationship between price and total revenue for given quantities using parts *a* and *c*.

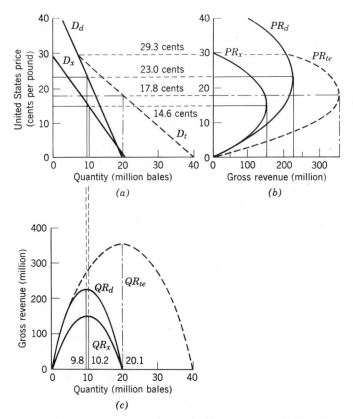

FIGURE 12.8   The domestic and export demand functions for United States cotton, projected 1975. Identification. (*a*) Demand functions (*D_i*). (*b*) Price-revenue functions (*PR_i*). (*c*) Quantity-revenue functions (*QR_i*). (*Note*. Revenue expressed in $5.00 units since 1 bale = 500 lb.)

The demand and revenue relationships necessary for analyzing discrimination among these spatially separated markets are given in Table 12.1. The demand curves for the export and domestic markets are shown in section A. If we assume that the price in these two markets is identical, then we are entitled to draw an aggregate demand curve D_t. For prices higher than 29.3 cents (the highest price at which any cotton will be sold abroad) the aggregate and domestic demand curves are identical. Equations in Table 12.1A, correspond with the demand curves shown in Figure 12.8a.

The equations for the price-revenue curves shown in Figure 12.8b, are provided in Table 12.1B. Again, we are entitled to produce a price-revenue relationship for the two markets together only so long as uniform

TABLE 12.1 Domestic and Export Demand for United States Cotton Projected 1975

Equation Description[a]	
A. *Demand functions*	
1. Export market	$Q_x = 20.5 - 0.70P_x$
2. Domestic market	$Q_d = 19.7 - 0.43P_d$
3. Aggregate market	$Q_t = 40.2 - 1.31P_t$ if $P_x = P_d$
	$= P_t \leqslant 29.3$
B. *Price-revenue functions*	
1. Export market	$PR_x = 20.5P_x - 0.70P_x^2$
2. Domestic market	$PR_d = 19.7P_d - 0.43P_d^2$
3. Aggregate market	$PR_t = 40.2P_t - 1.13P_t^2$ if $P_x = P_d$
	$= P_t \leqslant 29.3$
	$PR_t = 19.7P_d - 0.43P_d^2$ if $P_t > 29.3$
	and $Q_x = 0$
C. *Quantity-revenue functions*	
1. Export market	$QR_x = 29.3Q_x - 1.43Q_x^2$
2. Domestic market	$QR_d = 45.8Q_d - 2.33Q_d^2$
3. Aggregate market	QR_t is not unique but depends on distribution between domestic and export markets. If $P_x = P_d \leqslant 29.3$ and $Q_t \geqslant 7.1$, then $QR_t = 35.6Q_t - 0.88Q_t^2$.

Sources. For demand functions, *Cotton: Supply, Demand, and Farm Resource Use*, Arkansas Agricultural Experiment Station, Southern Cooperative Series 110 (Fayetteville, 1966), pp. 42–52. For price-revenue and quantity-revenue functions, computations were made from demand functions in section A.

[a]For convenience, price is expressed in cents per pound, quantity in millions of bales, and revenue, therefore, in $5.00 units (1 bale = 500 pounds).

prices are maintained in the two markets. These curves are simply the demand curves multiplied by price. The demand curve for United States cotton in the export markets has been adjusted for added marketing costs by adding 4 cents to the United States farm price.[5]

The quantity-revenue relationships shown in Figure 12.8c, are provided in equation form in Table 12.1C. Notice that the quantity-revenue curve for the two markets together is not unique since quantity-revenue relationships depend on how a given quantity is distributed between the domestic and export markets. Again, however, if we assume a distribution that will result in equal prices in the two markets, we can produce a quantity-revenue relationship shown as Equation C3.

If the United States cotton industry were in a position to set prices in the two markets, that is, to act as a price adjuster, the relevant information for decision purposes would be the revenue associated with alternative levels of price in each market. Changes in total revenue, illustrated in Figure 12.8b, can be described in terms of the marginal price-revenue curves provided in Table 12.2 for the export and domestic markets.

[5]That is, the export price P_x is expressed in United States farm price units but is actually P_d plus 4 cents, or $Q_x = 23.3 - 0.70(P_d + 4) = 23.3 - 2.8 - 0.70P_d = 20.5 - 0.70P_d$.

TABLE 12.2 Marginal Revenue Functions for United States Cotton Projected, 1975

	Equation Description[a]
D. *Marginal price-revenue functions*	
1. Export market	$MPR_x = 20.5 - 1.40P_x$
2. Domestic market	$MPR_d = 19.7 - 0.86P_d$
3. Aggregate market	Not unique but, if $P_x = P_d = P_t$ $\leqslant 29.3$, then $MPR_t = 40.2 - 2.26P_t$.
E. *Marginal quantity-revenue functions*	
1. Export market	$MQR_x = 29.3 - 2.86Q_x$
2. Domestic market	$MQR_d = 45.8 - 4.66Q_d$
3. Aggregate market	MQR_t is not unique but depends on distribution between export and domestic markets. If $P_d = P_x$ $\leqslant 29.3$ and $Q_t \geqslant 7.1$, then $MQR_t = 35.6Q_t - 1.76Q_t$.

Source.   Derived from equations in Table 12.1.
[a]For convenience, price is expressed in cents per pound, quantity in millions of bales, and revenue, therefore, in $5.00 units (1 bale = 500 pounds).

Should the decision be made to charge equal prices in the two markets, again we are entitled to produce Equation $D3$; but we must remember that this is not unique in the event that prices are not equal in the two markets and that it holds true only for prices no larger than 29.3 cents, as pointed out earlier.

A visual inspection of Figure 12.8b, shows that maximum revenue from sales on the domestic market are achieved at a price of 23 cents and at sales of 9.8 million bales. Maximum revenue on the export market would be achieved at a price of 14.6 cents per pound and sales would total 10.2 million bales.

If industry decisions are to be made on the basis of the quantity of cotton sold, then we are interested in marginal quantity-revenue relationships that are provided in the second portion of Table 12.2. The earlier qualifications concerning the relevant quantity-revenue relationship for the two markets taken jointly should be observed. Clearly, the quantities at which maximum revenue is achieved, as illustrated in Figure 12.8c, correspond exactly with the prices shown in Figure 12.8b, for the reason that they are derived from the identical demand relationships.

As a practical matter, we are interested in prices ranging from 15 to 35 cents per bale. The authors of the study from which these data are drawn conclude that United States producers of cotton would supply 1.5 million bales at the low price and 31 million bales at the high price. This suggests that we need to be concerned only with a rather narrow range of prices and quantities and that we need not be overly disturbed at the use of linear demand relationships at this point. However, the reader will recognize that, in other situations, nonlinear demand relationships may be much preferred. For ease of illustration and, in this case, for practical application, the linear relationships are satisfactory.

We now use this information to compare two price policies for United States cotton, one where equal prices (with proper adjustment for marketing cost differences) prevail in the two markets and the other where equal marginal revenue prevails in the two markets. Suppose that United States cotton production amounts to 16 million bales. This amount could be sold at a price of 21.5 cents, as shown in Figure 12.9. Domestic sales would total 10.4 million bales and export sales 5.6 million bales, as shown in the back-to-back diagram and the aggregate demand diagram. However, as shown in Figure 12.8b, 21.5 cents falls on the increasing range of the domestic price-revenue function but on the decreasing range of the export function. Clearly, revenue would be larger if the domestic price were raised and the export price were lowered by appropriate changes in quantities sold.

By using the back-to-back format of Figure 12.10, it will be observed

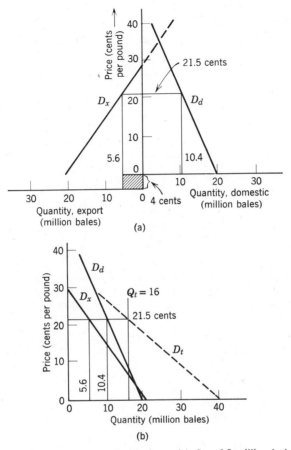

FIGURE 12.9 The equal net price equilibrium with $Q_t = 16$ million bales. (a) Back-to-back demand functions. (b) Aggregate demand function.

that equal marginal revenue equilibrium will occur at 7.2 cents with 8.3 million bales sold at 26.5 cents per pound in the domestic market and 7.7 million bales sold at 18.3 cents per pound in the export market. These values can be verified by using the equations in Tables 12.1 and 12.2. An obvious question to be answered is how a net price difference of 8.2 cents per pound can be maintained in the two markets. The answer is that some nonprice market regulator must be introduced—the topic of the next chapter.

The graphic solution to the equal marginal revenue case is illustrated best by Figure 12.11. Again, marginal revenue curves for each market are shown individually and in the aggregate. Notice that the aggregate

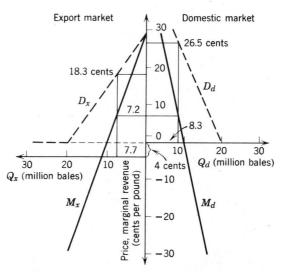

FIGURE 12.10 The equal marginal revenue equilibrium, back-to-back marginal revenue functions, $Q_t = 16$ million bales. (*Note.* D = demand function; M = marginal revenue function; d = domestic market; and x = export market.)

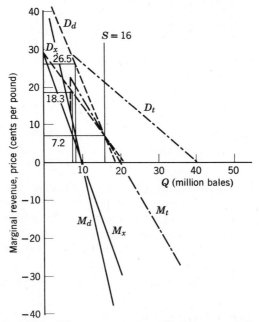

FIGURE 12.11 The equal marginal revenue equilibrium, aggregate marginal revenue function, $Q_t = 16$ million bales. (*Note.* D = demand function; M = marginal revenue function; d = domestic market; x = export market; and t = two-market aggregate.)

marginal revenue function has a sharp break at the quantity 7.1 million bales as do the aggregate demand and aggregate revenue functions at a price of 29.3 cents. Recall that any point on the marginal revenue function refers to the quantity read directly below it and to the price on the demand curve read directly above it.

Although this spatially separated market example has many additional intricacies that might be pursued, such as competition from synthetics and changes in trade policies and programs, they will be left to the reader and we shall move on to new ground.

12.6 PRICE DIFFERENTIATION AMONG MARKETS — FORM

To illustrate price discrimination among product forms, we return to the fluid milk and manufactured milk products markets. Our example, drawn from a study of northeastern milk markets, refers to the New York area in the early 1960's.[6] The demand functions for these two markets, illustrated in Figure 12.12, can be written as follows:

$$\text{Fluid milk: } Q_f = 6.15 - 0.12P_f$$

$$\text{Manufactured milk products: } Q_m = 9.10 - 0.96P_m.$$

In 1960, the observed price of fluid milk was $6.27 per hundredweight and sales were 5.4 billion pounds, while the price of manufactured milk products was $2.93 per hundredweight with total sales amounting to 6.3 billion pounds for the year. The elasticity of demand for these two markets at the 1960 price level was -0.14 and -0.45, respectively. Notice that in the fluid milk market the demand is very inelastic at "going" prices and that in the manufactured milk products market demand is more elastic.

It is obvious that at these prices substantial increases in total revenue could be achieved if it were possible to reduce the total quantity marketed. This is true for both the fluid milk and manufactured milk products markets. Unitary elasticity in the fluid milk market occurs at a price of roughly $25 per hundredweight. The reason why milk prices are not closer to $25 per hundredweight is quite simple. The milk from every cow east of the Rocky Mountains would immediately be shipped to the New York area. This may be a roundabout way of making the point that we are looking at only one-half of the factors that establish equilibrium

---

[6]D. A. West and G. E. Brandow, *Equilibrium Prices, Production, and Shipments of Milk in the Dairy Regions of the United States, 1960*, Pennsylvania State University, Department of Agricultural Economics and Rural Sociology, AE and RS No. 49 (University Park, 1964).

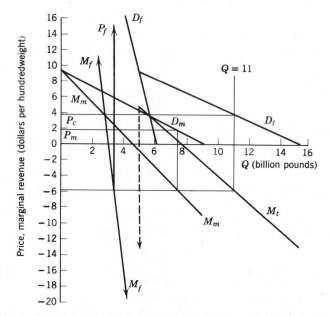

FIGURE 12.12 The fluid milk and manufactured-milk-products demand functions, New York area, 1960. (*Note.* D = demand function; M = marginal revenue function; f = fluid milk; m = manufactured milk products; and t = two-market aggregate.)

market prices (namely, the demand side) and have, to this point, ignored the simultaneous relationships that exist in the real world between demand and supply.

Let us suppose, for ease of computation, that 11 billion pounds of milk were provided to the New York market. With equal prices, equilibrium would be reached at a price of $3.96, or roughly $1.00 per hundredweight above the 1960 manufactured milk price. At this price, fluid milk sales would amount to 5.7 billion pounds and manufactured milk sales 5.3 billion pounds. Equating marginal revenues, on the other hand, would have produced prices of $22.51 and $1.63 and sales of 3.4 and 7.6 billion pounds, respectively. The observed prices, although not differing by more than $20 per hundredweight as in our second case, reflect the opportunity to increase the gross revenue from milk sales by charging different prices in these two product-form markets. The answer to the question of how this is possible again lies in nonprice constraints on milk markets—in this case, state and federal milk marketing orders that establish minimum prices based on use of the raw product.

The usual textbook example is concerned with equating marginal revenues in two markets, both of which have positive values. The usual case in agriculture will be the drive for equalization of marginal revenues in markets where elasticity is less than one, therefore, where marginal revenue is negative, as in Figure 12.12. Once the reader is convinced of the necessity for the presentation of marginal revenue curves with large negative values on the vertical axis, he will begin to understand some of the behavior of agricultural prices and an important underlying force that bears on modern United States agricultural policy and, in fact, agricultural policy the world over.

12.7 PRICE DIFFERENTIATION AMONG MARKETS – TIME

The avocado is a fruit for which the demand function, or quantity demanded, varies systematically throughout the year. In the 1950's, California provided 70 percent of the United States' total supply; Florida, about 20 percent; and Cuban shipments, 10 percent. When the Calavo Growers of California, a cooperative of avocado producers, was organized in 1924, its 100 members produced roughly 80 percent of the total California crop, although at the present time Calavo handles approximately 50 percent of the California output. Avocado production in California centers in the Los Angeles area where about 25 percent of the Calavo sales are made, with 20 percent sold in other California areas, 30 percent sold in other western areas, and 25 percent sold east of the Mississippi River.

From the turn of the century to the early 1960's imports have come predominantly from Cuba, although small amounts have been shipped from other countries in the Central America region. This is understandable, since Cuban shipments have been exempt from the import duty of 15 cents per pound set in 1930 and 7.5 cents per pound in 1947 under the Reciprocity Treaty of 1902 – amounts that usually exceed the value of the fruit. Furthermore, supplies could clear Cuban ports only from June 1 through September 30.

The annual demand for avocados can be expressed as follows:[7]

$$\hat{P} = -66.1 - 0.327C + 44.6 \log Y$$

where $\hat{P} =$ "predicted" season-average Calavo selling price, f.o.b. Los Angeles, in cents per pound
$C =$ million pounds of California avocados sold during the season
$Y =$ billion dollars of United States nonagricultural personal income.

[7]Stephen H. Sosnick, "Orderly Marketing for California Avocados," *Hilgardia*, Vol. 33, No. 14 (December, 1962), p. 731.

This function implies that for each additional million pounds of California avocados sold, the selling price decreases 0.327 cents per pound. By taking the average values of the variables for the two-decade period of the 1940's and 1950's, the price flexibility with respect to volume is −0.69, and the price flexibility with respect to income is 0.91 (the corresponding values for price elasticities are reported as −1.44 and 1.32, respectively).

Although the annual demand for avocados is elastic, the problem facing the avocado industry is to allocate the year's crop in such a way as to maximize returns to the growers. To do this, information is needed concerning seasonal variations in the demand for avocados.

There are three ways in which seasonal shifts in the demand may be considered. The first approach is to treat each subperiod as a completely separate set of observations. The second treats all observations as a single set and obtains a single regression equation containing dummy variables that allow the demand curve to shift while holding the slope of the function constant. The third treats all observations as a single set and obtains a single regression equation but treats changes from week to week in a nonlinear fashion.

By using the third approach, the following demand function was estimated for California avocados:

$$\hat{P} = -69.5 - 28.4C + 1.40CW - 0.0274CW^2 - 7.14N + 46.7 \log Y$$

where $\hat{P}$ = "predicted" weekly average Calavo selling price, f.o.b. Los Angeles, in cents per pound
   C = million pounds of California avocados sold during the week
   W = week of California season
   N = million pounds of Florida and imported avocados sold during the week
   Y = seasonally adjusted annual rate of nonagricultural personal income for the week, in billion dollars.

The variable C can be factored out of the second, third, and fourth terms of this equation, and the remaining values $(-28.4 + 1.40W - 0.0274W^2)$ can be treated as a new variable B_w.

The values of Calavo sales, the estimated Florida sales, and the estimated imports for the 1958–59 season are shown in Table 12.3 together with values for the coefficient described above, B_w. The slopes of the weekly demand functions estimated in this fashion range from 30 to 90 times the slope of the annual function. Price flexibilities for these mid-week demand functions for each month range from −0.30 in November

TABLE 12.3 Monthly Variations in Avocado Sales and Estimated Monthly Demand Shifters Selected Weeks, 1958–59 Season

	Avocado Sales (Thousand Pounds)				Demand Shifters	
	Calavo's	Non-California				
Week in middle of month	Sales of California Crop	Florida	Imports	Total	Value of W	Value of B_w
October	365	350	30	745	3	−24.4
November	416	620	0	1,036	7	−19.9
December	743	350	0	1,093	12	−15.5
January	700	350	0	1,050	16	−12.9
February	1,346	40	0	1,386	20	−11.3
March	1,578	0	0	1,578	24	−10.5
April	1,543	0	0	1,543	29	−10.7
May	1,222	0	0	1,222	33	−11.9
June	835	0	80	915	38	−14.6
July	918	110	800	1,828	42	−17.7
August	638	100	40	778	46	−21.7
September	409	590	490	1,489	51	−28.0
Twelve-week total	10,713	2,510	1,440	14,663		

Sources. Column 1: Stephen H. Sosnick, "Orderly Marketing for California Avocados," *Hilgardia*, Vol. 33, No. 14 (December, 1962), Appendix Table 2; *Column 2: Ibid.*, Appendix Table 6; *Column 3: Ibid.*, Appendix Table 7; and *Columns 5 and 6: Ibid.*, Table 9, p. 740.

to −0.82 in May (corresponding price elasticities are −3.3 for November and −1.2 for May). The 12 demand functions are illustrated in Figure 12.13.

The graphic solution to this problem is complicated, but it illustrates the procedure by which the orderly flow of avocados can be arranged in order to equate marginal revenue in each time period and so maximize grower returns (Figure 12.14). The 1958–59 output of Calavo avocados was 46.172 million pounds. If the quantity sold each week had been selected so as to result in equal marginal net income in all weeks, this would have resulted in an increase of 0.7 cents per pound and an increase in income of $300,000 or 8 percent. This volume was slightly larger than the 45 million pounds that profitably could have been sold fresh. If sales had been limited to this quantity, the processing, carry-over, or abandon-

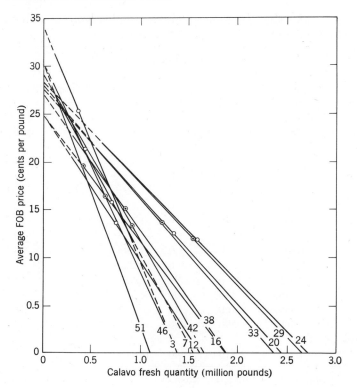

FIGURE 12.13   The weekly net regressions of Calavo price on Calavo quantity with intercepts inferred from actual 1958–59 season prices. [*Source.* **Stephen H. Sosnick,** "Orderly Marketing for California Avocados," *Hilgardia*, Vol. 33, No. 14 (December, 1962), p. 742.]

ment of the remaining one million pounds would have increased members' returns only about 0.007 cents per pound and would have increased the returns to independent growers by 0.3 cents per pound.

The potential payoff associated with a variety of alternative sales strategies is evaluated in the Sosnick study. Here an important nonprice factor is the marketing contract between member growers and Calavo. Under this contract they agree to deliver all commercial production to the Association, with harvesting schedules and warehousing decisions made by Calavo.

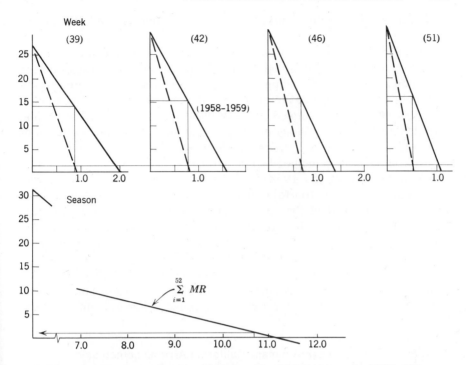

FIGURE 12.14   The generalized weekly demand function for avocados 1958–59 season (*Source.* Sosnick S. H, "Orderly Marketing for California Avocados," *Hilgardia*, Vol. 33, No. 14 (December, 1962), p. 740.)

12.8 PRICE DIFFERENTIATION AMONG MARKETS — FORM, TIME, AND SPACE

The lemon market provides an interesting combination of space, form, and time choices.[1] Lemon production in the United States is concentrated in the state of California where approximately 16 million boxes are produced annually. A much smaller quantity, usually less than one million boxes, are produced in Arizona and a still smaller quantity is grown in Florida. Approximately one-half of the California-Arizona output of lemons is sold as fresh lemons, and the remainder is sold as lemon products. The fresh market for lemons can be divided into three

[1]From Sidney Hoos and George M. Kuznets, *Impacts of Lemon Products Imports on Domestic Lemon Markets*, University of California, Giannini Foundation Research Report No. 254 (Berkeley, 1962) and Ben C. French and Raymond G. Bressler, "The Lemon Cycle," *Journal of Farm Economics*, Vol. XLIV, No. 4 (November, 1962), pp. 1021–1036.

submarkets: the winter market, the summer market, and the export market.

In 1958–59, fresh lemon sales during the winter season, extending from November to April, amounted to 2.7 million boxes, and sales during the summer season, extending from May to October, amounted to 4.5 million boxes. Export sales totaled 1.5 million boxes (Table 12.4). Lemon products production totaled 28.6 million gallons in 1958–59 and included 15.6 million gallons of concentrate juice, 8.7 million gallons of frozen lemon concentrate, the remainder being distributed among several other products which included single-strength juice and nonfrozen lemon concentrate. During the 1958–59 crop year, the output of concentrate juice doubled and the fourfold buildup of inventory of concentrate juice occurred at the end of the season. The average on-tree price for fresh lemons was $2.64 per box in 1958–59, although the average on-tree return for lemon products was − 38 cents per packed box equivalent. Again, in 1959–60, the on-tree return to lemon products was negative.

We now consider an analysis of the demands for lemons and lemon products and alternative strategies for product allocation among these four markets. Table 12.5*A* provides the market demand functions ex-

TABLE 12.4   Three-Year Summary, California-Arizona Lemon Sales

Item	1957–58		1958–59		1959–60	
	Quantity[a]	Price[b]	Quantity[a]	Price[b]	Quantity[a]	Price[b]
Crop allocation						
Fresh shipments	10.4	2.24	8.7	2.64	9.4	2.42
Lemon products	6.9	0.20	8.5	− 0.38	8.7	− 0.70
Total crop	17.3	1.43	17.2	1.16	18.1	0.93
Fresh product allocation						
Winter market	2.78	2.24	2.74	2.50	2.00	
Summer market	4.26	2.24	4.45	2.72	c	
Export market	3.36	2.24	1.51	2.64		
Total, fresh	10.40	2.24	8.70	2.64	9.40	2.42

Source. Sidney Hoos and George M. Kuznets, *Impacts of Lemon Products Imports on Domestic Lemon Markets*, University of California, Giannini Foundation Research Report No. 254 (Berkeley, 1962).
[a]Million-box equivalent.
[b]On-tree price in dollars per packed box equivalent.
[c]Blanks indicate no data available.

TABLE 12.5 The Demand for California-Arizona Lemons: A Form-Time-Space Example

Equation Description[a]	
A. *Market demand functions*[b]	
1. Fresh lemons, winter market	$P_{fw} = 10.20 - 1.84Q_{fw}$
2. Fresh lemons, summer market	$P_{fs} = 10.05 - 1.05Q_{fs}$
3. Fresh lemons, export market	$P_{fx} = 6.75 - 0.60Q_{fx}$
4. Processed lemon products	$P_p = 4.95 - 0.50Q_p$
B. *Derived on-tree demand functions*	
1. Fresh lemons, winter market	$P'_{fw} = 7.50 - 1.84Q_{fw}$
2. Fresh lemons, summer market	$P'_{fs} = 7.35 - 1.05Q_{fs}$
3. Fresh lemons, export market	$P'_{fx} = 3.55 - 0.60Q_{fx}$
4. Processed lemon products	$P'_p = 3.75 - 0.50Q_p$
C. *On-tree marginal revenue functions*	
1. Fresh lemons, winter market	$M'_{fw} = 7.50 - 3.68Q_{fw}$
2. Fresh lemons, summer market	$M'_{fs} = 7.35 - 2.10Q_{fs}$
3. Fresh lemons, export market	$M'_{fx} = 3.55 - 1.20Q_{fx}$
4. Processed lemon products	$M'_p = 3.75 - 1.00Q_p$

Sources. Sidney Hoos and George M. Kuznets, *Impacts of Lemon Products Imports on Domestic Lemon Markets*, University of California, Giannini Foundation Research Report No. 254 (Berkeley, 1962), and Ben C. French and Raymond G. Bressler, "The Lemon Cycle," *Journal of Farm Economics*, Vol. XLIV, No. 4 (November, 1962), pp. 1021–1036.

[a]Million-box equivalent; on-tree price in dollars per packed box equivalent.
[b]F.o.b. packinghouse.

pressed in terms of f.o.b. packinghouse prices and quantities in millions of 79-pound packed box equivalents. However, the cost of placing lemons on these four markets differs. For this reason, we need the derived on-tree demand functions shown in Table 12.5*B*. Fresh winter and fresh summer lemons involve a cost of $2.70 per box to cover the cost of picking, hauling, and packing. Equations 1 and 2 in Table 12.5*B*, therefore, are adjusted downward by this amount. We assume that export sales of fresh lemons involve an additional 50 cents per box, hence, Equation 3 has been adjusted downward by a total of $3.20. Finally, the processed lemon demand curve has been shifted downward by $1.20, which represents the costs of picking and hauling lemons for this market. In section *C* of 12.5, we find marginal revenue functions for each of the four markets. They are comparable to the equations in section *B*, but the slope of each is twice that of the corresponding demand curve (Figure 12.15).

We are now in a position to calculate the optimum distribution of a

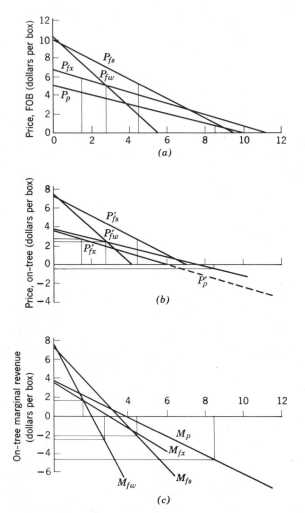

FIGURE 12.15   The California–Arizona lemon demand functions, 1958–59 season. (a) FOB demand functions. (b) On-tree demand functions. (c) On-tree marginal revenue functions. (Source. See equations in Table 12.5.)

crop the size of the 1958–59 crop—namely, 17.2 million boxes. If we specify that marginal revenue in every market must be the same, then we have four equations with five unknowns. The fifth equation is derived by setting down the fact that all lemons must be sold; that is, total quantity must be equal to the sales in all four markets. We then solve this system of five simultaneous equations and find that marginal revenue for a crop of this size is $1.91. The optimum allocation of the 17.2 million boxes among the four markets is as follows:

Lemon Market	Sales in Million Boxes	On-tree Price	F.o.b. Price
Fresh, winter	2.56	$2.79	$5.49
Fresh, summer	4.41	2.72	5.42
Fresh, export	4.56	0.81	4.03
Processed products	5.67	0.91	2.11

By comparing this allocation with the observed 1958–59 allocation, we find that the quantity sold as processed lemon products is substantially smaller and that the quantity exported is considerably larger, with minor changes in fresh winter and summer sales. The export demand function used here is probably the least reliable of the four, but serves well for illustrative purposes.

Notice that processed lemon products are not necessarily sold in the year in which they are processed and, therefore, there is always the opportunity for profit associated with storage and sale in a later year in the event of a short crop. However, since lemon production is reasonably uniform from year to year, the uncertain outlook for profit making as a result of a heavy inventory carried over into the following crop year (as in the 1958–59 crop year described above) suggests that new export or processed products sales must be developed or that a major shift must be made in the rate of output of lemon products in the California-Arizona area to approach a break-even price in these two markets.

12.9 SUMMARY

We have examined four cases in which industry groups and/or government have taken actions that tend to distort the perfect market equilibrium in form, time, and space. These distortions are perhaps the rule rather than the exception, but we believe that the model can deepen our understanding of the economic world in which we live, can encourage the consideration of a framework that goes beyond the pinhead economy, and can provide a benchmark with which to compare still more realistic situations in which firms do not behave purely as quantity adjusters, where government participates in the marketing process, and where the realms of political science and economics intersect.

SELECTED READINGS

Price Discrimination among Markets

Brandow, George E., *Interrelations Among Demands for Farm Products and Implications for Control of Market Supply*, Pennsylvania State University, Agricultural Experimental Station Bulletin 680, University Park (August 1961).

French, Ben C. and Raymond G. Bressler, "The Lemon Cycle," *Journal of Farm Economics*, Vol. XLIV, No. 4 (November 1962). pp. 1021–1036.

Forker, Olan D. and Brenda A. Anderson, "An Annotated Bibliography on Price Discrimination," Cornell University Agricultural Economics Research Mimeo. Report 241, Ithaca (February 1968).

Houck, James P. and Jitendar S. Mann, *An Analysis of Domestic and Foreign Demand for U.S. Soybeans and Soybean Products*, University of Minnesota Agricultural Experiment Station Technical Bulletin 256, St. Paul (1958).

Schneider, Erich, *op. cit.*, pp. 120–129.

Sosnick, Stephen H., "Orderly Marketing for California Avocados," *Hilgardia*, Vol. 33, No. 14, California Agricultural Experiment Station, Berkeley (December 1962).

Waugh, Frederick V., *Demand and Price Analysis*, United States Department of Agriculture Technical Bulletin, No. 1316, Washington (1964).

Waugh, Frederick V., Edgar L. Burtis, and A. F. Wolf. "The Controlled Distribution of a Crop Among Independent Markets," *Quarterly Journal of Economics*, Vol. 51, No. 1. (1936). pp. 1–41.

chapter 13

NONPRICE FACTORS AFFECTING TRADE

In Chapter 12, we described a variety of practices by which the prices that would result from the free and unhindered working of the marketing system may be modified. In addition, there are a variety of nonprice actions that may also influence the behavior of market prices and the character of interregional product flows. Some of them have the effect of accelerating change, but others retard change. Some serve to stabilize market prices, but others cause modification of product flows. In this chapter, we enumerate briefly some of these factors and provide several examples to indicate how selected models might be used in analyzing the effect of these forces on market prices and trade.

13.1 TYPES OF INTERVENTION

Situations may arise in which market price does not provide a sufficient incentive to bring about change at the socially desired rate. Some of these situations were mentioned early in this book. For example, bounties were paid to southern colonists for the production of indigo and naval stores by the British government. After the establishment of the Nation, free land was provided to encourage settlement of newly acquired territories.

Railroad companies were provided public lands to stimulate the extension of these critical ties with distant parts of the nation. Educational grants were extended to local governments to guarantee a minimum level of learning and technical skills, first at elementary and secondary levels and later through land-grant college legislation.

In other situations, efforts have been made to retard the rate at which change would otherwise occur. Early among them were the navigation acts, which were intended to slow the rate of expansion of the colonial shipping industry. Duties were imposed on certain classes of goods, and tariffs were levied on others. More direct efforts to retard change include the 17th-century nightriders of the Tidewater tobacco section and, more recently in the 20th century, civil unrest in the Kentucky and Tennessee burley tobacco areas. The range wars that were engaged in by cattlemen, sheepherders, and farmers in the West were clearly designed to modify changes being brought about through free market prices.

The efforts to stabilize market price have been widespread. They have included state and federal milk-control legislation, national price support and subsidy programs for a variety of agricultural products, and direct price control during World War II. Direct efforts have also been employed to regularize products flows. Market quotas clearly accomplish this, as do the market order and agreement programs for a variety of vegetables and fruits operating under both state and federal legislation.

Space limitations make it impossible for us to cover fully a representative sample of these types of market intervention. Our purpose, however, is to encourage the exploration of these lines of inquiry and to suggest that the perfect market model, having form, time, and space dimensions, may be a useful device by which the effects of this intervention may be better understood.

13.2 THE PINK MILK CAPER[1]

The laws of the state of Rhode Island give full power to the state's Department of Agriculture and Conservation to inspect and to register milk producers who make direct shipments of milk to local distributors. These registrations are renewable annually but, once granted, are normally revoked only for failure to meet the state farm inspection standards. In addition to registration, the so-called "Can Act," which was enacted in 1932, required milk from registered farms to be delivered to

[1]This section draws heavily on *State Control of the Rhode Island Milk Market*, A. L. Domike, Jr., Agricultural Experiment Station Bulletin 345, University of Rhode Island, Kingston, June 1959. Title credit also goes to Professor Domike.

plants for bottling and sale in Rhode Island in containers approved by the department. This law was viewed both as a health precaution and as a legal restraint on dealers' supply sources.

The power of the department to exclude producers from registration has aroused considerable legal dispute from time to time. Local producer organizations generally favored the restriction of registration to producers within and immediately surrounding the state, in the belief that the state's controls were more effective and viable when distributors were permitted to purchase their "balancing supply" from unregulated sources. Distributors who have been fully subject to the state supply and price regulations supported this position. Both unregistered producers desiring entry to the Rhode Island market and some distributors who were subject to pricing orders in other markets opposed restrictive licensing.

To enforce the registration and container laws, the department was empowered to color nonconforming supplies "by the use of vegetable coloring matter." This penalty was used once in 1937. On that occasion milk shipped in from an unlicensed source in Vermont was dyed with a pink vegetable coloring matter. Clearly unsuitable for sale for human consumption, the milk was disposed of to a local hog producer at a very modest price. It is said that this gentleman repeatedly requested similar supplies from the Director of Agriculture on the grounds that it was an excellent pig feed. However, the state courts permanently enjoined the use of this device to protect a local market.

The coloring penalty grew out of the department's efforts to restrict producer licensing to the immediately surrounding milkshed. Some Vermont producers had been registered in Rhode Island until 1937, but nearby registered supplies were more than adequate to meet the needs of Rhode Island distributors. A reduction in registrations was brought about, in spite of the court case, and the present boundaries to the milkshed were established. In 1941, under the pressure of growing milk demands, the Agriculture Department sought to reextend registrations to northern New England. In a court suit the local producer cooperative successfully fought the milkshed expansion as a violation of the Can Act. Thereafter, as supply needs of local distributors expanded during the war and postwar years, they were met with "permit" milk.

The expansion of milk production in the early 1950's was sufficiently rapid for local producers' cooperatives to request further restriction of "outside" supplies. Shortly after the new licensing restrictions were instituted, General Ice Cream Corporation, a Boston dealer with sales in Rhode Island, sought reinspection for all producers supplying its plant. The Agriculture Department withheld inspections on the basis that the producers were using bulk tanks, and these tanks had not been approved under the Can Act. The dealer gained a court injunction shortly afterward that compelled the state to register the producers.

This case cast doubt on the state's discretionary power in limiting producers' registrations, and it broke down restrictions on the use of bulk-tank storage and pickup of milk in the milkshed. Before 1955, the Agriculture Department had banned bulk pickup under the Can Act provisions, although exceptions were granted for unregistered supplies. The court ruling led to the rapid introduction of bulk tanks in the milkshed and permitted some distributors to expand direct bulk pickup from unregistered farms.

13.3 THE WORLD SUGAR MARKET

The usefulness of point trading models for gaining an understanding of price equilibrium in spatially separated markets was described in Chapter 5. Here, we show how that model may be employed to analyze the effects of barriers to trade as they are found in the world sugar market.

We can take exports and imports as given, estimate transfer costs and then compare actual flows with the ones that minimize total transfer costs. Bates and Schmitz calculate total costs for world sugar shipments at $89.0 million and $107.4 million in 1959 and 1963, respectively, for actual flows as compared with $65.5 million and $73.5 million with least-cost allocations. Actual costs are 136 and 146 percent of the least allocation, suggesting a substantial departure from a free market model (Table 13.1). This is further supported by a comparison of actual and calculated shadow prices for selected importing points (Table 13.2). Not only is the least-cost price surface much flatter than the actual price surface, as might be expected since other costs incurred in the movement of sugar that might vary with length of haul have not been included, but nearby markets such as New York and Montreal reflect substantial price differences ($126.51 versus $85.42).

Some of the reasons for these divergencies are not difficult to find.[2] The international sugar market can be divided into two parts, free and nonfree. "Free market" trade consists of all sugar trade except the following flows, which are defined as "nonfree market."

1. The internal movements between overseas territories and their mother countries (with the exception of the ones between the United Kingdom and her dependencies).

2. The exports of foreign countries to the United States.

3. The exports of Czechoslovakia, Hungary, and Poland to the U.S.S.R.

[2]*Ibid.*, pp. 5–7.

TABLE 13.1   Shipping Costs with Optimal Allocations of World Sugar Supply and Comparison with Actual Costs 1959 and 1963

Purchasing Region	Shipping Cost with Optimal Allocation (Million Dollars)		Actual Cost as Percent of Optimum	
	1959	1963	1959	1963
United States	23.8	26.4	120	122
Commonwealth Sugar Agreement countries	15.2	14.7	152	175
France	2.7	1.0	230	424
Portugal	0.7	0.8	136	142
Residual	23.1	30.6	131	144
World total	65.5	73.5	136	146

Source.   Bates and Schmitz, 1969, *A Spatial Equilibrium Analysis of the World Sugar Economy*, Gianinni Foundation Monograph No. 23, University of California, Berkeley, Tables 13 and 14, p. 21.

TABLE 13.2   Comparison of Actual and Shadow Prices of Sugar at Selected Destinations, 1959

Destination	Price of Sugar (Dollars per Metric Ton)		
	Actual	Shadow Price	Difference
Bordeaux, France	128.32	99.56	+ 28.76
New York, United States	126.51	97.97	+ 28.54
Lisbon, Portugal	103.27	99.34	+ 3.93
Antwerp, Belgium	86.97	99.67	− 12.70
Montreal, Canada	85.42	98.16	− 12.74
Wellington, New Zealand	72.61	95.48	− 22.87

Source.   Bates and Schmitz, *op. cit.*, Table 12, p. 20.

Nonfree market trade from 1954 to 1962 averaged about 7 million metric tons, or about 38.9 percent of the total world exports, but declined relatively, dropping from 43.2 percent of the total world exports in 1954 to 31.4 percent in 1961. Exports under internal movements averaged 2.7 million metric tons from 1954 to 1962, dropping from 18.4 to 13.5 percent of world trade during this period. The movements between the United States offshore areas and the United States mainland were far and away the most important of all internal movements, accounting for 65.2 percent of the total. Second in importance was trade within the French Community at 27.9 percent, and third was that trade between Portuguese overseas provinces to Portugal, at 5 percent.

In the period 1954 to 1962, the free-market trade averaged 10.9 million metric tons, or 61.1 percent of total world trade. By definition, all trade between dependent territories and the countries of the British Commonwealth is part of the free market. However, a rather large part of this trade is subject to regulation under the Commonwealth Sugar Agreement and, as such, is subject to special conditions. Exports under this agreement, in the period 1954 to 1962, averaged 12.9 percent of world exports. The balance of free-market trade constitutes a "residual" free-trade market; the residual market share in total world exports was 42.3 percent in 1954 and 54.1 percent in 1962, averaging 48.2 percent over the period.

From 1954 to 1961 the free-market trade was regulated by the 1953 and 1958 International Sugar Agreements, although trade outside the free market was not subject to the provisions of these agreements. Aside from the United States market, the markets of the French Community and of Portugal are the only ones of those excluded from the provisions of the International Sugar Agreements that are comprehensively regulated.

The highlights of the present United States sugar policy are sketched by Bates and Schmitz.[3] The following provisions of a 1965 bill to amend and to extend the provisions of the Sugar Act of 1948, as amended, are of particular interest.

1. The Sugar Act is extended for five years to December 31, 1971.

2. The mainland beet-sugar quota was increased by 375,000 short tons, and the mainland cane-sugar quota by 205,000 short tons. The domestic sugar-producing areas now have the following quotas as compared with the 1962 amendments.

[3]*Ibid.*, pp. 31–32.

Area	1962 Amendment	1965 Amendment
	(Thousand short tons)	
United States		
Domestic beet sugar	2650	3025
Mainland cane sugar	895	1100
Hawaiian Islands	1110	1110
Puerto Rico	1140	1140
Virgin Islands	15	15
	5810	6390

To or from the above total of 6,390,000 short tons, raw value, there will be added or subtracted, as the case may be, a quantity equal to 65 percent of the amount by which the Secretary of Agriculture's determination of requirements of consumers for the calendar year exceeds 10,400,000 short tons or is less than 9,700,000 short tons, raw value. This amount will be apportioned between the domestic beet area and the mainland cane area.

3. A quota will be given to the Philippines in the amount of 1,050,000 short tons, raw value, plus 10.86 percent of the amount, not exceeding 700,000 short tons, raw value, by which the Secretary's determination of requirements for consumption for the calendar year exceeds 9,700,000 short tons, raw value.

4. The Cuban share of 50 percent was prorated to the various foreign countries listed, in accordance with their basic quotas, until such time as Cuba's quota is restored following its return to the free world, except that the portion of the Cuban share arising from consumption requirements in excess of 10 million short tons, raw value, will be prorated only to countries that are members of the Organization of American States.

5. Assigned to the Philippines was a share amounting to 47.22 percent of all deficits under the above quotas, beginning in 1966, except that a deficit of a country that is a member of the Central American Common Market will first be allocated to other member countries. The remainder of deficits arising in a domestic area or any Western Hemisphere country will be prorated to other Western Hemisphere countries. The remainder of deficits arising elsewhere will be prorated to other non-Western Hemisphere countries. Special consideration will be given to the countries that purchase United States agricultural commodities.

Space does not permit a full review here of how these constraints will affect world sugar prices and trade flows, but the reader will find the Bates-Schmitz study of considerable interest. Suffice it to say that the perfect market model falls considerably short of providing a true representation of the world sugar trade, but it can provide a framework around which the details of this market can be assembled and analyzed.

13.4 NORTHEAST MILKSHEDS AND THE CANADIAN BORDER[4]

Some empirical situations are better understood by using a spatially dispersed production model like that outlined in Chapter 7. Our example is drawn from a study of the effects of the virtual exclusion of Canadian fluid milk and cream supplies from consumer centers in the northeastern part of the United States.

In the period immediately following World War II, Bredo and Rojko found that Boston would be affected more than any other Northeast market by the entry of Canadian supplies, but that New York milk and cream prices were not measurably affected. Exclusion of the nearby Canadian dairying area was responsible for an uneconomical extension of the Boston milk supply area along the Rutland line into the New York counties adjacent to Canada. Without entry of Canadian supplies, the Boston market reached out for milk 350 miles, almost to the western border of Franklin County, Maine, a distance of 370 miles from Boston. The introduction of Canadian supplies would have brought about a contraction of 40 miles, bringing the Boston milk zone on the west to Clinton County in New York State and to Brownville, Maine on the Bangor and Aroostook Railroad (Table 13.3).

Opening the border would also have brought about a decline in the Boston milk price of 2 cents, or 7 cents under New York City. This causes an equivalent reduction of the price in all the New England secondary markets except Connecticut. At the peak of the 1947 fall season, savings arising from unhindered entry of milk to these New England markets would have amounted to $1146 per day. By this reallocation, the Boston cream supply area in Franklin and St. Lawrence counties in upstate New York would extend into Canada, both into the counties across the St. Lawrence River and also into the eastern townships of Quebec (see Figure 13.1).

[4]This section draws heavily on William Bredo and Anthony S. Rojko, *Prices and Milksheds of Northeastern Markets*, Massachusetts Experiment Station Bulletin 470, Amherst, August 1952.

TABLE 13.3 Effect of Free Entry of Canadian Fluid Milk and Cream on Boston Prices Relative to New York City and on Market Boundaries

Item	New York City Market	Boston Market	
		Canadian Milk and Cream Excluded	Free Entry from Canada
Relative prices *(cents per hundred-weight)*			
Fluid milk	114.0	109.0	107.0
Cream-powder	41.6	42.6	42.6
Distance to product boundary (*miles*)			
Fluid milk: truck,	350	290	270
rail	380	350	310
Cream-powder:			
rail	908	1015	1015

Source. W. Bredo and A. S. Rojko, *Prices and Milksheds of Northeastern Markets.* Northeastern Regional Publication No. 9, University of Massachusetts Agricultural Experiment Station Bulletin No. 470, Amherst. Table 19, p. 54 and Table 24, p. 69.

Large supplies of milk were available in this area for use in the form of cream which, otherwise, would be diverted into the manufacture of butter, cheese, evaporated milk, and other milk products. If permitted unhindered entry into the United States in the form of cream, milk manufactured in Quebec and Ontario was of sufficient volume to meet the total demand of the Northeast. It was estimated that Northeast markets could obtain a supply-consumption equilibrium for cream by absorbing the "surplus" supplies available in an area extending from St. Thomas and London, Ontario in the western part of the Niagara Peninsula to the eastern townships of Quebec. If the Philadelphia market were to reach into the Niagara Peninsula instead of to Chicago, the costs of inshipping cream could be reduced by 4 cents per hundredweight. It is not unreasonable to suggest that the whole cream and milk price structure of the Northeast was at least 4 cents per hundredweight higher than it would otherwise have been as a result of the virtual exclusion of Canadian cream. Based on cream consumption alone, the saving for the region would have been about $4090 per day in the period of lowest production.

A. Imports of Canadian milk and cream prohibited

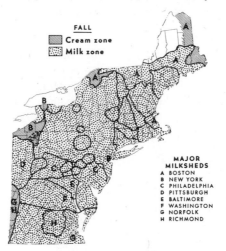

B. Free entry of Canadian milk and cream

FIGURE 13.1 The effect of prohibition of the Canadian fluid milk and cream imports on the Northeast milksheds. (*Source.* W. Bredo and A. S. Rojko, *Prices and Milksheds of Northeastern Markets*, Agricultural Experiment Station Bulletin 470, University of Massachusetts, Amherst, 1952. Based on supply-consumption relationships of November-December, 1947.)

This example illustrates how a spatially-dispersed production model can be used to measure the effects of a variety of market-exclusion practices. It shows clearly how these practices can influence the site-price surface, can modify product flows, and can raise the cost of supplying consumer centers with specified quantities of closely related products.

13.5 FRESH VEGETABLES IN MIDWINTER

The effect of tariffs on prices and trade can be illustrated by considering the midwinter supply of fresh vegetables in the United States. Few regions in the country have a good climate for winter vegetable production, as Figure 13.2 indicates. Only in the lower Rio Grande River valley

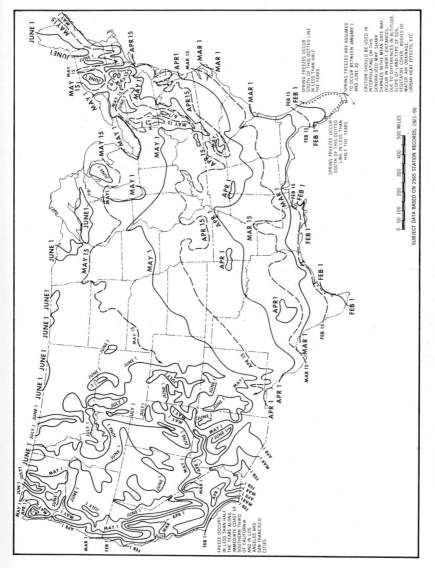

FIGURE 13.2 The mean date of the last 32° temperature in the spring in the continental United States. [*Source. Supplying U.S. Markets with Fresh Winter Produce.* United States Economic Research Service, Agricultural Economic Report No. 154 Washington (April 1969). Figure 14, p. 133.]

269

and in southern Florida does the last winter frost in less than half the years occur earlier than February 1. However, fresh vegetables can be produced during the winter months in some areas of the Caribbean and in parts of Mexico. However, this production is subject to United States import duties, as is shown for the selected crops in Table 13.4. The United States tariff schedules for these crops are arranged so that the amount of the duty varies with the season of the year. For example, tomatoes entering the United States between March 1 and July 14 or between

TABLE 13.4   United States Import Duties on Selected Crops 1969

Crop and Time Period	Duty in Cents per Pound
Cucumbers	
If entered during the period from December 1 in any year to the last day of the following February, inclusive.	2.2
If entered during the period from March 1 to June 30, inclusive, or the period from September 1 to November 30, inclusive, in any year.	3.0
If entered during the period from July 1 to August 31, inclusive, in any year.	1.5
Eggplant	
If entered during the period from April 1 to November 30, inclusive, in any year.	1.5
Other.	1.1
Peppers	2.5
Strawberries	
If entered during the period from June 15 to September 15, inclusive, in any year.	0.4
If entered at any other time.	0.75
Tomatoes	
If entered during the period from March 1 to July 15, inclusive, or the period from September 1 to November 14, inclusive, in any year.	2.1
If entered during the period from July 15 to August 31, inclusive, in any year.	1.5
If entered during the period from November 15, in any year, to the last day of the following February, inclusive.	1.5

Source.   Tariff Schedules of the United States Annotated (1969), U.S. Tariff Commission. TC Pub. 272. Reproduced in *Supplying U.S. Markets with Fresh Winter Produce*. Agricultural Economic Report No. 154 United States Economic Research Service, Washington (April 1969), Table 3, p. 13.

September 1 and November 14 are subject to a 2.1 cent per pound duty, although tomatoes imported during other periods of the year are subject to a 1.5 cent per pound duty.

The effect of United States import duties and other costs associated with importing vine-ripe tomatoes from Mexico is summarized in Table 13.5. A comparison of south Florida and northwest Mexico reveals that the total production and harvesting costs are far lower in Mexico ($0.49) than in south Florida ($1.31). Mexican packing and selling costs are

TABLE 13.5 Production and Marketing Costs for Vine-Ripe Tomatoes, South Florida and Northwest Mexico, 1967–1968 Season

Item	Production Area (Dollars per 20 Pound Lug)	
	South Florida	Northwest Mexico
Preharvest cost	0.84	0.31
Harvesting cost	0.47	0.18
Total production and harvesting cost	1.31	0.49
Packing and selling cost	0.82	0.44
Mexican export cost to Nogales, Arizona:		
Union and association dues	0.00	0.02
United States import duty	0.00	0.39
United States customs and other services	0.00	0.02
Mexican taxes, duties, and services	0.00	0.07
Freight and related costs	0.00	0.30
Labor, materials, and miscellaneous expenses	0.00	0.02
Sales commission and promotion	0.00	0.20
Total marketing costs	0.82	1.46
Delivery cost to:		
New York	0.45	0.93
Chicago	0.50	0.61
San Francisco	0.80	0.39
Total costs delivered to:		
New York	2.58	2.88
Chicago	2.63	2.56
San Francisco	2.93	2.34

Source. Compiled from *Supplying U.S. Markets with Fresh Winter Produce. Ibid.* Table 38, p. 82; Table 40, p. 84; Table 61, p. 107; and Table 67, p. 111.

roughly one-half the Florida level, but when exports costs are added, including the United States import duty of $0.39 per 20 pound lug, we find that marketing costs total $0.82 in south Florida and $1.46 in northwest Mexico. By using Nogales, Arizona as the import point, we add delivery costs to New York, Chicago, and San Francisco to arrive at a total delivered cost in these three cities. In New York City, the total costs for Mexican tomatoes exceed costs for Florida tomatoes by $0.30, but are $0.07 below Florida in Chicago and $0.59 below Florida in San Francisco.

The relative shares of Florida and Mexico tomato shipments in selected cities in the United States in 1967 are shown in Figure 13.3. In view of our findings above, we would expect that the Mexican supplies would dominate in western markets and that the Florida supplies would dominate along the east coast. This is, in fact, what occurs. However, notice that, although Buffalo obtains 90 percent of its supplies from Florida, Toronto and Montreal purchase about equal quantities from Mexico and from Florida, reflecting certain differences in the United States and the Canadian import duty structures. In the absence of a $0.39 import duty from Mexico, supplies from that country could sell at a lower price than Florida supplies in every major United States city. Clearly, the importance of import duties varies from one commodity to another and from one season to another, making generalizations hazardous. However, the general impact of import duties on product prices and flows are illustrated by the vine-ripe tomato case.

13.6 ADMINISTERED PRICING

An almost unlimited number of examples might be cited to show the effect of administered pricing in one form or another on the prices of agricultural commodities. Similarly, a wide variety of examples might be provided concerning the ubiquitous nature of government intervention in the free flow of many commodities from region to region and from country to country with the corresponding impact on prices and the distribution of revenues among landowners, operators, and laborers. One of these examples deals with the effects of the federal government support of the price of flue-cured tobacco.

The price of flue-cured tobacco sold by United States farmers is supported through purchases by the Agricultural Stabilization and Conservation Service of the United States Department of Agriculture. Since the quantity of tobacco that would be produced at support prices far exceeds the quantity that can be marketed at these prices, it is necessary

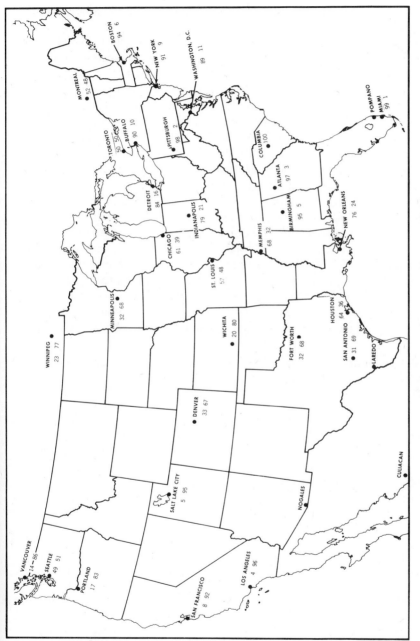

FIGURE 13.3 The relative shares of Florida and Mexico tomato shipments to selected markets in 1967. Notice that the first number is the percent from Florida and that the second number is the percent from Mexico. [*Source: Supplying U.S. Markets with Fresh Winter Produce*].

to limit the amount of tobacco that is produced. This is done through acreage allotments and through marketing quotas on individual farming units.

The average flue-cured tobacco acreage allotment is about three acres. There are important economies of size in tobacco production, and many farmers rent an additional allotment from other farmers. For sometime it was required that a tobacco allotment rented in this way be used on the farm where the allotment rests. However, in 1962 the transfer of tobacco allotments among farms within a given county was first allowed. By 1966, one out of every four owners of a flue-cured tobacco allotment transferred some or all of their allotment to other producers in their county. The proportion of allotments rented out in this way varied from 20 percent in the Carolinas to more than 40 percent in Florida.

The value of tobacco allotments can be approximated by comparing the annual rent paid for these allotments with the average price received by growers for their tobacco. The dollar value of these allotments ranged from 14.5 cents in Virginia and North Carolina to more than 18.5 cents in Georgia (Table 13.6). When expressed in terms of the average price received, the rent varied between 23 percent in Virginia to 28 percent in South Carolina and Georgia. In addition to providing information concerning the value of these restrictions on output, these data suggest the pressure for the movement of tobacco allotments toward South Carolina,

TABLE 13.6 Average Rent Paid for Flue-Cured Tobacco Allotments Transferred by Owners to Other Producers 1966

Production Belt	Rent per Pound of Marketing Quota (Cents per Pound)	Rent as Percent of Average Price Received (Percent)
Old Belt, Virginia and North Carolina Type 11*a*	14.5	22.6
Middle Belt, North Carolina Type 11*b*	14.5	23.1
Eastern North Carolina Type 12	17.7	28.3
South Carolina and border North Carolina Type 13	18.5	28.3
Georgia, Florida and Alabama Type 14	17.6	26.6
All belts	17.0	26.6

Source. Dale M. Hoover, *Lease and transfer of flue-cured tobacco marketing quota among farms*, North Carolina State University, Raleigh. Economics Information Report No. 6 (December 1967), Table 1, p. 8, and Table 2, p. 17.

Georgia, and Florida relative to Virginia and North Carolina. If transfer restrictions are removed so as to allow unlimited transfer among farms and across county lines, the total value and importance of these allotment leases can be expected to increase substantially.

SELECTED READINGS

Nonprice Factors Affecting Trade

Bates, Thomas H. and Andrew Schmitz, *A Spatial Equilibrium Analysis of the World Sugar Economy*, University of California, Giannini Foundation Monograph No. 23, Berkeley (May 1969).

Christiansen, Martin K, *The Impact of Milk Holding on Midwestern Markets*, University of Minnesota Agricultural Experimental Station Bulletin 493, St. Paul (1969).

Fliginger, John C. et al., *Supplying U.S. Markets with Fresh Winter Produce: Capabilities of U.S. and Mexican Production Areas*, United States Economic Research Service Agri. Econ. Report No. 154. Washington (April 1969).

Gray, Roger W. et al., *An Economic Analysis of the Impact of Government Programs and the Potato Industry of the U.S.*, University of Minnesota Agricultural Experiment Station Technical Bulletin 211, St. Paul (June 1954).

Jamison, John A., *Marketing Orders, Cartels, and Cling Peaches: A Long-Run View*, Food Research Institute Studies, Vol. VI, No. 2, Palo Alto (1966). pp. 117–142.

Johnson, Harry G., "Trade Preferences and Developing Countries," in W. W. McPherson (ed.), *Economic Development of Tropical Agriculture*, University of Florida Press, Gainesville (1968). pp. 112–132.

U.S. Department of Agriculture, "Barriers to Trade Between States," *Marketing, The 1954 Yearbook of Agriculture*, Washington (1954). pp. 288–295.

U.S. Department of Agriculture, *Farm Labor in a Changing Agriculture*, published as Part 4, Senate Hearings, Department of Agriculture and Related Agencies Appropriations, 90th Congress, First Session. United States Government Printing Office, Washington (1967).

U.S. Department of Agriculture, *Regulations Affecting the Movement and Merchandizing of Milk*, Agricultural Marketing Service, Marketing Research Report No. 98, Washington (June 1955).

University of Illinois, Trade Barriers in Milk Distribution," *Papers in Dairy Marketing, Agricultural Industries Forum*, February 1960, Department of Agricultural Economics, Urbana.

PART IV

REGIONAL SPECIALIZATION AND TRADE

chapter 14

SHORT-RUN TRADE FLOWS

For ease in exposition, we have postponed our discussion of multiple products until the treatment of single-product market models could be extended to include spatial, form, and temporal dimensions of market price. In Chapter 5, we warned that the benefits from trade could be shown only by simultaneous consideration of two or more products. The reason for this is clear. It is that some of the resources devoted to product A in the no-trade case must be shifted by *producers* to other products when trade results in a lowering of the price of product A in region X. Also, *consumers* of product A will shift some of their expenditures in the no-trade case away from other products and will purchase more of product A when its price falls as a consequence of the opening of trade with region Y.

To introduce the analysis of regional specialization and trade, we first consider a two-region situation in which the supply of the two products is taken as given. In later chapters, we modify these stock models and allow output of the two products to vary with price. Eventually, we treat models in which inputs and product outputs in multiple regions are all treated as variables, thus, approaching a general equilibrium analytical framework.

279

14.1 THE CONCEPT OF UTILITY

The analytical apparatus used to demonstrate the effects of trade in the short-run case of fixed product supplies will be familiar to most readers but will be reviewed here very briefly. We have observed that the individual's demand schedule reflects his particular tastes and preferences — or the ability of the commodity to satisfy his particular wants. The satisfaction of wants necessarily is a subjective matter for the individual and, as such, is difficult to measure. The characteristics of commodities (and services) that satisfy wants we label *utility*, and this is an important concept even though we cannot measure utility in objective terms. In spite of this, we can think of an individual receiving a certain amount of utility from the possession or consumption of a particular set of commodities. Let us consider a simple illustration: A person obtains certain utility or satisfaction from the combination of four apples and three oranges. His utility is increased (so long as both apples and oranges yield positive rather than negative utility) if he is given an additional apple, an additional orange, or one of each. Contrariwise, his total satisfaction will be decreased if we take away an apple, an orange, or one of each. Since each of these commodities bears a positive relation to the consumer's total utility, it follows that a decrease in the amount of one can be offset by an increase in the other.

This is illustrated in Figure 14.1. The original combination of four apples and three oranges is represented by *A*. Points *B*, *C*, and *D* show increases in either or both commodities and, hence, represent points of greater total utility. Points *E*, *F*, and *G*, on the other hand, represent

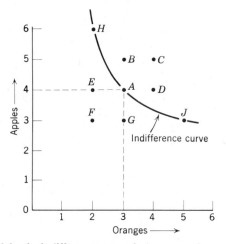

FIGURE 14.1   An indifference curve between apples and oranges.

smaller amounts of one or both commodities and so lower total utility. This person indicates, however, that his utility would be unchanged if he were given six apples and two oranges or three apples and five oranges. Thus, *H* and *J* represent combinations equivalent to *A* in terms of total utility. A curve joining these points, and many other similarly determined points, represents a constant utility curve or contour. If the consumer actually receives the same total satisfaction or utility from any combination represented by points on this curve, then his particular position on the curve will be a matter of complete indifference. For this reason, such isoutility curves are called *indifference* curves.

As long as the possession of more of the commodities in question yields positive utility, then indifference curves must be negatively inclined; a gain in the quantity of one commodity must be offset by a reduction in the quantity of the other to hold constant the total utility. In addition, indifference curves can be expected to be convex to the origin, as shown in Figure 14.1. This property is a reflection of the principle of diminishing marginal utility—that added units of a commodity will normally add less and less to total utility. The slope at any point on an indifference curve represents the inverse ratio of marginal utilities. In the present example, this means that the slope at any point on curve *HAJ* represents the marginal utility of oranges divided by the marginal utility of apples. When we move toward *J*. the marginal utility of oranges decreases, the marginal utility of apples increases, the ratio of marginal utilities thus decreases and, hence, the slope of the curve becomes less and less steep. This slope is also called the *personal rate of substitution*.[1]

Since we could start with any combination of apples and oranges (for instance, *B*, *C*, or *F*) and trace out indifference curves, it is apparent that our diagram might be filled with these curves and that every point on the diagram falls on one and only one curve. This family of indifference curves is called an indifference or preference map. The curves themselves will all be negatively inclined and convex to the origin; they will not cross or intersect for this would require that greater quantities have less utility than lesser quantities of the commodities in question. Each curve will represent a constant total level of utility or satisfaction. Each higher curve (up and to the right) represents greater total utility. For this reason, we can order the curves from lower to higher total utility even though we cannot measure the amount of utility in objective terms. Stated another way, we can rank combinations of commodities in terms of their total utility to the individual, indicating that some are preferable

---

[1]Commonly referred to as marginal rate of substitution—a phrase which fails to distinguish between personal and technical rates of substitution.

to others even though we cannot say by how much more they are preferred.

The particular shape of indifference curves will reflect the tastes and preferences of the individual consumer. If he is very fond of apples and not especially fond of oranges, it will take a large number of oranges to offset the loss in utility from a single apple; and so the indifference curves would be relatively flat. On the other hand, a consumer greatly addicted to oranges would have relatively steep indifference curves. If the two products are nearly perfect substitutes over a wide range, then the indifference curves will approximate negatively inclined straight lines. At the other extreme, products that are very poor substitutes will be characterized by quite convex indifference curves.

14.2 CONSUMER EQUILIBRIUM

Let us now consider what this indifference curve apparatus can add to our understanding of the nature of consumer choice and of demand. Every consumer evaluates a large number of alternative commodities and, thus, we would need indifference surfaces with as many dimensions as commodities. The essential nature of the process may be revealed, however, by aggregating all commodities in money terms and by considering indifference curves between money and a particular commodity. In this case, it is understood that the marginal utility of money does not represent utility of the monetary unit itself but instead the utility of alternative commodities that can be purchased with the money. Figure 14.2 shows a hypothetical indifference map between income and a given commodity

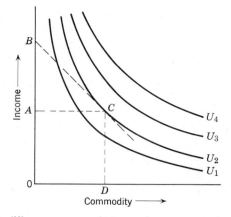

FIGURE 14.2 The indifference curves between income and quantity of a particular commodity.

for an individual consumer. A few of the indifference curves are shown: $U_1, \ldots, U_4$ where the subscripts refer not to the absolute level of utility or satisfaction but to the rank from lower to higher total satisfaction.

Suppose that the individual has an income represented by OB and that he is confronted by a price P for the commodity. As long as this price remains fixed, the individual can exchange dollars of income for units of the commodity in a fixed proportion. More specifically, the individual can buy $1/P$ units of the commodity for $1.00; and within the limits of his income, he can elect to buy as much or as little of the commodity as he chooses at this fixed exchange rate. In the diagram, we represent these exchange possibilities—income for commodity—by the line BC. Notice that the line starts from B representing the consumer's income, that it is a straight line corresponding to the fixed exchange rate P, and that the slope AB/AC equals the exchange rate P. In this diagram, then, we are representing (1) the consumer's tastes and preferences—the indifference map, (2) the consumer's income, and (3) the price of the product relative to other prices—money.

In this situation, the consumer will maximize his satisfactions by exchanging money for the commodity until he reaches the highest possible indifference curve. Starting at B, he moves along the price line toward C. At first, each move in this direction brings him to higher indifference curves; but, finally, at C he has reached the highest curve available with his given income and the given price. If he moves beyond C, he finds himself on lower indifference curves. Point C must then represent the best possible solution to the consumer's purchase problem: his satisfaction is as large as possible if he gives up AB of income in order to obtain AC of the commodity. Notice that the price line BC intersects all lower indifference curves but is tangent to curve U_2. From this we can conclude that the consumer's equilibrium position requires that price ratios must be equated to the marginal rates of substitution. If the marginal utility or satisfaction obtained from expenditure of an added dollar on commodity X is greater than from the last dollar spent on commodity Y, then the consumer can improve his position by reallocating his expenditures until the marginal satisfactions per dollar spent on each and every commodity are equal.

14.3   BARTER BETWEEN INDIVIDUALS

We can now improve our analysis of the interdependent and reciprocal flow or exchange of commodities by using the indifference curve apparatus discussed above. Let us consider two individuals with present stocks of two commodities. For simplicity, assume that Mr. Green has a stock or supply of commodity A and that Mr. Brown has a stock of commodity B. This is indicated graphically in Figure 14.3 where Green's stock is *oc* of commodity A and where some of Green's indifference curves for commodities A and B are represented by curve *ceh* and others like it which are convex to the origin O. Brown's stock of B and his indifference curves are also represented, but in this case we have rotated the diagram 180° so that the origin is located at O′ with the quantities of B measured to the left of his origin and the quantities of A measured vertically below O′. This "Edgeworth-Bowley box" diagram is so constructed, in other words, that the sides measure the total stock *oc* of A that Green possesses and the total stock *o′c* of B in Brown's possession. Any point within this box is attainable, in that it involves only the available quantities of the two commodities; and any such point will represent a distribution of the two commodities between the two individuals. Point O, for example, indicates that Green would have zero quantities of both commodities, while Brown would have the entire supplies.

Assume that these are the only two commodities involved; this simplifies the graphic presentation, but it should be emphasized that the general conclusions that we are able to obtain will hold true for multiproduct cases. With this construction, both Green and Brown start at position *c*. Will it be possible to exchange commodities to the benefit of both persons? Notice that in the absence of exchange, Green finds himself on his indifference curve *ceh* while Brown is on his curve *cgh*. Any position above and to the right of *ceh* would place Green on a higher indifference curve,

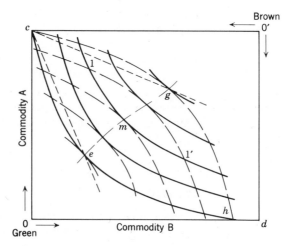

FIGURE 14.3   The superimposed indifference maps for two individuals.

just as any position below and to the left of *cgh* would improve Brown's satisfactions. It is apparent, therefore, that any movement from point *c* into the concave area *cehgc* would permit both Green and Brown to better their positions as compared to the situation at *c* in the absence of trade. Suppose that they start to barter, Green offering to exchange some of his A for B and Brown offering to give up some B in order to obtain some A. By this process, they arrive at point *l* where both have increased their satisfaction or total utility.

But this movement from *c* to *l* does not exhaust the possibilities of exchange with mutual benefit, since now any move from point *l* into the smaller concave area between *l* and *l'* will again permit each individual to move to a higher indifference curve. This will continue until some position, such as *m*, is reached on the *contract line emg*, which consists of all combinations where the two sets of indifference curves are tangent — where Green's personal rate of substitution is exactly equal to Brown's personal rate of substitution. An inspection of the diagram will indicate that any change from *m* to some point not on the contract line must involve decreased satisfactions for one or both individuals, although moves from *m* up or down the contract line will improve one person's position only by reducing the satisfactions for the other individual (Figure 14.4). As pointed out above, the final position in equilibrium must lie within the concave area formed by the indifference curves *ceh* and *cgh*; in fact, stable equilibrium will not be obtained until a position is reached somewhere on the contract line between *e* and *g*. The diagram also indicates

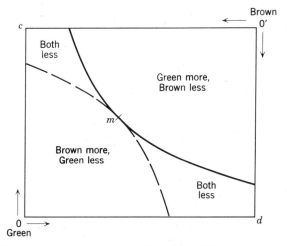

FIGURE 14.4 The changes in satisfactions for two individuals, compared to situation at some point *m* on contract line.

the extreme limits for the barter terms of trade—the quantities of A that will be exchanged for a unit of B. If Green is the more skillful bargainer, the barter terms of trade will approach the slope of the straight line cg while, if Brown is more adept, the terms of trade will approach the slope of line ce.

14.4 INDIVIDUAL "OFFER" CURVES

As long as we remain in a barter economy with two individuals, the final solution will be indeterminate, falling between e and g at some point, reflecting the relative bargaining abilities of the two. But let us introduce a simple rule in this game of exchange—that terms of trade will be "announced" and that each person will then adjust his offers to buy and to sell to these terms of trade. This is equivalent to saying that prices exist in a market economy with individuals buying and/or selling at these prices. And observe that the barter terms of trade of so many units of A per unit of B are equivalent to the inverse ratio of prices P_b/P_a in a price economy. With this rule, a low price for B relative to the price of A, equivalent to a relatively flat terms-of-trade line, would induce Green to demand a large quantity of B in exchange for a moderate amount of A. But this price ratio would be disadvantageous to Brown, and we observe that he would be willing to give up only a small amount of B. This discrepancy would represent a disequilibrium position, and the excess of the amount of B demanded over the amount offered for exchange would force an upward revision in the price of B. Eventually, a price ratio would be discovered that would equate the offers of the two individuals, and this would represent the final and determinate equilibrium.

All of these adjustments can be indicated readily by an elaboration of the diagram just presented. In Figure 14.5 we show the box diagram with indifference maps for Green and Brown. In addition, we show curves cfk and cfj, summarizing the offers of Green and Brown to exchange goods at various price ratios or terms of trade. Suppose the P_b/P_a ratio is represented by the slope of line cr. At these relative prices, Brown would offer to exchange B for A so as to reach point n, since this combination would place him on his highest attainable indifference curve. Green's best position would be at r, however, involving larger quantities of both commodities. Since the quantities demanded do not equal the quantities supplied, they cannot represent equilibrium prices.

Under the conditions stated, the equilibrium position is found at the intersection f of the two *offer* or *supply-demand* curves. At this point, Green's offer to supply cs of A is just equal to Brown's demand ft, while

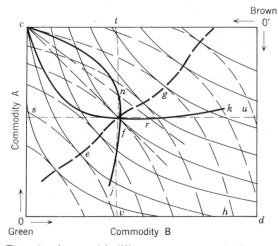

FIGURE 14.5 The superimposed indifference curves and offer curves for two individuals.

Brown's offer *ct* of B coincides with the quantity *fs* demanded by Green. Exchange takes place at the equilibrium price ratio represented by the slope of the straight line from *c* to *f*; and observe that at *f*, this line is tangent to an indifference curve for Green and also an indifference curve for Brown. From this we deduce the general conditions for equilibrium: that the personal rates of substitution (or the inverse ratio of marginal utilities) must be equal for all individuals and equal to the inverse ratio of product prices.

Notice that exchange or trade opportunities are measured from point *c*, the original position for each individual before trade. The final consumption pattern is indicated by point *f*. Green consumes *os* of A and *ov* of B, Brown consumes *o't* of A and *o'u* of B, and these quantities exactly exhaust the total available supplies. This solution in no way depends on our original assumption that each individual had a stock of one commodity only. Figure 14.6 shows the situation for an individual who starts with some of both commodities—point *c'*. This places him on indifference curve *dc'e*; and at an exchange rate tangent to this curve at *c'*, he would find it impossible to better his position through trade. In short, with terms of trade indicated by the slope of line *hk*, this person would be forced to lower indifference curves if he moved from point *c'*. At any other price ratio, however, he could engage in trade to his benefit. With higher prices of B relative to A, he could move into the area bounded on the left by the segment *c'd* of the indifference curve and on the right by the vertical line through *c'* (representing an infinitely high value for P_b relative to P_a). His

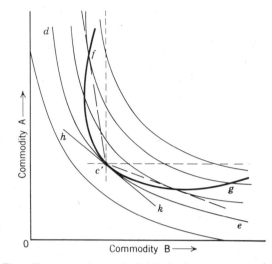

FIGURE 14.6 The offer curve for an individual who possesses stocks of two commodities.

offer curve in this range is indicated by the curved line $c'f$. With lower prices for B, the reverse would be true, and his offer curve would be $c'g$. His total offer curve then is $fc'g$, reflecting the fact that in certain price ranges he will sell A and buy B while in others he will buy A and sell B.

This simple model has brought out the fact that trade is basically concerned with the exchange of *goods for goods* instead of *goods for money*. Of course, with many commodities involved for every individual, direct barter of goods would be quite cumbersome and difficult. Here, the introduction of money as a medium of exchange is most useful. Goods are then traded for money and vice versa, but it must be emphasized that money merely represents a claim on goods and, as such, is only a facilitating device.[2]

14.5 SHORT-RUN REGIONAL OFFER CURVES

If we redefine our original problem to represent two regions rather than two individuals, the above analysis might be considered appropriate for interregional trade. In a strict sense, however, regional indifference curves cannot be used, since it is not possible to add together the preference maps of individuals. This stems from the subjective character of

[2]Money and monetary policies have a more active role in international trade than this suggests, but these aspects may be neglected in our presentation of the theory of interregional trade.

utility and the fact that the individual's indifference curves can only be ranked from lower to higher without specific measurement of the total utility or satisfaction involved. We might proceed on the heroic assumption that all individuals in a region had exactly the same tastes and preferences since, in this case, the regional preference map would merely be an individual preference map scaled upward in direct proportion to the number of individuals in the region.

A more useful approach, however, is based on the fact that we can add together individual offer curves because they are defined entirely in objective and measurable quantities. For any selected price ratio, we can sum together the quantities of A that all individuals offer to sell, the quantities of A that all offer to buy (and at any price some will be buyers and others sellers), the quantities of B offered for sale, and the quantities of B that all individuals offer to buy. With these four sets of quantity data for any assigned price ratio, it is a straightforward matter to construct regional offer curves similar to the individual offer curves. If we are concerned with trade between and among regions, however, these offer curves will be "gross" in that the indicated supply and demand conditions will be balanced off, at least in part, by trade *within* each region. If we consider a region in isolation, the aggregate offer curves just described will intersect to determine regional prices; and, at these prices, the buying and selling operations within the region will be in balance for each commodity. This means that at these prices the region would trade entirely on an internal or domestic basis without the export or import of any commodities. If we subtract the quantities that would be sold from the quantities that would be bought within the region at any specified price ratio, however, we can obtain "net" or *external* offer curves for the region.

This is illustrated in Figure 14.7 where we have assumed that our friends Brown and Green form the total inhabitants of a region. Our previous analysis then shows the internal trade equilibrium for this region, and the equilibrium ratio P_b/P_a is now shown by the slope of line *od*. At this price ratio the region would not find it profitable to trade with other regions. If the price of B increases relative to A, the price line becomes steeper than *od* with the result that there would be "surpluses" of selling offers for B and buying offers for A. These surpluses provide the opportunity for external trade and are summarized for various price ratios by the external offer curve *oc*. In a similar way, lower values for P_b/P_a are represented by price lines flatter than *od* and would result in net regional offers to sell A and buy B and external offer curve *oe*. To summarize, each region will have two external offer curves. One will fall *above* the internal equilibrium price ratio and will summarize offers to export B in exchange for A imports, and the other will fall *below* the

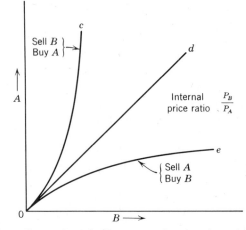

FIGURE 14.7   The net or external offer curves for a region, showing quantities of commodities offered for export and demanded for import. (*Source.* Derived from Figure 14.5.)

internal equilibrium price ratio and will show the region's offers to export A in exchange for B imports.

With this tool of external regional offer curves, we can complete our analysis of short-term interregional trade. Consider two regions, X and Y, for each of which we have the internal equilibrium price ratio and the pair of external offer curves. This is illustrated in Figure 14.8 where region X is represented by the internal price ratio *od* and the associated pair of offer curves and where region Y is similarly represented by *oe* and its

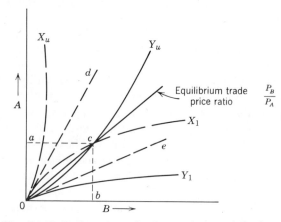

FIGURE 14.8   The external offer curves for two regions and the interregional trade equilibrium.

associated pair of external offer curves. Now if trade is to occur between these two regions, the product price ratio with trade will fall somewhere between the price ratios in isolation so that trade possibilities lie between the limits *od* and *oe*. This means that only one offer curve is now pertinent for each region: the *lower* offer curve for region X where the region exports A and imports B and the *upper* offer curve for region Y showing imports of A and exports of B.

The intersection of these two curves at *c* then defines the interregional trade equilibrium. The terms-of-trade or price ratio is shown by the slope of line *oc*. At this price, region X will ship *oa* of A to region Y, and this will be "paid for" by the shipment *ob* of B from region Y to X.

SELECTED READINGS

Short-Run Trade Flows

Braff, Allan, *op. cit.*, pp. 241–252.

Lloyd, Cliff, *op. cit.*, Chapter 2, "The Theory of Exchange and Pareto Optimality," pp. 80–97.

Newman, Peter, *The Theory of Exchange*. Prentice-Hall, Inc., Englewood Cliffs (1965). pp. 50–125.

Schneider, Erich, *op. cit.*, pp. 299–313.

Waugh, Frederich V., "A Partial Indifference Surface for Beef and Pork," *Journal of Farm Economics*. Vol. 38, No. 1 (February 1956). pp. 102–112.

chapter 15

REGIONAL PRODUCTION POTENTIALS

The above analysis has been short run in nature for we have taken stocks of commodities as given and appraised exchange possibilities in terms of the distribution of these available stocks among individuals or regions. This is only a first step, however, for important and significant problems in interregional trade involve the adjustments of regional production patterns in order to take full advantage of the special productive resources in any region. Regions and individuals are differently endowed — with abilities, skills, intelligence, physical power and agility, and training and experience for individuals and with quantitative and qualitative differences in climate, soils, mineral deposits, location, and population in the case of regions. An exchange economy is characterized by the development of economic specialization or the division of labor. On the individual level, some men are mechanics, some butchers, some teachers, some doctors, some lawyers, and some professional athletes. Some regions predominate in heavy industry, some in light industry, some in the production of cereal crops, some in fruits and vegetables, and some develop as trading and commercial centers. The gain to the individual from specialization in an exchange economy is obvious — consider the utter impossibility of each individual producing for himself the quantities of all the different goods and services that contribute to our modern living. In a similar way, regional specialization gives rise to important economies and efficiencies in production. We initiate our inquiry into long-run trade adjustments, therefore, with a consideration of the production possibilities in regions.

15.1 ALTERNATIVE PRODUCTION OPPORTUNITIES

Let us return to Mr. Green and assume that he and his family were pioneers on the Ohio frontier at the beginning of the 19th century. He has been developing a farm in an isolated valley, and there he and his family have been struggling to produce a subsistence for themselves. Their productive resources include the labor and skills that they can provide, some simple tools, a span of oxen, and 50 acres of cleared land. It is certain that these limited resources (including climatic and soil conditions) place hard outside limits on the quantities and kinds of outputs they can produce. It is also clear that if they use most of their resources to produce corn, there will be few remaining with which to produce beans or potatoes. In short, this family has a limited range of production opportunities and, in general, will be able to expand the output of certain lines only by contracting or reducing the output in others. Its economic problem is that of deciding how to use these limited resources so as to yield the greatest satisfaction.

For convenience in graphic presentation, assume that the Green family produces and consumes only two commodities (remembering that the analysis, if not the graphic procedure, is applicable to the case of many goods and services). And suppose that the farmland differs in quality as indicated in Table 15.1. For ease in computation, we have illustrated the case where the farm is divided into five-acre tracts with all land exactly the same within each tract but quite different from the land in other tracts. These between-tract differences are indicated by the yields of commodities A and B. Notice that the tracts differ not only in an absolute sense (Z is better than Y for both crops) but they also differ relative to the particular crop (V is fairly good for A but very poor for B, while X is very good for B but quite poor for A). Our problem is to show the A and B production possibilities with these tracts of land and the associated bundle of other resources.

It can readily be determined that Green could produce 530 bushels of A if he used all of his land for A or 650 bushels of B if all land were devoted to that crop. It is also clear that he can move between these two extremes by progressively shifting land from A to B production. Suppose he shifts the land from A to B by following down the order of tracts as

TABLE 15.1 Land Tracts in the Green Farm, with Yields per Acre for Crop A and Crop B[a]

Tract	Acres	Yields (Bushels per Acre)		
		A	B	A/B
V	10	11	2	5.50
W	10	15	7	2.14
X	10	6	23	0.26
Y	10	4	13	0.39
Z	10	17	20	0.85

[a]Hypothetical data. Yield data drawn and arranged at random from numbers from 1 to 25.

TABLE 15.2 Production Combinations as Land is Shifted From Crop A to Crop B[a]

Order No. 1			Order No. 2			Order No. 3			Order No. 4		
	Total Production (Bushels)			Total Production (Bushels)			Total Production (Bushels)			Total Production (Bushels)	
Tract	Crop		Tract	Crop		Tract	Crop		Tract	Crop	
	A	B		A	B		A	B		A	B
–	530	0	–	530	0	–	530	0	–	530	0
V	420	20	Y	490	130	X	470	230	X	470	230
W	270	90	X	430	360	Z	300	430	Y	430	360
X	210	320	V	320	380	Y	260	560	Z	260	560
Y	170	450	W	170	450	W	110	630	W	110	630
Z	0	650	Z	0	650	V	0	650	V	0	650

[a]Based on Table 15.1. This is ordered as follows. No. 1. As given in Table 15.1. No. 2. From lowest to highest A yields. No. 3. From highest to lowest B yields. No. 4. From lowest to highest ratio of A yields to B yields.

listed in the table. With all land in A, his output would be 530 bushels of A and zero bushels of B. After shifting tract V to B, the results would be 420 bushels of A plus 20 bushels of B. Transferring the W land would reduce A to 270 bushels and increase B to 90, and further moves down the table would give combinations of 210 and 320 bushels, 170 and 450 bushels and, finally, zero bushels of A and 650 bushels of B. These production possibilities are summarized as Order No. 1 in Table 15.2 and Figure 15.1.

It takes little thought to indicate that this order, although possible, would be a particularly unfortunate way to go about allocating resources between A and B. Farmer Green recognizes this at once and realizes that a better plan would be to first shift the poorest A land to B, then the next poorest, and so on. This indicates that tract Y should first be transferred to B, followed in order by X, V, W, and Z. The results of this Order No. 2 are clearly superior to Order No. 1 throughout most of the range. But Green is still dissatisfied, since it occurs to him that an alternative ordering would have been to array the tracts from the best to the poorest B land instead of from the poorest to the best A land. The results of Order No. 3, shown in the table and diagram, do prove to be substantially better than Order No. 2.

We could forgive Green if he stopped at this point, since he has

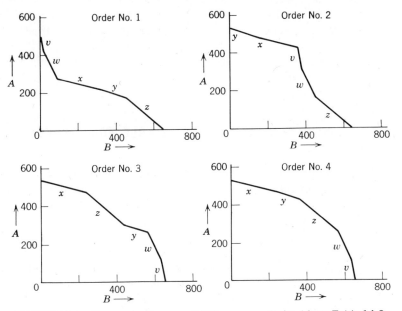

FIGURE 15.1   The production possibilities curves derived from Table 14.2.

considered ordering the land transfer both from the standpoint of A yields and B yields and worked out quite an improved program. But pioneers pay directly for inefficiency, and Green finally realizes that the really important consideration is not the absolute yields of either crop but the comparative yields of A relative to B. He wants to transfer his land from A to B so as to reduce as much as possible the cost of increasing B when measured in the foregone opportunity of producing A. He calculates the ratios of the yields of A to the yields of B as shown in the last column of Table 15.1 and makes an array from the lowest to the highest values of this ratio. This final Order No. 4 does prove to be better than Order No. 3 and, in fact, is the best possible under the stated circumstances. Green now has four schedules or curves showing possible production patterns, but the last is as good as or better than all the others at all the points on the curve.

This curve showing the most efficient production possibilities is called the *opportunity cost curve* because, as explained above, it shows the cost of producing one commodity in terms of the foregone opportunity of producing the other. If we had considered a case with a large number of grades of land and with more or less continuous variation in yields, the opportunity cost curve would become smooth and continuous instead of being made up of a few straight-line segments; but it would retain the same general shape—concave to the origin. With such a smooth curve, the slope of the curve at any point would represent the opportunity cost ratio. In the present case, where factors other than land are held constant, the slope of the opportunity cost curve represents the ratio of yield per acre of A to yield per acre of B—the ratio that Green used to obtain his final and most efficient ordering.

15.2 OPPORTUNITY COST CURVES — SINGLE HOMOGENEOUS FACTOR

The foregoing illustration of the derivation of a concave opportunity cost curve is based on *qualitative* differences in a single productive factor. Although this is realistic, it is important to realize that these concave opportunity cost curves will result with *homogeneous* factors if production is characterized by the law of diminishing physical returns. Consider the case of the production opportunities that are based on a single homogeneous factor that may be used in the production of two alternative commodities. First, assume that the production function for each factor shows constant returns—that the law of diminishing returns does not hold true.

Constant Returns. This situation is illustrated in Figure 15.2 where, in the top portion of the figure, we show the production functions for the two commodities. The output of commodity A is represented by the straight line sloping upward and to the right, and apparently it reflects a basic production function of the type $Q_a = AF_a$ where F_a represents the use of the single factor F in the production of commodity A and the constant A represents the uniform output of Q_a per unit of F_a. The same diagram shows the production function for commodity B: $Q_b = BF_b$ where we have reversed the curve so that the origin is at the right of the diagram and with the length of the base line $0_a 0_b$ representing the total available F. From this construction it is clear that any vertical line on the

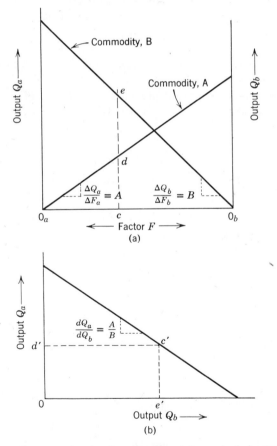

FIGURE 15.2   The linear production functions involving a single homogeneous factor and the corresponding opportunity cost curve. (*a*) Production functions. (*b*) Opportunity cost curve.

diagram will represent a particular allocation of the total available F between the two alternative uses, so that $F = F_a + F_b$. It is also clear that a shift of a unit of F from the production of A to the production of B will represent a constant reduction of A units of A in order to obtain a constant increase of B units of B. The corresponding opportunity cost curve, then, is shown in the lower part of the diagram. As indicated above, this opportunity cost curve will be linear, with slope equal to $-A/B$.

Notice that every point on the opportunity cost curve corresponds to a particular allocation of F between A and B. Thus, if we allocate the total F with $0_a c$ to A and $0_b c$ to B, this will result in outputs of cd of A and ce of B shown in Figure 15.2a. In Figure 15.2b, showing the opportunity cost curve (or the product transformation curve), these quantities are represented by point c' — and every other point on the opportunity cost curve will correspond to a particular allocation of F between the two alternative uses.

Although this is an almost trivial case, it is instructive to trace through the mathematical relationships involved. We are given two products, A and B, each produced in direct proportion to inputs of a single factor F. Thus, the two production functions are of the form:

$$Q_a = AF_a \tag{15.1}$$

$$Q_b = BF_b. \tag{15.2}$$

We also know that the total available amount of the factor F is fixed, so that

$$F = F_a + F_b. \tag{15.3}$$

The production functions (15.1) and (15.2) can be rewritten to obtain

$$F_a = \frac{Q_a}{A} \tag{15.4}$$

$$F_b = \frac{Q_b}{B}. \tag{15.5}$$

By substituting in Equation 15.3, we find that

$$F_a = F - \frac{Q_b}{B}. \tag{15.6}$$

By equating the two expressions for F_a, Equations 15.4 and 15.6, we obtain

$$Q_a = AF - \frac{AQ_b}{B}. \tag{15.7}$$

This, then, is the equation for the opportunity cost curve — a straight line with intercept AF and with slope $-A/B$. This slope of any point on the opportunity cost curve is

$$\frac{dQ_a}{dQ_b} = \frac{-A}{B} = \frac{-MPP_a}{MPP_b}. \tag{15.8}$$

In short, the slope of the opportunity cost curve represents the (negative) ratio of the marginal physical productivities of the factor in the two alternative employments: $(dQ_a/dF)/(dQ_b/dF)$. Since linear production functions are used in this example, the marginal productivities are constant; the slope of the opportunity cost curve must also be constant throughout — the curve is a negatively sloping straight line.

It is important to recognize that the slope of the opportunity cost curve also represents the inverse ratio of marginal costs. In the present example, only one variable factor is involved and, thus, the marginal cost will represent the factor price divided by the marginal physical productivity. Thus, we may express the slope of the opportunity cost curve in these alternative ways:

$$\frac{dQ_a}{dQ_b} = \frac{-MPP_a}{MPP_b} = \frac{-\left(\dfrac{P_f}{MPP_b}\right)}{\left(\dfrac{P_f}{MPP_a}\right)} = \frac{-MC_b}{MC_a}. \tag{15.9}$$

Decreasing Returns.   Consider now the situation with two products and a single factor fixed in total supply but with the production subject to (eventually) diminishing physical returns. The graphic representation of this situation is essentially similar to the previous case as illustrated in Figure 15.3. Again, we have the fixed factor F and the production functions for A and B; but now we illustrate the situation where each output at first increases at an increasing rate with applications of the factor, but eventually the increase occurs at a decreasing rate. Any allocation of the given factor F between the two alternatives is again represented by a vertical line in Figure 15.3a, and points on the opportunity cost curve in Figure 15.3b are represented by these pairs of A and B outputs.

We have already discovered that the slope at any point on the opportunity cost curve represents the marginal productivity ratio, but now we are confronted with a situation where the marginal productivities in A and B are changing as we shift the factor from use in one enterprise to the other. The result is an opportunity cost curve that is curvilinear, as illustrated in Figure 15.3b. Throughout most of the range of this curve, both outputs are subject to diminishing returns; as a consequence, the opportunity cost curve is concave to the origin. At the extremes of the curve where production is nearly specialized in either A or B, however,

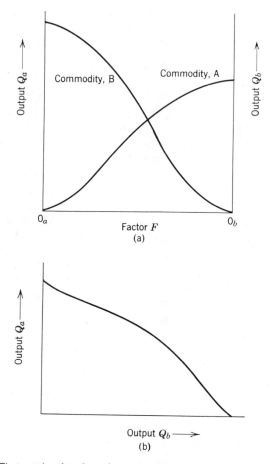

FIGURE 15.3 The production functions showing increasing and decreasing returns and the corresponding curvilinear opportunity cost curve. (a) Production functions. (b) Opportunity cost curve.

the increasing returns phase of one production relationship becomes dominant and, as a result, these portions of the opportunity cost curve are actually convex to the origin.

Mathematical representation of this situation parallels the previous case, but because of diminishing returns in the production relationships the mathematics is more complicated. In simple form, these production functions might be represented by

$$Q_a = AF_a{}^n \tag{15.10}$$

$$Q_b = BF_b{}^m \tag{15.11}$$

where the exponents n and m have values less than 1.0.[1] As before, these production functions can be transformed to give two F_a equations:

$$F_a = \left(\frac{Q_a}{A}\right)^{1/n} \tag{15.12}$$

$$F_b = \left(\frac{Q_b}{B}\right)^{1/m} \tag{15.13}$$

$$F_a = F - \left(\frac{Q_b}{B}\right)^{1/m}. \tag{15.14}$$

By equating these F_a expressions, we obtain the equation for the opportunity cost curve:

$$Q_a = A\left[F - \left(\frac{Q_b}{B}\right)^{1/m}\right]^n. \tag{15.15}$$

Although this is a somewhat complex form, clearly, it defines the opportunity cost curve as concave to the origin, with slope decreasing at an increasing rate.

The slope of any point on this opportunity cost curve, of course, is represented by the derivative dQ_a/dQ_b. The opportunity cost function (15.15) is of the general form $Q_a = AU^n$ where U is a function of Q_b. The derivative, therefore, takes the form $dQ_a/dQ_b = \partial Q_a/\partial U \cdot \partial U/\partial Q_b$ where $U = F - (Q_b/B)^{1/m}$, i.e. $= F_a$.

$$\partial Q_a/\partial U = nAU^{n-1} = nAU^n/U = nQ_a/U \tag{15.16}$$

$$\begin{aligned} \partial U/\partial Q_b &= -1/m(1/B^{1/m})Q_b^{1/m-1} \\ &= -1/m(Q_b^{1/m}/B^{1/m})1/Q_b \\ &= -1/m(F_b/Q_b). \end{aligned} \tag{15.17}$$

From Equations 15.16 and 15.17 it follows that

$$\begin{aligned} dQ_a/dQ_b &= -nQ_a/U(F_b/mQ_b) \\ &= -nQ_a/F_a(F_b/mQ_b) \\ &= -(nAF_a{}^n/F_a)(F_b/mBF_b{}^m) \\ &= -(nAF_a{}^{n-1})/(mBF_b{}^{m-1}). \end{aligned} \tag{15.18}$$

But this is the ratio of the derivatives of our original production functions (15.10) and (15.11), with respect to F_a and F_b; so again we observe that the slope of any point on the opportunity cost represents the (negative)

---

[1] These functions do not include phases with increasing returns, but they permit us to illustrate the concavity of the opportunity cost curve without unduly complicating the mathematics.

ratio of marginal physical productivities. As before, this also means that the slope represents the inverse ratio of marginal costs.

15.3 OPPORTUNITY COST CURVES – MULTIPLE FACTORS

We now discuss the more general case in which production involves several factor inputs. Although the analysis is appropriate for the many-factor, many-product case, for obvious reasons the graphic presentation is limited to two inputs and two products. Consider, then, the case in which two factors are involved in the production of any commodity, and in which they are substitutable one for the other but subject to diminishing returns. Isoquants showing factor substitution in the production of *unit quantities* of two commodities are given in Figure 15.4. We know that the slope at any point on an isoquant represents the production rate of substitution or the inverse ratio of marginal physical productivities of the two factors. Now, as we use less of factor 1 and correspondingly more and more of factor 2, the marginal productivity of factor 1 increases but the marginal productivity of factor 2 decreases. The result is that as the MPP_2/MPP_1 ratio declines, the slope of the isoquant decreases, and the isoquants are convex to the origin as shown. Moreover, we have selected two commodities with somewhat different factor requirements: crop A is a relatively heavy user of factor 2 and, thus, is called F_2-intensive, and crop B is F_1-intensive.[2]

Let us suppose that Farmer Brown proposes to produce these two crops and that he has available $O_a k$ of factor 1 and $O_a j$ of factor 2. His production possibilities for crop A are illustrated by the system of isoquants convex to origin O_a in Figure 15.5. They have been developed from the unit isoquant for crop A in Figure 15.4 with the assumption that Brown's total output is subject to first increasing and then diminishing returns as a consequence of his limited managerial factor. Consider any fixed proportions in factor combinations represented by any straight line, such as $O_a f$, through the origin. If Brown's total output was characterized by constant returns, then equal increments or additions to output could be obtained by directly proportionate increases in both factors at

[2]Since the proportions of factor inputs vary as we move from point to point on the unit isoquants, this is an ambiguous definition. Consider the production function

$$Q = AF_1{}^n F_2{}^m$$

where the exponents n and m have values less than 1.0. If $n > m$, the process is F_1-intensive; if $n < m$, it is F_2-intensive. Notice also that when $n+m > 1.0$, there are increasing returns to scale; when $n+m < 1.0$, there are decreasing returns to scale; and that when $n+m = 1.0$, there are constant returns to scale.

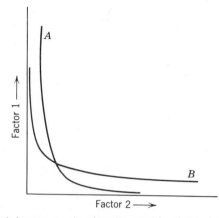

FIGURE 15.4   The unit isoquants showing the combinations of two factors to produce one unit of F_2-intensive crop A and one unit of F_1-intensive crop B.

this fixed combination ratio. This means that isoquants representing equal increments would cut the line $O_a f$ at equal intervals. But with increasing and then decreasing returns. equal increases in inputs will bring more than proportionate increases in output in the low-volume range and less than proportionate increases in the high-volume range. Thus, the distance $O_a c$ is larger than cd to reflect increasing returns, although de, ef, and so on are larger and larger to show diminishing returns.

With given and fixed quantities of F_1 and F_2 available. it is possible

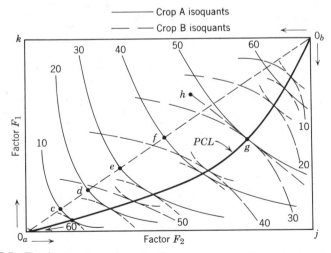

FIGURE 15.5   The isoquants and production contract line (*PCL*) for two factors and two commodities.

to represent all production possibilities by an "Edgeworth box" diagram with sides equal to the available resources. This is also shown in Figure 15.5. where isoquants representing crop B have been added by using O_b as the origin. Brown can produce A and B at any point within this box. Suppose that he chooses a point such as h. This is a possible point. but an inspection of the diagram indicates that this would be an inefficient allocation of resources. Brown could increase the output of both A and B by shifting down and to the right from point h. When he reaches a point where A and B isoquants are tangent. however. this will no longer be possible. Changes from some point such as g cannot involve increases in the output of both commodities but must result in decreases in both or decreases in one with increases in the other. A point of tangency between A and B isoquants means that the slopes of the two isoquants are equal. and so we define an efficient production point as one where the inverse ratios of marginal productivities of factors used in the production of the two commodities are equal. The locus of all such efficient points is indicated by the production contract line O_agO_b.[3]

Since every point on this contract line represents a specific pair of A and B isoquants. it is a straightforward matter to read off efficient production combinations and to plot an opportunity cost curve. The opportunity cost curve based on the contract line in Figure 15.5 is given in Figure 15.6. It should be emphasized that this curve represents efficient production. Inefficient points. for instance. point h in the previous diagram. will fall between this opportunity cost curve and the origin. No possible reallocation of factors can result in production combinations that fall farther from the origin than the opportunity cost curve.

We have now learned that qualitative differences in factors are not necessary to give concave opportunity cost curves. since the law of diminishing returns will have a similar effect even with homogeneous resources. But the opportunity cost curve in Figure 15.6 is concave to the origin only through part of its range and becomes convex near either end. Just as diminishing returns result in concave curves. so increasing returns will result in production possibility curves convex to the origin. This is true in our illustration. since we have assumed. as in the previous single-factor example. that production is subject to increasing returns in the low-output ranges.

The opportunity cost curve just derived is based on the production possibilities for an individual producer. The short-run opportunity cost

[3]The contract line is convex to the lower right corner of the box diagram because we have plotted the F_2-intensive crop from the O_a origin. If we had used O_a as the origin for crop B. the contract line would have fallen to the left of the diagonal and would have been convex to the upper left corner of the box.

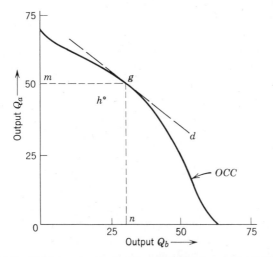

FIGURE 15.6   The opportunity cost curve (*OCC*) derived from Figure 15.5.

curve for a region would simply be the aggregation of these individual curves, obtained by selecting values for the marginal productivity ratios and by adding together all outputs by individuals to obtain points on the regional curve.[4] Since the selected points on each individual curve will have slope equal to the selected ratio of marginal physical productivities (or marginal costs), it follows that the slope of the regional curve at this aggregated point will also have this slope. The short-run regional curve would look something like Figure 15.6, representing in effect a weighted combination of all individual curves.

15.4   THE LONG-RUN OPPORTUNITY COST CURVE

Given time for economic adjustments to work out, we can expect factors used by individual producers to come into optimum adjustment — that each firm will operate at its most efficient point. Under these conditions, long-run changes in the commodity output of a region will be obtained by appropriate shifts in the numbers of efficiently organized firms. As a consequence, proportional increases in all factor inputs will be associated with directly proportional increases in outputs. The regional production functions, in other words, may be expected to reflect diminishing returns

[4]Under perfect market conditions, all producers in the region would face identical product prices. As we will learn later, with any given set of prices each individual would find it economical to produce that combination of outputs which would equate the ratio of marginal productivities to the (inverse) ratio of product prices.

as we increase the relative use of any particular factor, but constant returns when all factors are increased in proportion. These production functions are called "linearly homogeneous" or "homogeneous of degree one." With these production functions, the resulting long-run regional opportunity cost curves will be concave to the origin throughout their entire ranges; and, in general, they will exhibit less pronounced curvature than will the individual and regional short-run curves. Regional curves convex in the low output ranges are possible, but this requires external economies of scale for the industries involved.

Graphic Formulation.   Since the essential features of the graphic analysis will not be changed, we will not repeat the parallels to Figures 15.5 and 15.6. We point out that all isoquants in the equivalent of Figure 15.5 will be exact scalar images of the unit isoquants given in Figure 15.4. This means that, if we select some factor proportion, the equivalent straight line through the origin will cut any set of isoquants that represent constant increments in output at constant distances along the line, since this will represent directly proportional increases in all inputs and in output. Notice also that any such straight line through the origin represents the locus of constant MPP_2/MPP_1 ratios — that all isoquants have equal slope along such a line. As already indicated, the outputs of the two commodities will be read from the pairs of tangent isoquants along the contract line, and the resulting opportunity cost curve will look much like Figure 15.6 but without the convex segments near each end. With diminishing returns limited to individual inputs and not appropriate for total output, it can be expected that the long-run regional opportunity cost curves will be somewhat less curvilinear than the individual short-run curves.

It is interesting to notice that, with linear-homogeneous production functions, the construction of the production contract line (PCL) and the opportunity cost curve (OCC) can be illustrated in a single box diagram. In Figure 15.7 we show a conventional Edgeworth box, with available quantities of F_1 measured by the height and available F_2 quantities by the length of the box. Line $O_a c O_b$ represents the contract line; for simplicity, we have omitted all isoquants except for the pair tangent at point c.

Remember that, with these production functions, any straight line through the origin will show constant increases in output by constant incremental distances along the line. This means that the straight-line diagonal $O_a O_b$ can be scaled from O_a up and to the right to represent outputs of Q_a and, also, that it can be scaled from O_b down and to the left to represent equal additions to Q_b. Let us convert the top half of the box

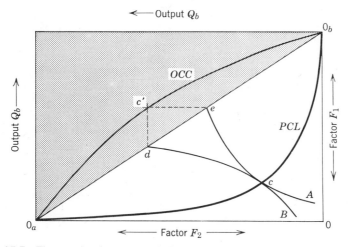

FIGURE 15.7   The production contract line (*PCL*) and the opportunity cost curve (*OCC*).

diagram to a diagram representing outputs, with origin at point 0 at the lower right-hand corner. The vertical axis now is scaled to represent the output of Q_a, with scale transferred horizontally from the appropriate points on the diagonal; and a similar scaling permits us to measure Q_b along the horizontal axis.

Consider the pair of A and B outputs represented by the isoquants tangent at point c. The A isoquant intersects the diagonal at point e, likewise the B isoquant intersects the diagonal at point d. In terms of our new Q_a and Q_b scales, it is apparent that this pair of outputs can be represented by point c'. This is a point on the opportunity cost curve, and the fact that it falls on the far side of the diagonal from origin 0 (at lower right) clearly indicates that the opportunity cost curve must be concave to this origin. The addition of other pairs of isoquants will permit us to trace out the complete opportunity cost curve $O_a c' O_b$.

Mathematical Formulation.   Before leaving this discussion of opportunity cost curves, we turn once again to more formal mathematical expression, with a warning that the detail may be tedious. We are considering the case of two factors, F_1 and F_2, in fixed total supply and two products, A and B, with linear homogeneous production functions. By extending our earlier single-factor analysis of Section 15.2, we define these functions as

$$Q_a = A F_{1a}^{n_a} F_{2a}^{m_a} \qquad (15.19)$$

$$Q_b = BF_{1b}^{n_b}F_{2b}^{m_b} \tag{15.20}$$

where $n_a + m_a = 1.0$ and $n_b + m_b = 1.0$.

The production contract curve is defined as the locus of all points where the (inverse) ratio of marginal factor productivities in A are equal to the (inverse) ratio of marginal productivities in B. Thus

$$\frac{\partial Q_a/\partial F_{2a}}{\partial Q_a/\partial F_{1a}} = \frac{Am_a F_{1a}^{n_a} F_{2a}^{m_a-1}}{An_a F_{1a}^{n_a-1} F_{2a}^{m_a}} = \frac{m_a F_{1a}}{n_a F_{2a}} \tag{15.21}$$

and, also,

$$\frac{\partial Q_b/\partial F_{2b}}{\partial Q_b/\partial F_{1b}} = \frac{m_b F_{1b}}{n_b F_{2b}}. \tag{15.22}$$

By equating Equations 15.21 and 15.22 and by substituting $F_1 - F_{1a} = F_{1b}$ and $F_2 - F_{2a} = F_{2b}$,

$$\frac{m_a F_{1a}}{n_a F_{2a}} = \frac{m_b(F_1 - F_{1a})}{n_b(F_2 - F_{2a})} \tag{15.23}$$

$$F_{1a} = \frac{n_a m_b F_1 F_{2a}}{n_b m_a F_2 + (n_a m_b - n_b m_a) F_{2a}}. \tag{15.24}$$

Then, in terms of the variables F_{1a} and F_{2a}, this is the equation for the production contract curve. Observe that when Q_a is F_2-intensive and Q_b is F_1-intensive (the situation assumed in our graphics), this shows F_{1a} increasing with F_{2a} at an increasing rate. If Q_a were F_1-intensive and Q_b F_2-intensive, the curve would increase but at a decreasing rate, and the contract line would fall above and to the left of the diagonal in Figure 15.7.

Now, we consider the opportunity cost function. We can convert the Q_b production function to

$$F_{1b} = \left(\frac{Q_b}{BF_{2b}^{m_b}}\right)^{1/n_b}. \tag{15.25}$$

By substituting $F_1 - F_{1a}$ for F_{1b},

$$F_{1a} = F_1 - \left(\frac{Q_b}{BF_{2b}^{m_b}}\right)^{1/m_b} \tag{15.26}$$

and by substituting in the production function for Q_a, we have this expression for the opportunity cost curve:

$$Q_a = AF_{2a}^{m_a}[F_1 - (B^{-1}F_{2b}^{-m_b}Q_b)^{1/n_b}]^{n_a}. \tag{15.27}$$

We wish to define the slope dQ_a/dQ_b of any point on the opportunity cost curve, and we observe that the above expression is of the general form

$$dQ_a/dQ_b = \partial Q_a/\partial U \cdot \partial U/\partial V \cdot \partial V/\partial Q_b$$

where $U = (F_1 - V^{1/n_b})$
and $V = (B^{-1}F_{2b}^{-m_b}Q_b)$.

The several partial derivatives yield

$$\partial Q_a / \partial U = n_a Q_a / U \qquad (15.28)$$

$$\partial U / \partial V = -V^{1/n}b/n_b V \qquad (15.29)$$

$$\partial V / \partial Q_b = B^{-1}F_{2b}^{-m_b}. \qquad (15.30)$$

Thus the slope of any point on the opportunity cost curve is

$$dQ_a / dQ_b = (n_a Q_a / U)(-V^{1/n_b}/n_b V)(B^{-1}F_{2b}^{-m_b})$$

$$= (n_a Q_a / [F_1 - (B^{-1}F_{2b}^{-m_b})^{1/n_b}])(-[B^{-1}F_{2b}^{-m_b}Q_b]^{1/n_b}/$$

$$n_b[B^{-1}F_{2b}^{-m_b}Q_b])(B^{-1}F_{2b}^{-m_b})$$

$$\qquad (15.31)$$

$$= (n_a Q_a / F_{1a})(-F_{1b}/n_b Q_b).$$

But we have already defined the marginal productivities, and with further substitution we obtain

$$\partial Q_a / \partial F_{1a} = n_a A F_{2a}^{m_a} F_{1a}^{-n_a} / F_{1a} = n_a Q_a / F_{1a} \qquad (15.32)$$

$$\partial Q_b / \partial F_{1b} = n_b Q_b / F_{1b}. \qquad (15.33)$$

Thus we find that the slope of the opportunity cost curve represents the ratio MPP_{1a}/MPP_{1b}. Moreover, if we had followed this same sequence but substituted in the production function for Q_b, we would have demonstrated that the slope of the opportunity cost function is also equal to the ratio MPP_{2a}/MPP_{2b}.

15.5   FACTORS AFFECTING THE OPPORTUNITY COST CURVE

We have learned that the opportunity cost curve is an effective device for summarizing the production possibilities of any region. The foregoing analysis has stressed the impact of the technical production functions on the shape or curvature of the opportunity cost curve. We have found that, with given resource endowments, the slope of the opportunity cost curve will reflect the ratios of marginal factor productivities in the several alternative enterprises. But we must emphasize that the curvature of the opportunity cost function is a reflection of the relative factor intensities of the several production functions.

Factor Intensities. Consider the equation that we have derived to express the production contract curve in the Edgeworth box diagram:

$$F_{1a} = \frac{n_a m_b F_1 F_{2a}}{n_b m_a F_2 + (n_a m_b - n_b m_a) F_{2a}}. \tag{15.24}$$

If the two production functions are identical in factor intensities — if $n_a = n_b$ and $m_a = m_b$ — then this reduces to

$$F_{1a} = F_1 F_{2a}/F_2 \tag{15.34}$$

a straight-line function that is represented by the diagonal $O_a O_b$ in Figure 15.7.[5] Moreover, the greater the difference in factor intensity in the alternatives, the greater the departure of the production contract curve from this straight-line diagonal. We illustrate this in Figure 15.8 where the contract line PCL_1 passing through the points $O_a c O_b$, is taken from Figure 15.7 and where $n_a = m_b = 0.2$ and $n_b = m_a = 0.8$. We have also included a contract curve where differences in factor intensities are not so pronounced — $n_a = m_b = 0.33$ and $n_b = m_a = 0.67$ — the PCL_2 curve $O_a f O_b$. Finally, as we pointed out above, any equal factor intensity situation will result in a production contract curve that is the straight-line diagonal ($O_a O_b$ in this diagram).

[5]Notice that the production contract line will be the straight-line diagonal for all cases of equal factor intensities even if $n + m \neq 1.0$. If $n + m > 1.0$, however, the corresponding opportunity cost curve will be convex, likewise, if $n + m < 1.0$, the opportunity cost curve will be concave.

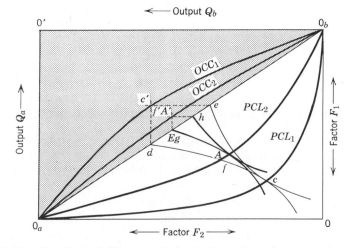

FIGURE 15.8 The effect of differences in factor intensity on the production contract line and the opportunity cost curve.

From this diagram we can observe that, the greater the difference in factor intensity in the alternative production functions, the greater the curvature of the production contract curve. In fact, this curve is concave to the line O_aO_b in the diagram and, in the limit as n_a and m_b approach zero and n_b and m_a approach 1.0, the production contract curve converges on the axes O_a0O_b.

This diagram also illustrates the fact that the opportunity cost curve becomes more curvilinear as differences in factor intensities increase. We have observed that the contract curve is the straight-line diagonal in the box diagram when factor intensities are identical. Under these conditions, the equation for the opportunity cost function becomes

$$Q_a = F_1{}^n F_2{}^m Q_b. \qquad (15.35)$$

When the production functions are linear and homogeneous ($n + m = 1.0$), and with appropriate allowance for scaling, this is also a linear function represented by the diagonal in the diagram. As the differences in factor intensities increase, the opportunity cost curve takes shapes like $O_a f' O_b$ and (with greater differences) $O_a c' O_b$. In the limit, as n_a and m_b approach zero, the opportunity cost curve converges on a single point $0'$, since in this situation Q_a will require only F_2 and will use all of the available supply but Q_b will require only F_1 and will use all of that factor available.

Factor Endowments.   Although differences in factor intensities are largely responsible for the curvature or convexity of opportunity cost curves, their general shape and size reflect differences in the endowments of factors. These effects are illustrated in Figure 15.9 where opportunity cost curves based on identical production functions have been generated from a variety of assumed factor endowments. It should be quite clear that regions well supplied with all resources will have opportunity cost curves that show greater production possibilities than will regions with relatively scarce resources (compare curve B with curve E). Regions with relatively abundant supplies of resources well adapted to the production of A (that is to say, abundant resources of which A is an intensive user) will have opportunity cost curves similar to curve A in the diagram, while regions with few resources well adapted to A but abundant resources well adapted to B will have curves somewhat like D in the diagram.

We close this chapter by pointing out that our illustrations of differences in factor intensities and in factor endowments have been entirely hypothetical but that even the extreme examples used do not begin to match real differences in intensities and endowments. Within agriculture, examples such as wheat production in the Dakotas, poultry production in Delaware, or vegetable production in California suggest some of the more

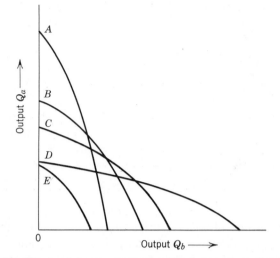

FIGURE 15.9   The effects of changes in resource endowments on the opportunity cost curve. (*Note.* For all curves the production functions are identical: $Q_a = F_1^{0.2}F_2^{0.8}$; $Q_b = F_1^{0.8}F_2^{0.2}$. The factor endowments vary as follows: $A:F_1 = 5, F_2 = 30$; $B:F_1 = 10$, $F_2 = 15$; $C \cdot F_1 = 15, F_2 = 10$; $D \cdot F_1 = 30, F_2 = 5$; $E \cdot F_1 = 5, F_2 = 7.5$.)

extreme variations in land, labor, and capital proportions and intensities. These illustrations also suggest important differences in relative factor endowments, although perhaps the most pronounced differences here are to be found in comparisons of industrial metropolitan areas with extensive farming areas. Thus we may expect opportunity cost curves to exhibit a wide variation in curvature and in general form—factors of primary importance as we move on to a consideration of interregional trade possibilities.

SELECTED READINGS

Regional Production Potentials

Arrow, Kenneth et al., "Capitol-Labor Substitution and Economic Efficiency," *Review of Economics and Statistics*, Vol. 43 (August 1961). pp. 225–250.

Brown, Murray. *The Theory and Empirical Analysis of Production.* National Bureau of Economic Research, New York (1967), "Introduction." pp. 3–13.

Farrell, Maurice J., "The Measurement of Productive Efficiency." *Journal of the Royal Statistical Society*, Vol. 120, Part III, Series A (1957). pp. 253–281.

Heady. Earl O.. *Economics of Agricultural Production and Resource Use*. Prentice-Hall. Inc.. New York (1952) Chapter 22. "Location of Production: Interregional Resource and Product Specialization," pp. 639–671.

King. Richard A.. "Product Markets and Economic Development." in W. W. McPherson. *Economic Development of Tropical Agriculture*. University of Florida Press. Gainesville (1968). pp. 78–92.

Leontief. Wassily W.. "An International Comparison of Factor Costs and Factor Use: A Review Article," *American Economic Review*, Vol. 54 (June 1964). pp. 335–345.

Mighell. Ronald L. and John D. Black. *Interregional Competition in Agriculture*. Harvard University Press, Cambridge (1951). pp. 13–57.

Zarembka. Paul. "Manufacturing and Agricultural Production Functions and International Trade: United States and Northern Europe." *Journal of Farm Economics*. Vol. 43. No. 4 (November 1966). pp. 952–966.

chapter 16

LONG-RUN REGIONAL SPECIALIZATION

16.1 PRODUCTION ADJUSTMENTS AND INDIVIDUAL OFFER CURVES

Given an individual's opportunity cost curve and his preference map, we can proceed with the analysis of the interdependent adjustments in production, consumption, and exchange. The previously derived opportunity cost curve for Brown is repeated in Figure 16.1 along with indifference curves from Brown's preference map. In the absence of exchange opportunities, it is clear that Brown will elect to produce and consume oa of A and ob of B for this combination will place him at point c on the highest attainable indifference curve. But suppose that exchange opportunities do exist and that they are represented by specified exchange rates P_b/P_a. If the exchange rate is shown by the slope of line hc, Brown would discover that his best position would remain that of self-sufficiency. At any other relative prices, however, he would find it possible and profitable to trade.

Consider the case where the "outside" prices show P_a higher relative to P_b so that the terms of trade are represented by the slope of line cf. The immediate effect of these prices is to provide Brown with profitable trade opportunities that are based on his stocks of Q_a and Q_b already in

314

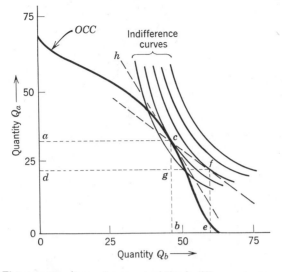

FIGURE 16.1   The opportunity cost curve and the indifference curves for Mr. Brown (short-run adjustments).

hand. Thus, he will find it to his advantage to exchange *cg* of *A* in order to obtain *gf* of *B* for this will take him from point *c* to point *f* on the highest attainable indifference curve in the short run. Notice that the "trade triangle" is *cgf* with the price ratio represented by the slope of the hypotenuse *cf*. This corresponds to a point on the short-run offer curves depicted in Figure 14.6.

But now Mr. Brown has the opportunity to adjust his production program as well as his short-run trade and consumption patterns. This long-run situation is illustrated in Figure 16.2 where the slope of the line *np* is the same as *cf* in the previous diagram, representing the trade price ratio P_b/P_a. This price line is tangent to Brown's opportunity cost curve at point *n*, indicating that Brown would find it economical to shift production from *c* to *n*. With this adjustment, he would be able to trade along the price line *np*, eventually arriving at *p* on the highest attainable indifference curve.

Brown would maximize his position, therefore, by shifting production from *c* to *n* and then trading *qn* units of *A* for *qp* units of *B*. His final consumption pattern, *oj* of *A* and *om* of *B*, would differ considerably from his production pattern, *oi* and *ok*; and this is the essence of specialization and trade. In general, the initiation of trade will bring an increase in the production of the relatively high-priced product and a decrease in its local consumption. Trade frees the consumption pattern of each individual from

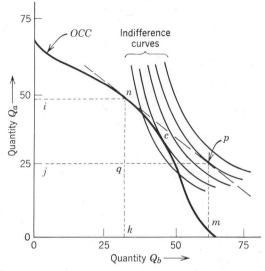

FIGURE 16.2 The opportunity cost curve and the indifference curves for Mr. Brown (the long run).

direct dependence on his own resources and abilities, and it permits him to gain by adjusting both his production and his consumption patterns.

The above exchange possibilities constitute an offer by Brown to sell qn units of A and at the same time to buy qp units of B at the established exchange ratio P_b/P_a. Other price ratios would bring forth other combination offers, and they can be summarized in a no-trade price ratio and a pair of offer curves exactly as in Figure 14.7. In the present case, however, the individual's offer curves represent the combined effects of production and consumption adjustments instead of the simple effects of changes in consumption with given and fixed stocks of the commodities. Consequently, the exchange possibilities will be greatly expanded; compare the short-run trade triangle cgf in Figure 16.1 with the long-run triangle nqp in Figure 16.2. With these long-run individual offer curves, the exchange equilibrium between two individuals will follow lines exactly the same as the ones already discussed.

16.2 REGIONAL PRODUCTION AND TRADE

The aggregation of individual offer curves to obtain regional offer curves will parallel the discussion in Section 14.5. Through these procedures we can determine trade equilibrium positions for individuals or regions. They will involve the equalization of product prices (neglecting transportation costs) in the several regions and the determination of trade flows and production patterns. With these production patterns, represented by points on opportunity cost curves, we can move back to the basic isoquants and production contract lines and, thus indicate the equilibrium allocation of resources.

This whole matter may be summed up through the use of box diagrams similar to the one used to illustrate the case involving individuals. Consider two regions, X and Y, with differing endowments of two homogeneous resources. Assume that technology is perfectly mobile between the two regions: that they have identical production functions and that proportionate increases in all inputs result in directly proportionate increases in output.[1] This is suggested by the double-box diagram in Figure 16.3 where factors used for commodities A and B are measured from origins O_a and O_b, respectively, for region X and from origins

[1]As we have observed, such production functions are called linearly homogeneous or homogeneous in the first degree. Functions of the Cobb–Douglas type ($Q = AF_1{}^n F_2{}^m \ldots$) are homogeneous in the first degree when the exponents $n, m, \ldots$, sum to 1.0. In the present example. the isoquants were generated from relationships of this type. with n and m equal to 0.2 and 0.8 for commodity A and 0.8 and 0.2 for commodity B.

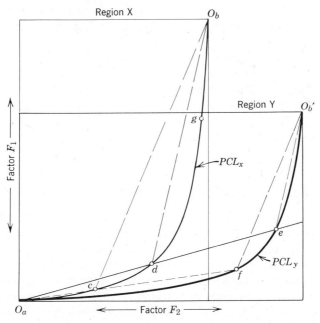

FIGURE 16.3 The resource allocations in two regions with equal technology but different factor endowments.

O_a and O'_b for region Y. Isoquants have been omitted, but production contract lines connecting points where the marginal productivity ratios are equal for the two commodities are shown by $O_a c d O_b$ for region X and $O_a f e O'_b$ for region Y.

Opportunity cost curves based on these production contract lines are given in Figure 16.4. Because region X has relatively more of factor 1 and less of factor 2, its opportunity cost curve indicates that it is better adapted than region Y for the production of F_1-intensive commodity B. In both cases, however, the curves are not greatly concave; opportunity costs are not greatly variable. This reflects the homogeneous nature of the resources, the availability of identical technology in the two regions, the absence of total diminishing returns in the production relationships, and especially the fact that factor intensities do not differ greatly in this hypothetical case.

We need not repeat the detailed analysis of consumer and trade reactions in the two countries for it is adequate for present purposes to remember that reciprocal trade flows will continue until relative product prices in the two regions are brought into equilibrium. Let us suppose these equilibrium prices with trade are represented by the identical slopes at points d' and e' on the opportunity cost curves. They indicate the combinations of A and B that will be produced in the two regions. Corresponding to these production patterns, resources will be allocated at point d in region X and at point e in region Y (Figure 16.3). Given basic technological relationships, consumer preferences, and the regional endowments of productive resources, therefore, this analysis has indicated the competitive determination of production patterns and trade flows, of consumption patterns, and of product prices with trade among regions. It also involves the determination of factor prices in the several regions, but this topic is discussed in the following section.

16.3   PRODUCT PRICES AND FACTOR PRICES

We have learned that the direct cause of interregional trade is differences in product prices in the several regions. More fundamentally, our analysis indicates that the causes of trade are differences in the resource endowments. Even with identical resources patterns, however, trade could profitably take place between regions if there were differences in consumer tastes and preferences since they would give rise to differences in product prices. The fundamental causes of regional specialization and of interregional trade, then, are differences in consumer demands and preferences *relative* to the resource endowments of the several regions.

We have also observed that a direct result of interregional trade is the equating of product prices in the several regions, disregarding costs of commodity transfer. Now, the demands for factors of production are derived from the demands for products. Since interregional trade has the effect of transferring the demands of one region to the outputs of another region, it seems reasonable to suppose that this trade must affect not only product prices but also factor prices. To be more specific, interregional trade has the effect of transferring demands on resources that are scarce and expensive in one region to resources that are relatively abundant and inexpensive in other regions. Consequently, resource or factor prices in the several regions move toward one another and tend to equate.

We have already noticed that interregional trade will bring product prices together as indicated by the equal slopes at points e' and d' on the regional opportunity cost curves in Figure 16.4. Moreover, we have observed that these patterns of production correspond to resource allocations at point e on the contract line for region Y and at point d on the contract line for region X (Figure 16.3). We know by construction that these production contract lines represent points where isoquants for products A and B are tangent — where the ratios of marginal factor

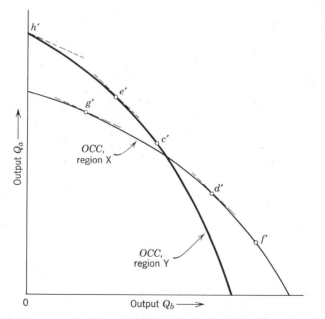

FIGURE 16.4   The opportunity cost curves for two regions, based on Figure 16.1. (*Note.* Except for scaling, they are the same as curves B and C in Figure 15.9.)

productivities are equal. In these equilibrium positions, factor prices in the given region are also determined. The inverse ratio of factor prices is equal to the slope of the isoquants at points like d and e.

Let us consider a situation where factor prices deviate from this equilibrium ratio. Then, firms would find it economical to combine factors in proportions other than the ones indicated by points along the contract line; and, as a necessary consequence, not all of the available resources would be utilized. Such a nonequilibrium situation is illustrated in Figure 16.5 where the factor endowments and one pair of production isoquants for region X have been repeated. The production contract line based on the complete utilization of the available resources is given by $O_a d O_b$. The equilibrium allocation of resources with trade is given by point d on this line, and the competitive equilibrium value for the inverse ratio of factor prices is represented by the slope of line ed, which is tangent to commodity A and commodity B isoquants through point d. Now suppose that factor prices deviated from these equilibrium values: that the price of F_1 was higher relative to the price of F_2, as suggested by the slope of lines such as fg. Under these conditions, firms producing commodity A would find it economical to combine resources along the line $0_a h$ where the ratio of marginal factor productivities is equal to the given ratio of factor prices.

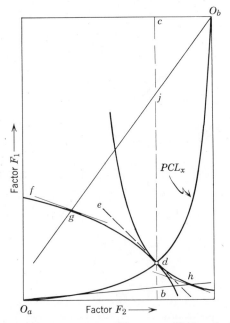

FIGURE 16.5   The allocation of resources with nonequilibrium factor prices, region X.

Similarly, producers of commodity B would expand output along line 0_bg.

Eventually the expanding outputs of A and B would absorb all of the relatively cheap F_2 available; for example, line bc with 0_ab of F_2 used to produce A and the balance 0_bc used for B. But at this point, the production of A would require only bd of F_1, and B would require only cj. In short, the amount dj of F_1 would be unutilized. Clearly, this could not be a stable competitive equilibrium, with a relatively high price for F_1 but with a substantial proportion of the factor unused. Under competitive conditions, partial utilization of any available factor is possible only if the factor is a free good. As a consequence, the price of F_1 will decline relative to the price of F_2 until a true equilibrium position is reached somewhere on the contract line, with all available factor supplies used. Observe that these factor prices in equilibrium correspond to the slopes of the isoquants and that, as any equilibrium position on the contract line moves upward and to the right, the isoquant slopes and, hence, the factor price ratios are increasing. This means that every possible equilibrium position for commodity prices corresponds to a particular and unique ratio of factor prices, with P_2/P_1 increasing as the output of B increases and the output of A decreases.

Returning to Figure 16.4, suppose we select points d' and e' on the opportunity cost curves as representing equal commodity price equilibrium positions with trade. These commodity outputs in the two regions correspond to factor allocations at points d and e on the regional contract curves in Figure 16.3. We notice that these points d and e fall along a single straight line O_ae and also that the lines O_bd and $O_b'e$ are parallel. This means that, in equilibrium, commodities A and B are being produced with identical factor proportions in the two regions. More than that, since unit isoquants are identical in the regions, identical factor proportions must mean identical absolute factor inputs per unit of output. From this it must follow that trade will not only equate product prices among regions (disregarding transfer costs) but also that it will completely equalize factor prices.

Notice that, under competitive conditions, equilibrium will involve equating the price of any commodity to its cost of production:

$$P_a = p_1 f_{1a} + p_2 f_{2a} \cdots$$

where P_a = price of commodity A
  p_1 and p_2 = factor prices
  f_{1a} and f_{2a} = factor input per unit of output.

Now P_a, f_{1a}, and f_{2a} will be equal in each region as we have just observed.

It follows, therefore, that p_1 and p_2 must be equal in every region.[2] Alternatively, we may point out that, under competitive conditions, the price of any commodity will equal its marginal cost of production. For any commodity, marginal cost is represented by the price of a given factor divided by its marginal productivity in producing the commodity. Now, just as equilibrium involves equal factor inputs, so it must involve identical absolute marginal productivities. Thus we have

$$P_a = p_1/MPP_{1a} = p_2/MPP_{2a} \cdots.$$

If the marginal productivities are identical in all regions and the product prices also identical, it must follow that factor prices will be completely equalized.

The conclusion that product mobility in international trade is a perfect substitute for factor mobility and results in the complete equalization of factor prices among regions holds true only under severely restricted conditions. We have made note of some of them: that resources are homogeneous in the several regions, that technology is identical, and that production functions are linear and homogeneous. A further restriction is that the competitive equilibrium must not involve the complete specialization of any region. In Figure 16.4, we have selected a second set of equal prices corresponding to points c' and f' and, again, in Figure 16.3 we find that these equal commodity prices will result in identical factor proportions and so in equal factor prices in the two regions. But if demand conditions result in much different product prices, one or the other region will find it economical to specialize its production. With relatively high prices for A, for example, region X would produce A and B at point g', but region Y would produce only A at point h'. In Figure 16.3, this would correspond to factor allocations at point g for region X, but all available factors would be used for A in region Y (point $0'_b$). From the construction, it is clear that factor proportions will now differ in the two regions, that factor marginal productivity ratios cannot be equal and, hence, that factor prices will not equalize. Equilibrium factor prices will be determined in region X, and product prices will equalize in the two regions. But factor prices in region Y will now move inversely to factor proportions in the two regions in order that product prices in region Y will equal marginal costs of production.

---

[2]It may be argued that factor prices in the second region could vary inversely with the factor inputs and still maintain the equality of price and cost of production, but this would involve relative factor prices inconsistent with the necessary equilibrium conditions. If the ratios of factor prices must be equal, only one set of absolute prices will equate production cost to commodity price.

16.4 REGIONAL DIFFERENCES IN PRODUCTION TECHNOLOGY

A comment on the simplifying assumption of identical technology is in order. In an abstract sense, this may be taken to mean that technology is mobile: that knowledge of technical processes can spread from region to region so that each region will have available the identical production processes. But the complete production function involves inputs beyond the ones generally considered in an economic analysis—factors that are usually thought of as free goods or services. In agricultural production, these other inputs include things such as temperature, rainfall, sunshine, and length of frost-free season. It is true that we do not pay for these inputs directly, but neither are they subject to our control. For each region, they enter into the productive processes in unique "quantities."

Suppose that we state the general production function as

$$Q = q(f_1, f_2, f_3, \ldots, c_1, c_2, c_3, \ldots)$$

where the f's represent inputs of economic factors and the c's the uncontrolled inputs of climatic factors. Since the c's will vary characteristically from region to region; and since they have quite significant effects on production, it follows that the partial production function based only on economic inputs must differ from region to region. Even if every controllable aspect of technology is perfectly mobile as between regions, the economic production functions will not and cannot be identical. It follows that factor prices will differ from region to region, with the price differences in essence representing indirect payments for differences in uncontrolled, noneconomic factors.

16.5 THE GAINS FROM TRADE

To conclude this chapter, we repeat that the direct causes of interregional trade are interregional differences in commodity prices, although the fundamental causes are differences in consumer demands and preferences relative to resource endowments. The direct effects of trade are the equalization of commodity prices among the regions and, under restricted conditions, the equalization of factor prices. Given the realistic facts that resources are not homogeneous among regions, that technology is not identical, and that some regions may be completely specialized as far as some commodities are concerned, a more generally applicable conclusion is that trade transfers demands from resources scarce in a region to the ones that are abundant and relatively cheap in another region and, hence, reduces (but normally will not completely eliminate) disparities in factor prices among regions.

A more fundamental result of regional specialization and interregional trade, of course, is that it permits the individuals involved to increase their satisfactions and welfare. This aspect has been stressed in the foregoing analyses — individuals engage in trade when it permits them to reach higher indifference curves. In a similar way, production is carried on more efficiently; the aggregate output of the combined regions is increased. This is suggested in Figure 16.6. Consider a region with opportunity cost curve *afb* producing at point *c* in the absence of trade and with relative commodity prices represented by the slope of line *ec*. The opportunity cost curve for a second region has been inverted and superimposed on this diagram (the curve *pcq* with its production in isolation is represented by point *c* and prices by line *dc*). By this construction, the combined but independent outputs of the two regions are represented by point *h*. If trade is established between the two regions, product prices will equalize at some intermediate values, like the ones that are represented by the slope of line *gf*, and each region will produce at point *f* where opportunity costs are equal to the inverse price ratio. But this displaces the opportunity cost curve for the second region to *rfs*, and the combined outputs of both commodities are increased to point *j* on the opportunity cost curve *mjn*

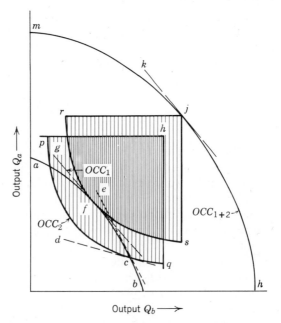

FIGURE 16.6 The regional and combined opportunity cost curves illustrating production gains from regional specialization and trade.

for the combined regions.[3] In short, point h is inefficient in relation to the combined production possibilities for the regions, and the move from h to j is indicative of the gain in production efficiency.

We conclude, therefore, that interregional trade will permit increases in production and in productive efficiency and that this, plus the better adjustment of consumption patterns to tastes and preferences, will result in a general improvement in satisfactions and welfare. We must recognize, however, that some individuals may have their positions worsened through trade. Consider the case of an individual who obtains all of his income from the ownership of a resource scarce and expensive in a particular region. When trade begins, the value of this resource will be reduced and the individual's income will correspondingly decline. This decline will be offset, in part, by changes in product prices, but there is no reason to assume that the real income of such an individual will not be reduced as a consequence of trade. Moreover, if the adjustment of resources to new employment involves some lags (a situation not considered in the previous analysis), the resulting "technological" unemployment will have obvious immediate disadvantages for the displaced resources. The final conclusion, then, is that trade opens the possibilities for increases in the general welfare even though some individuals may not share, at least immediately, in the general benefit.

SELECTED READINGS

Long-Run Regional Specialization

Caves, Richard E., *Trade and Economic Structure*. Harvard University Press, Cambridge (1950).

Chipman, John S., "A Survey of the Theory of International Trade: Part 1, The Classical Theory," *Econometrica*, Vol. 33, No. 3 (July 1965), pp. 477–519; Part 2, "The Neo-Classical Theory," *Econometrica*, Vol. 33, No. 4 (October 1965), pp. 685–760; and Part 3, "The Modern Theory," *Econometrica*, Vol. 34, No. 1 (January 1966), pp. 18–76.

Haberler, Gottfried V., *Survey of International Trade Theory*, revised and enlarged edition. Princeton University (1961).

Johnson, Harry G, *Money, Trade and Economic Growth*. Harvard University Press, Cambridge (1967). Chapter II, "Comparative Costs and Commercial Policy", pp. 28–45.

Kemp, Murray C., *The Pure Theory of International Trade*. Prentice-Hall, Inc., Englewood Cliffs (1964).

[3]Notice that the slope of the combined curve at j is the same as the slopes of the individual opportunity cost curves at f: that the inverse ratios of marginal physical productivities are all equal.

Land, A. H., "Factor Endowments and Factor Prices," *Economica*, NS., Vol. 26 (May 1959), pp. 137–144.

Leontief, Wassily W., "The Use of Indifference Curves in the Analysis of Foreign Trade," *Quarterly Journal of Economics*, Vol. XLVII, No. 3 (May 1933), pp. 493–503.

Meade, James Edward, *A Geometry of International Trade*, Allen and Unwin, Ltd., London (1952).

Ohlin, Bertil, *Interregional and International Trade*. Harvard University Press, Cambridge (revised edition, 1967) Especially, "Reflections on Contemporary International Trade Theories," pp. 305–319.

Samuelson, Paul A., *The Collected Scientific Papers of Paul A. Samuelson*, Vol. II. Book Three, Part IX, "Trade." The M.I.T. Press, Cambridge (1966), pp. 773–1037.

PART V

SPATIAL ARRANGEMENT OF ECONOMIC ACTIVITY

chapter 17

LAND-USE EQUILIBRIUM MODELS

A brief review of earlier topics will be helpful in placing the present section in proper perspective. In Part II our models dealt with a single product whose output was taken as given, although spatially distributed. This analysis was extended in Part III to include multiple forms of a single product as well as to introduce the time dimension of market price. The effects of specialization and trade, considered in Part IV, became clear only after two-commodity models were substituted for the single-product models used earlier. It is our intention now to expand those two-commodity models and to apply them to more interesting but more complicated questions.

In Chapter 17, we concentrate on alternative uses of a single fixed input—land. We assume that all other inputs are available in unlimited supply at established prices that are independent of production site. In Chapter 18, land enters only in terms of the potential sites at which production may take place. Other inputs are regarded as mobile with transportation treated as costless only for ubiquitous raw materials. In Chapter 18, however, we are forced to revert to a one-commodity output world. In Chapter 19, we treat multiple-product and multiple-input situations that lead toward a general equilibrium model.

17.1 THE NOMADIC, NO-CHOICE CASE

In many primitive societies, the provision of an adequate food supply was the all-important force that influenced the organization of economic activity. Often, instead of assembling resources at one site or another to produce food or instead of transporting food from one place to another, man was forced to travel to his food supply, even though it was found only in widely separated locations. An interesting example of this type of society existed in the Tehuacán Valley of Mexico in the period 6500 to 1500 B.C. In this valley, it is believed, maize was first domesticated.

The environment of the Tehuacán Valley of 8000 years ago is sketched in Figure 17.1. The alluvial valley floor consisted of a level plain sparsely covered with mesquite, grasses, and cacti, and offered fairly good possibilities along the Rio Salado for primitive maize agriculture that was wholly dependent on rainfall. The western slope of the valley provided niches useful for growing maize and tomatoes and for trapping cottontail rabbits. A thorn forest was located on the eastern side of the valley with abundant seasonal crops of wild fruits. Deer were also abundant in the fall, and cottontail rabbits and skunks were to be found year-round. In the upper reaches of the eastern slopes were eroded canyons, unsuitable for exploitation except for limited hunting of deer and acorns in the fall but

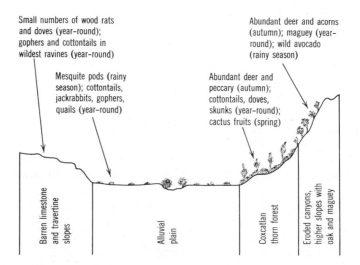

FIGURE 17.1 An idealized west–east transection of the central part of the Tehuacan Valley, Puebla, Mexico, showing microenvironments and the seasons in which the food resources are exploited. (West is to the left; the length of the area represented is about 20 kilometers.) [*Source.* Michael D. Coe and Kent V. Flannery, "Microenvironments and Mesoamerican Prehistory," *Science*, Vol. 143 (February 14, 1964), p. 652.]

providing routes up to the fields where the maguey plant could be found, the leaves of which were often part of the diet.

The inhabitants of the valley were more collectors of seasonally gathered wild plant foods than they were big game hunters and traveled in small bands in an annual wet-season-dry-season cycle from one micro-environment to another as food supplies changed. Coe and Flannery describe life in the valley during the Formative Period (1500 B.C. to 200 A.D.) as follows:[1]

> Most of the peoples of the Formative Period apparently lived in large villages on the alluvial valley floor during the wet season, from May through October of each year, for planting had to be done in May and June, and harvesting, in September and October. In the dry season, from November through February, when the trees and bushes had lost their leaves and the deer were easy to see and track, some of the population must have moved to hunting camps, princi-pally in the Coxcatlan thorn forest. By February, hunting had become less rewarding as the now-wary deer moved as far as possible from human habita-tion; however, in April and May the thorn forest was still ripe for exploitation, as many kinds of wild fruit matured. In May it was again time to return to the villages on the valley floor for spring planting.

The gradual improvement of agriculture seems to have made few alterations in the settlement pattern of the valley, and even after irrigation was introduced, perhaps between 200 and 900 A.D., it was still necessary for food production to be supplemented with extensive plant collecting and hunting. Although drastically changed with the coming of irrigation and improved agricultural techniques, the migrating patterns of this early Mexican population are not unlike those found as late as the mid-19th century among Shoshonean bands living in the Great Basin of the Ameri-can West. The wide variety of choices concerning the location of economic activity which we in the 20th century take for granted is thus to be regard-ed as a relatively recent state of affairs. We now consider a variety of models that provide insights concerning these choices.

17.2 SITE-RENT SURFACE

We have learned how the geographic structure of prices around a market center can be described in terms of a site-price surface for a single product or in terms of several site-price surfaces for multiple forms of a single raw product. However, it is clear that a direct comparison of site-price surfaces

[1]Michael D. Coe and Kent V. Flannery, "Microenvironments and Mesoamerican Pre-history," *Science*, Vol. 143 (February 14, 1964), p. 652.

for a variety of products cannot be made when the inputs used per unit of output vary from product to product. Neither will a site-price surface be a direct measure of differences in net revenue for a single product in the event that it is profitable to change the input mix as the price received by the producer varies from nearby to more distant sites.

To make interproduct comparisons, it is necessary to transform site prices into a measure of annual net returns per unit of land. We use the term *site rent* to describe this measure.[2] Site rent is the maximum return per unit of land expressed as the difference between receipts (site price multiplied by output) and outlays for the mobile factors used in the production of a given product at a specified site. Site rent includes, but is not necessarily limited to, land rent in the sense of payment for land used as an input in the production process, since it encompasses returns to all those characteristics of spatially separated sites that cannot be duplicated at will elsewhere at zero cost.

We can now construct a *site-rent surface* for any given product. A site-rent surface is a representation of the spatial pattern of site rents that accrue to the fixed factor, land, expressed as an annual rate of return when a given product, i, is produced. Each point on the surface thus represents a properly weighted combination of product and factor site prices that will make annual returns comparable among products.

Two cases may be encountered. The first, in which land is the only fixed factor, offers no problem. The second, in which one or more fixed factors other than land are present, is somewhat more complicated; but we can view the problem as that of maximizing returns to the fixed *bundle* of inputs, *any one* of which can be selected as a numeraire. We assume that the goal of the enterprise is to maximize return to land.

17.3 EQUILIBRIUM MARKET PRICE

At this point the spatial features of the structure of farm prices must be explored in greater detail. The first section of Figure 17.2 shows the price at the farm as a function of distance from market center and emphasizes the connection between farm prices and market price through transfer cost. The second section of the figure shows average and marginal cost curves for a farm; they do *not* include an allowance for land costs. We as-

---

[2]Other writers have used the terms location rent and economic rent in referring to this same concept. Hoover's definition of location rent: "The local differential accruing to immobile factors of production in some places by virtue of their exclusive advantages of location"; see Edgar M. Hoover, Jr., *Location Theory and the Shoe and Leather Industries* (Cambridge: Harvard University Press, 1937), p. 14, footnote 4.

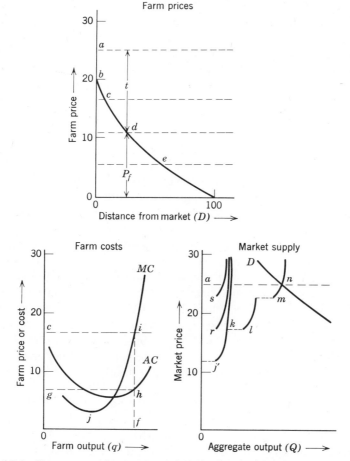

FIGURE 17.2 The geographic structure of at-the-farm prices, farm cost curves (for inputs other than land), and the determination of market supply curves.

sume that these cost relationships are appropriate at every farm location. According to familiar theoretical reasoning, a farmer located a short distance from market who is confronted with an at-the-farm price of *oc* would adjust to this by producing the quantity *of*, thus, equating his marginal costs to price and so maximizing net returns as represented by the rectangle *cghi*.

As market price P_m varies, the price to this farmer P_f will vary by identical absolute amounts, always maintaining a difference equal to transfer cost. It is clear, therefore, that changes in the market price will induce changes in the volume produced by this farmer and that these changes will be represented by movements along his marginal cost curve. It is also apparent that he will continue to produce, at least in the short run, so long as the at-farm price is as high as or higher than the lowest point j on his marginal cost curve. (We assume for convenience that this is also the lowest point on his average variable cost curve, although this would require a linear total variable cost function and, therefore, constant marginal cost for outputs to the left of this point.)

This minimum price at which he will produce corresponds to a market price equal to the sum of marginal cost at point j plus farm-to-market transfer cost. Therefore, we can represent this farmer's responses in terms of market prices by elevating his marginal cost curve by the appropriate transfer cost. This is indicated by the curve starting at point j' and passing through the point k in the third diagram in Figure 17.2. Here, point j from the middle diagram has been moved upward by the appropriate transfer costs as explained above. Notice also that the quantity scale in this last diagram has been condensed to measure aggregate output of all producers.

By similar argument, farms more distant from the market (as suggested by points d and e in the first section) would be represented in terms of market prices by transformed marginal cost curves starting at points r and s in the third section of the figure. Now, if these three farms are the only ones supplying the market, it is a simple matter to construct a curve showing the total quantities that would be delivered in response to changes in the market price. This merely involves the horizontal summation of the three transformed marginal cost curves; the resulting market supply curve would be the discontinuous function $j'klmn$. With any given market demand curve, such as D in the diagram, the equilibrium market price oa would be determined. With many farmers at varying distances from market, of course, the aggregation of transformed marginal cost curves would result in a reasonably smooth and positively inclined market supply curve.

17.4 FACTORS INFLUENCING SITE RENTS

In constructing the average and marginal cost curves described above, all inputs and costs other than land were included. We assumed that these curves were appropriate for farms at any location, that land was perfectly homogeneous throughout the region, and that at-farm prices for all other inputs were constant and equal throughout the region. Under these conditions the net returns, as represented by rectangle $cghi$ in Figure 17.2, would be due entirely to the particular location of the farm; and similar net returns at other locations would fall off as distance from market increased. Recognition of the higher net returns available to nearby farms would induce other farmers to bid for these more advantageous locations. This bidding would continue so long as costs, including payment for location, were lower than gross farm returns for the given production period. In short, these net returns are economic rents resulting from superior locations, and the operation of the land market will (under perfect competition) bring about a regular geographic structure of such site rents.

The spatial variation in site rent is illustrated in Figure 17.3. Land immediately adjacent to the city will command the highest rent, as suggested by point *a*, since it has the lowest product transfer cost. The nearby farm that we considered in our previous example has an economic rent represented by point *b* in Figure 17.3. Here the vertical dimension of this point corresponds to the size of the profit rectangle *cghi* in Figure 17.2. Eventually, a site will be reached along any radius where the at-farm price is just sufficient to cover nonland average costs at the minimum point on the average cost curve. Here there is no surplus or net return and, hence, this location shown as point *c* defines the "no rent" margin. At points more distant from market than point *c*, production may be carried on in the short run; but returns will not be adequate to cover total costs, and this land

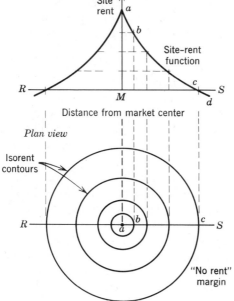

FIGURE 17.3   Site rent as a function of distance from market.

will eventually be retired from use in this *submarginal* line of production. Notice that the *land* is not submarginal, only this *use* is submarginal.

From this discussion it should be apparent that the site-rent structure is directly dependent on market price, on nonland production costs, and on product transfer cost. It follows that changes in market price will induce upward or downward movements in the entire structure of rents. It also follows that differences in production costs must modify rents. Consider the case where prices of input factors are not constant but increase (because of higher transfer costs for inputs) with distance from the central market. This will cause the level of the cost curves to rise as we move away from the market and thereby bring about a more rapid decline in the rent surface. Moreover, differences in land quality may modify input-output relations and, thus, give rise to differences in net returns at any given distance from market. Such qualitative differences will result in rents attributable to the land itself — Ricardian rents. In the real world, then, land rents combine two elements — pure site rents and rents that result from qualitative differences in the land input.

17.5 SITE RENTS AND PRODUCTION ZONES

The site rents discussed thus far represent earnings available from a single, particular crop (or fixed rotation of crops). Other crops will yield characteristically different geographic rent structures and so will have differing abilities to compete for land of any given quality at any given location. For any product or set of joint products, we can construct a site-rent surface representing the net returns over nonland costs that result from advantageous or disadvantageous locations. Moreover, the particular structure of potential rent earnings around a market will vary from product to product, in part, reflecting bulkiness, perishability, and other factors affecting transport costs and, in part, the adaptability of the land to production. These differences are basic to the development of regional specialization.

Let us first abstract from land differences by considering the case of an isolated city located in a plain that has uniform fertility and with transport facilities equally available and at equal unit costs in every direction. Each potential use for this agricultural land will then generate a conelike structure of site rents centered on the city and decreasing with distance from market. These rents represent the ability of the particular use to compete for the land and, in a perfect market, will give rise to concentric zones of optimum product uses. The uses that result in heavy yields per acre will bear heavy transfer costs and, hence, will locate near the market, but uses that involve smaller and more concentrated outputs will tend to be located in more distant zones. Perishability of the product will also be important for this influences transfer costs directly in the added costs of protecting the product and indirectly in the increased losses due to deterioration with increasing length of haul and time in transit. Market prices will directly affect the rent structures for each alternative use, of course, and the eventual allocation of the producing area among the several products will represent an interdependent supply and demand equilibrium.

These principles of the location of agricultural production were first given systematic expression by Johann Heinrich von Thünen in 1826. At that time, overland transportation was by wagon, and transport costs exerted compelling influences even over relatively short distances. Thünen observed that these transport costs would quickly consume any net returns from the production of bulky and perishable products as distance from the central city increased. His general scheme of efficient production is indicated in Figure 17.4. Various intensive and perishable crops, for example, potatoes, fresh vegetables, and fluid milk, would be produced in the zone immediately adjacent to the city.

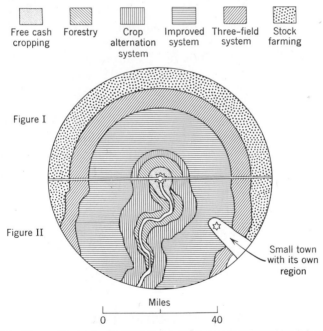

FIGURE 17.4   The optimum land utilization patterns as developed by Johann Heinrich von Thünen in 1826. [*Source.* Johann Heinrich von Thünen, *Von Thunen's Isolated State: An English Edition of Der Isolierte Staat*, translated by Carla M. Wartenberg and edited by Peter Hall (New York: Pergamon Press, 1966), 304 pp.]

The radius of this ring was calculated by Thünen to be 4 miles, each the equivalent of 4.6 English miles. Beyond this would come a zone for forest crops, for wood was the essential fuel in those days and its transport was expensive. The forestry ring was used to provide the firewood supply for the town. The higher quality fuel timber was produced somewhat further from town and was followed by building timber toward the outer edge of the ring, which was located 7.3 miles from town.

The forestry ring was followed by three rings having enterprise combinations that included small grains but consisted of different cropping systems because of changing relative prices of the products. Ring three—a zone of grain and root culture that included crops such as barley, potatoes, hay and legumes, and root crops—was included in the illustration, but Thünen's calculations showed that it would not be a profitable rotation under his assumptions. Ring four was devoted to a rotation of grain, pasture, and fallow extending 24.7 miles from town. The limit of cultivated farming was the historic three-field system with grain and fallow, as in the previous zones, but with much permanent pasture and meadows.

Beyond 31.4 miles came the final agricultural ring devoted to grazing—a use that was made possible by the fact that livestock could be driven to market. Thünen also noted that wool could be sheared and butter manufactured at a profit at this distance because of their high value and small bulk. Beyond these agricultural zones would be a wilderness area with hunting and trapping and the shipping of valuable and easy-to-transport furs.

Thünen also recognized the important influence of water transportation where available with rates per ton-mile much lower than wagon rates. The modifications to product zones and optimum uses that would result are suggested by the lower half of the diagram in Figure 17.4 where water rates are one-tenth the land freight charges. Here, transport costs from any point to the city will represent the most economical combination of land and water routes, and the availability of low-cost water movement will greatly elongate the zones along the river. The boundary between any two zones, however, will involve combined transfer costs, as was the case with the wagon transfer costs in the upper half of the figure.

17.6 THE EFFECTS OF DIFFERENCES IN LAND QUALITY

The introduction of qualitative differences in land will, to some extent, obscure the effects of site-rent differences by destroying the symmetry of the utilization zones, but the impact of location and of transport costs will remain. The general nature of these effects is suggested by the hypothetical example summarized in Table 17.1. Here, we assume that there are three different grades of land — A, B, and C — and three products — 1, 2, and 3. In general, Product 1 results in the lowest product-weight per acre, Product 2 in an intermediate product-weight, and Product 3 in the highest product-weight per acre; but the relative weights vary among the several land classes. Yields per acre are given in the first row of the table.

Equilibrium prices for the products delivered to the central market are shown in the second row, and gross values per acre in terms of those market prices are given in the third row. Production costs per acre for all inputs except land are summarized in row 4, and equivalent site rents *at the market center* are given in the following row. The costs of transporting the product of one acre for a distance of one mile are given in row 6. We have assumed that transport costs are linear functions of distance and that they amount to 10 cents per mile for a unit of any product. The final rows indicate the distances from the market center to the various boundaries between product zones and to the no-rent margin for each product.

The geographic structures of land rents corresponding to these situations are indicated in Figure 17.5. Because Product 3 yields the greatest product-weight per acre, it carries the largest transport cost and so shows the most rapid decline in site rent as distance from market increases. Product 1, on the other hand, has the lowest product-weight and transport costs and a rent structure that reflects this through a more gradual decline with distance. Product zones are always ordered from the heavy product-weight near the market to the light product-weight at a distance from market for any land class, but differences in yields on the several land classes may completely eliminate the production of some products. Thus, all three products would be produced on land class A, but only Products 1 and 3 would occur on land class B, and only Products 1 and 2 on land class C. Inspection of the yield data in Table 17.1 indicates that this is because Products 2 and 3 are relatively poor alternatives on land classes B and C, respectively. Notice that this is true even though the highest *absolute* yields for Product 3 are obtained from class C land.

The final organization of zones around the market as indicated in Figure 17.6 emphasizes the disruption to regular and even product zones that will result from qualitative differences in the land resource. Needless to say, the appearance of these zones would be even more chaotic if the several land classes were found in irregular and scattered patterns through the producing territory. In addition, a less regular and more realistic structure of transport costs would further complicate matters. In spite of these disturbances to the apparent regularity of the zonal

TABLE 17.1 Example Illustrating the Combined Effects of Location and of Qualitative Differences in the Land Resource on Optimum Land Utilization

Item	Land Class A			Land Class B			Land Class C		
	Product			Product			Product		
	1	2	3	1	2	3	1	2	3
1. Bushels per acre	20	40	60	25	30	50	20	50	65
2. Market price (dollars)	3.00	2.50	2.00	3.00	2.50	2.00	3.00	2.50	2.00
3. Value per acre (dollars)[a]	60.00	100.00	120.00	75.00	75.00	100.00	60.00	125.00	130.00
4. Cost per acre (dollars)[b]	10.00	20.00	30.00	11.00	17.00	25.00	10.00	23.00	32.00
5. Site rent at market (dollars)[c]	50.00	80.00	90.00	64.00	58.00	75.00	50.00	102.00	98.00
6. Transport cost per mile (dollars)[d]	2.00	4.00	6.00	2.50	3.00	5.00	2.00	5.00	6.50
Distance to product boundaries (miles)[e]									
Product 1	15.0			25.6			25.0		
Product 2		15.0				4.4		17.3	
Product 3			5.0			4.4			17.3
No-rent margin	25.0	20.0	15.0	25.6	19.3	15.0	25.0	20.4	15.1

[a]The gross value at market prices for the products.

[b]Costs other than land costs. They are indicated as varying among land classes primarily as a consequence of yield variations and corresponding changes in harvest costs.

[c]The gross value at market prices less nonland costs expressed as dollars per acre.

[d]The transport cost per mile for the total product of one acre, based on a uniform transport rate of 10 cents per mile per bushel.

[e]The distance from market center to the indicated boundaries between product zones and to the no-rent or extensive margin for each product.

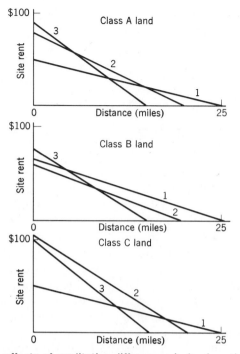

FIGURE 17.5   The effects of qualitative differences in land on the structure of site rents and on boundaries between product zones. (The numbers refer to products. See Table 17.1.)

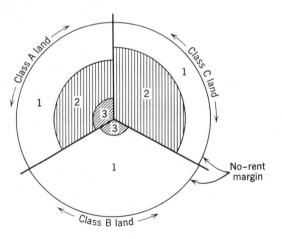

FIGURE 17.6   The effects of qualitative differences in land on optimum land utilization patterns.

structure, however, the basic influences of location and of transport costs, although less obvious, will continue to operate. The simplified models help us to understand these influences, but the more complicated models warn us that many factors and influences, in addition to transfer costs, must be considered in any attempt to explain real geographic production patterns.

17.7 LAND-USE EQUILIBRIUM WITH MULTIPLE MARKETS

It is a relatively simple matter to expand the *concept* of site-rent structures and product zones around a single market to include many alternative markets, although the resulting systems of site prices, site rents, and production patterns may be quite complex. We have learned that a producer at any particular location considers the production alternatives available to him and selects that one which will maximize his returns. In a competitive market he is forced to this optimum selection by the bidding up of resource values—by the site rents. His physical production opportunities are defined by the resources at his disposal and by available technology. If he is located in a semiarid country without irrigation, water limits his opportunities to a small list of enterprises that can be carried on successfully under dry land conditions. To produce fresh fruits and vegetables for winter markets, he must be located in regions where winter temperatures are moderate enough to permit this culture. If his operation depends on some unique resource, then he must locate where this resource is available, coal mines must be at coal deposits! In general, then, we state that the possible alternative production opportunities are determined by physical conditions, by resources and differences in resources, and by the physical technology that tells us how best to combine these resources to obtain desired products.

Given a list of potential enterprises and the physical inputs and outputs involved in each, the selection of the particular enterprise or enterprises to follow depends on economic considerations. These economic forces are presented to the individual producer in the form of product prices f.o.b. the farm location (site prices), cost rates and prices for inputs, and alternative opportunities as reflected in site rents. In the single market case, all of them refer to conditions in the central market, and the whole system is brought into equilibrium through the interaction of market demands for the several products and the product zone and supply allocations. When several market centers are involved, each product must be considered with reference to each market outlet, and the producer makes *disposal* responses as well as production and utilization responses.

In brief, we visualize multiple product zones and the associated site-rent surfaces around every market with them all interacting and impinging on product demands in every market. With any given set of product prices for each market, every point in the producing territory will be characterized by a particular site rent *for each product in every market.* Through a free-choice system, producers at every point will consider these alternatives and select that which yields the highest rent. Through this process the entire region will be allocated among markets and among products. If this allocation does not result in a supply-demand balance for each product in every market consistent with the original market prices, adjustments in prices, rents, and supply area allocations will continue until the final equilibrium is attained. We have already stressed that this is an interdependent system; if any single product in any market is out of line, the subsequent adjustment will have direct or indirect influences on all products in all markets.

This interdependent system is suggested by the hypothetical product zones in Figure 17.7. Here, we have assumed a vast producing territory with land somewhat differentiated by irregular bands of Class A, Class B, and Class C land running roughly from north to south. Four markets are located in the area: a large market in the south-central district, a major secondary market in the north, and small markets to the east and west. Product zones are somewhat irregular and discontinuous around any market because of land differences, as previously illustrated in Figure 17.6. They are further modified by the competition among markets along lines similar to the ones discussed in Chapter 7. Rents are not directly shown in Figure 17.7, except that the extensive or zero-rent margin is represented by the outside boundaries of the diagram; beyond these boundaries the land would not be cultivated. Within these boundaries, site rents would rise slowly through the zones producing the low-weight per acre products more rapidly in the medium-weight product zones and most rapidly in the heavy-weight zones near the market centers. The geographic site-rent surface would be discontinuous, of course, reflecting the abrupt changes from one land class to another.

Let us suppose that the system illustrated in the diagram is in equilibrium and that we then introduce an increase in the demand for the heavy-weight product in the small market at the western side of the region. The immediate impact of this would be the rise of this product's price in this market. As a consequence, the boundary between Product 3 and Product 2 would be pushed farther from the market center. But this would reduce market supplies for Product 2, and its price would move upward. In turn, the margin between Product 2 and Product 1 would be affected and, hence, the price of Product 1 would be increased and the extensive margin expanded somewhat.

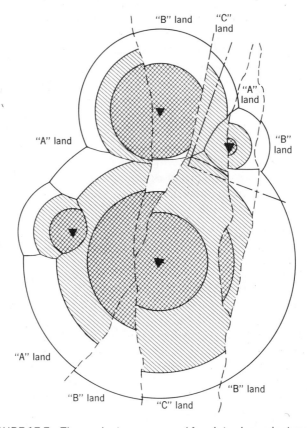

FIGURE 17.7 The product zones around four interdependent markets.

But these price increases in the small western market would also push out its boundaries with the major southern market, setting in motion a whole chain of interdependent price and zone adjustments in that major market. Finally, these "ripples" would reach the markets to the north and the northeast, affecting at least in some small degree the prices, site rents, and final product zones in those districts. In this way, a change in demand for any product in any market will have effects felt throughout the entire system and will give rise to a new and different equilibrium. In a similar way, changes in production technology or in transfer costs will interact and will modify the entire regional structure of prices, site rents, and market-product zones.

17.8 COMPARATIVE ADVANTAGE, SPECIALIZATION, AND TRADE

The Law of Comparative Advantage is frequently referred to in a discussion of the utilization of resources and of the development of exchange and trade. In general terms, this law states that a producer (individual, region, or nation) will tend to specialize in the production of the commodities in which it has the highest comparative advantage or the least comparative disadvantage and to obtain by trade the commodities in which it has the least comparative advantage or greatest comparative disadvantage.

Suppose that Brown can produce corn for 50 cents per bushel and potatoes for $1.00 per bushel but that Green's costs are 60 cents and 90 cents, respectively. Brown, thus, has a comparative and absolute advantage in producing corn, while Green has a comparative and absolute advantage in producing potatoes. It would clearly be to their mutual advantage if each specialized in the crop where he is most "efficient" and obtained the other by exchange or trade.

But suppose that Green's costs were higher than Brown's for both commodities: 60 cents per bushel for corn and $1.50 for potatoes. Now Brown has the absolute advantage in both crops, but he has the greatest *comparative* advantage in potato production ($1.50/$1.00), and Green has his least comparative disadvantage in corn (60 cents/50 cents). If Green were to reduce his potato production by 2.0 bushels, he would save $3.00 and, assuming costs are constant at the indicated levels, this would permit him to expand his corn output by 5.0 bushels. He now offers this extra corn to Brown in exchange for potatoes. Since Brown finds that 5.0 bushels of corn are the cost equivalent to him of 2.5 bushels of potatoes, it is apparent that any exchange rate between 2.0 and 2.5 bushels of potatoes for 5.0 bushels of corn would permit both parties to gain from this transaction.

Let us consider a similar situation that confronts two regions with a monetary exchange system rather than one of direct barter. Region A can produce corn and potatoes for 50 cents and $1.00 per bushel, respectively, and Region B's costs are 60 cents and $1.50, respectively. When trade opens between these two regions, it will be profitable (neglecting transfer costs) to ship both corn and potatoes from A to B. This will reduce supplies of both commodities in Region A and increase them in Region B. Moreover, there will be a monetary flow from Region B to Region A. Both the commodity flow and the money flow will increase prices in Region A and decrease them in Region B. As this continues, the price of corn in Region B will eventually fall below the price in Region A, and shipments of corn will correspondingly move from B to A.

In equilibrium, prices will be so adjusted that A ships potatoes (where it has greatest comparative advantage), B ships corn (where it has least comparative disadvantage), and the monetary value of the trade flows are in balance.

If this equilibrium involves a lowering of prices in Region B, however, it may be protested that the region produces and ships corn at returns lower than production costs. But costs reflect the physical inputs and prices of factors of production, and factor prices are derived from product demands and product prices. The indicated reductions in commodity prices in Region B and increases in commodity prices in Region A, therefore, will give rise to related adjustments in factor prices. The final equilibrium thus involves a lowering of costs in Region B through a devaluation of factor prices and an increase in costs in Region A through the inflation of factor prices.

In fact, the detailed trade and location theory that we have been considering provides us with the real meaning of the Law of Comparative Advantage, and we may well restate the law to read that each producer will specialize in the commodities from which the site rents to his productive factors are greatest. Consider the situation in a region like the one surrounding the market in the northeastern section of the diagram in Figure 17.7. Physical production possibilities are limited to the three products considered in this example, and input-output ratios for each of them are differentiated by the assumed three classes of land. Producers in this region must decide on which products to produce and whether to produce for the domestic (internal) market or for export to other markets in other regions. As we have already explained, equilibrium adjustments in this area are not independent but are determined as an integral part of the major regional adjustment. This equilibrium for the northeast area is shown on an expanded scale in Figure 17.8.

Site rents in this frontier area in general are highest along the western and southern boundaries, reflecting the important influences of major markets in adjacent areas. Rents decline to the northeast, finally reaching zero along the extensive margin of cultivation; beyond this lies an undeveloped wilderness. The declining rent structure is interrupted, however, by an inverted cone of increasing rents around the small town located in this area. In fact, site rents immediately surrounding this town are the highest in the region. The general nature of the total rent surface is indicated by the *isorent contours* shown as dotted lines in Figure 17.8 as well as by product boundaries for the given markets.

From this diagram it is apparent that a significant portion of the land resources of the region will be used to produce products for the local market. Land along the western border, however, is devoted to Products

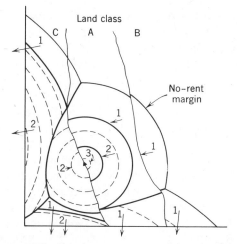

FIGURE 17.8 The specialization in an area, as determined by market demands, location, and land class. [*Note*. Numbers refer to products and arrows indicate direction of trade flows (enlarged northeast section of Figure 17.7).]

1 and 2 for export to the large secondary market beyond this border. Although the major market to the southeast is far from this area, it is profitable to devote some land along the southern border to export crops for this distant market.

Of course, this illustration of product and market zones is very much simplified, but it should suggest the nature of competition—interenterprise and interregional—for the available resources and the final allocation as determined by site rents. In the present example, exports from the region are indicated but without balancing imports. A more realistic model would have included products that require specialized resources not available in this region, for example, particular soils or climatic conditions and, as a consequence, would have indicated a much more elaborate pattern of multilateral trade. Even more important, this model has stressed the agricultural land resource and has neglected industrial production. A more complete model would have included these nonagricultural products, and would have probably indicated imports of industrial products by the small region to balance its exports of farm products.

17.9 OPPORTUNITY COST CURVES AND TRANSFER COSTS

This discussion of alternative production possibilities and of comparative advantage should remind us of the production possibilities or opportunity cost curves used in Part IV. There we suggested that the resource and technological endowment of a region would define a particular opportunity cost curve that summarized the production possibilities in the region. With these curves for several regions and with consumer demands, we were able to derive regional offer curves and to determine the patterns of production in each region, the trade flows, the product prices, and the prices for factors of production. All of this ignored location and transfer costs, although processing or production costs were directly included through the opportunity cost concept.

The preceding pages have indicated how space and form must be inserted in the general analysis of regional specialization and interregional trade. Without attempting a complete revision of the opportunity cost and offer curve analysis to insert transfer costs, we will indicate one or two major aspects. The opportunity cost curve for some Region X is indicated in Figure 17.9 for the simple two-commodity case. Suppose that some other Region Y contacts Region X with intent to trade. The prices in Y are indicated in the diagram by the slope of the price line P_{by}/P_{ay}. This is the familiar inverse ratio of product prices. If trade is established and these prices made effective in Region X, the optimum production pattern would fall at d on the opportunity cost curve.

But this ignores transfer costs. If Region X imports Product A and exports Product B, the effective prices in the region will be $(P_{ay} + t_a)$ and $(P_{by} - t_a)$ where t_a and t_b represent the costs of interregional transfer. With these prices, Region X will find its best production position at c on the opportunity cost curve. Similarly, e would represent the optimum production adjustment if Region X exported Product A and imported Product B. As a result of transfer costs, commodity prices in the two regions can differ over a substantial range without giving rise to profitable trade opportunities. This range is represented by the segment from c to e on the opportunity cost curve; prices in the two regions must differ by more than the combined transfer costs to make interregional trade advantageous.

To place this properly in its locational framework, consider Region X to be located at any of a number of alternative sites relative to Region Y. As distance and transfer costs between the two regions increase, the range within which prices could fluctuate without permitting profitable trade will increase, and the opportunity for trade will diminish. In the extreme case, of course, transfer costs are sufficiently great to more than offset potential gains from regional specialization, and trade is not established. On the other hand, two regions located close together and connected with low-cost transportation routes can engage in a wide variety of exchange to their mutual benefit. Notice also that increasing

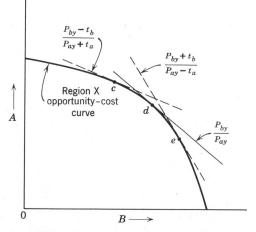

FIGURE 17.9   The effects of transfer costs on interregional trade possibilities.

distance and transfer costs will have a differential effect on product prices, reflecting product characteristics such as bulkiness and perishability. Consequently, and in conformity with our earlier location models, bulky products with high transfer costs will be traded among nearby regions, but concentrated and low transport-cost products can be traded over long distances. Some exceptions to this generalization are found where production requires specialized and localized resources not generally available in all regions. Trade flows based on bulky and perishable tropical fruits provide obvious examples.

This analysis is also revealing in the case of a region that has been expanding its output of a particular product. As long as local production is less than domestic consumption, the industry operates on the basis of a price that exceeds the "world" price by the transfer costs on the imported product. But when the growth of the industry has resulted in an exportable surplus, the domestic price will fall to the world price *minus* transfer costs. If transfer costs are relatively important, this abrupt price change will be severe and may well explain why certain industries expand within the limits of the domestic market but still are unable to compete effectively in world markets. Moreover, this situation may be quite unstable; with domestic production and consumption about in balance but subject to some variation, the domestic price may oscillate wildly between the transfer cost *plus* and the transfer cost *minus* positions.

17.10 TWO ILLUSTRATIONS

As an example of the multiple product form-space complex, we urge the reader to reexamine the map that shows the major type-of-farming areas in the United States (presented earlier). With minor exceptions, this complex organization is the result of the choices made by individual farmers in seeking profitable employment for labor, capital, and land resources. Our theoretical discussions of resource endowments and alternative opportunities of transfer costs and production-processing costs and of market and product zones provide an appreciation of the general forces that have shaped and that continue to modify the agricultural evolution. Population growth and improvements in marketing and transportation encouraged the expansion of the agricultural frontier and gradually forced farming in the East to concentrate on bulky and perishable products where nearness to market meant comparative advantage. The ultimate expansion of cereal production into the semiarid lands of the Great Plains was dictated by least comparative disadvantage. These lands are far less productive in wheat than the fertile and well-watered areas to the east, but cereals are one of the few alternative uses for the dry lands and their production is made economical by an appropriate evaluation of the basic land resource. The Cotton Belt and the areas of fruit and vegetable production in the Southwest have obvious connections with climatic conditions. Winter vegetable production in Florida, Texas, and California is economical in spite of long distances and high transport costs to market because normal production is impossible during the winter season in other parts of the country, and market prices must be high enough to cover abnormal production and marketing costs if out-of-season produce is to be available.

These broad farming areas, of course, cover a wide diversity of use patterns within any region. The major dairy regions are in the northeastern and the Great Lakes states with fluid milk dominating near the great metropolitan areas and manufactured dairy products in the Minnesota–Wisconsin–Iowa area. But dairy production is one of the most widely scattered of farm enterprises and is important in every state. In general, fluid milk requirements tend to be produced locally, since here bulk and perishability put a premium on closeness to market. In a similar way, every small region exhibits a particular pattern of land use that results from the trial-and-error search by farmers for profitable enterprises. In the extensive areas this is observed at the margin of cultivated agriculture, and abandoned homesteads are evidence of past errors in judgment. Small tracts of intensive potato and vegetable production in the scrublands of southern New England attest to the effectiveness of farmers in searching out and developing unusual resources, as do the small irrigated valleys scattered throughout the Mountain and the Pacific states.

In the more intensive areas, the working of the market in form and space is reflected in the patterns of alternative crops. Here again, the finding and exploiting of particular advantages is amazing testimony of the effectiveness of the enterprise system. The evolution of the Central Valley in California from grazing land to dryland cereal production and to irrigated intensive agriculture reflects broad technological changes in production, transportation, and marketing, coupled with expanding regional and national markets. But the detailed pattern of present land utilization and the adjustment to relatively minor differences in soils and climate represents an economical exploitation of natural resources that far surpasses the ability of the Forty-Niner to discover and to extract gold from the foothills of the Sierra Nevada.

Land-use equilibrium models are by no means limited in applicability to agricultural choices, but they can be readily adapted to other forms of enterprise. As illustrated in Figure 17.10, economic rents for commercial, residential, and industrial activities also are related to distance from market centers, resulting in concentric land-use zones that are the exact counterparts of the ones in Figure 17.7.

As in our agricultural examples, the smooth isorent boundaries between zones would be modified by irregularities in terrain, the occurrence

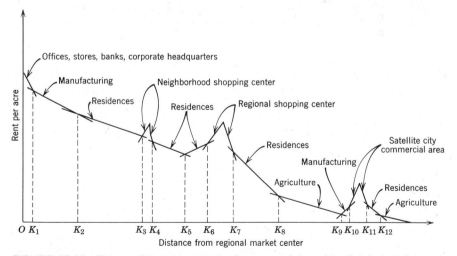

FIGURE 17.10 The spatial arrangement of commercial, residential, industrial, and agricultural activity around a regional market center. [*Source.* Hugh O. Nourse, *Regional Economics* (New York: McGraw-Hill, 1968), p. 120.]

of water barriers, the pattern of transport connections and, in some cases, by political boundaries. The peculiarities of spatial distribution of nonland inputs would also influence the site rent from and, therefore, the location of certain activities while leaving others unaffected. Furthermore, the extension of the single-market center case to cover a variety of central and satellite places is quite straightforward.

SELECTED READINGS

Land-Use Equilibrium Models

Alonso, William, *Location and Land Use: Toward a General Theory of Land Rent*. Harvard University Press, Cambridge (1964). pp. 1–75, 130–142.

Hall, Peter, "Introduction," in *Von Thünen's Isolated State* (ed.), Peter Hall. Pergamon Press, New York (1966), pp. xi–xliv.

Hoover, Edgar M., Jr., *The Location of Economic Activity, op. cit.*, pp. 67–102.

Hoover, Edgar M., Jr., *Location Theory and the Shoe and Leather Industries*. Harvard University Press, Cambridge (1937). pp. 7–33.

Isard, Walter, *Location and Space-Economy, op. cit.*, pp. 1–54, 188–206.

Lösch, August, *op. cit.*, Chapter 5, "The Theory of Agricultural Location," pp. 36–67.

Nourse, Hugh O., *Regional Economics*, McGraw-Hill Book Co. New York (1968), Chapter 5, "Land Use," pp. 83–125.

Von Thünen, Johann Heinrich, *Von Thünen's Isolated State: An English Edition of Der Isolierte Staat*, translated by Carla M. Wartenberg and edited by Peter Hall, Pergamon Press, New York, pp. 7–11, 18–40, 96–158.

chapter 18

SPATIAL EQUILIBRIUM WITH MOBILE RESOURCES

We have observed how site-rent surfaces can be used to determine the spatial arrangement of a wide range of forms of economic activity under the assumption that all inputs, except land with its related unique characteristics, are either ubiquitous or available in unlimited quantities at specified prices. Optimum product zones are defined by the site-rent surface that dominates all others at each point in the region. To relax this assumption, we limit our discussion to a single product that requires multiple inputs, one or more of which are available only at specified locations. Although they are mobile, they can be moved from place to place only at a cost that is specified by an appropriate transfer cost function. These localized factors, therefore, have price surfaces that are not perfectly flat throughout the region, as we assumed in Chapter 17.

Beginning with a single localized raw product, the analysis rapidly becomes more complex as more inputs are considered, requiring the abandonment of graphic analysis in favor of strictly mathematical formulations for complex real-world situations. But this must be deferred until a later chapter.

18.1 SPATIAL DISTRIBUTION OF RAW MATERIALS

Natural resources are termed *localized* if they exist at only a few concentrated locations; they are called *ubiquitous* if widely scattered and generally available at all locations. Deposits of coal, gas, and minerals are usually localized. Air is ubiquitous; climate exists everywhere and thus might be called ubiquitous, but differences in temperatures, rainfall, and other aspects are qualitatively important. Within any region, land and water are usually ubiquitous, but with important quantitative and qualitative differences. Certain types of agricultural land, together with the associated climatic conditions, may well be treated as a localized resource or, at least, may be restricted to subareas of any region. Similarly, water is localized at an oasis in the middle of a desert, but water is ubiquitous in much of Europe and the United States.

18.2 PRODUCTION LOCATION: SINGLE, LOCALIZED RAW MATERIAL

In our first model we explore the conditions governing the location of production of a particular commodity that involves a single raw material input, with this raw material localized at some point A while the market for the product is localized some distance away at point B. Assume that the process is *weight losing*. The use of $1\frac{1}{2}$ tons of raw material, for example, results in 1 ton of the finished product. Let us further assume that transfer costs *per ton* are the same for raw material and for finished product and that these transfer costs increase with distance but at a decreasing rate. Under these conditions we inquire as to the most economical location for production — at the raw-material site, at the market, or at some other location.

Least-Cost Site. The analysis of this simple problem is indicated in Figure 18.1. In the cross-section view at the top of this figure, we have located points *A* and *B* on the straight line *RS*; and above this base we have plotted transfer costs. Above *B*, for example, we show the structure of transfer costs for 1 ton of product and have indicated both terminal costs β and costs related to distance. Above *A*, on the other hand, we have plotted the costs of transferring the equivalent $1\frac{1}{2}$ tons of raw material that include terminal costs α plus costs related to distance. These two sets of transfer costs are added together to show the combined total transfer costs that would characterize each possible location for production along the line *RS*. Thus, if production were located at the raw-material site, the costs of transferring the finished product to the

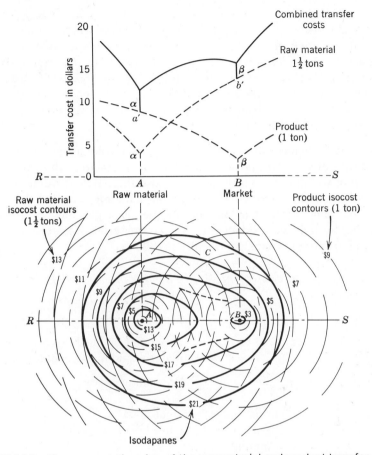

FIGURE 18.1   The cross-section view of the raw material and product transfer costs, and the plan view of isocost contours and isodapanes (raw material source at *A* and market at *B*).

market are represented by point *a'*. If production were to be located at the market, on the other hand, only the raw material would have to be transported, and its transfer cost is indicated by point *b'*. At any other location along the line *RS*, both product and raw material would have to be moved. The combined costs appropriate for any location along the straight line through *A* and *B* are indicated by the solid curves in the cross-section view.

By inspection, we can determine that the lowest possible combined transfer costs will be incurred when production is carried on at the raw material site *A*. For a plant at any other location on the line *RS*, combined transfer costs would be greater. As a general rule, then, we may conclude that weight-losing processes tend to be material rather than market-oriented, provided that only one raw material is involved and that transfer costs are the same per unit weight for product and raw material. If transfer costs are higher for the finished product, as is frequently true, then production will be market oriented in the event that product transfer costs exceed material transfer costs per ton by more than the ratio of material weight to product weight.

Weight-Equivalent Relationships. In common language, we are merely stating the obvious proposition that it costs less to ship product than material in weight-losing processes because there is less weight to transport (1 ton as compared to $1\frac{1}{2}$ tons in our example) but that this weight advantage can be offset in part or completely if transfer costs per unit are higher for finished products than for raw materials. These relationships can be simply expressed algebraically as follows.

If the weight-equivalent relationship is:	*Then the process will be located at:*
$W_p t_p > W_m t_m$	Market center
$W_p t_p = W_m t_m$	Any point on line between raw material and market center
$W_p t_p < W_m t_m$	Raw material source

where W_p = weight per unit of product
W_m = weight of raw material used per unit of raw product
t_p, t_m = constant unit transfer costs.

In our example, W_p is 1 ton and W_m is $1\frac{1}{2}$ tons.

Expressed as ratios, these relationships may be written as

$$t_p/t_m > W_m/W_p \qquad \text{Market oriented.}$$
$$t_p/t_m = W_m/W_p \qquad \text{Any point on line } AB.$$
$$t_p/t_m < W_m/W_p \qquad \text{Raw material oriented.}$$

Finally, it is a simple matter to substitute nonlinear transfer cost functions for the constant unit cost terms in these equations.

Location-Cost Relationships. The lower section of Figure 18.1 shows these transfer costs in plan view for all locations throughout the area surrounding A and B as well as along their straight-line connector RS. The structure of increasing transfer costs for the product is represented by the set of concentric circles centered on the market location at *B*. These circles are contour lines on the cost surface, each showing the locus of points with equal product transfer costs. Thus, successive circles centered at *B* correspond to transfer costs of $3, $4, $5, . . . per ton of product. The circles centered on *A*, on the other hand, represent equal transfer cost contours for the equivalent weight ($1\frac{1}{2}$ tons) of raw material to produce 1 ton of product.

Notice that these cost contours are perfect circles as a result of our assumption that transfer costs are uniformly related to airline distances; if topography, road and rail networks, and traffic volumes distort and modify the relationship between cost and airline distance, then equal transfer cost contours will be correspondingly distorted and irregular. Notice also that the radii of these circles increase at an increasing rate: that the added distances corresponding to equal increments in cost become larger as we move away from the market. This reflects the assumption that transfer costs increase at a decreasing rate with distance.

Isodapanes.   We have sketched in a few of the product and material transfer cost contours to show the method of generating the combined material-plus-product transfer cost surface. If production were located at *C*, for example, it would cost $12 to move $1\frac{1}{2}$ tons of raw material from *A*, $7 to transport the resulting ton of finished product to the market at *B*, or a combined transfer cost of $19. In this way, we can construct a system of equal combined cost contours called *isodapanes*. They are represented by the heavy, more or less oval curves in Figure 18.1. An examination of these isodapanes will reveal that the combined cost surface somewhat resembles a trough with low points falling along the line connecting *A* and *B*. The cost "elevation" along the line *AB*, of course, is indicated by the solid curves at the top of the upper diagram. Finally, at *A* and at *B* this surface is "punched out" with costs dropping below the general level of the cost surface by amounts representing the fixed or terminal costs of transfer.

Some Generalizations.   It may be observed that the optimum location for production will usually be at either the material site or the market and not at an intermediate location. If costs are a *linear* function of distance but with zero terminal costs (a straight line passing through the origin), then the optimum location will be at either the material site, if weight losing, or the market site if the process is weight gaining. Transfer costs will be identical at all points on the line that connects the material site and the market if the process is weight constant and the unit transfer costs for product and raw material are identical. If transfer costs increase with distance at a *decreasing* rate, as assumed above, or if they are a linear function of distance but with positive terminal costs, the transfer-cost that minimizes location will always be at either the material site or the market. If transfer costs increase with distance at an *increasing* rate—an improbable situation—then the optimum location will be at some point between the raw material site and the market, unless weight gains or losses are relatively very large. Again, restatement of the problem in terms of equivalent weights is needed.

18.3 PRODUCTION LOCATION: ONE LOCALIZED AND ONE UBIQUITOUS RAW MATERIAL

Let us complicate our model by assuming that there are two raw materials used in the process. To produce *2* tons of product now requires 1½ tons of a raw material localized at *A* plus 1 ton of a second but ubiquitous raw material. Wherever production is located, the second material will be available without transfer cost, but its addition influences total transfer costs through the added weight of the finished product. This new situation is represented in Figure 18.2. In essence, the addition of the ubiquitous material has changed our case from a weight-losing to a weight-gaining process—comparing the weight of the finished product to the weight of the localized raw material—and, as a consequence, the optimum location will now be at the market *B*. Since optimum location must be at *A* or *B* or on the line connecting them, as in the previous case, we dispense with the cross-section view and the construction of isodapanes.

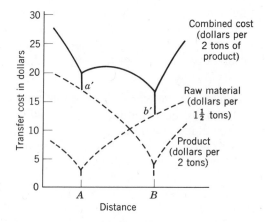

FIGURE 18.2   The effect of the increase in product weight as a result of the addition of 1 ton of a ubiquitous material to the process illustrated in Figure 18.1.

18.4 PRODUCTION LOCATION: TWO LOCALIZED RAW MATERIALS

As a further modification, consider the situation where the second raw material is not ubiquitous but localized at some point C. Here, we have the basic problem discussed by the earliest writers on industrial location. In view of its historical significance, as well as its current usefulness, we give below the essential features of the "classical" three-point solution as first developed by Launhardt in 1882 and then, independently, by Weber and his mathematical associate Pick in 1909.[1]

Consider, as in section 18.3, an industrial process with a localized market at some point B, a localized raw material at some point A, and a second raw material now assumed to be localized at some point C. The process requires $1\frac{1}{2}$ tons of raw material from A plus 1 ton of raw material from C to produce 2 tons of the finished product to be delivered to the market at B. As in the classical treatment, we assume that transfer costs per ton-mile are equal and constant in all directions, for all distances, and for all materials and products; the transfer cost function is uniform and linear through the origin. Under these circumstances, the locational "pull" of any material or market site will be proportional to the weight of the material or product involved, and this force will act in the direction of the straight line connecting any selected site with the location of the market or the raw material. Where these forces exactly balance off or are in equilibrium, total transfer costs will be at a minimum.

Weight Triangle.   Geometric representation of these forces for our assumed situation is developed in Figure 18.3. Part I of this figure shows the "weight triangle," with sides proportional to the specified raw material and product weights: the line directed toward a represents the $1\frac{1}{2}$ tons of raw material A; the line toward c represents the 1 ton of raw material C; but the line directed toward b represents the resulting 2 tons of finished product to be delivered to the market B. By this construction, the three forces are brought into equilibrium, as illustrated by the locational force vectors in Part II. Notice that the two raw material vectors da and dc resolve into the component db' and that this is equal to but opposite in direction to the product vector db. Apparently, then, the determination of the cost-minimizing location for this activity amounts to selecting some point d so that the vectors as given in Part II will point directly to the appropriate market and material locations at A, B, and C.

Before moving on to the determination of this cost-minimizing

---

[1]This and the following three sections draw heavily on R. O. Been, "A Reconstruction of the Classical Theory of Location" (unpublished Ph.D. dissertation, Department of Agricultural Economics, University of California, Berkeley, 1965).

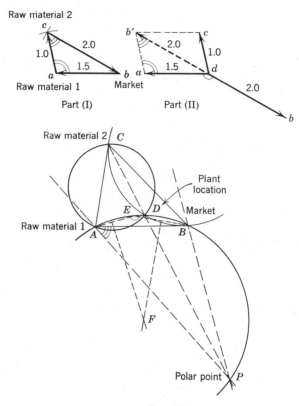

FIGURE 18.3   The optimum plant location—the three-point solution. (*Part I*) Weight triangle. (*Part II*) Locational force vectors. (*Part III*) Minimum cost location (point *D*).

location, we must point out that the given weights will always establish a unique weight triangle (and so the conditions for the equilibrium resolution of force vectors) unless one of the weights exceeds the total of the others. In these cases it will be impossible to construct the weight triangle, and the cost-minimizing solution will coincide with the location of the weight-dominant material or product. In the above illustration, if the process had required 4 tons of the raw material at *A*, this would have exceeded the combined weights of raw material *C* and product *B*; and, hence, the optimum location would have been at point *A*.

Location Triangle.   Part III illustrates the final determination for specific locations at designated points *A*, *B*, and *C*, defining the "location triangle" *ABC*. We seek that point *d* within this triangle that will give force directions similar to the ones in the diagram of vectors in Part II. Although this may be determined by superimposing the vector diagram on the location triangle and by adjusting until the vectors extend exactly through the A, B, and C locations, the point can be obtained geometrically as follows: Lay off line AE through A in an arbitrary direction "northeast" of point A. Construct a line through B to a line through A so that at E the angle AEB is equal to angle adb in the Part II vector diagram.[2] Drop perpendicular bisectors of AE and EB to intersect at F. With this as center, circumscribe circle through A, E, and B. We know that, in equilibrium, the forces operating through A and B must form an angle equal to AEB; we also know that every inscribed angle through A and B and any selected point on arc AEB will be equal and equal to angle AEB. Therefore, the equilibrium solution must fall somewhere on arc AEB. The construction of a similar circumscribed circle on leg AC or CB of the location triangle will determine the locus for central angles bdc or adc, and the intersection of these circles will determine the cost-minimizing location at D.

Polar Point.   An alternative construction of considerable interest is to find the "polar point" to point C of the location triangle. This is accomplished by constructing line BP with angle ABP equal to angle cab in the weight triangle (Part I) and line AP with angle BAP equal to angle bca. Their intersection determines polar point P; the circle circumscribed through A, B, and P is the same as the previously described circle through A, E, and B. Now draw the line connecting P with C; this will intersect arc AEB at the cost-minimizing point D.[3]

A valuable characteristic of this polar point is that it is determined completely by the three weights and by the specific locations of A and B; point P, in short, is the polar point for any C location. In Figure 18.3, Part III, any location for C above line AB that falls within the angle APB will give a cost-minimizing solution, such as point D where the line connecting C and P cuts the arc AEB, thus, giving solutions within the location triangle. C locations to the right of line BP and above AB indicate a "corner" solution at B: the process should be located at market B. Points to the left of line AP and above AB give optimum solutions at raw material site A. If C is located below AB, the whole construction is inverted.

---

[2]If the selected angle BAE is too large, it may prove to be impossible to construct angle AEB; in this case, select a smaller angle BAE.

[3]If point D has already been determined, of course, an alternative construction is to extend line CD until it intersects the circumscribed circle at polar point P.

18.5 UNEQUAL AND NONPROPORTIONAL TRANSFER COSTS

In the previous section, we treated the localizing forces or vectors as proportional to the respective weights of product and raw materials. In fact, these forces are transfer costs—more precisely, they are marginal transfer costs. If we consider any possible site D, the forces attracting this location to market and material are the weights multiplied by appropriate marginal transfer costs per ton-mile. When we assume that transfer costs are direct linear functions of distance and are the same for product and all raw materials, the weights are multiplied by a uniform cost per ton-mile—the slope of the transfer cost function. In the more general case where costs are not the same for all products and materials or where functions are nonlinear, the localizing forces will not be proportional to the weights.

Under the assumption that transfer cost functions are linear and pass through the origin but that rates differ for products and/or materials, the modification to the foregoing analysis is slight. Suppose that we continue our example of $1\frac{1}{2}$ tons of material A, 1 ton of material C, and 2 tons of product B; but now assume that transfer rates on A and B equal 10 cents per ton-mile, but for C the rate is 20 cents, perhaps because the material is perishable, difficult to handle, bulky, or requires special handling and shipping equipment. The locational forces will then be as follows: for material A, $1\frac{1}{2}$ tons × 10 cents per ton-mile or 15 cents per mile; for material C, 1 ton × 20 cents per ton-mile or 20 cents per mile; and for product B, 2 tons × 10 cents per ton-mile or 20 cents per mile. These transfer costs are used to construct the transfer cost triangle in Figure 18.4. With this triangle substituted for the weight triangle in Figure 18.3, the determination of the optimum location proceeds as before.

Under the assumption that transfer costs are equal for all products

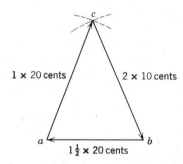

FIGURE 18.4 The transfer-cost triangle with rates of 10 cents per ton-mile for Material A and Product B and 20 cents per ton-mile for Material C. (*Note.* Compare with Figure 18.3, Part I.)

and materials and in all directions but are not directly proportional to distance, two general cases can be distinguished: (1) constant transport cost per ton-mile with a fixed terminal cost, and (2) transport costs that increase with distance but (normally) at a decreasing rate with or without terminal charges. Such nonproportional rate structures were discussed earlier. The straight line *od* through the origin in Figure 18.5 illustrates the directly proportional cost functions used in the previous sections. Straight line *ae* has the same "marginal" cost per ton-mile, but differs from *od* by the fixed terminal charge (loading, unloading, etc.) of *oa* per ton. Finally, the curve *obc* shows transfer costs per ton increasing with length of haul but at a decreasing rate, the marginal cost decreasing as we move from nearby points, such as *b*, to more distant points, such as *c*.

If transfer cost functions are linear but include terminal costs, the previous analysis will still determine the minimum cost location for any point *within* the location triangle; at any such internal point, the transport costs will simply be increased by a constant representing the aggregate terminal charges. If terminal charges of $1.00 per ton for all products and materials were involved, the previous example would simply have all costs increased by $4.50, corresponding to the 1.5 tons of material A, 2.0 tons of product B, and 1.0 tons of material C. This will not be true, however, for plant locations at any corner of the triangle since these locations will avoid both transport and terminal costs for one material or for the finished product.[4]

[4]Although such a corner location will avoid the terminal transfer costs for the material localized at that point, there may be some partially offsetting local handling costs. These costs have been ignored in the above treatment.

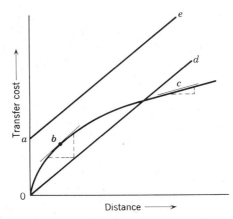

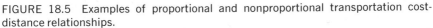

FIGURE 18.5 Examples of proportional and nonproportional transportation cost-distance relationships.

It will be necessary, therefore, to check the combined transport plus terminal costs for point D with the corresponding costs at each of the corner locations. This procedure is suggested in Table 18.1, where distances in miles have been scaled from Figure 18.3 and where the transfer cost function is assumed to involve terminal costs of $1.00 per ton and transport costs of 10 cents per ton-mile. These calculations indicate a total transport cost at D of $17.85. This is lower than for any other point within the location triangle. The addition of terminal costs, however, increases this to $22.35 as compared to $22.70 for plant location at A,

TABLE 18.1   Total Transfer Costs for Plant Locations[a]

Origins	Plant Location			
	D	A	B	C
Tons shipped from				
A	1.5	0.0	1.5	1.5
B	2.0	2.0	0.0	2.0
C	1.0	1.0	1.0	0.0
Miles from				
A	37	0	70	57
B	35	70	0	82
C	53	57	82	0
Transport costs[b]				
A	$ 5.55	$ 0.00	$10.50	$ 8.55
B	7.00	14.00	0.00	16.40
C	5.30	5.70	8.20	0.00
Subtotal	$17.85	$19.70	$18.70	$24.95
Terminal charges[c]				
A	$ 1.50	$ 0.00	$ 1.50	$ 1.50
B	2.00	2.00	0.00	2.00
C	1.00	1.00	1.00	0.00
Subtotal	$ 4.50	$ 3.00	$ 2.50	$ 3.50
Total transfer costs	$22.35	$22.70	$21.20	$28.45

[a] At points A, B, C, and D in Figure 18.3, *supra*, p. 360.
[b] 10 cents per ton-mile.
[c] $1.00 per ton.

$21.20 at *B*, and $28.45 at *C*. Thus, the inclusion of terminal costs has changed the cost-minimizing location from point *D* to point *B*, and, hence, the optimum plant location would be at the market.

We have already pointed out that the locational forces acting at any point are not the material-product weights, but these weights multiplied by the appropriate marginal transfer costs. The assumption of linear but unequal cost-distance functions for the several products and materials requires a relatively simple adjustment, since the marginal transfer costs per ton-mile for any single product or material would be constant over all distances. With curvilinear cost functions, however, marginal transfer costs (the slope of the total cost-distance function) will change continuously with distance changes. This means that every possible location will be characterized by a particular set of distances to raw materials and to market and, hence, by a unique set of marginal transfer costs. Consequently, the force vectors will differ in magnitude with every change in location. Although there is no way to determine the optimum location directly, it can be discovered through a process of successive approximation. Since the locational problem with more than three points must also be approached by such an iterative process, the treatment will be suggested in the following section.

18.6 OPTIMUM LOCATION WITH MORE THAN THREE POINTS

We have observed that, with linear transfer cost functions, three fixed points and the associated material-product weights permit the construction of a unique weight triangle or transfer cost triangle and the equivalent equilibrium force vector diagram. From this we can move directly to the determination of the optimum plant location. With four or more fixed sites and corresponding weights, however, no unique force polygon or vector diagram can be obtained and, therefore, it is necessary to find the optimum location through a trial-and-error or successive approximation approach. Suppose that we illustrate this by adding to our earlier example of one market and two raw materials a third raw material localized at some point *D* which contributes 1 ton of material to the process; we retain the assumption of equal and constant transfer costs per ton-mile.

Vector Analysis.   Such a configuration is shown in Figure 18.6 where *A*, *B*, and *C* locations and weights are the same as in Figure 18.3 but where we have added the new raw material at point *D*. *ABDC* is then the locational polygon and, since the figure is not concave, we expect to find the optimum plant location within this polygon or at one of its

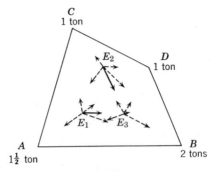

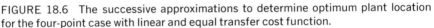

FIGURE 18.6 The successive approximations to determine optimum plant location for the four-point case with linear and equal transfer cost function.

corners. A consideration of the several weights involved suggests that this optimum location probably is in the "southeast region" of the polygon, and we might well select a point in that region to start our iterative process. To clarify the procedure, however, we deliberately select point E_1 as our initial position. At this point, construct the vector diagram with each vector (the broken lines) acting in the direction from E_1 to the appropriate corner and scaled in proportion to the weights (marginal transfer costs). By the usual methods, we determine that this is a nonequilibrium situation and that the resultant vector sum is represented by the solid arrow extending from E_1 in an easterly direction. Notice that this represents the net force acting at E_1, that its length represents the magnitude of this force (scaled as are the other vectors), and that it points in the "general" direction of the optimum location.

We might well select a second point to the east of E_1 and, by following this procedure, gradually converge on the desired point of minimum transfer cost. As an alternative, however, we have selected E_2 with the full realization that this will not be a close approximation to the optimum location. Plotting vectors again reveals a nonequilibrium situation (see the solid arrow extending to the southeast of E_2). To select our third approximation, we take E_3 at the intersection of the vector sums from E_1 and E_2. This will not normally represent the exact optimum location because the vector sums will change directions somewhat as we move from E_1 or E_2 toward E_3, but it should be a fairly close approximation and, thus, permit us to converge rapidly on the desired location. Construction of the vector diagram at E_3 confirms that this is not an equilibrium position but also that the disequilibrium, as represented by the vector sum, is quite small. Further trials, although not carried out here, will permit us to locate the optimum site with any desired degree of precision.

Mechanical Analogs.   The use of line vectors to analyze this and the previous three-point example, where transfer costs are linear functions of distance, may well remind the reader of the mechanical device used to illustrate the equilibrium of forces in elementary physics classes. Suppose that we mount a map of our region on the top of a table and that at each material or market site we bore a hole through the table. If we suspended weights on strings passed through each hole and tie all strings to a ring at the table surface, the system would come into equilibrium (disregarding friction) with the location of the ring indicating the cost-minimizing plant location. The weights used, of course, must be proportional to the locational forces—to the product or material weights if transfer cost functions are linear through the origin and equal for all materials or to these weights multiplied by the appropriate transfer costs per ton-mile if they are linear but unequal. Notice that this crude mechanical analog computer will work for any number of localized market and material sites. This is a fact that might make its construction a practical consideration as an alternative to the tedious work involved in the geometry of multiple vectors for a number of successive approximations! Notice that physiographic barriers can be introduced easily in these models.

Isodapanes with Multiple Inputs.   With curvilinear transfer cost functions the vector approach follows the procedures just outlined but with the serious complication that the magnitude of each vector must be recalculated for every new location. Distances to the material sources and market must be determined for each location and used to determine the appropriate marginal transfer costs (the slopes of the cost function). Given these marginal rates per ton-mile, the appropriate locational forces are calculated by multiplying by the corresponding material or product weights. Vector diagrams are then constructed, the vector sum determined, and a new location selected as suggested by the direction and magnitude of this vector sum. Needless to say, the work involved is greater and the rapidity of convergence on the optimum solution slower than with linear cost functions.

Perhaps, for this reason the solution to these problems with either linear or curvilinear cost functions is often reached through the use of isodapanes. It will be recalled that they are contours that connect points of equal total transfer costs. Figure 18.7 suggests the method of construction of isodapanes for our "three-point" example. Again, we represent the location triangle ABC. For any of the three locations, constant transfer costs for the material in question will be represented by a set of concentric circles, spaced to reflect the material weight and the cost function. We illustrate the linear cost case, but the procedure is identical

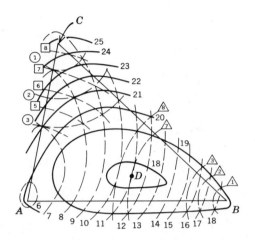

FIGURE 18.7   The construction of constant transfer cost isodapanes for the three-point problem with linear transfer cost functions. [*Note.* Circled values identify isocost contours around point C, values in squares the isocost contours around A, and triangles the contours around market B. The heavy contours are isodapanes (compare with Table 18.1).]

for curvilinear functions. A few of these individual transfer cost circles for points A and C are shown near the top of the diagram. From them, isodapanes of constant A plus C transfer costs have been constructed (see the broken lines in the diagram). Now we draw concentric circles representing product transfer costs centered on B and add them to the A–C isodapanes to obtain the A–B–C isodapanes shown by the heavy solid lines; they are labeled to show costs in dollars per ton under distance and rate assumptions as specified in Table 18.1, excluding all terminal charges.

Examination of this diagram indicates that total transport costs would be relatively high (approaching \$25) for plant locations near point C, that they would be reduced to \$19 to \$20 near point A, and that they would be less than \$19 near the market at B. In fact, costs would be less than \$18 somewhere west of B, and we observe that this \$18 contour surrounds the optimum location at point D as determined previously. Table 18.1 shows that at D the combined cost is \$17.85. It should be clear that, with sufficient patience and drafting skill, it would be possible to add other contours to define more exactly the optimum position— \$17.95, \$17.90, \$17.88, \$17.87, and so on. But it is also clear that the process is not only tedious but that it is unusually sensitive to very minor drafting errors in the region immediately adjacent to the optimum position. Actually, in this and in many other cases, the cost surface has a relatively shallow "depression," and there is a substantial area where it is nearly flat. The entire area within the $18 isodapane, for example, has combined transfer costs within one percent of the true minimum at point D.

In summary, mechanical problems make it difficult to determine optimum location with the precision suggested by the theoretical concepts — a practical defect perhaps offset by the fact that resulting errors in estimated costs will be very minor. We emphasize again that, when functions are curvilinear or involve fixed terminal charges, it is always necessary to compare the combined costs for any location, for instance at point D, with the costs for locations at market or material sites. In fact, gains or losses in weight coupled with terminal charges and nonlinear transfer cost-distance functions will usually result in optimum locations at some corner position on the location polygon.

An early study of the competitive position of eastern poultry farmers illustrates the potential uses of isodapanes as an analytical device. Prices for first-grade eggs of comparable quality in Chicago, New York, and Boston during the years from 1935 to 1939 indicated a pronounced tendency to move together and to be interrelated through transport costs; correlation coefficients ranged from 0.90 to 0.98. At the same time, prices for standard poultry feeds in these markets also closely approximated perfect market location patterns: correlations for corn, middlings, bran, and soybean meal gave coefficients ranging from 0.90 to 0.99. These findings were combined to indicate the effects of feed and egg transportation costs in a weight-losing process that involved 390 pounds of feed for every 100 pounds (gross) of eggs. The resulting isodapanes are

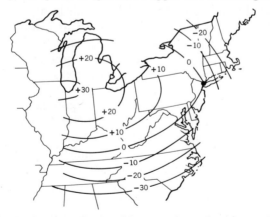

FIGURE 18.8   The isodapanes showing differences in aggregate transfer costs for 390 pounds of feed and 54 dozen eggs, (100 pounds gross). [*Source.* S. K. Seaver, "Location Factors Affecting the Competitive Position of Connecticut Egg Producers" (unpublished thesis, University of Connecticut, 1942), p. 60.]

shown in Figure 18.8. Feed transport costs and prices increase with distance from Chicago, and egg prices decrease with distance from New York City. The combined effect is a transport disadvantage of about 50 cents (roughly 1 cent per dozen) for southern New England as compared with the Midwest. Of course, this is only a partial analysis of locational advantages or disadvantages, but it well illustrates the general approach.

18.7 ALTERNATIVE RAW MATERIAL SOURCES AND NONTRANSFER COSTS

If alternative sources of a particular raw material are available, the selection of the source to be used simply involves a comparison of total transfer costs for each alternative source. In the case discussed previously (Figure 18.3), we discovered that transfer cost minimization would involve locating production at point D, transporting two raw materials from points B and C and the finished product to market at B. Now let us suppose that alternative sources for raw material C were available. Clearly, the alternative source would be used in preference to C if it were located closer to D and, thus, involved lower transfer cost, but the source at point C would be more favorable if new localized deposits were located farther from D.

With alternative sources, however, it will usually be true that the cost of the raw material at the site will differ from source to source. We may be considering coal mines, and the minehead cost of a ton of coal will vary from mine to mine as a result of factors such as size and depth of coal seams. If this is true, then a new mine located farther from the market than point C may still be the most economical source, since lower costs at the mine may more than offset the higher transfer costs. The optimum selection of material sources and of production location, there-fore, depends on differences in production costs as well as on transfer costs.

As a market increases in size, its coal requirements may exceed the supply available from the most economical mine. It will then be forced to obtain part of its supply from the next most economical source, consider-ing both production and transfer cost. But under competitive conditions, coal will command a single price at the market, and this price apparently will be just high enough to pay production costs and transfer costs from the "marginal" mine. Market price less transfer cost will now yield a return higher than production cost at the most economical mine, and this excess will represent abnormal profits. These profits are attributable either to advantageous location or to advantageous production conditions and, in any event, give rise to economic rent. In brief, operators become aware of the abnormal profits available from mine 1 and through competitive bidding the rent (or royalty) at this mine is bid up until it approximates the unusual profit possibilities. These rents and royalties, in turn, would be capitalized into a superior price for the mine if it were to be sold. We shall return to this subject later and shall discuss in greater detail the relation between location and rents.

18.8 LABOR AS A MOBILE RESOURCE

Labor is an important element in most productive processes, and wages vary from place to place and from region to region. This will be true even for labor of comparable quality, and these wage differences will have an important influence on production costs and, thus, on economical location. These locational differences in wages, however, will usually fail to exhibit any simple and regular space pattern. It is true that transfer costs have an influence on wages, but this is indirect through the impact on general industrial location and the transportation of materials entering into living costs. Certainly, climatic differences modify the cost of living and, hence, affect wages. In any short-run analysis, however, labor may be considered as a localized resource available at the going wage at any particular location. In long-run situations, like the ones that will be discussed later, industries that are drawn to particular locations because of plentiful and cheap labor will find wages increasing. Two factors are involved in this tendency for wages to equalize among regions: (1) the migration of industry in response to low wages increases the local demands for labor, and (2) the local supply of labor is decreased in low wage areas through slow but persistent human migration.

A brief mention must be made of the effect of low wages in localizing certain types of secondary or "parasitic" industry. In the early days of the textile industry in New England, firms depended mainly on workers from farm families — on the proverbial farmer's daughter. Even today there are many situations where employment opportunities for men attract families to particular locations and, as a result, a pool of potential workers — wives and children — builds up. These family workers are not qualified for employment in the primary industry, so their labor is available for "light" industry at low wages. The wage situation may be further complicated by the fact that family workers are willing to be employed at lower wages, since by so doing they add to the total family income. Secondary industries move to the location of these primary industries, therefore, to exploit the available and cheap labor supply. Of course, one aspect of this is the combination of farming and industry where part-time farmers, and some family members are occupied only partially in agriculture and are available for supplementary employment in industrial plants. The movement of the cotton textile industry from New England to the cotton South following the Civil War was dictated in part by transfer costs on raw cotton and finished products and, also, by the availability of lower cost labor. The continuing industrialization of the South Atlantic States is based on similar considerations and may be expected to continue as long as substantial wage differentials persist.

18.9 SOME UNRESOLVED ISSUES

Even with comparable resource costs and wages, differences in costs may occur that are important localizing forces. Let us suppose that we had complicated our previous analysis by including two market locations. Suppose also that production is subject to important economies of scale: that production costs per unit decrease rapidly with increases in volume. These economies may well outweigh transfer cost considerations so that the optimum organization might involve a single large plant serving both markets instead of two smaller plants.

Related in effect to economies of scale are external or agglomerating economies. Economies of scale refer to efficiencies internal to individual plants or firms. External economies, on the other hand, are advantages that accrue to all producers and industries at a particular location and that have their origins in the aggregate size of the city or producing district. As many firms locate at one site, it becomes economical to develop specialized service industries. Construction and repair services are readily available and at lower cost. Transportation services improve to accomodate the growing metropolis, often with favorable rates. A large, dependable, and diversified labor force becomes available. These external economies may be offset after a point by diseconomies, for example, the higher costs involved in obtaining food supplies and the generally higher costs of living and of within-city transportation. But, until they are offset, they represent economic forces that lead to agglomeration or to the concentration of economic activities at particular points. These agglomerizing forces, coupled with favorable transfer sites on waterways at good harbors, or at the junction of major elements in the transportation network, explain in large measure the development of super cities, of secondary cities, and of local centers in the complex of economic geography.

SELECTED READINGS

Spatial Equilibrium with Mobile Resources

Friedrich, Carl Joachim, "Editor's Introduction: The Theory of Location in Relation to the Theory of Land Rent," *Alfred Weber's Theory of the Location of Industries*. University of Chicago Press, Chicago (1929), pp. xiii–xxxiii.

Hoover, Edgar M., Jr., *Location Theory and the Shoe and Leather Industries, op. cit.*, pp. 34–59, 75–88.

Isard, Walter, *Location ..., op. cit.*, pp. 172–182, 254–281.

Krzyzanowski, Witold. "Review of the Literature of the Location of Industries," *Journal of Political Economy*, Vol. 35, No. 2 (April 1927). pp. 278–291.

Lösch, August, *op. cit.*, Chapter 4. "Industrial Location Theory," pp. 16–35.

Thoman, Richard S., Edgar C. Conkling, and Maurice H. Yeates, *The Geography of Economic Activity*, McGraw-Hill Book Co., New York, second edition (1968), Chapters 9–12, pp. 147–215.

Weber, Alfred, *Theory of the Location of Industries, op. cit.*, pp. 48–94, 102–112.

chapter 19

GENERAL EQUILIBRIUM IN AN ISOLATED REGION

We developed the general theory of regional specialization and inter-regional trade in Part IV, gradually complicating our theoretical models so as to explain the simultaneous and interdependent determination of product prices, factor prices, production and consumption patterns, and interregional trade flows. Although attention was centered on the two-region case, our models represented a considerable extension of the treatment of single-product markets in space, time, and form. Emphasis thus far in Part V has been on agriculture and on the land resource, but it should be apparent that, again, this analysis is reaching toward a general theory of economic interdependence. In this chapter these interrelationships will be examined for an isolated region. Multiple region models will be discussed in Chapter 20.

19.1 A SIMPLE GENERAL EQUILIBRIUM SYSTEM

Although we do not pretend to develop here a complete theory of general equilibrium, it may be useful to begin by presenting a set of simultaneous equations of the Walras-Cassel type often used to describe such an equilibrium in an isolated region. The specific equations presented in this

374

section are drawn directly from Ohlin, although we have taken the liberty of using a slightly different nomenclature.[1] In the following chapter, which deals with two or more regions, we introduce spatial identifications as subscripts. We use superscripts only in the present chapter.

In our region there are H inhabitants (households) having $R^1, R^2, \ldots,$ R^F fixed total amounts of the F basic resources (factors) and with given ownership patterns of these resources by individuals. We let k represent the commodities that are produced and consumed with $k = 1, 2, \ldots, K$.

Technical Coefficients.   Production functions are taken as given. The technical coefficients, a^{kf}, relate factor inputs to product outputs: a^{11}, $a^{12}, \ldots, a^{1F}$ are the inputs of each of the F factors used to produce one unit of the first product; $a^{k1}, a^{k2}, \ldots, a^{kF}$ the inputs of each factor used to produce one unit of the kth product, and so on. The technical coefficients of the K commodities are not fixed, however, but depend on the relative prices v^f of the F factors. These functional relationships are indicated by the following set of equations:

$$a^{11} = f^{11}(v^1 v^2 \ldots v^F)$$

$$\cdot$$
$$\cdot \qquad\qquad\qquad\qquad\qquad (1)$$
$$\cdot$$

$$a^{KF} = f^{KF}(v^1 v^2 \ldots v^F)$$

where the v's represent the several factor prices.

Product Prices.   Under perfect market conditions, product prices P^k will equal costs of production, and cost of production for any product will be the sum of unit factor inputs a^{fk} multiplied by factor prices v^f. In equations

$$P^1 = a^{11}v^1 + a^{12}v^2 + \cdots + a^{1F}v^F$$

$$\cdot$$
$$\cdot \qquad\qquad\qquad\qquad\qquad (2)$$
$$\cdot$$

$$P^K = a^{K1}v^1 + a^{K2}v^2 + \cdots + a^{KF}v^F.$$

Market Demands.   The demands for the K commodities are determined by basic tastes and preferences and can be expressed as functions

[1]Bertil Ohlin, "Simple Mathematical Illustration of Pricing in Trading Regions," *Interregional and International Trade*, Appendix I (rev. ed.; Cambridge: Harvard University Press, 1967), pp. 297-300.

of commodity prices and of the distribution of incomes among the households:

$$D^1 = f^1(P^1 \ldots P^K, Y^1 \ldots Y^H)$$

$$\begin{matrix} \cdot \\ \cdot \\ \cdot \end{matrix}$$

$$(3)$$

$$D^K = f^K(P^1 \ldots P^K, Y^1 \ldots Y^H).$$

Individual Incomes.   In Equation 3 the Y's represent household incomes. These incomes are generated, however, from factor prices and the given resource ownership patterns. Thus, if O^{hf} represents the amount of factor f owned by individual h, we can specify these incomes as

$$Y^1 = O^{11}v^1 + O^{12}v^2 + \cdots + O^{1F}v^F$$

$$\begin{matrix} \cdot \\ \cdot \\ \cdot \end{matrix}$$

$$(4)$$

$$Y^H = O^{H1}v^1 + O^{H2}v^2 + \cdots + O^{HF}v^F.$$

Resource Use.   The aggregate requirements for every factor can be specified in terms of the quantities X^k of the products produced and the technical coefficients a^{fk}. In equilibrium, the total use of factors must exactly equal the amounts R^f of the factors available; if use is less than the available quantity, the factor becomes a free good and, thus, drops out of the system. In equation form, we have

$$R^1 = a^{11}X^1 + a^{21}X^2 + \cdots + a^{K1}X^K$$

$$\begin{matrix} \cdot \\ \cdot \\ \cdot \end{matrix}$$

$$(5)$$

$$R^F = a^{1F}X^1 + a^{2F}X^2 + \cdots + a^{KF}X^K.$$

Demand and Supply.   Finally, we have the equilibrium condition that the quantities of products produced must equal the quantities consumed, or

$$X^1 = D^1$$

$$\begin{matrix} \cdot \\ \cdot \\ \cdot \end{matrix}$$

$$(6)$$

$$X^K = D^K.$$

Equilibrium.   We now have completed the circle of interdependent relationships. Notice that the fifth set of equations can be redefined as follows: in terms of D from Equations 6; in terms of P and Y from Equations 3; and finally in terms of v from Equations 1, 2, and 4. In short, this system can be reduced to a set of F equations involving only the F unknown factor prices.

In this system, one equation is not independent of the others. If we have specified the outputs of $K-1$ products, the output of the final product is already determined by the residual resources available for its production. As a consequence, the solution of the set of equations will not yield a set of absolute prices but a set of relative prices. We can designate one commodity (for instance, gold) as the base for the monetary system and with a price equal to one, in which case all other prices will be expressed in terms of this monetary unit. By the usual test of counting equations and unknowns, then, the system is presumed to be determinate. Once the set of factor prices is obtained, it is a relatively simple matter to work back through the system to determine the related sets of product prices, incomes, resource allocations, and outputs of the several commodities.

These equations have not been presented for their operational value. As noted earlier, the particular relationships involved are extremely complicated and, with the addition of space considerations, could be reduced to algebraic form only with great difficulty. But they do serve to illustrate the concept of general interdependence. From the above equations, it can be seen that any technical change for a particular commodity will have repercussions throughout the entire system, as would any change in income distribution, in demand, or in the basic endowment of natural resources. Furthermore, we have observed how a change that affects any commodity in any market will set in motion a wave of influences that eventually affects all commodities in all markets. Since it is beyond our abilities to know everything and to enter all relationships in proper form, practical research must proceed on the basis of simplification, with partial or particular equilibrium models. The validity of our research results, it follows, will depend on our wisdom (and good fortune) in making simplifications and aggregations that do not seriously distort our particular findings.

19.2   A MODIFIED GENERAL EQUILIBRIUM SYSTEM

One possible simplification of the single region system is the following.[2] First, we take the technical coefficients a^{fk} as given instead of variable, as in equation set(1). Second, we allow inequalities between unit costs and

[2]We follow Dorfman, Samuelson, and Solow in much of this chapter. See Robert Dorfman, Paul A. Samuelson, and Robert M. Solow, *Linear Programming and Economic Analysis* ("The Rand Series." New York: McGraw-Hill Book Company, Inc., 1958), Chapter 13, pp. 346–389.

commodity prices in addition to the equalities required in equation set(2). Should the factor cost of any commodity exceed its price, the output of that commodity would be zero:

$$a^{11}v^1 + a^{21}v^2 + \cdots + a^{Fl}v^F \geqslant P^1$$

$$. \tag{7}$$

$$a^{1K}v^1 + a^{2K}v^2 + \cdots + a^{FK}v^F \geqslant P^K.$$

Third, we substitute factor prices for individual incomes in the market demand equations [set (3)] as a method for allowing changes in demand induced by shifts in the level and distribution of income. We now write

$$X^1 = f^1(P^1, \ldots, P^K, v^1, \ldots, v^F)$$

$$. \tag{8}$$

$$X^K = f^K(P^1, \ldots, P^K, v^1, \ldots, v^F).$$

and delete the income equations shown above as set (4).

Next, we allow the market to determine which, if any, of the available resources will not be fully utilized. This is expressed algebraically by rewriting equation set (5), by using inequalities:

$$a^{11}X^1 + a^{12}X^2 + \cdots + a^{1K}X^K \leqslant R^1$$

$$. \tag{9}$$

$$a^{F1}X^1 + a^{F2}X^2 + \cdots + a^{FK}X^K \leqslant R^F.$$

Finally, we drop the demand-supply relations (6) and add a new resource supply relation that expresses resource availability as a function of product and factor prices:

$$R^1 = G^1(P^1, \ldots, P^K, v^1, \ldots, v^F)$$

$$. \tag{10}$$

$$R^F = G^F(P^1, \ldots, P^K, v^1, \ldots, v^F).$$

In the four sets of equations, (7) through (10), we have $2F$ plus $2K$ equations, although sets (8) and (10) contain only $F + K - 1$ independent equations. Unknowns consist of the v's (F), P's (K), X's (K), and R's (F). As noted in the previous section, one product price may be selected as numeraire, leaving $2F + 2K - 1$ unknowns, which is equal to the number of independent equations. A rigorous statement of conditions necessary to assure existence and uniqueness is given by Dorfman et al.[3]

19.3 LINEAR PROGRAMMING FORMULATION WITH FIXED RESOURCE SUPPLIES[4]

It is instructive to look at the linear programming specification of the above model, as outlined by Dorfman et al., before adding the complications of spatial aspects and alternative production processes.[5] To simplify the presentation, we assume that factor supplies are given: that is, supplies described in Equation 10 are perfectly inelastic at given levels. For the general equilibrium system under competitive conditions with all firms acting as price-takers (that is, quantity adjusters), we wish to maximize the value of output with given product prices. This value must be equivalent to factor returns which will be at their minimum, a condition that is assured in the direct and dual problems of linear programming. More formally, we may state the problem as follows:

Maximize
$$\sum_{k=1}^{K} p^k x^k.$$

Subject to
$$A x^k \leq r^f$$
$$x^k \geq 0.$$

In order that x^k attain a maximum ($\bar{x}^k$), it must also satisfy the condition that the direct problem maximum must equal the value of the dual, or

$$p^k \bar{x}^k = v^f r^f$$

for some vector v of imputed factor prices, which must satisfy

$$v^f \geq 0$$
$$v A \geq p^k.$$

By writing out the problem in full, we have the following linear programming problems.

Direct. (Maximize the value of output)

Maximize:
$$\sum_{k=1}^{K} p^k x^k$$

[3]*Ibid*, pp. 366–375.

[4]The remainder of this chapter is drawn from an unpublished report by Gordon A. King, "Analysis of Location of Agricultural Production and Processing" (University of California, Davis, 1965).

[5]Dorfman et al., *op. cit.*, p. 370.

Subject to   (a) $x^k \geq 0$

(b) $a^{11}x^1 + a^{12}x^2 \ldots a^{1K}x^K \leq r^1$

$a^{21}x^1 + a^{22}x^2 \ldots a^{2K}x^K \leq r^2$ (11)

. . . .

$a^{F1}x^1 + a^{F2}x^2 \ldots a^{FK}x^K \leq r^F.$

Dual. (Minimize total factor returns)

Minimize: $\sum_{f=1}^{F} r^f v^f$

Subject to   (a) $v^f \geq 0$

(b) $a^{11}v^1 + a^{21}v^2 \ldots a^{F1}v^F \geq P^1$

$a^{12}v^1 + a^{22}v^2 \ldots a^{F2}v^F \geq P^2$ (12)

. . . .

$a^{1K}v^1 + a^{2K}v^2 \ldots a^{FK}v^F \geq P^K.$

The problem is solved by assuming a set of product prices p^k and by obtaining the set of other unknowns (x^k, v^f). The remaining step is to check this set of prices and quantities with the demand equations (8) for consistency. If consistent, the solution is complete. If not, we must revise prices and rerun the linear programming problem. This method is familiar, as we have used it earlier in dealing with the quantification of spatial equilibrium models with demand functions specified.

19.4 LINEAR PROGRAMMING FORMULATION WITH ALTERNATIVE PRODUCTION PROCESSES

This model of production was generalized by Koopmans (1951) to include alternative production processes as well as various intermediate commodities that are not desired by consumers as such but that are used in producing final commodities. The introduction of alternative production processes requires the distinction between outputs (x^k) and process levels, which we shall refer to as x^{ks}, where superscript k refers to the commodity and s to the process or system used in its production. That is, in association with each commodity, we now allow alternative techniques that require different amounts of the inputs. Our unit level input-output coefficients also now require an added superscript to identify the process. That is, a^{fks} represents the amount of input f used to produce one unit of commodity k by process s. The symbol x^k still represents output of commodity k and will be a measure of production by process x^{k1}, x^{k2}, or whatever process is selected in the linear programming solution. The (*b*) restraint in the direct linear programming problem thus is modified as

follows:
$$a^{111}x^{11} + a^{112}x^{12} + a^{121}x^{21} + a^{122}x^{22} \ldots a^{1KS}x^{KS} \leqslant r^1$$
$$a^{211}x^{11} + a^{212}x^{12} + a^{221}x^{21} + a^{222}x^{22} \ldots \qquad\qquad \leqslant r^2$$

$$\cdots\cdots\cdots\cdots\cdots\cdots\cdots\cdots\cdots\cdots\cdots\cdots\cdots\cdots\cdots$$

$$a^{F11}x^{11} + a^{F12}x^{12} + a^{F21}x^{21} + a^{F22}x^{22} \ldots a^{FKS}x^{KS} \leqslant r^F.$$

(13)

The program thus selects the activity that will maximize the value of output and will minimize total factor returns. Modification is required in the dual restraint (*b*) in 19.3, similar to that shown above for the direct problem.

19.5 INTRODUCTION OF INTERMEDIATE COMMODITIES

Let us consider a simple economy with two final commodities. There are two processes available for the production of each that require two resources (for instance, land and labor) plus an input of a previously produced commodity, that is, an intermediate commodity. An example might be broiler production that requires land, labor, and an intermediate commodity, feed grains. The production of the intermediate commodity, feed grains, requires only land and labor resources for its production in this simple case.

In Figure 19.1, we illustrate the production conditions for an even more elementary situation in which the final commodity requires only one resource and one intermediate commodity. The inputs required to produce one unit of output *x* by process 1 are given by point (a^{11}, y^{11}); and similarly for process 2 $(\bar{a}^{11}, \bar{y}^{11})$. For the production of the intermediate commodity, resource input per unit output by process 1 is (b^{11}, b^{22}) and by process 2 is $(\bar{b}^{11}, \bar{b}^{22})$.

We can write out the set of equations required to obtain an equilibrium in prices and levels of processes for final and intermediate commodities and for resource flows. To save space, the alternative processes will not be written out but can be considered as an added term for each commodity as, for example, in the equation system shown in the previous section.

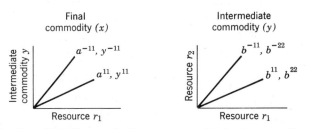

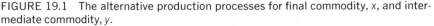

FIGURE 19.1   The alternative production processes for final commodity, *x*, and intermediate commodity, *y*.

There are 12 equations in this system: they relate to the demand for resources (2); the demand for intermediate commodities (2); the market demand for final commodities (2); the supply of resources (2); the supply of intermediate commodities (2); and a unit cost condition for each commodity (2).

Demand for Resources

$$a^{11}x^1 + a^{12}x^2 + b^{11}y^1 + b^{12}y^2 \leqslant r^1 \tag{14}$$
$$a^{21}x^1 + a^{22}x^2 + b^{21}y^1 + b^{22}y^2 \leqslant r^2$$

Demand for Intermediate Commodities

$$b^{11}x^1 + b^{12}x^2 \leqslant s^1 \tag{15}$$
$$b^{21}x^1 + b^{22}x^2 \leqslant s^2$$

Market Demand for Final Commodities

$$x^1 = F(P^1, P^2, p^1, p^2, v^1, v^2) \tag{16}$$
$$x^2 = F(P^1, P^2, p^1, p^2, v^1, v^2)$$

where quantity is a function of final commodities (P^k), intermediate commodities (p^m), and resource prices (v^f).

Supply of Resources

$$r^1 = G(P^1, P^2, p^1, p^2, v^1, v^2) \tag{17}$$
$$r^2 = G(P^1, P^2, p^1, p^2, v^1, v^2)$$

Supply of Intermediate Commodities

$$s^1 = S(P^1, P^2, p^1, p^2, v^1, v^2) \tag{18}$$
$$s^2 = S(P^1, P^2, p^1, p^2, v^1, v^2)$$

Unit Cost Relation

$$a^{11}v^1 + a^{21}v^2 + b^{11}p^1 + b^{21}p^2 \geqslant P^1 \tag{19}$$
$$a^{12}v^1 + a^{22}v^2 + b^{12}p^1 + b^{22}p^2 \geqslant P^2$$

where now the final commodity price is equal to the sum of the resource cost $(a^{11}v^1 + a^{21}v^2)$ plus the intermediate commodity cost $(b^{11}p^1 + b^{21}p^2)$. With alternative processes, the programming solution selects that process which provides maximum final commodity output consistent with minimum factor cost.

We now sketch out this problem in activity analysis format. If we had only one process, both for final and intermediate commodities, and one limiting resource of labor, the problem could be reduced to the Leontief input-output case, as indicated by Dorfman et al.[6] Alternatively, if

[6] *Ibid*, p. 355.

resources and intermediate commodity supplies are given, our problem reduces to the one considered in section 19.3. A demand function could be introduced into that problem, and the resulting quadratic programming problem could be solved. However, we shall proceed in a stepwise fashion by assuming prices for commodities but treating resource supplies $\bar{r}^{t}$ as fixed.

We wish to maximize the value of output, subject to certain restraints. These restraints are presented in Table 19.1 in an activity analysis framework, in the equations, and in matrix notation for comparative purposes. Notice that prices are inserted in the objective function for final commodity and for intermediate commodities. For final commodity, there is an additional demand function for each good. A price (P^k) and quantity (D^k) consistent with the demand function are inserted into the program. With an equilibrium result the "rents" (u_5, u_6) that are associated with the final commodity quantities will be equal to zero, indicating a consistent set of prices and quantities. A similar procedure is followed for the intermediate commodity supplies (S^s). The prices (p^s) which are inserted into the objective function must be consistent with a supply function for intermediate commodities. With an equilibrium solution, the rents associated with these intermediate commodities (u_3, u_4) must be consistent with the prices inserted in the objective function. The rents associated with the resources are indicated by u_1, u_2.

TABLE 19.1   Final and Intermediate Commodity Model for Simplified Two-Product Case

Rent	Equation Number	Production Activity								Restriction
		Final Commodity				Intermediate Commodity				
		x^1	$\bar{x}^1$	x^2	$\bar{x}^2$	y^1	$\bar{y}^1$	y^2	$\bar{y}^2$	
	0	P^1	$\bar{P}^1$	P^2	$\bar{P}^2$	$-p^1$	$-\bar{p}^1$	$-p^2$	$-\bar{p}^2$	
u_1	1	a^{11}	$\bar{a}^{11}$	a^{12}	$\bar{a}^{12}$	b^{11}	$\bar{b}^{11}$	b^{12}	$\bar{b}^{12}$	$\leq r^1$
u_2	2	a^{21}	$\bar{a}^{21}$	a^{22}	$\bar{a}^{22}$	b^{21}	$\bar{b}^{21}$	b^{22}	$\bar{b}^{22}$	$\leq r^2$
u_3	3	b^{11}	$\bar{b}^{11}$	b^{12}	$\bar{b}^{12}$	1	1			$\leq S^1$
u_4	4	b^{21}	$\bar{b}^{21}$	b^{22}	$\bar{b}^{22}$			1	1	$\leq S^2$
u_5	5	-1	-1							$\leq -D^1$
u_6	6			-1	-1					$\leq -D^2$

Note. The bar is used to identify second processes (for example, x^1 and $\bar{x}^1$). See discussion in text.

The symbols in Table 19.1, which treats the two-intermediate commodity and the two-final commodity case, each with two production
processes, may be interpreted as follows.

Maximize total value of final commodity

$$= P^1x^1 + P^2x^2 - p^1y^1 - p^2y^2$$

when $x^1, y^1 \geq 0$.

Subject to

Resource Demand and Supply Relation

(1) $a^{11}x^1 + \bar{a}^{11}\bar{x}^1 + a^{12}x^2 + \bar{a}^{12}\bar{x}^2 + b^{11}y^1 + \bar{b}^{11}\bar{y}^1 + b^{12}y^2 + \bar{b}^{12}\bar{y}^2 \leq r^1$

(2) $a^{21}x^1 + \bar{a}^{21}\bar{x}^1 + a^{22}x^2 + \bar{a}^{22}\bar{x}^2 + b^{21}y^1 + \bar{b}^{21}\bar{y}^1 + b^{22}y^2 + \bar{b}^{22}\bar{y}^2 \leq r^2$

Intermediate Commodity Demand and Supply

(3) $b^{11}x^1 + \bar{b}^{11}\bar{x}^1 + b^{12}x^2 + \bar{b}^{12}\bar{x}^2 + 1y^1 \quad + 1\bar{y}^1 \qquad\qquad\quad \leq S^1$

(4) $b^{21}x^1 + \bar{b}^{21}\bar{x}^1 + b^{22}x^2 + \bar{b}^{22}\bar{x}^2 \qquad\qquad\qquad + 1y^2 \quad + 1\bar{y}^2 \quad \leq S^2$

Final Commodity Demand and Supply

(5) $1 \cdot x^1 - 1 \cdot \bar{x}^1 \qquad\qquad\qquad\qquad\qquad\qquad\qquad\qquad \leq -D^1$

(6) $\qquad\qquad\qquad 1 \cdot x^2 - 1 \cdot \bar{x}^2 \qquad\qquad\qquad\qquad\qquad\quad \leq -D^2$

In matrix notation the problem may be written as follows.

Maximize $\qquad\qquad\qquad\qquad\qquad Px.$

Subject to: $\qquad\qquad\qquad\qquad\quad x \geq 0$

$\qquad\qquad\qquad\qquad\qquad\qquad Ax \leq R$

where the x vector is choice variables of outputs (x) and intermediate
commodities (y); P is a vector of given prices; A is a matrix of coefficients
for input per unit of output by various processes; and (R) is the vector of
restraints.

The dual of the above program is given in Table 19.2, where the objective is to minimize returns to resources. Notice that the final commodity
price for some activity will be equal to the cost of the intermediate commodity plus the imputed resource cost. It also specifies the intermediate
commodity price as equal to cost for production activities in the program.

The symbols in Table 19.2 may be interpreted as follows.

Minimize returns to resources

$$= u_1r^1 + u_2r^2 + S^1u_3 + S^2u_4 + D^1u_5 + D^2u_6$$

when $u_i \leq 0$.

Subject to

TABLE 19.2   Dual of Problem Given in Table 19.1

Equation Number	Rents						Restriction
	u_1	u_2	u_3	u_4	u_5	u_6	
1	a^{11}	a^{21}	b^{11}	b^{21}	-1		$\geqslant P^1$
2	$\bar{a}^{11}$	$\bar{a}^{21}$	$\bar{b}^{11}$	$\bar{b}^{21}$	-1		$\geqslant P^1$
3	a^{12}	a^{22}	b^{12}	b^{22}		-1	$\geqslant P^2$
4	$\bar{a}^{12}$	$\bar{a}^{22}$	$\bar{b}^{12}$	$\bar{b}^{22}$		-1	$\geqslant P^2$
5	b^{11}	b^{21}	1				$\geqslant p^1$
6	$\bar{b}^{11}$	$\bar{b}^{21}$	1				$\geqslant p^1$
7	b^{12}	b^{22}		1			$\geqslant p^2$
8	$\bar{b}^{12}$	$\bar{b}^{22}$		1			$\geqslant p^2$

Final Commodity Price Equal to Cost of Resources and Intermediate Commodities

$$(1)\ \ u_1 a^{11} + u_2 a^{21} + u_3 b^{11} + u_4 b^{21} - u_5 \cdot 1 - u_6 \cdot 0 \geqslant P^1$$
$$(2)\ \ u_1 \bar{a}^{11} + u_2 \bar{a}^{21} + u_3 \bar{b}^{11} + u_4 \bar{b}^{21} - u_5 \cdot 1 - u_6 \cdot 0 \geqslant P^1$$
$$(3)\ \ u_1 a^{12} + u_2 a^{22} + u_3 b^{12} + u_4 b^{22} - u_5 \cdot 0 - u_6 \cdot 1 \geqslant P^2$$
$$(4)\ \ u_1 \bar{a}^{12} + u_2 \bar{a}^{22} + u_3 \bar{b}^{12} + u_4 \bar{b}^{22} - u_5 \cdot 0 - u_6 \cdot 1 \geqslant P^2$$

Intermediate Commodity Price Equals Cost

$$(5)\ \ u_1 b^{11} + u_2 b^{21} + u_3 \cdot 1 \qquad\qquad\qquad \geqslant p^1$$
$$(6)\ \ u_1 \bar{b}^{11} + u_2 \bar{b}^{21} + u_3 \cdot 1 \qquad\qquad\qquad \geqslant p^1$$
$$(7)\ \ u_1 b^{12} + u_2 b^{22} + \qquad\qquad u_5 \cdot 1 \qquad \geqslant p^2$$
$$(8)\ \ u_1 \bar{b}^{12} + u_2 \bar{b}^{22} + \qquad\qquad\qquad u_6 \cdot 1 \geqslant p^2$$

In matrix notation the dual problem may be written as follows.

Minimize $\qquad\qquad\qquad uR$

Subject to $\qquad\qquad\qquad u = 0$
$$uA = P$$

where u is a vector of rents or imputed values to fixed factors; R is a vector of restraint coefficients; A is the matrix of input-output coefficients; and P is the vector of prices for product (P) and intermediate commodity (p).

Because of the difficulty of specifying a supply function for intermediate commodities, one simplification might be to specify the cost of the intermediate commodity ($u_3 b^{11} + u_4 b^{21}$). The result of this simplification is that in Equation 1 the unit resource cost is equal to the value added, or $P^1 - (u_3 b^{11} + u_4 b^{21})$.

19.6 CONSIDERATION OF JOINT PRODUCTION

Many agricultural production processes involve the output of more than one commodity. In livestock production, meat, hides, and by-products are commodity outputs. In crop production, rotation of crops is common to reduce disease problems and to maintain soil fertility. Alternative production processes can be defined that give differing output combinations but that maintain conditions of constant returns to scale for any given process. Agricultural economists frequently encounter such problems for individual firms under which the prices of the product are considered as given. In moving to the aggregate industry in this model, the demand function for each of the commodities must be specified. In the framework of Section 19.5, a process would now have associated with it two or more outputs, each of which would have a quantity demanded specified as a restraint. The price associated with the process would be the weighted average of the two output prices. In equilibrium, these quantities and individual prices would have to be consistent with the demand functions for the products.

SELECTED READINGS

General Equilibrium in an Isolated Region

Dorfman, Robert, Paul A. Samuelson, and Robert M. Solow, *op. cit.* Chapter 13, "Linear Programming and the Theory of General Equilibrium," pp. 346–389.

Lloyd, Cliff, *Microeconomic Analysis*, Richard D. Irwin Inc., Homewood (1967). Chapter 9, "The General Equilibrium of the Entire System," pp. 237–256.

Ohlin, Bertil, "Simple Mathematical Illustration of Pricing in Trading Regions," *Interregional and International Trade*, Harvard University Press, Cambridge, (revised edition 1967), Appendix I. pp. 297–300.

Schneider, Erich, *op. cit.*, "Total Equilibrium in a Closed Economy," pp. 324–363.

chapter 20

MULTIPLE-REGION PRODUCTION AND TRADE MODELS[1]

In this chapter the spatial dimension of resource availability, productive activity, and trade are added to the single-region analysis of Chapter 19. Although they fall short of full general equilibrium systems, the models that are presented are both logically consistent and of proven empirical usefulness.

The first two sections treat the case of a single fixed resource — first by using an output orientation, and second by a resource-use orientation. The emphasis is placed on information that concerns equilibrium prices provided by the dual linear programming solution, especially as it bears on site rents. Models with multiple resource restraints are introduced, followed by models that allow trade in intermediate products. A brief summary of an empirical application is presented and reference is made to other studies that may be of interest to readers who wish to carry out similar production and trade analyses.

---

[1] Much of the material in this chapter is drawn directly from an unpublished report by Gordon A. King, "Analysis of Location of Agricultural Production and Processing" (University of California, Davis, 1965).

20.1 AN OUTPUT-ORIENTED FORMULATION

The following simple model of regional production, consumption, and trade illustrates several important aspects of spatial equilibrium analysis. Assume that there are two markets for two commodities, each of which may be produced in two producing areas. The production technology consists of one activity for each commodity in each region, or four production activities. Inputs consist of one fixed resource—say, land—and a bundle of other inputs that will be expressed in value terms, or "cost of production excluding land rent." Each process has the properties of combining inputs in fixed proportions, of being divisible, and of exhibiting constant returns to scale. It is assumed that all firms in the two regions are quantity adjusters and that they behave according to the rules of pure competition.

The formulation of this problem parallels exactly that of the general equilibrium case discussed in Chapter 19 with the exceptions that (1) the transportation costs are introduced and (2) the cost of production, excluding land rent, replaces the supply equations. The objective function is stated in order to maximize the net value of output, which is the market value less transfer and production costs. The primal problem is illustrated in Table 20.1.

The relationships in Table 20.1 may be restated as follows.

TABLE 20.1 Maximization of Net Value of Output[a]

Rent	Equation Number	Production and Shipment Activity								Restriction R
		Commodity 1				Commodity 2				
		x_{21}^1	x_{31}^1	x_{22}^1	x_{32}^1	x_{21}^2	x_{31}^2	x_{22}^2	x_{32}^2	
	0	N_{21}^1	N_{31}^1	N_{22}^1	N_{32}^1	N_{21}^2	N_{31}^2	N_{22}^2	N_{32}^2	
u_1	1	a_2^1		a_2^1		a_2^2		a_2^2		$\leq r_2$
u_2	2		a_3^1		a_3^1		a_3^2		a_3^2	$\leq r_3$
u_3	3	-1	-1							$\leq -D_1^1$
u_4	4			-1	-1					$\leq -D_2^1$
u_5	5					-1	-1			$\leq -D_1^2$
u_6	6							-1	-1	$\leq -D_2^2$

[a]The net value of output is net returns per unit of output multiplied by output. Model situation consists of single fixed resource, two final commodities, two producing areas, two markets, and one production process for each product in each region.

Maximize net value of output (market value less transfer and production costs)

$$= \sum_i \sum_j \sum_k N^k_{ij} x^k_{ij} = \sum_i \sum_j \sum_k P^k_{ij} x^k_{ij} - \sum_i \sum_j \sum_k t^k_{ij} x^k_{ij} - \sum_i \sum_j \sum_k q^k_i x^k_{ij}$$

where $x^k_{ij} \geqslant 0$.

Subject to

Demand and Supply of Resource by Region

$$(1) \quad a_2{}^1 x^1_{21} + a_2{}^1 x^1_{22} + a_2{}^2 x^2_{21} + a_2{}^2 x^2_{22} \leqslant r_2$$
$$(2) \quad a_3{}^1 x^1_{31} + a_3{}^1 x^1_{32} + a_3{}^2 x^2_{31} + a_3{}^2 x^2_{32} \leqslant r_3.$$

These equations require that the availability of a resource in a region must equal or exceed production requirements for all commodities.

Demand and Supply of Final Commodity

$$(3) \quad -x^1_{21} - x^1_{31} \qquad\qquad\qquad \leqslant -D_1{}^1$$

$$\cdot$$
$$\cdot \quad \dots\dots\dots\dots\dots\dots\dots\dots$$
$$\cdot$$

$$(6) \quad -x^2_{22} - x^2_{32} \qquad\qquad\qquad \leqslant -D_2{}^2.$$

These equations require that the supply of a final commodity produced and shipped to market (1 or 2) in equilibrium must equal the quantity demanded at the specified market price.

The following notation has been used in Table 20.1.

x^k_{ij} = quantity of kth final commodity produced and shipped from i to j.
N^k_{ij} = net return per unit of output of kth final commodity produced in region i and shipped from i to j.
$P_j{}^k$ = price per unit for commodity k at market location j.
t^k_{ij} = transfer cost per unit of commodity k shipped from i to j.
$a_i{}^k$ = resource input required per unit of output of k in region i.
$q_i{}^k$ = cost of production (exclusive of fixed resource) for one unit of the kth commodity in the ith region.

Notice that in the primal problem the objective functions contains, in place of the price of each product, the *net return per unit of output* for the kth commodity produced in region i and shipped from i to j. However, market prices must be consistent with a demand function for the final product, and the associated quantity for each product in a given market is inserted as a restriction. This procedure has been shown by Takayama and Judge (1964) to be consistent with a quadratic programming formulation with the demand function specified in the objective function and has proven to be satisfactory for quantitative work with partial equilibrium models.

We find it useful to consider briefly the dual formulation of this problem, which deals directly with the prices or rents associated with the resource and market restrictions. The dual is sketched in Table 20.2.

TABLE 20.2   Minimization of Returns to Resources[a]

Equation Number	Rents						Restriction R
	u_1	u_2	u_3	u_4	u_5	u_6	
0	r_2	r_3	$-D_1{}^1$	$-D_2{}^1$	$D_1{}^2$	$D_2{}^2$	
1	$a_2{}^1$		-1				$\geq N^1_{21}$
2		$a_3{}^1$	-1				$\geq N^1_{31}$
3	$a_2{}^1$			-1			$\geq N^1_{22}$
4		$a_3{}^1$		-1			$\geq N^1_{32}$
5	$a_2{}^2$				-1		$\geq N^2_{21}$
6		$a_3{}^2$			-1		$\geq N^2_{31}$
7	$a_2{}^2$					-1	$\geq N^2_{22}$
8		$a_3{}^2$				-1	$\geq N^2_{32}$

[a]This is the dual problem to the one in Table 20.1.

We may write out the relationships shown in Table 20.2 as follows. Minimize returns to resources

$$= u_1r_1 + u_2r_2 + u_3D_1{}^1 + u_4D_2{}^1 + u_5D_1{}^2 + u_6D_2{}^2$$

where $u_i \geq 0$.

Subject to

$$(7) \quad u_1a_2{}^1 - u_3 \geq N^1_{21} = P_1{}^1 - t^1_{21} - q_2{}^1$$
$$(8) \quad u_2a_3{}^1 - u_3 \geq N^1_{31} = P_1{}^1 - t^1_{31} - q_3{}^1$$
$$(9) \quad u_1a_2{}^1 - u_4 \geq N^1_{22} = P_2{}^1 - t^1_{22} - q_2{}^1$$
$$(10) \quad u_2a_3{}^1 - u_4 \geq N^1_{32} = P_2{}^1 - t^1_{32} - q_3{}^1$$
$$(11) \quad u_1a_2{}^2 - u_5 \geq N^2_{21} = P_1{}^2 - t^2_{21} - q_2{}^2$$
$$(12) \quad u_2a_3{}^2 - u_5 \geq N^2_{31} = P_1{}^2 - t^2_{31} - q_3{}^2$$
$$(13) \quad u_1a_2{}^2 - u_6 \geq N^2_{22} = P_2{}^2 - t^2_{22} - q_2{}^2$$
$$(14) \quad u_2a_3{}^2 - u_6 \geq N^2_{32} = P_2{}^2 - t^2_{32} - q_3{}^2.$$

Equations 7 through 14 state that net returns at each producer location should be equal to unit rent for the corresponding resource. Net returns per unit of output at a producer location are equal to rent to the fixed resource for one activity in the program. The value u_1 is rent per unit fixed resource, which gives rent per unit of output when multiplied by the input-output coefficient. Each of the values u_3 through u_6 is an artificial rent that will equal zero when assumed market price is equal to equilibrium market price.

Equations that are associated with the dual problem, as given in Table 20.2, provide a clearer statement as to the relationship between net returns and rents, u_1 and u_2, that accrue to the fixed resource by region. There are four possible activities associated with land rent in each region, as shown in the first two columns of the dual (or the first two equations in the primal). Take region 1 as an example. Commodity 1 can be produced and then shipped either to market 1 or market 2. A similar procedure is followed for commodity 2. In the solution, the rent associated with the fixed resource, land, will be determined by the activity or activities selected in the program. In equilibrium, the rent associated with land in region 1 will be equal for any of the activities that are included in the solution: that is, for the u_1 in Equations 1, 3, 5, or 7 given in Table 20.2. As pointed out, the imputed values of u_3 through u_6 will be zero with the demand price-quantity equilibrium conditions. The solution that maximizes the net value of output also minimizes returns to the fixed resource, which is the well-known outcome of linear programming problems.

In matrix notation the direct and dual problems of Tables 20.1 and 20.2 may be written as follows.

Direct

Maximize $\qquad\qquad Px$

Subject to $\qquad\qquad x \geqslant 0$

$\qquad\qquad\qquad\quad Ax \leqslant R$

Dual

Minimize $\qquad\qquad uR$

Subject to $\qquad\qquad u \geqslant 0$

$\qquad\qquad\qquad\quad uA \geqslant P$

where P is a vector of prices at region of production; x is a vector of choice variables for production and shipment; R is a vector of restraints; A is a matrix of input-output coefficients; and u is a vector of imputed prices or rents to fixed factors.

20.2   A RESOURCE-ORIENTED FORMULATION

With the single resource restraint, an alternative formulation of the objective of maximization of net value of output may be of interest. This can be expressed as net return per unit fixed resource multiplied by the quantity of the fixed resource. This quantity is equivalent to the net returns per unit of output multiplied by total output when constrained by resource availability and quantity demanded. The formulation of the problem in this way is given in Table 20.3 and approximates the one suggested by Beckmann and Marschak (1955) as a representation of a discrete production von Thünen model. The researcher may encounter a variety of problems where it is appropriate to simplify to a single resource, single production process case.

TABLE 20.3   Resource-Oriented Approach to Maximization of Net Value of Output[a]

Rents	Eq. No.	Commodity 1				Commodity 2				Restriction
		r^1_{21}	r^1_{31}	r^1_{22}	r^1_{32}	r^2_{21}	r^2_{31}	r^2_{22}	r^2_{32}	
	0	n^1_{21}	n^1_{31}	n^1_{22}	n^1_{32}	n^2_{21}	n^2_{31}	n^2_{22}	n^2_{32}	
u_1	1	1				1				$\leq r_2$
u_2	2		1				1			$\leq r_3$
u_3	3	$-y_2^1$	$-y_3^1$							$\leq -D_1^1$
u_4	4			$-y_2^1$	$-y_3^1$					$\leq -D_2^1$
u_5	5					$-y_2^2$	$-y_3^2$			$\leq -D_1^2$
u_6	6							$-y_2^2$	$-y_3^2$	$\leq -D_2^2$

[a]Net returns per unit fixed resource multiplied by fixed resource.
Note. Assumptions are single fixed resource, two products, two producing areas, two markets, and one production process for each product in each region.

The relationships described in Table 20.3 can be summarized as follows.

We wish to maximize the net value of output (net return per unit fixed resource multiplied by a quantity of fixed resource) which is

$$\sum_i \sum_j \sum_k n^k_{ij}\, r^k_{ij} = \sum_i \sum_j \sum_k [(P^k_j - t^k_{ij} - q_j^{\,k}) y^k \cdot r^k_{ij}]$$

where $r^k_{ij} \geq 0$.

Subject to

Demand and Supply of Resource by Region

$$(1)\ \ 1 \cdot r^1_{21} + 1 \cdot r^2_{21} \leq r_2$$
$$(2)\ \ 1 \cdot r^1_{31} + 1 \cdot r^2_{31} \leq r_3$$

The availability of fixed resource must equal or exceed requirements for producing commodities 1 and 2 in region 2 (F_2) or in region 3 (F_3).

Demand and Supply of Final Commodity

$$(3) -y_2{}^1 r_{21}^1 - y_3{}^1 r_{31}^1 \leqslant -D_1{}^1$$

$$. . . . .$$

$$(6) -y_2{}^2 r_{22}^2 - y_3{}^2 r_{32}^2 \leqslant -D_2{}^2$$

The supply of final commodity produced and shipped to market (1 or (2) in equilibrium must equal the quantity demanded at the specified market price $P_j{}^k$.

The following notation has been used.

$r_{ij}^k =$ quantity of fixed resource used to produce the kth final commodity in region i and shipped to region j.

$n_{ij}^k =$ net return *per unit of fixed resource* used to produce the kth final commodity in region i and shipped from region i to j (equal to net return per unit output divided by input-output coefficient).

$y_i{}^k =$ output per unit of input for production of kth commodity in region (equal to reciprocal of the input-output coefficient $a_i{}^k$ in Table 20.1).

20.3 LOCATION RENTS

Our discussion thus far has considered land in a given region to be homogeneous, and the rents derived are strictly location rents. A move toward reality would be to introduce land of varying quality in the restraints. The imputed rents would then be in terms relevant to the particular quality of land in the given region. Actually, land quality varies even on a given field on one producing unit, and the gain in reality would be open to debate. The point to be reemphasized here is that a given rent structure — for instance, around a given market — depends on the market price, the transfer costs for the product, the quality differentials in land, and the nonland costs of production. It will be a smooth function only with homogeneous land, constant factor prices, and transfer costs that are continuous with distance.

The introduction of the variable, nonland costs of production, replaces several relations that would be included in a general equilibrium framework discussed in the previous chapter. What has been done is to lump all nonland costs into a single figure instead of specifying in a production relation the inputs of resources other than land and any intermediate commodities used in production and then, by assuming prices of these items are given and fixed, to obtain the value of nonland costs.

Let us designate the *nonland cost per acre* as (c^k), which is equal to yield per acre (y^k) multiplied by the nonland cost of production for one unit of the kth commodity (q^k). The supply function for this bundle of inputs is thus perfectly elastic at the determined cost, as shown in Figure 20.1. The supply function for land is perfectly inelastic at the given level (r). For this single commodity case, land rent is generated only if the available supply is employed; and the level of rent is a function of the demand for the product.

In the short run, the supply function for land is relatively inelastic. But in the long run, new areas may be brought into production (within limits) through irrigation projects, reclamation of alkaline soil, clearing, and so forth. Let us assume for the moment that in the area under consideration all land is under cultivation, so that an inelastic supply function for the region is relevant.

Suppose that we wish to determine how the present pattern differs from that of an efficient spatial production pattern. Another way of stating the problem is to ask: What is the level of land rent for a particular location as compared with that under the "optimum" pattern? We consider first the determination of the equilibrium land rent and then discuss some of the problems of such a comparison with "present" land rents.

Let production technology for each individual crop or crop combination be represented by three alternative technologies that consist of different combinations of land and nonland inputs per unit of output (Figure 20.2). Notice that yield per acre is the reciprocal of the coefficient (a^k), the land input per unit of output. Therefore, yield and nonland costs are positively related in a linear or nonlinear fashion. The exact form of this relationship is vital in determining the production process selected for each crop and region.

In this formulation, land costs are taken to be zero, and we obtain imputed rent to the single fixed resource, land. As was done previously, with given transfer costs and an assumed price in each market, we proceed to maximize net value of output subject to resource and quantity demanded restraints. The dual provides the rent per acre for a particular

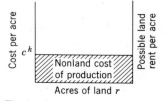

FIGURE 20.1   The land rent per acre under a simplified case.

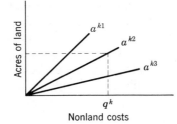

FIGURE 20.2   The production activities for one unit of output.

commodity k and process s, one of which will be a maximum for a particular piece of land. This can be expressed as

$$u^{ks} \quad \cdot \quad a^{ks} \quad \geqslant \quad N^k \quad = \quad P^k \quad - \quad t_{21}^k \quad - \quad q^{ks}$$

$$\begin{bmatrix} \text{Rent} \\ \text{per} \\ \text{acre} \end{bmatrix} \cdot \begin{bmatrix} \text{Land per} \\ \text{unit of} \\ \text{output} \end{bmatrix} \geqslant \begin{bmatrix} \text{Net return} \\ \text{per unit} \\ \text{of output} \end{bmatrix} = \begin{bmatrix} \text{Market} \\ \text{price} \\ \text{per unit} \\ \text{of output} \end{bmatrix} - \begin{bmatrix} \text{Transfer} \\ \text{cost per} \\ \text{unit of} \\ \text{output} \end{bmatrix} - \begin{bmatrix} \text{Nonland} \\ \text{cost per} \\ \text{unit of} \\ \text{output} \end{bmatrix}$$

With a given price at a producer's location (that is, $P_j^k - t_{ij}^k$), there will be only one relevant production process for each commodity that will provide maximum returns. However, if we do not know to which market commodities will be shipped, net producer prices will not be known. Similarly, the levels of the market prices will not be known. Thus, we cannot specify in advance which production activity should be included in the program. It would be expected that the areas located farther from the market (and thus having lower net price per unit of output because of higher transfer costs) would select production processes requiring relatively more land and less nonland costs, with the associated lower yield per acre. In any case, our equilibrium model will provide the imputed land rent per acre (u^{ks}) associated with the kth commodity and the production process or system s.

These rents would correspond to actual market rents under very restrictive conditions of a static framework in which the land rental market was strictly competitive. Actual land rents and associated production patterns could be compared with the ideal production patterns and imputed rents. If land were rented out to farmers rather than following the typical ownership pattern, producers would treat land rents as a cost per acre; and, in a perfectly competitive situation, these rentals would correspond to the imputed rents. Also, the production pattern, selection of activities, and shipment patterns would correspond to the equilibrium solution.

In looking at data from actual production patterns, the rental levels and the production activities reflect adjustments to actual market prices, transfer costs, mill locations for processed commodities, and shipment patterns. Selection of given levels of nonland costs for use in an equilibrium model raises theoretical questions, especially when these nonland costs might include intermediate commodities that are not produced in the region but are shipped in. Thus the level of these costs will vary depending on the distance shipped, for example, which may depend on the absolute level of production in a particular region. Thus, the assumed supply function that is completely elastic at a given cost level may be relevant for the analysis of certain types of agricultural production but would not be general enough for others.

20.4 MULTIPLE RESOURCE RESTRAINTS

This production model is easily modified to include multiple resource restraints as well as alternative production processes. The objective function is now formulated so as to maximize the net value of output defined as net returns per unit of output multiplied by output. Table 20.4 is modified to include two production processes and two resource restraints for each region. For simplicity, production processes for commodity 1 only are shown here. Notice that the input-output coefficients

TABLE 20.4 Alternative Production Processes With Multiple Resource Restraints

Equation Number	Production in Region 2				Production in Region 3				Restraints
	x_{21}^{11}	x_{21}^{12}	x_{22}^{11}	x_{22}^{12}	x_{31}^{11}	x_{31}^{12}	x_{32}^{11}	x_{32}^{12}	
0	N_{21}^{11}	N_{21}^{12}	N_{22}^{11}	N_{22}^{12}	N_{31}^{11}	N_{31}^{12}	N_{32}^{11}	N_{32}^{12}	
1	a_2^{111}	a_2^{112}	a_2^{111}	a_2^{112}					$\le r_2^1$
2	a_2^{211}	a_2^{212}	a_2^{211}	a_2^{212}					$\le r_2^2$
3					a_3^{111}	a_3^{112}	a_3^{111}	a_3^{112}	$\le r_3^1$
4					a_3^{211}	a_3^{212}	a_3^{211}	a_3^{212}	$\le r_3^2$
5	-1	-1			-1	-1			$\le -D_1^1$
6			-1	-1			-1	-1	$\le -D_1^2$

Column group header: Production and Shipment Activities for Single Commodity in Two Regions

a_i^{fks} have superscripts indicating the amount of resource f required per unit of output of the kth commodity produced by process s. The subscript refers to region of production.

20.5 TRADE IN INTERMEDIATE COMMODITIES

Following Beckmann and Marshak (1955), commodities now are divided in three classes: (1) resources or primary commodities, (2) intermediate commodities, which are produced commodities emerging from a production process as an output and then entering some other process as an input, and (3) commodities that are produced or final commodities desirable in themselves. Resource flows per unit of time include items such as land, labor, and a catchall "capital." Certain resources are fixed in both the long and short runs, such as land, but labor is mobile to some extent in the long run, and migratory farm labor by definition is mobile among regions in the short run. Capital mobility is an interesting topic for research in itself, and we bypass this admittedly difficult area, only suggesting its importance for "further work" in models that incorporate technological change and in growth models.

Intermediate commodities and final commodities can be shipped among regions. Notice that the transportation industry "produces" an intermediate commodity of space transfer, and Lefeber (1958) incorporates the transportation production process directly into the spatial equilibrium framework. The scope of intermediate commodity production is very wide. For example, in the Leontief *closed* input–output model, all commodities are considered as intermediate, with final commodities considered as inputs for the production of personal services. The *open* input–output model specifies "final commodity" demand as a separate sector determined outside the system.

In agricultural economics research, there has been considerable specialization of analysis that centers on the production processes for intermediate commodities at the farm level or production processes at the processing level—to cite two areas that have received much attention in the past. Admittedly, it is often useful to make concentrated efforts on one phase and live with "assumed" prices or costs in other sectors. Perhaps the ability to analyze large quantities of data with current computer techniques will encourage more comprehensive approaches to problems that require recognition of the interrelationships among the various sectors of the agricultural complex.

In fact, intermediate commodities can be further divided into various subgroups. Takayama and Judge (1964) refer to *primary* intermediate commodities as the ones "emerging from a farm-level production process as an output and entering some other (production) process as an input—for example, feed grains or feeder cattle." *Secondary* intermediate commodities are defined as the ones that are "produced commodities emerging from a farm-level production process as output and entering the processing activities as an input—for example, commodities such as cattle or hogs which are ready for consumption after they are processed." Rather than specify various levels of intermediate commodities, it seems more appropriate to treat them as a group, except when we may wish to designate a processing production process that requires certain intermediate commodities as well as resources as inputs. Actually, it is hard to imagine any commercial agricultural production that does not require purchased intermediate commodities and, hence, there is no need to press the point further. What we really want to consider here is the implications of a model in which *intermediate commodities may be produced and shipped between regions* and, therefore, it must be considered explicitly in the location of the production process in the next stage toward production of the final commodity.

The shipment of intermediate commodities is particularly important in the feed-livestock economy. This implies that the equilibrium pattern of grain prices cannot be determined without the consideration of the location of livestock production and, similarly, for livestock production. The processing locations for grain and for livestock also must be considered, but it will be deferred to a subsequent section. We thus specify the spatial equilibrium counterpart to the general equilibrium discussion in Chapter 19. For practical reasons, the discussion will center on a model with a single market, two producing areas, each with a single resource restraint for the production of a single intermediate commodity, and two products. This can easily be generalized but at some loss of clarity.

This problem is stated below as a set of equations and in a programming format that parallels previous developments in Table 20.5 and, hence, needs no particular comment. However, it should be noted that the objective function requires selection of not only product prices (P) but also intermediate commodity prices (p). If we added resource supply as a function of price, the situation would become even more difficult. With a single production process, a single market, and only two commodities, selection of prices (P, p) that would be feasible does not appear difficult, utilizing the known interrelationships of unit cost and prices inherent in the dual. But, as the problem grows in size and complexity, the choices would be formidable, based on experience with a one commodity-model that ignored intermediate commodity prices as such.

TABLE 20.5 Spatial Equilibrium Model with Trade in Intermediate Commodities

	Activities for Production and Shipment							
	Final Commodities				Intermediate Commodities			
Equation Number	Region 2		Region 3		Region 2		Region 3		Restraints
	x_{21}^1	x_{21}^2	x_{31}^1	x_{31}^2	y_{22}	y_{23}	y_{33}	y_{32}	
0	P_{21}^1	P_{21}^2	P_{31}^1	P_{31}^2	p_{22}	p_{23}	p_{33}	p_{32}	
1	a^1	a^2			a^y	a^y			$\le r_2$
2			a^1	a^2			a^y	a^y	$\le r_3$
3	b^1	b^2			1	-1		1	$\le s_2$
4			b^1	b^2		1	1	-1	$\le s_3$
5	-1		-1						$\le -D^1$
6		-1		-1					$\le -D^2$

Note. This model includes two final commodities, one market, one intermediate commodity, one resource, and two producing regions.

The following notation has been used in Table 20.5.

$x_{ij}^k =$ quantity of kth final commodity produced and shipped from i to j.
$y_{ij} =$ quantity of intermediate commodity produced and shipped from i to j.
$P_{ij}^k =$ price per unit of kth commodity at production region i if shipped to region j, and equal to market price P_j less transfer cost t_{ij}.
$p_{ij} =$ price per unit of intermediate commodity at region j; if $i = j$ and $t_{ii} = 0$, then net and gross price are equal, with $i \ne j$ equal to $p_i - t_{ij}$.
$a^i =$ resource input per unit output of final commodity.
$b^i =$ intermediate commodity input per unit output of final commodity.
$r_i =$ quantity of resource available in ith region.
$s_i =$ quantity of intermediate commodity *produced* in region i.
$D^k =$ quantity of commodity k consumed at price P_j^k.

The objective here is to maximize the net value of output, subject to certain restraints. The usual competitive conditions are assumed, with transportation cost between regions given and independent of volume shipped. This is an assumption that requires further attention in itself. We divide the restraints into three groups: the first are the ones used in the direct; the second, the ones used in the dual; and the third, the implicit functions related to the prices introduced into the objective function.

For the primal problem, we may write the following equations (see also Table 20.5).

Resource Demand and Supply (assumed given by region)

$$\text{(1)} \quad a^1 x^1_{21} + a^2 x^2_{21} + a^y y_{22} + a^y y_{23} \leqslant \bar{r}_2$$

$$\text{(2)} \quad a^1 x^1_{31} + a^2 x^2_{31} + a^y y_{33} + a^y y_{32} \leqslant \bar{r}_3$$

Intermediate Commodity Demand and Supply

$$\text{(3)} \quad b^1 x^1_{21} + b^2 x^2_{21} + 1 \cdot y_{22} - 1 \cdot y_{23} + 1 \cdot y_{32} \leqslant S_2 = s_2 \pm \text{shipments}$$

$$\text{(4)} \quad b^1 x^1_{31} + b^2 x^2_{31} + 1 \cdot y_{23} + 1 \cdot y_{33} - 1 \cdot y_{32} \leqslant S_3 = s_3 \pm \text{shipments}$$

Final Commodity Supply and Demand

$$\text{(5)} \quad -1 \cdot x^1_{21} - 1 \cdot x^1_{31} \leqslant -D^1$$

$$\text{(6)} \quad -1 \cdot x^2_{21} - 1 \cdot x^2_{31} \leqslant -D^2$$

The dual conditions of equilibrium can be written as follows.

Final Commodity Price Equal to Unit Cost (Intermediate commodity plus imputed cost of resource for activity included.)

Intermediate Commodity Price Equal to Unit Cost (Imputed cost of resource for activity included. Obviously, several resources and other "intermediate commodities" are required under a more realistic situation.)

The following side analyses are used in establishing price-quantity relationships.

Demand for Final Commodity

$$\text{(1)} \quad D^1 = f(P^1_1 P^2_1 \ldots)$$

$$\text{(2)} \quad D^2 = f(P^1_1 P^2_1 \ldots)$$

Supply of Intermediate Commodity

$$\text{(1)} \quad s_2 = F(P^1_1 - t_{21}, P^2_1 - t_{21}, \ldots)$$

$$\text{(2)} \quad s_3 = F(P^1_1 - t_{31}, P^2_1 - t_{31}, \ldots)$$

Clearly, a problem of a size having relevance for decision-makers would be very large and complex. Our purpose here has been to illustrate how various research problems have been formulated to indicate some of the implicit assumptions of partial equilibrium analyses. Realistically, quantification of spatial models will be less than general, and equilibrium will never be fully specified. But the insights gained by these partial analyses hold considerable promise. Since the types of simplifying assumptions that are made for one kind of production analysis may not be relevant for another, we have not singled out any particular model as most suitable. That is the first task of the economist who ventures into the unknown of applied economics.

SELECTED READINGS

Multiple-Region Production and Trade Models

Beckmann, Martin J. and Thomas Marschak, *An Activity Analysis Approach to Location Theory*, Cowles Foundation for Research in Economics, New Haven, Paper No. 99 (1956). pp. 331–377.

King, Gordon A., "Effects of Transportation on the Location of Grain and Livestock Activities in the Western States," in Jack R. Davidson and Howard W. Ottoson (eds.), *Transportation Problems and Policies in the Trans-Missouri West*, University of Nebraska Press, Lincoln (1967), pp. 81–103.

King, G. A. and L. F. Schrader, "Regional Location of Cattle Feeding—a Spatial Equilibrium Analysis," *Hilgardia*, Vol. 34, No. 10, University of California Agricultural Experiment Station, Berkeley (July 1963). pp. 331–416.

Isard, Walter, *Location...op. cit.* pp. 207–220.

Isard, Walter, and Associates, *Methods of Regional Analysis: An Introduction to Regional Science*. John Wiley & Sons, New York (1960). Chapter 10, "Interregional Linear Programming," pp. 413–492.

Lefeber, Louis, *Allocation in Space: Production, Transport, and Industrial Location*, North Holland Publishing Company, Amsterdam (1958).

Ohlin, Bertil., *op. cit.* pp. 300–304.

Takayama, T. and G. G. Judge, "Equilibrium Among Spatially Separated Markets: A Reformulation," *Econometrica*, Vol. 32, No. 4. (October 1964), pp. 510–524.

Zusman, P., A. Melamed, and Katzim, *Possible Trade Effects of EEC Tariff and "Reference Price" Policy on the Market for Winter Oranges*, University of California, Giannini Foundation Monograph 24, Berkeley (1969).

chapter 21

EFFICIENCY IN MARKETING

At first glance, the concept of efficiency would seem to be relatively simple. If we know what inputs are used in a particular process and we know what output results, a simple ratio of output to input provides a measure of productivity. An increase in this ratio from one time period to another would clearly seem to be an improvement in the efficiency of the process. However, many plants produce two or more products and, thus, we encounter a problem in measuring the aggregate output of the several products. We may find that it is difficult not only to measure outputs but also to measure inputs associated with output during a particular time period. This is related to the fact that some inputs produce streams of services that extend over several production periods, although other inputs are consumed immediately. Another difficulty is associated with the measurement of changes in efficiency brought about by the substitution of capital for human labor. If we simply consider changes in the inputs used, we may overlook some of the costs incurred in shifting resources out of this process and, in particular, the costs incurred by the persons who formerly were employed in the process and are now forced to find other lines of employment. Finally, we may find that there is a relationship between the particular marketing system in use and the set of prices that emerge. Since prices are the allocators of resources and of products in a market economy, we clearly must give consideration to the pricing aspect of efficiency as well as to the production process itself. This is the task that we face in this final chapter.

21.1   EFFICIENCY OF MARKETING FIRMS[1]

How does one measure the relative efficiency of different firms in an industry? To simplify matters, we limit our discussion to the case of a single plant, single product firm. One answer is to construct simple input-output ratios, such as labor used per unit of output or capital investment per unit of output. The difficulty with simple ratios of this type is that, although a firm may rank high in efficiency when measured in terms of output per unit of labor, it may do this only at the cost of a large amount of capital per unit of output. That is to say, the firm with a low labor/output ratio may have a high capital/output ratio and *vice versa*. Clearly a method is needed by which all of the important inputs can be considered simultaneously.

Figure 21.1 is an illustration of the two-input, single output case. The two axes represent the rate of use of each input per unit of output. The curve SS' is to be regarded as the *efficient unit isoquant*. This curve represents the smallest quantity of factor 1 that can be used to produce one unit of output as the amount of factor 2 used is varied. All points on this line and the ones more distant from the origin are attainable, but all points between the line SS' and the origin are not attainable.

Now consider a firm represented by point P. We draw line OP from the origin to that observation. This line intersects the efficient unit isoquant at point Q. The length QP then is a measure of the excess use of the two

---

[1]This section draws heavily on a paper by M. J. Farrell, "The Measurement of Productive Efficiency," *Journal of the Royal Statistical Society*, Vol. 120, Part III, Series A (General), p. 253–281.

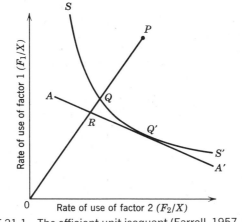

FIGURE 21.1   The efficient unit isoquant (Farrell, 1957, p. 254).

factors relative to what is technically feasible, represented by the length OQ. We measure *technical efficiency* as the ratio of the length OQ to the length OP. All points on the efficient unit isoquant are 100 percent technically efficient, and all points lying above the line are less than 100 percent efficient.

Let the relative prices of factor 1 and factor 2 be represented by the slope of line AA' which is tangent to the efficient unit isoquant at point Q'. It is clear that although point Q lies on the efficient unit isoquant, the resources required at this point are more costly than the resources that would be required at point Q'. This is true because any factor price line parallel to the line AA' but farther from the origin represents a larger outlay for the factors F_1 and F_2. The length RQ is a measure of the price inefficiency associated with the selection of the technically efficient but more costly point Q as compared with the minimum outlay point Q'. We construct the index of *price efficiency* by forming the ratio OR/OQ.

We may now combine these two indexes to obtain a measure of *economic efficiency*. This is the ratio OR/OP. It is equivalent to the product of technical efficiency and price efficiency $OQ/OP \times OR/OQ$. In summary then, given the efficient unit isoquant, the relative prices of the factors, and any observed position of a firm either on that isoquant or above it and to the right of the isoquant, it is possible to form an index of technical efficiency, an index of price efficiency, and the product of the two — economic efficiency.

Estimating the Efficient Unit Isoquant. To empirically estimate an efficient unit isoquant requires data on individual firms within an industry, like the ones illustrated in Figure 21.2. One procedure for describing these firms would be to estimate a regression line for the scatter of observations by least-squares or some similar procedure. On occasion, the Cobb–Douglas function has been used for this purpose. The disadvantage of this procedure is simply that it describes the *average* of all firms instead of providing information about the *most efficient* firms.

The proposal made by Farrell is that we describe the relationship for the most efficient plants by constructing an envelope-type curve that passes through the points nearest the origin. In Figure 21.2 the efficient unit isoquant is drawn through the observations for firms a, b, c, and d. Firm a lies furthest to the left of all observations, indicating that it uses least of factor 2. The isoquant is therefore drawn vertically from point a. Similarly, firm d uses least of factor 1 per unit of output, so that the isoquant is drawn horizontally to the right of this observation. Between these two points, the curve consists of a series of line segments that connect the four firms a through d.

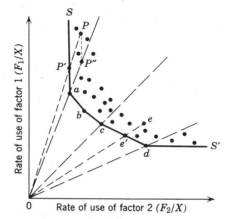

FIGURE 21.2   A hypothetical example of the "pessimistic" estimate of the efficient unit isoquant – two inputs (Bressler, 1967, p. 5).

The technical efficiency of firm *e* which does not lie on the efficient unit isoquant, is found by drawing a line to this point from the origin. The line *oe* crosses the efficient unit isoquant at point *e'* which lies on the line segment *cd*. Technical efficiency is measured by the ratio *oe'/oe*, as suggested earlier. Two choices are open for estimating price efficiency. One procedure is to use the tangent representing market prices of the factors. However, if there is reason to believe that substantial differences exist among firms in the relative price of factors, it is possible to substitute a factor price line that represents "own" prices for the line representing "market" prices of factors.

Scale and Efficiency.   Of particular interest to economists is the relationship between efficiency and scale of operation. Individual firm data may be sorted by size group and efficient unit isoquants that are constructed for each group, as outlined above for the industry as a whole. It is then possible to separate the efficiency index of each firm into components associated with its performance relative to other firms in its size group, as well as with the performance of one size group relative to other groups.

Economic efficiency is equivalent to the inverse ratio of average cost (Bressler, 1967). The relationship between the index of economic efficiency and the index of average cost is illustrated in Figure 21.3. The horizontal axis represents the scale of operation of the firm measured in terms of output per production period. Firm observations are arrayed along this axis with the vertical distance *below* the 100-index line a measure of the economic efficiency of each firm relative to the firm having the highest

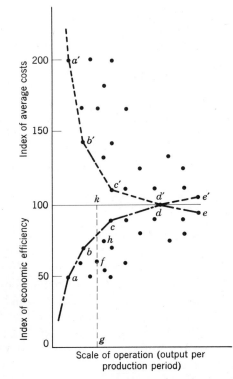

FIGURE 21.3 A hypothetical example of the relation of economic efficiency to scale of operation and to the usual concept of economies of scale (Bressler, 1967, p. 7).

economic efficiency index. We then construct an envelope curve "from above." The inverse of the efficiency index of a firm is an index of average cost and is measured vertically *above* the 100-index line in Figure 21.3. As previously, the average cost for each firm is measured relative to that of the firm having the lowest average cost. We then construct an envelope curve "from below."

The envelope curve to economic efficiency observations is strictly equivalent to the envelope curve to average cost observations. Notice that both economic efficiency and average cost indexes are independent of *proportional* changes in factor prices but that, in general, they are not independent of changes in relative factor prices.

Industry Efficiency. It may be of interest to compare the efficiency of two or more industries. For this purpose it is necessary to weight individual firm observations by their contribution to industry output. Measures of both technical and price efficiency are possible as well as the overall or economic efficiency of the industry. This method eliminates the necessity of devising a common measure of output for the several industries. Instead, comparisons are made with efficient firms in the same industry where outputs are more homogeneous. Interindustry comparisons of indexes are then possible.

The measurement of changes in efficiency within a given industry over time is also possible where individual firm data are available for several production periods. Shifts in the efficient unit isoquant might well provide a more sensitive measure of the effects of efforts to raise productivity in an industry than methods that rely on shifts in all firms in the industry such as have been generally employed.

Technological Change and Efficiency. The effect of technological change on the efficiency of production is also a matter of widespread interest. Technological change can be visualized as a drifting of the efficient unit isoquant toward the origin over time.

With respect to development prospects in many regions of the world, it is important that measures be developed that make it possible to identify those sectors and industries where substantial improvement is possible. Figure 21.4 illustrates the potential for change in the production of barley in the sierra region of Peru. Coffey (1966) has identified four levels of technology: the traditional, the transitional, the modern, and the potential. They are represented by the corner points on the rectangular

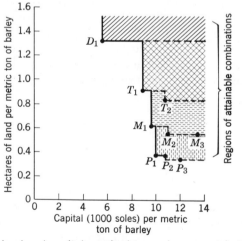

FIGURE 21.4   The land and capital required to produce a metric ton of barley in the Peruvian sierra under various levels of technology [Technology code: D = traditional, T = transitional, M = modern, and P = potential; 1 = nonmechanized, 2 = partially mechanized, and 3 = fully mechanized (Coffey, 1966, p. 51).]

isoquants in Figure 21.4. The isoquants are rectangular because it is assumed that no variation in factor proportions is possible within a given technology. The technological changes illustrated here do suggest that it is not possible to produce a unit of barley with less of *all* inputs but that it is possible to reduce substantially the amount of land required per unit of output.

The effect of technological change, then, is to expand sequentially the set of input combinations that are attainable. Only occasionally will it be possible to make the type of breakthrough where the isoquant will shift toward the origin in such a way as to dominate all previous input combinations. The shifts illustrated in Figure 21.4 represent, by far, the most common type of technological change that occurs in the real world. This has important economic implications. Notice that the incentive to adopt new technology will depend on the relative prices of the factors of production.

Suppose that technology levels D and T are attainable. If the relative price line passes through points D_1 and T_1, this indicates that the two techniques are equally profitable. If, on the other hand, the price of capital is higher than the one suggested by the line D_1T_1, this would increase the slope of the factor price line and would indicate that the traditional method is more efficient. The separation of technological changes that dominate existing methods from the ones that offer new profit opportunities only within specific ranges of relative prices would be highly desirable.

The Farrell approach to the estimation of the technical, price, and economic efficiency of firms offers an opportunity to improve substantially our ability to measure interfirm differences in efficiency, to measure the rate of adoption of new technology, to study the relationship between scale and efficiency, and to make interregional or interindustry comparisons. Although we have dealt only with the single product, two input case, the logic is directly applicable to the more general case.

21.2 ALTERNATIVE MARKETING SYSTEMS

Market organization is a general term embracing all aspects of a particular marketing system. There are three generally recognized components of market organization. *Market structure* refers in a descriptive way to the physical dimensions involved: that is, the approximate definitions of industry and markets, the number of firms and/or plants in the market, the distribution of firms or plants by various measures of size and concentration, the descriptions of products and product differentiation, the conditions of entry, and the like. All of these descriptions, to be sure, are geared in some way to our concepts and value judgments of elements that affect market competition. *Market conduct* refers to the behavior of firms under a given market structure and, especially, to the types of decisions that managers can make under varying market structures. Finally, *market performance* refers to the real impact of structure and conduct as measured in terms of variables such as prices, costs, and volume of output. Performance is the significant element in this classification scheme. In fact, descriptive studies of structure are of value only in so far as they explain performance.

Microtheory provides us with analyses of firm operations under a variety of market settings that range from competition at one extreme to monopoly at the other. Each of these situations is characterized by descriptions of the institutional setting within which the firm operates — descriptions in terms of numbers and size of firms, product characteristics, conditions of entry, and so on. These theoretical developments have been utilized by students of market structure to construct the familiar classification system or tableau — competition, monopolistic competition, dominant firm, dominant oligopoly, oligopoly, duopoly, bilateral monopoly, monopoly, and so on.

Given fairly readily available characteristics of an industry — number and size of firms, the degree of product differentiation, the proportions of the total business handled by the largest or the 4 largest, or the 20 firms — the industry can be assigned to its appropriate place in this classification system. Theoretical analyses are then used to develop generalizations about conduct and performance and particularly to contrast the expected or suspected performance with the results anticipated under competitive conditions. At either end of the market classification tableau (competition or monopoly), generalizations about conduct and performance derived from structural descriptions seem most valid, although even here it is seldom appropriate to conclude that the advantages of competition would come from the breaking up of a monopolistic firm into many small (and inefficient) firms.

The area intermediate between competition and monopoly is most characteristic of real life, and it is also the area where our theoretical conclusions and value judgments as to the relations between structure and performance are most suspect. What does theory tell us about performance in a market where the top 4, 10, or 20 firms control 60 percent of the business? In the absence of direct collusion, which reduces the case essentially to one of monopoly, it is difficult to find clear-cut guidelines in theory. Yet, hundreds of studies have been made that describe changes in the number of firms in an industry and in the concentration ratio — the percentage of total business handled by the top firms. It is perhaps most revealing that research work and application in this area have found it convenient to constantly increase the number of firms considered in the "dominant" group—from 1, to 4, to 10, to 20—while also implying that a stated percentage of the total business in the hands of the 20 largest firms is just as much a cause for public concern as would be that percentage in the hands of 1 or 2 firms.

The "numbers game" can be well illustrated by two divergent facts. Recently, the FTC ruled against a merger of two small food chains when the combined volume of the two was well under 10 percent of the *local* market and, of course, a very much smaller proportion of the national total of retail food-store sales. At about the same time, studies of 6000 retail stores operated by 9 major chains failed to reveal significant relationships between the percent of local market business and any of the variables that might be expected to accompany changing degrees of local market concentration (see recent studies by the National Commission on Food Marketing).

The foregoing is not intended to make the point that "market organization" is unimportant in agricultural markets but instead to stress that the connection between market structure and market performance is often too tenuous to be of great value. As we have observed, the classic approach is to study structure and then to attempt to draw generalizations about performance. In what follows, we urge the reverse attack: that is, to study market performance, at least in some aspects, and then, as required, to move into detailed studies of the institutional factors that might properly be called structure. Although performance is more difficult to study than descriptive structure, nevertheless, at least two major dimensions can be researched effectively in most agricultural markets. These studies will provide meaningful bases for industry decisions and public policy in these fields. These two dimensions are (1) productive efficiency and (2) pricing efficiency.

21.3 EFFICIENCY OF MARKETING SYSTEMS

The question of efficiency runs even deeper than that of firms and industries. It has to do with how well a particular job might be done under alternative systems. We have identified two attributes of an efficient marketing system. They are (1) to provide efficient and economical services and ownership transfers in the movement of commodities from seller to buyer, and (2) to provide an effective price-making mechanism. In a sense, the first is merely a specific aspect of the second. That is, the creation of marketing services does not differ from other productive processes which, given the efficient operation of the pricing mechanism, bring about the economical allocation of resources. The direct objective of the marketing system, therefore, can be described as providing for and participating in price formation with the understanding that the pricing system has as its prime function the guiding of the flow of resources into production (including marketing) and of goods and services into consumption. It will be convenient to consider separately the productive efficiency aspect and the pricing efficiency aspect of marketing systems.

Productive Efficiency.   In the creation of marketing services, productive efficiency has two dominant aspects: (1) the extent to which firms in the industry make reasonably full use of their available facilities—(the "load" factor or the amount of excess or unutilized capacity—and (2) the extent to which firms and/or plants are organized to take full advantage of economies of scale—the "scale" factor. We might add (3), the technical progressiveness of the industry, but here we encounter the difficulty of distinguishing between the problems of industry application and of basic scientific and technological development. This area of productive efficiency possesses real potential for improvements in marketing efficiency and, thus, is an area where major emphasis should be placed by marketing economists.

"Structuralists" have been known to view with alarm the fact that the number of country creameries in the Midwest has decreased during the past 25 years by approximately one-half. Although this decrease may seem to be a basis for major concern to one whose stock in trade is the numbers game, to a "performist" who knows anything at all about the nature of this industry, such a change can only be a cause for rejoicing. It seems clear that many country creameries of a past decade were using only part of their available capacities and that many were much too small to realize the potential economies of scale. Moreover, technological change within the plant but especially in transportation equipment and highway quality has made for rapid increases in the scale of operation that would give reasonable approximations to minimum costs.

Perhaps it is premature to suggest a "taxonomy" based on "scale and load" factors, but something like this is required. For any particular agricultural marketing industry, the marketing economist should have *general* information as to the influence of scale and load on costs and efficiency. Notice that they are *performance* and not structural factors. He can collect information on volume distributions and, more difficult to be sure, capacities. With them, he should be able to make a preliminary appraisal of the performance of the group of plants in a particular locality.

If his preliminary analysis indicates reasonably efficient levels of performance, then he would be well advised to move on to other localities and/or other fields. If, however, the preliminary classification suggests a combination of too small scale and too much excess capacity, then specific studies of the particular local situation are in order. For example, the study of the optimum number, size, and location of pear-packing plants by Stollsteimer and Sammet referred to the specifics of a single producing district in California and drew on detailed researches on costs, efficiency, and economies of scale that had been completed previously. The essential approach was to describe the geographic location of production in the district and, through elaborations of the transportation model, to check the effects of numbers and the location of plants on the combined costs of assembly and plant operation. By comparison with the existing organization, this provided an appraisal of the present scale and load efficiency, an indication of desirable directions for future evolution, and an estimate of the cost of savings that could be expected from this rationalization.

A second example that illustrates this approach concerns the consolidation of orange packinghouses in another small district of California. The general nature of orange packing operations and the effects of volume and scale on packinghouse costs were well known. Preliminary investigations in the district in question, where total fruit volume was decreasing as a result of urban encroachment, suggested that plants were not large enough to be efficient and that, even more important in this situation, most plants were operating well below 50 percent of capacity even in peak seasons. This "diagnosis" of trouble and its probable causes is about what marketing economists can expect from general research.

The development of an action program, then, depended on the careful exploration of a number of local factors: the available facilities and capacities of plants, the present and future trends in available fruit, present and probable future levels of unit costs, the financial situation in each house; the possibilities for liquidation of physical assets, and a host of "personal" questions, including the present and possible composition of boards of directors, the positions of present managers, and the disposition of present labor forces. This particular project considered a half dozen plants and finally resulted in the actual merger of three (two cooperatives and one private plant), with a more than doubling of plant volume, a satisfactory disposal of unneeded facilities, and a significant reduction in costs and/or increase in returns to growers. This represents a substantial improvement, even though it falls short of the "ideal" that pure research might suggest. Of all the institutional factors that stand in the way of load and scale improvements in performance, the most difficult and pervasive seem to be the personal factors.

Pricing Efficiency.   Pricing efficiency can be thought of as the positive aspect of the main concern of market structure: that is, what happens to prices. Pricing efficiency studies attempt to appraise this directly by contrasting actual prices with the ones that are generated by some "efficiency" model (The reader is reminded that efficiency models are closely related to and sometimes identical with competitive models.) Our theoretical constructs here must come largely from the theory of the perfect market in space, form, and time. To repeat, we expect that an efficient market will establish prices that are interrelated through space by transportation costs, through form by costs of processing, and through time as a consequence of the costs of storage. Although such models are admittedly simplifications of reality, nevertheless, they can often be used to spot distortions in pricing performance.

Suppose it is alleged that prices paid dairy farmers for milk delivered to local creameries are "inefficient": that is, these prices do not accurately reflect market demands for finished products, with appropriate allowances for processing and transportation costs. The perfect market concept gives us a diagnostic tool by which we can test this hypothesis; the results either indicate reasonable performance or wave a red flag that warns us something is amiss. In the latter case, careful and specific explorations of local institutions are in order.

Again, research gives only the general picture. A good example of these general results is the study of pricing efficiency in the manufactured dairy products industry (Hassler). His findings indicated that this market operated with a relatively high degree of consistency and pricing efficiency. More important in our present context, they suggested an approach and provided much of the information needed to appraise local specific situations. Thus, it might be true that the "national" market for butter operated efficiently as judged by price comparisons among major cities, but it also could be true that wholesale butter prices and/or returns to farmers for milk were depressed below "normal" levels in parts of California or Iowa. Specific studies would then be required to determine how these price results could be explained and, hence, to suggest what might be done about it.

To encourage efficient marketing, the economist must make special or local studies of this kind and then, if the results so indicate, mount action programs to improve the situation. This last may not be easy when dealing with a marketing system. Yet, effective programs are often possible. If prices are depressed locally as a result of trade barriers that discriminate against the products of the district, publicity and public action seem indicated—perhaps even action through the courts to throw out barriers to interstate commerce. If prices are low because of the structure of the local industry (and we must always recognize that efficient size will usually pose the dilemma of numbers too small in the local district to insure aggressive competition), then continuing publicity that compares local prices with "computed normal" prices may be sufficient to bring the local industry into line. In many cases, although this is less true now than in the past because of improved communications, the development of an effective market news system may be the answer. And in some cases, the traditional establishment of a cooperative to serve as a competitive yardstick may be effective. Although the use of public regulatory power is not common in agricultural markets, this also is a possibility (for example, the establishment of maximum charges for marketing services under state milk control).

21.4 THE "IDEAL MARKET" AND MARKETING RESEARCH

To summarize, we return to the "ideal market" model and its relevance for research. The objectives for the marketing system have been defined in terms of "efficiency" and "economy." However, these are relative or comparative words. A marketing firm, function, or system cannot be judged as efficient or economical in any absolute sense, but only with respect to alternatives or to some standard. Studies may be designed to show how the existing marketing methods could be improved, that is, made more efficient and less costly. To be more useful, however, marketing research should be oriented with reference to a concept of an ideal or perfect market. Such a concept should make possible the most meaningful appraisal of the existing system both in terms of the delineation of problem areas and of the indications of the magnitude and importance of the distortions. Also, it should provide a framework within which individual studies could be fitted, past work evaluated and integrated, and future research planned.

What, then, can we use as a model of perfection? A partial answer is suggested by the above-mentioned objectives for the marketing system, since they correspond in general to the results that would characterize an economy of perfect competition. For such an economy, economic theory describes an interdependent system of pricing for factors of production, for goods, and for services. Within this system, factors will be shifted among alternative employments in response to higher and more profitable returns. In turn, these returns will change and adjust with changes in technology and with shifts in consumer tastes and preferences. In equilibrium, the costs of production (including the production of marketing services) will be at the minimum consistent with the given conditions of resources, technology, and demands. Prices for goods and services will reflect and differ only by these production and marketing costs.

Competitive economic theory can thus provide the framework for our ideal market. Confronted with any marketing and pricing problem, the research worker can plan his attack by asking himself questions such as: How would this marketing process be organized if it operated under the conditions of perfect competition? This does not imply that competitive conditions could be completely attained nor that the solution to marketing problems is simply a "return" to the system of free and perfect competition. A realistic view of the industrial economy of today indicates that it would be both *undesirable* and *impossible* to attain many of the characteristics of a competitive market. Two main types of modifications are necessary: first, the inclusion of welfare considerations that modify the distribution of income, such as progressive income taxes and minimum wages; and second, the possible advantages of a limited number of firms in those areas where economies of large-scale operation are important. In this last case, these are the significant questions: What organization of this process would minimize costs? How can these costs be reflected in prices?

Attempts to improve marketing by approximating competitive conditions will be appropriate in many instances. They include steps such as the curbing of large-scale organization where its effects are primarily to exact charges not commensurate with costs and perfecting knowledge through research, education, and market news. In certain other areas, however, this approach will not be productive and, here, the stress must be on approximating the *results* of competition in terms of costs and prices. As previously mentioned, large-scale organization may frequently result from technological factors that give rise to economies of scale, and the curbing or breaking up of these large units would necessarily lead to higher costs. This is a much more common situation in marketing than is sometimes supposed, since economies of scale are frequently of sufficient importance relative to the size of local markets to result either in (1) a considerable degree of local and spatial monopoly or in (2) a number of small and high-cost competing firms. In country marketing and processing plants, for example, this conflict is clear. The problem may be one of how to achieve and to regulate low-cost monopolies in the public interest.

The following list suggests some of the benefits that this ideal market concept can bring to marketing research.

1. It makes it possible to judge the existing system by standards of socially desirable results or ends. This is not to deny that welfare considerations will sometimes define other results, but in most instances the

competitive model appears consistent with the general welfare in terms of results.

2. The underlying principles are well developed and widely understood, and with careful thought they can be expanded to apply to such detailed problems as the organization and operation of local marketing facilities or to such broad issues as the allocation of resources among marketing and the other major sectors of the economy.

3. It stresses the importance of theorizing and of logical analysis in the planning phases of research; relationships are not determined by random gathering and tabulating of data, but must be inserted as well-conceived hypotheses and then tested by carefully designed empirical studies.

4. By suggesting the general form for particular studies, it will help insure that the findings can be used in succeeding and more advanced studies. This should facilitate and promote effective integration of research and cooperation among research workers.

5. By stressing the important interrelationships and interdependencies in the workings of the economic system, the ideal market concept should encourage researchers to go beyond superficial and gross relationships. The real market mechanism is complex, and an appreciation of these complexities is essential if research simplifications are not to destroy the usefulness of the estimates of basic relationships.

6. Finally, by providing a "goal" that will frequently differ significantly from the *status quo*, the ideal market concept should encourage the exploring and developing of new areas of knowledge. Innovation is essential to progress, and research that contributes to progress is simply a scientific approach to innovation.

It has been said that economists often view the existing market organization as given but invariably turn over to the next generation a far different organization. Hopefully, these chapters will provide a foundation for a systematic evaluation of some of these alternative systems.

SELECTED READINGS

Efficiency in Marketing

Bressler, R. G., "Agricultural Economics in the Decade Ahead," *Journal of Farm Economics*, Vol. 47, No. 3 (August 1965). pp. 521–528.

Bressler, R. G., "The Measurement of Productive Efficiency," in M. V. Waananen (ed.), *Western Farm Economics Association, Proceedings, 1966*. Washington State University, Pullman (January 1967). pp. 1–10.

Brewster, John M., "The Impact of Technical Advance and Migration on Agricultural Society and Policy," *Journal of Farm Economics*, Vol. 41, No. 5. (December 1959). pp. 1169–1184.

Brownlee, O. H., "Marketing Research and Welfare Economics," *Journal of Farm Economics*, Vol. XXX, No. 1 (February 1948). pp. 55–68.

Coffey, Joseph D., "Prospects of Transforming Peru's Traditional Agriculture," unpublished Ph.D. thesis, North Carolina State University at Raleigh (1966). University Microfilms, Ann Arbor, Mich.

Koopmans, Tjalling, *Three Essays on the State of Economic Science*, McGraw-Hill Book Co, New York (1957). II, "The Construction of Economic Knowledge," pp. 127–166.

Sosnick, Stephen H., "Toward a Concrete Concept of Effective Competition," *American Journal of Agricultural Economics*, Vol. 50, No. 4 (November 1968), pp. 827–853.

AUTHOR INDEX

SUBJECT INDEX